Peace Psychology Book Series

D1795668

Series Editor
Daniel J. Christie, Marion, OH, USA

The scope of threats to human security at the dawn of the 21st century is daunting. Terrorism, weapons of mass destruction, nuclear proliferation, failed states, ideological struggles, growing resource scarcities, disparities in wealth and health, globalizing trends, violations of human rights, and the continued use of force to advance individual, group and national interests, are all complex problems. At the same time, we are witnessing countervailing trends in the growing recognition and endorsement of nonviolent means of resolving differences, the importance of reconciliation processes in human relations, the promotion of cultures of peace, and the building of societal structures and global institutions that promote peace, human rights and environmental sustainability. During the past 20 years, peace psychology has emerged as a specialty in psychology with its own knowledge base, perspectives, concepts, and preferred methodologies to grapple with threats to human security and seize opportunities to promote human well-being. In regard to the problem of violence, peace psychology scholars and activists place human psychology and its links to other disciplines at the center of their efforts to prevent and mitigate episodes of violence and structural forms of violence. In addition to reducing violence, peace psychologists seek to develop theory and practices that promote relational harmony across levels (from interpersonal relations to global networks) and equitable human well-being. The Peace Psychology Book Series recognizes that the emerging and multi-faceted problems of human security challenge us as scholars and activists to develop psychologically-informed theory that will deepen our understanding of the major threats to human security, and create practices that will help us address some of the most urgent and profound issues that bear on human well being and survival in the 21st century.

Series Advisory Board
Herbert Blumberg, Goldsmiths College, United Kingdom **Daniel Bar-Tal**, Tel Aviv University, Israel **Klaus Boehnke**, International University Bremen, Germany **Peter Coleman**, Columbia University, USA **Cheryl de la Rey**, University of Cape Town, South Africa **Shelley McKeown Jones**, University of Bristol, United Kingdom **Yayah Khisbiyah**, Universitas Muhammadiyah Surakarta, Indonesia **Siew Fang Law**, Victoria University, Australia **Wilson Lopez Lopez**, Pontificia Universidad Javeriana, Colombia **Winnifred Louis**, University of Queensland, Australia **Anthony Marsella**, University of Hawaii, USA **Fathali Moghaddam**, Georgetown University, USA **Maritza Montero**, Central University of Venezuela, Venezuela **Cristina Montiel**, Ateneo de Manila University, Philippines **Ann Sanson**, University of Melbourne, Australia **Mohamed Seedat,** University of South Africa **Michael Wessells**, Columbia University and Randolph-Macon College, USA

More information about this series at https://link.springer.com/bookseries/7298

Elizabeth Lira • Marcela Cornejo
Germán Morales

Editors

Human Rights Violations in Latin America

Reparation and Rehabilitation

 Springer

Editors
Elizabeth Lira
Universidad Alberto Hurtado
Santiago, Chile

Marcela Cornejo
Pontificia Universidad Católica de Chile
Santiago, Chile

Germán Morales
Pontificia Universidad Católica de Chile
Santiago, Chile

ISSN 2197-5779   ISSN 2197-5787   (electronic)
Peace Psychology Book Series
ISBN 978-3-030-97544-9   ISBN 978-3-030-97542-5   (eBook)
https://doi.org/10.1007/978-3-030-97542-5

This Springer imprint is published by the registered company Springer Nature Switzerland AG
The registered company address is: Gewerbestrasse 11, 6330 Cham, Switzerland

Acknowledgments

When different authors from different countries work together on the same book, a complex process of dialogues, communications, texts revisions, and exchanges takes place until the final manuscript is produced. The result is an exercise of reflection, humility, and reciprocal learning, joining ideas and experiences to achieve a shared work.

This book is possible by collaborating with many people, first and foremost the authors who shared their ideas and experiences and their commitment to this task.

This project began with the invitation of Patricio Cumsille from Pontificia Universidad Católica de Chile and Judith L. Gibbons, Professor Emeritus of Psychology at Saint Louis University, a few years ago to write a book that would reflect the work done in psychology in the field of human rights in Latin America.

Several people collaborated in the editorial revision of the chapters translated into English, among them Maxine Lowy, Anne Pérotin-Dumont, and Paula Jorquera. We also benefited from the careful work of Marais del Río in the revision of the APA Standards.

One of the authors, Wilson López of the Pontificia Universidad Javeriana de Bogotá, contacted Dan Christie, Series Editor of Peace Psychology Book Series, making it possible to link our work to an editorial project generated by colleagues from different parts of the world.

We want to thank all those who have contributed to the realization of this book. The writings belong to Latin America's collective memory and of all those who have worked in recent decades to recognize and rehabilitate victims. The contribution of their voices in the construction of democratic coexistence is the best guarantee of stable and lasting peace in political life and everyday spaces.

Elizabeth Lira
Marcela Cornejo
Germán Morales

Contents

Part VI Political and Psychosocial Challenges of Transitions

About the Authors

José Manuel Bezanilla Psychologist, PhD in Family Sciences, Group Psychotherapist and Clinical Psychodramatist, Founder and General Manager of Psicología y Educación Integral A.C. Founder of PEI (international journal), Clinical Psychologist and Adjunct Visitor at Comisión Nacional Derechos Humanos México, founding member of the Mexican Team of Psychosocial Treatment and Support (EMAAPSI). Equipo Mexicano de Atención y Acompañamiento Psicosocial, Naucalpan, México

Mariana Biaggio BSc in Social Work (UBA, Universidad de Buenos Aires) and MSc in Social Anthropology (UNSAM, Universidad Nacional de San Martín). She was awarded a PhD in Social Sciences by the Universidad de Buenos Aires in 2014. She has worked on identity reconstruction processes, as part of the search for and restitution of grandchildren appropriated during the last Argentine military dictatorship and within the context of identity-based resistance processes involved in the implementation of policies aimed at people classed as "homeless." She is part of the Mental Health Team of the CELS (Centro de Estudios Legales y Sociales) since 2006 and is a professor at UCES (Universidad de Ciencias Empresariales y Sociales) and Universidad Lomas de Zamora (UNLZ). CELS, Centro de Estudios Legales y Sociales, Buenos Aires, Argentina

Carlos Felipe Buitrago-Panader Psychologist (Universidad Pontificia Javeriana) and MSc (c) in Methodology of Behavior and Health Sciences (Universidad Complutense, Madrid, UNED—Universidad Nacional de Educación a Distancia). He is working on the implementation of a training program for public servants in charge of delivering mental health support to people affected by the armed conflict; in addition, he is part of a project aimed at characterizing the mental health situation of Venezuelan migrants who have settled in some regions of the USA and Colombia. Pontificia Universidad Javeriana, Bogotá, Colombia

María Luisa Cabrera Pérez-Armiñan PhD in Social Psychology (Universidad Complutense de Madrid), resident of Guatemala since 1988. She conduct social research in indigenous communities, implementing humanitarian psychosocial interventions with a psychosocial approach (Massacre of Xamán, Guatemala, 1995), and treating victims of violence and catastrophes (Indonesian Tsunami, 2004), human rights violations, and violence against women. She has several publications and articles about historical memory, transitional justice and conflicts, gender violence, and health. Undergraduate (Diploma courses) and postgraduate professor (Master's programs). She has over 30 years of professional experience in psychosocial reconstruction, victim treatment and reparation, and transitional justice with a psycho-legal approach applied to cases. She is a member of and researcher at the Guatemalan Center for Research on Conflicts, Power, and Violence (CENDES) and collaborates as a psychosocial consultant with the Team of Community Research and Psychosocial Action (ECAP) in Guatemala. Guatemalan Center for Research on Conflicts, Power and Violence (CENDES), Antigua, Guatemala

Angélica Caicedo-Moreno Student of the Doctoral Program in Psychology. Department of Social Psychology, Faculty of Psychology, Universidad del País Vasco, Donostia, España. Collaborator of the research group Culture, Cognition and Emotion from the same department in the line of research on peace and armed conflict studies. Her thesis analyzes how newspapers and social media impact the creation of social representations of peace and transitional justice in Colombia. Universidad del País Vasco, San Sebastián-Donostia, España

María Isabel Castillo Clinical Psychologist (Universidad de Chile). Psychoanalyst (ICHPA). PhD in Psychoanalysis (UAB). Since 1980, she has delivered psychotherapeutic treatment to victims of human rights violations. She is one of the founders of the Instituto Latinoamericano de Salud Mental y Derechos Humanos (ILAS), created in 1988. As a member of the clinical and research team, she received the National Psychology Award in 2003. She has been professor and undergraduate and postgraduate supervisor in several universities. She is a member of several organizations, including the Chilean Association of Group Psychoanalytic Psychotherapy and the Chilean Chapter of the International Association of Psychotherapy and Relational Psychoanalysis (IARPP-Chile). She has authored multiple publications (books and articles) about mental health and human rights. Her latest book, *El (im) posible proceso de duelo: Familiares de detenidos desaparecidos: violencia política, trauma y memoria—The (Im)possible Mourning Process: Relatives of Detained-Disappeared Persons. Political Violence, Trauma, and Memory*, was published in 2013. ILAS Instituto Latinoamericano se Salud Mental y Derechos Humanos, Santiago, Chile

Pablo Castro-Abril Student of the Doctoral Program in Psychology. Department of Social Psychology, Faculty of Psychology, Universidad del País Vasco, Donostia, España. Member of the well-established research group on Culture, Cognition, and Emotion from the same department. He is currently researching changes in attitudes of the public regarding emotions and transcendent emotions focused on the importance of forgiveness and reconciliation in victims, perpetrators, and the public for the construction of a peace-based culture. Universidad del País Vasco, San Sebastián-Donostia, España

Alexei Conte Indursky Psychoanalyst, Member of the Psychoanalytic Association of Porto Alegre (APPOA) PhD in Psychoanalysis and Psychopathology (Université Paris 7, Sorbonne, Denis-Diderot). Coordinator of the Testimony Clinics Project, in association with the Ministry of Justice, the Amnesty Commission, and Association Psychoanalytic of Porto Alegre APPOA (2016–2017). Member of the Center for the Psychic Reparation of State Violence During the Democratic Period, in association with the British Council, Newton Fund, and Institute APPOA (2016). Psychoanalytic Association of Porto Alegre (APPOA), Porto Alegre, Brasil

Marcela Cornejo Psychologist (Universidad Católica de Chile) and PhD in Psychological Sciences (Université de Louvain, Belgique). She is an associate researcher at the Millennium Institute for Research on Violence and Democracy, VIODEMOS [ANID—Millennium Science Initiative Program—ICS2019_025], and an adjunct researcher at the Center for the Study of Conflict and Social Cohesion, COES [CONICYT/FONDAP/15130009]. She is currently Chair of the Department of Psychology of the Universidad Católica de Chile. Her research interests focus on psychosocial trauma related to political violence; individual and collective processes of psychological working-through of trauma; collective and autobiographical memory; the generational approach to understanding psychosocial phenomena; and the rationales and practices of qualitative social research. In these areas, she has conducted research projects in collaboration with Chilean and foreign researchers, participating in and organizing conferences and symposiums, publishing articles in various journals, and supervising doctoral theses in Chilean and foreign universities. Pontificia Universidad Católica de Chile, Santiago, Chile

Andrea Correa-Chica PhD student of the Doctoral Program in Psychological Processes and Social Behavior. Department of Social Psychology, Basic Psychology, and Methodology, Faculty of Psychology, Universidade de Santiago de Compostela, Santiago de Compostela, España. Member of the research group "Social Behavior and Applied Psychometry" (COSOYPA), from the same department. Member of the International Society of Political Psychology and the Spanish Scientific Society of Social Psychology. Universidad de Santiago de Compostela, Santiago de Compostela, España

Clemencia Correa Psychologist. Founder and current director of Aluna Acompañamiento Psicosocial A.C. She has delivered psychosocial support to victims of political violence and human rights organizations for over 30 years, 10 of which she spent in Colombia with relatives of disappeared people and communities displaced as part of resistance processes. In Mexico, since 2002, she has accompanied relatives of disappeared people and journalists. She has also worked as a consultant for various at-risk organizations in contexts of political violence. She has carried out psychosocial expert opinions before the Inter-American Court on sexual torture and forced disappearance. She was a professor of Social Psychology in Colombia and has written several articles on mental health and human rights from a psychosocial perspective. And she was a judge in the court of conscience: sexual violence as a crime against humanity under the Ortega-Murillo regime carried out in 2020. ALUNA Acompañamiento Psicosocial A.C., Ciudad de México, México

Bárbara De Souza Conte Psychoanalyst. PhD in Psychology (Universidad Autónoma de Madrid). Full member of the Sigmund Freud Psychoanalytic Association—SIG (POA/RS). Coordinator of SIG project Psychoanalytic Interventions, consisting in group listening activities with teachers. External consultant for TeCMe (Clinical Territories of Memory), Buenos Aires, Argentina. Teacher, Latin American Seminar State Violence and Comprehensive Reparation Policies produced by TeCMe and Universidad de La Plata (online) (2019–2020–2021). Member of the Testimony Clinics project, Association Psychoanalytic of Porto Alegre—APPOA (2016–2017). Coordinator of pilot project Testimony Clinics, SIG (2013–2015). Member of the Center for the Psychic Reparation of State Violence during the Democratic Period, in association with the British Council, Newton Fund, and APPOA Institute (2016). Member of the Human Rights Commission of the Federal Psychology Council (2013–2016). Author of articles on State violence published in Brazilian newspapers and other publications. Sigmund Freud Psychoanalytic Association, Porto Alegre, Brasil

Rosa Matilde Díaz Jiménez Psychologist, Universidad Santo Tomás (Colombia, 2000). Specialist in Legal Psychology trained in the same university (2005). She studied Human Rights at the Inter-American Institute of Human Rights (2006). In Colombia, she worked in the Comisión Colombiana de Juristas (2007–2011), Corporación de Asistencia Psicosocial a Víctimas, (AVRE, 2005–2006), and the Fundación Menonita Colombiana para el Desarrollo (2001–2005), combining psycho-legal support and assistance to her duties as a representative and defender of the human rights of communities and groups affected by sociopolitical violence and armed conflicts. In Argentina, she is working at the Dirección General de Acompañamiento, Protección y Orientación a las Víctimas (DOVIC, Procuración General de la Nación). She was a member of the Mental Health Team of the CELS (Centro de Estudios Legales y Sociales, 2010–2017). Procuración General de la Nación Argentina, Buenos Aires, Argentina

Laura Espinosa Psychology Intern (Universidad Nacional Autónoma de México), with a specialization in Human Rights and Gender Perspective. She has experience in psychosocial work. Since 2011, she has assisted victims of severe human rights violations and has been part of Aluna Psychosocial Support since 2014. Currently, she is the coordinator of Aluna's Psychosocial Support area. ALUNA Acompañamiento Psicosocial A.C., Ciudad de México, México

Ângela Flores Becker Psychologist. Trained in Psychoanalysis; Associate Member of the Sigmund Freud Psychoanalytic Association (POA/RS). Member of the Testimony Clinics project/Association Psychoanalytic of Porto Alegre—APPOA (2016–2017). President of the Fiscal Deliberative Council of the Rio Grande do Sul Psychological Society. Sigmund Freud Psychoanalytic Association, Porto Alegre, Brasil

Florencia González Pla BSc in Psychology, MSc in Psychoanalysis, Universidad de Buenos Aires (UBA). Professor of Psychology, Ethics, and Human Rights, Faculty of Psychology, UBA. Professor in charge of the professional experience module "Psychology in the Legal Domain: clinical-ethical reflections through qualitative case studies," Faculty of Psychology, UBA. Doctoral researcher at Scientific and Technical Program (2018–2020); topic: "Psychoanalysis and Human Rights." Member of research project "A right to identity: testimonies of grandchildren appropriated and returned upon detection of forged birth documentation. Ethical-psychological aspects" (2017–2019) at the Research Institute of the Faculty of Psychology, UBA. Universidad de Buenos Aires, Buenos Aires, Argentina

Evelyn Hevia Jordán Psychologist, Universidad de Arte y Ciencias Sociales (ARCIS), and Master's in History, Universidad de Chile. Currently, she is a PhD student at the Lateinamerika Institut of the Freie Universität Berlin. She is preparing her doctoral thesis entitled: "From the 'El Lavadero' Hospital to the 'Villa Baviera' Hospital: historiographic reconstruction of the hospital of the former Colonia Dignidad in Chile." She is a collaborator and editor at the Psicología Hoy bulletin of the Faculty of Psychology of Universidad Alberto Hurtado and belongs to the Interdisciplinary Program in Memory and Human Rights at the same university. She has worked on several projects with Human Rights, Oral Archives and Memory Sites in Chile and Germany. She has published as author, co-author, and editor about the dictatorship in Chile, the former Colonia Dignidad, the situation of victims of human rights violations, and the memory construction processes of the recent Chilean past. Universität Berlin, Deutschland/Universidad Alberto Hurtado, Santiago, Chile

Elizabeth Lira Psychologist (Universidad Católica de Chile, 1971), MSc in Ciencias del Desarrollo (Instituto Latinoamericano de Doctrina y Estudios Sociales, 1977); Family Therapist (Instituto Chileno de Terapia Familiar, 1989). She was a member of the Political Prison and Torture Commission of the Government of Chile: 2003–2005 and 2010–2011. She has published several books, chapters, and articles on human rights, reparation policies, reconciliation, and memory. Her last book published in 2020 with Brian Loveman (SDSU) is *Poder Judicial y Conflictos Políticos. Chile 1973–1990*. [Judicial Power and Political Conflicts. Chile 1973–1990]. She received the National Psychology Award, Chile, in 1983, the International Humanitarian Award from American Psychological Association in 2002, and the National Prize of Humanities and Social Sciences 2017 in Chile. She is Full Professor of the Faculty of Psychology at the Univerisdad Alberto Hurtado.

Co-researcher of the Fondecyt project: *Beyond the victim's paradigm: genealogies of performing devices of subjects of political violence. Chile, 1973–2018 [ANID— Fondecyt 1190834].* Universidad Alberto Hurtado, Santiago, Chile

Juan López Lawyer, Notary, and court clerk with a postgraduate degree in penal law (Universidad de Girona). Twenty years of experience in the defense and promotion of human rights, both in public service and in civil organizations. He is the current Area Director of the Crime Victim Assistance Program of the CNDH and a founding member of the Mexican Team of Psychosocial Treatment and Support (EMAAPSI). Equipo Mexicano de Atención y Acompañamiento Psicosocial, Naucalpan, México

Wilson López-López PhD in Basic and Social Psychology (Universidade de Santiago de Compostela). Professor, Pontificia Universidad Javeriana, Faculty of Psychology. Leader of a research group on social ties and cultures of peace. Editor of *Universitas Psychologica*. Recipient of the Inter-American Psychology Award (2017) of the Inter-American Society of Psychology. Two-time winner (2015 and 2017) of the Research Award of the Universidad Javeriana for outstanding studies. Recipient of the Colombian National Psychology Award (2018) in the Research category. He is a member of several international psychology organizations. Member of the international network of studies on the psychology of peace, councilor of the Global Network of Psychologists for Human Rights, and member of the administrative council of the Colombian College of Psychologists. Pontificia Universidad Javeriana, Bogotá, Colombia

Mireya Lozada PhD in Psychology. Université de Toulouse II, France; Magister Scientiarium in Social Psychology. Universidad Central de Venezuela; Director of the Institute of Psychology (2009–2013). Coordinator of the Master's in Social Psychology (2009–2016). Full Professor, Institute of Psychology, Universidad Central de Venezuela (UCV). Current member of the coordination team of project "Democratic coexistence, citizenship, and social reparation in Venezuela" and the Psychological Support Network of the Universities: Universidad Central de Venezuela (UCV); Universidad Católica Andrés Bello (UCAB); Universidad Metropolitana (UNIMET). Universidad Central de Venezuela, Caracas, Venezuela

Marcelo Marmer Medical doctor specialized in Psychiatry and Psychoanalyst. Graduate of the Escuela Argentina de Psicoterapia para Graduados. Member of the Mental Health Team, CELS (Centro de Estudios Legales y Sociales). Secretary, Fundación de Docencia e Investigación Psicofarmacológica (FundoPsi). Member, Asociación de Psiquiatras Argentinos (APSA). Former Physician of the Judiciary Power. He has published articles about trauma and mourning in relatives and friends of victims of forced disappearance. Author of the book *Encierros involuntarios* [Involuntarily Locked Up], (Ed. Paradiso, 2019, Bs. As.). CELS, Centro de Estudios Legales y Sociales, Buenos Aires, Argentina

Paula María Martínez Velázquez Psychologist, university professor, therapist, and human rights advocate; she specializes in gender and feminisms. She has considerable experience in the study of violence and sexual torture. After 2004, she has worked in the fields of community mental health, psychosocial intervention, and psycho-legal support in cases of severe human rights violations in Guatemala. She has participated in forensic examinations, conducted academic studies, designed projects, and produced educational material for the recovery of historical memory about political violence and the prevention of gender violence, especially in Maya towns. She has given talks in several international forums and seminars held in Nepal, Switzerland, Spain, Germany, Peru, Colombia, Mexico, and the United States, among other countries. She worked for 16 years at the Team of Community studies and Psychosocial Action (ECAP), coordinating the Program for the Construction of Gender Equity. She currently works for Protection International Mesoamérica. Equipo Estudios Comunitarios y Acción Psicosocial (ECAP)/ Protection International, Huehuetenango, Guatemala

Juan Jorge Michel Fariña BSc and PhD in Psychology (Universidad de Buenos Aires). He pursued postgraduate studies at Universitè Paris VI, France. Between 1983 and 1989, he coordinated the assistance program for victims of State terrorism. He has been visiting professor and guest speaker in France, the United States, South Africa, Norway, Switzerland, Spain, and several Latin American countries. He has authored several publications within his field of expertise, including five volumes about Ethics and Human Rights topics viewed through cinema. He co-directs *Ethics&Film Journal* and the Spanish edition of *JAHR*, the European Bioethics Journal. He is Full Professor at UBA, where he teaches the course Psychology, Ethics, and Human Rights at the Faculty of Psychology. He is also a Class I Researcher in UBA's Scientific and Technical Program. Universidad de Buenos Aires, Buenos Aires, Argentina

María Amparo Miranda Psychologist, MSc in Clinical Psychology, Director of Clinical Services at PEI.AC and Director of PEI (international journal), Professor-Researcher at the Universidad del Valle de México Lomas Verdes and the Universidad Bancaria de México, and founding member of the Mexican Team of Psychosocial Treatment and Support (EMAAPSI). Equipo Mexicano de Atención y Acompañamiento Psicosocial, Naucalpan, México

Germán Morales Clinical Psychologist and MSc in Clinical Psychology, Universidad Católica de Chile. Postgraduate degree in Family Therapy, Instituto Chileno de Terapia Familiar. He has worked as a psychotherapist in several institutions that serve low-income areas and victims of human rights violations such as the clinical team of the Instituto Latinoamericano de Salud mental y Derechos Humanos (ILAS), which received the Chilean National Psychology award (2003). He has taught at several universities and, since 2001, he has been an Associate Professor at the Pontificia Universidad Católica de Chile. In addition, he belongs to several organizations, including the Chilean Association of Group Psychoanalytic Psychotherapy, the Youth Systemic Relational Network, and the Chilean Chapter of the International Association of Psychotherapy and Relational Psychoanalysis (IARPP-Chile). He has authored several publications on trauma, adolescence, self-care, and professional burnout. Pontificia Universidad Católica de Chile, Santiago, Chile

Rodrigo Morales BSc in Psychology (Universidad Nacional Autónoma de México) and currently enrolled in the Master's in Psychosocial Approaches for the Construction of Cultures of Peace (Pontificia Universidad Javeriana, Colombia). He has extensive experience in psychosocial work; for instance, he has produced psychosocial assessments in cases of severe human rights violations and has prepared workshops and conferences informed by a psychosocial perspective. Collaborator in the Psychosocial Support Area of Aluna Acompañamiento Psicosocial. ALUNA Acompañamiento Psicosocial A.C., Ciudad de México, México

Sonia Mosquera BSc in Psychology and MSc in Social Psychology (Faculty of Psychology, Universidad de la República, Uruguay). Adjunct Professor at the Institute of Social Psychology. Professor and researcher in the field of human rights and gender, with experience in imprisoned women and the recent past: the current echoes of the dictatorships, intergenerational transmission, and identity construction. Member of the coordination team of the National Plan of Comprehensive Support and Assistance for Uruguayan claimants in the trials "Systematic Children Theft" and "Condor Plan" (Argentina), in association with the "Dr. Fernando Ulloa" Assistance Center for Human Rights Victims, part of the Secretariat of Human Rights (Argentina, 2011–2013). Regional Uruguayan consultant for TecMe (Clinical Territories of Memory), a civil association bringing together professionals with experience in human rights issues connected with memory, truth, justice, and reparation. Universidad de la República, Montevideo, Uruguay

Susana Navarro García Spanish psychologist, resident of Guatemala for nearly 25 years. BSc in Psychology (Universidad Autónoma de Madrid). Social Psychologist specialized in gender studies. Human rights advocate. For 15 years, she coordinated the project "Psychosocial work in processes involving the search and exhumation of victims of forced disappearance," conducted by the Team of Community Research and Psychosocial Action—ECAP. Current Executive Director of ECAP. She has participated in international forums and seminars. In addition, she has written for and collaborated with multiple research projects examining the psychosocial impact of forced disappearance and exhumation processes. These publications include "Resistances against oblivion," which she co-authored, and the collective creation process of the "World Consensus and Basic Norms for psychosocial work in forensic search and investigation processes for cases of forced disappearances and arbitrary or extrajudicial executions." Equipo de Estudios Comunitarios y Acción Psicosocial (ECAP), Ciudad de Guatemala, Guatemala

Carlos Augusto Piccinini MSc in Social and Institutional Psychology. Psychologist. Member of the Testimony Clinics Project, in association with the Ministry of Justice, the Amnesty Commission, and Sigmund Freud Psychoanalytic Association (2013–2015)/Psychoanalytic Association of Porto Alegre APPOA (2016–2017). Member of the Center for the Psychic Reparation of State Violence during the democratic period, in association with the British Council, Newton Fund, and Institute APPOA (2016). Psychoanalytic Association of Porto Alegre (APPOA), Porto Alegre, Brasil

Lísia Da Luz Refosco Psychologist. Psychoanalyst. Effective member of the Sigmund Freud Psychoanalytic Association. MSc in Clinical Psychology (Pontifícia Universidade Católica do Rio Grande do Sul). Member of the Testimony Clinics project/Institute APPOA (2016–2017) and Testimony Clinics/Sigmund Freud Psychoanalytic Association (2013–2015). Author of articles about State violence, trauma, and psychic reparation. In the clinical domain, she has experience in group and individual treatment for victims of the Brazilian dictatorship. Editor of the *SIG Psychoanalysis Journal* (2018–2020). Sigmund Freud Psychoanalytic Association, Porto Alegre, Brasil

María Celia Robaina Psychologist (Universidad Católica del Uruguay); MSc in Clinical Psychology (Universidad de la República—Uruguay); Diploma in Relational Psychoanalysis (Asociación Uruguaya de Psicoanálisis de las Configuraciones Vinculares); Specialist in Psychosocial Actions in Political Violence and Catastrophes (Spain—U. Complutense Madrid y GAC); Diploma in Psychotherapy in Health Care Services (UDELAR). Psychologist of the National Institute of Human Rights and Ombudsman (INDDHH, State agency—Uruguay, since 2016); Member of the Interdisciplinary Team of the "Site of Memory of the former Training Center for Reserve Officers"—CGIOR (since 2021). External consultant for Clinical Territories of Memory (TECME—2018 to date). Adjunct Professor at the Faculty of Psychology of Universidad de la República (1996–2017) in psychology and human rights. Individual and group psychotherapist, founder of the Cooperative of Mental Health and Human Rights (COSAMEDDHH—2009–2016) and the Social Rehabilitation Service (SERSOC—1985–2009). Delivered psychosocial support to a group of 28 former women political prisoners who filed a lawsuit for sexual violence during the State terrorism period (2010–2013). Author of numerous articles. Institución Nacional de Derechos Humanos y Defensoría del Pueblo (INDDHH), Pontifícia Universidade Católica do Rio, Montevideo, Uruguay

Karine Szuchman PhD student and MSc in Social and Institutional Psychology (Universidade Federal do Rio Grande do Sul). Psychologist. Member of the Testimony Clinics Project, in association with the Ministry of Justice, the Amnesty Commission, and Sigmund Freud Psychoanalytic Association (2013–2015)/ Psychoanalytic Association of Porto Alegre APPOA (2016–2017). Member of the Center for the Psychic Reparation of State Violence during the democratic period, in association with the British Council, Newton Fund, and Institute APPOA (2016). Universidade Federal do Rio Grande do Sul, Porto Alegre, Brasil

Viviana Valz Gen BSc in Clinical Psychology (Pontificia Universidad Católica del Perú); Psychoanalyst, specialist in adult, child, and adolescent (Peruvian Institute of Psychoanalysis, part for the Peruvian Psychoanalysis Society); rehabilitation courses for torture survivors (Rehabilitation and Research Center for Torture Victims, Denmark); Diploma: "Mental Health in Contexts of Political Violence and Catastrophes," GAC and Universidad Complutense de Madrid. Coordinator of the Mental Health Unit of the Truth and Reconciliation Commission; co-founder of the Wiñastin Association; member of the Peruvian Association of Child and Adolescent Psychoanalytic Psychotherapy; member of the Mental Health group of the National Human Rights Agency; member of the Psychosocial Support Group for Anthropological-Forensic Research Processes; member of the Contigo Psychologists' Association. Wiñastin Salud Mental Comunitaria, La Aurora, Peru

Ruth Vargas-Forman Psychotherapist and forensic psychologist. PhD in Clinical Psychology (Universidad de Salamanca, España). For fifteen years, she offered clinical services to refugees and asylum seekers at the Torture Treatment Center in the Intercultural Psychiatric Program at the Oregon Health & Science University (OHSU). Pro tem instructor in the Counseling Psychology Doctoral Program at the University of Oregon. Both in Chile and the United States, she has taught graduate students and professionals in areas such as Trauma, Resilience, and Interculturality. She has worked extensively with international human rights organizations promoting culturally sensitive psycho-forensic documentation. In Chile, she has provided training in the Istanbul Protocol: a forensic assessment tool to document consequences of human rights abuses. Dr. Vargas has presented expert testimony at the United States Immigration Court and at the Inter-American Court of Human Rights. Author of the book Pewmas Dreams of Justice: Lonkos and Mapuche Leaders vs Chile at the Inter-American Court. Testimonies and Psycho-Forensic Evidence of the Effects of the Anti-Terrorist Law (2017). *[Pewmas / Sueños de Justicia: Lonkos y dirigentes mapuches vs Chile en la Corte Interamericana. Testimonios y evidencia psico-forense de los efectos de la Ley Antiterrorista*s]. Center for Legal Defense and Research/Centro de Investigación y Defensa Sur (CIDSUR), Temuco, Chile/ Eugene, United States

Vera Vital-Brasil Psychologist (Universidade Gama Filho, UFG), Rio de Janeiro, 1981; Community-Based Mental Health Project: Community Schools in a Favela of Rio de Janeiro, Municipal Secretariat of Social Development, 1981–1984. Specialization in Psychological Theory and Practice in Public Institutions— Transdisciplinary Clinic, Universidade Federal Fluminense, 1993–1994; Institutional clinical psychologist at the "Instituto de Assistência aos Servidores do Estado do Rio de Janeiro," State Secretariat of Health, 1991–2010. Member of the Clinical Group "Torture: Never Again/RJ"; Projects for treating victims of State terrorism, supported by FNUVT (UN) and the European Commission, 1991–2010; Coordinator, Testimony Clinics project, Rio de Janeiro, Amnesty Commission, 2013–2015; Member of the "Human Rights Commission of the Federal Psychology Council," 2014–2015; Professor, "Latin American Seminar on State Violences and

Comprehensive Reparation Policies," Universidad de La Plata, Argentina, 2019–2021; Regional Advisor, "Clinical Territories of Memory" (TeCMe), 2018. Author of book chapters and articles published in local and international journals. Clinical Territories of Memory (TeCMe), Rio de Janeiro, Brasil

Mariana Wikinski Psychoanalyst. Attended the Universidad Central de Venezuela and the Universidad de Buenos Aires. Member of the Mental Health Team of the CELS (Centro de Estudios Legales y Sociales, 1984 to date). Member and former president of the Colegio de Psicoanalistas, Buenos Aires. Supervisor of the Program for child and adolescent victims of mistreatment and sexual abuse. Dirección General de Acompañamiento, Protección y Orientación a las Víctimas (DOVIC, Procuración General de la Nación). Supervisor (2016–2017) at the "Dr. Fernando Ulloa" Centro de Asistencia a Víctimas de Violaciones de Derechos Humanos (Ministerio de Justicia y Derechos Humanos). Author of the book *El trabajo del testigo. Testimonio y experiencia traumática* [The Work of the Witness. Testimony and Traumatic Experience] (2016, Ed. La Cebra, Bs. As, translated to Portuguese). Co-compiler of the book *Clínica Psicoanalítica ante las Catástrofes Sociales* [Psychoanalytic Clinic in the face of Social Catastrophes] (2002, Ed. Paidós, Bs. As.). CELS, Centro de Estudios Legales y Sociales, Buenos Aires, Argentina

Sol Yáñez Born in the Basque Country, Spain. PhD (Universidad del País Vasco, UPV) and Professor-Researcher (Universidad Centroamericana, UCA) in El Salvador. Her lines of research, teaching, and work with people are focused on psychosocial support for victims of human rights violations, historical memory processes, comprehensive reparation, and reconstruction of the psychosocial fabric after armed conflicts and catastrophes. She fulfills advisory and support roles in human rights organizations, relatives of victim's organizations, and institutions in Latin America and Europe. She has conducted several psychosocial forensic assessments and has made recommendations regarding comprehensive reparation issues before the Inter-American Court of Human Rights in cases of forced disappearance, massacres, and extrajudicial executions, among others. She has authored several publications about her lines of research and her book *Heridas abiertas* [Open Wounds], edited by the Ministry of Health of El Salvador, is a reference point for working with victims of human rights violations. Universidad Centroamericana "José Simeón Cañas", San Salvador, El Salvador

Chapter 1
Psychology and Human Rights: An Introduction

Elizabeth Lira, Marcela Cornejo, and Germán Morales

During the twentieth century, Latin America witnessed military coups, civil wars, massacres, and long dictatorships in several countries. The Dominican Republic, Haiti, Nicaragua, Guatemala, Colombia, and El Salvador were the scenes of political violence for decades. In 1959, the Cuban revolution began overthrowing a corrupt dictatorship, inspiring revolutionary movements in different countries—the reaction against these movements spread throughout the continent. Political repression reached women, men and children, guerrillas, students and trade unionists, activists, religious, social, and political leaders. Thousands of people were persecuted, openly and covertly, in the name of the common good, order, and internal security of the countries (Herman, 1982).

The clandestine disappearance, kidnapping, and extermination of people described as "dirty war" occurred in several countries (Martín-Baró, 1989). Torture, cruel and degrading treatment, material, and social losses have had profound psychological and psychosocial effects, prolonged over time, affecting generations. The extension of the conflict and repressive violence spread fear. Thousands of individuals and families abandoned their homes and were forced to be displaced within their country's territory in Colombia, Guatemala, and Peru. Thousands of others dispersed worldwide, assuming the personal and family cost of losing the right to live in their homeland, becoming political refugees and exiles.

Describing a conflictive society, with thousands of victims of torture, forced disappearance, and dead, it can state that almost all the members have been affected to

E. Lira (✉)
Universidad Alberto Hurtado, Santiago, Chile
e-mail: elira@uahurtado.cl

M. Cornejo · G. Morales
Pontificia Universidad Católica de Chile, Santiago, Chile
e-mail: marcela@uc.cl; gpmorale@uc.cl

some extent. The social psychologist and Jesuit priest Ignacio Martín-Baró (1990) conceptualized the disruption of social relations as psychosocial trauma. He analyzes the impact of violence and terror caused by threats, killings, disappearance, death, not only for its consequences on the victims but also for its effects on society, including political polarization. He pointed out that a social sector, almost always a minority, reacts moral and practically, trying to provide protection and help to the victims, struggling to respect people's rights, and attempting to change the political conditions to end such violations and promote political transformations. In some countries, church-based solidarity initiatives provided legal, medical, and psychological services (Cienfuegos & Monelli, 1983). Psychologists who took on the responsibility of working with the victims did so despite the difficulties, often in conditions of risk and vulnerability (Lira, 2017). However, a sector has also supported the repressive policy as necessary in defense of the common good and social order, arguing that the violence exercised was indispensable for ending the conflict while minimizing the personal and social costs and certainly the restriction and violation of rights (Martín-Baró, 1989).

When violence lasts for years or decades, it generates habituation. Paradoxically, the constant decrying of abuses and atrocities produces saturation, making it easier for them to become socially invisible. Trauma and suffering become a private affair of the victims (Weinstein et al., 1987).

The political transitions from de facto regimes to constitutional governments in Latin America and peace negotiations to end armed conflicts began in political contexts marked by the effects of these violent pasts. Political agreements were required to consolidate democratic regimes without jeopardizing the governability of the transition (Acuña & Smulovitz, 2007). Most countries sought to close the past by dictating amnesty laws, hoping that juridical forgetting (and impunity) would guarantee peace. Major and minor crimes vanished from the political horizon along with the victims and perpetrators. In Argentina, the law of national pacification; in Uruguay, the law of expiration of the State's punitive pretension; the amnesty laws in Brazil, Chile, and El Salvador were dictated in the name of social peace and political reconciliation. However, despite impunity as a condition for social stability, some countries had simultaneous internal and international pressure to establish the truth about the recent past and recognize the victims.

Truth commissions were set up in most countries of the region to establish the facts and recognize the victims. Most of the reports of these commissions expressly pointed out the moral and psychological damage to the victims, and some proposed specific recommendations regarding health and mental health. In Argentina, the National Commission on the Disappeared (CONADEP, 1984), in Chile the National Commission on Truth and Reconciliation (CNVR, 1991), in El Salvador From Madness to Hope (1993). In Guatemala, there were two commissions: the Commission for the Recovery of Historical Memory (REMHI, 1998) carried out by the Catholic Church, and the Historical Clarification Commission (CEH, 1999); in Peru, the Truth and Reconciliation Commission (CVR, 2004), and in Uruguay the Commission for Peace (2003) on the cases of the disappeared. In Brazil, it was the National Truth Commission (2014). In Colombia, there are several reports that have documented the consequences and victims of violence (CNMH, 2013; Ruta Pacífica de las Mujeres, 2013). The Peace Accords created a Truth Commission in Colombia, expecting the final report in 2022. In several countries, the forced disappearance of people included the appropriation of their children, who were handed over and grew up in families that hid their history and origin from them. The National Commission for the Right to Identity resulted from joint work between the State and civil society in the recovery of the identity of dozens of appropriated children (CONADI, 2007).

The struggle of victims' organizations against impunity in different latitudes contributes to linking democratic construction and social peace processes with the recognition and reparation of victims. The French magistrate Louis Joinet proposed an ethical, legal, and political framework to ground comprehensive reparation policies for victims, which the United Nations adopted (Joinet, 1997). Restitution, compensation, rehabilitation, and guarantees of non-repetition have been modalities within the concept of comprehensive reparation by the United Nations. This comprehensiveness implied establishing the right to truth, justice, and reparation for the victims' grievances, damages, and physical and psychological harm. The consequences are irreparable for many of them. Reparation requires identifying the effects on individuals and their families, the restitution of their rights and the implementation of various measures to improve the lives of the victims.

Psychosocial and therapeutic interventions are part of reparation strategies, described as rehabilitation processes. Reparation policies in different countries have been based mainly on monetary compensation ranging from one-time payments to life-long contributions delivered monthly. Victims have demanded in various instances the need to guarantee comprehensive reparations. Among their demands, they have insisted on rehabilitation as a form of reparation. The demand for rehabilitation often arose from the experience of the victims themselves, who received health and mental health care, support, and individual or community psychosocial accompaniment in very critical and afflictive conditions, and close to the occurrence of the acts of violence. Since the political transitions, some States have created public reparation policies that have gathered experiences of various professional groups in different Latin American countries, which have theoretically and practically based intervention models, especially in the clinical and psychosocial fields.

Since the late 1970s, some psychologists denounced the effects of the human rights violations they observed in international and national instances, held work and discussion meetings, and documented their professional practice. Articles and books compiled the work done by mental health professionals, psychiatrists, psychologists, physicians, anthropologists, and social workers, sometimes in the same country or countries of exile, documenting their experiences, work models, and emerging economies theories.

As editors of Human Rights Violations in Latin America, we invited colleagues whom we had met at congresses and seminars over the years to write to us to gather their experiences and reflections on their professional actions in contexts of human rights violations. NGO networks, in which professional groups have worked with victims since the 1980s and 1990s, allowed us to know the value of the work done. Preparing this publication took several years and responds to recording and sharing the contribution of psychology in reparation and rehabilitation of victims, the policies on truth and justice, political memory, and symbolic reparation.

Outline of the Book

This book contributes to the knowledge and understanding of the psychological practices in Latin America with victims of political violence and violations of human rights in the last decades. The book is divided into six sections, starting with "History, situations, concepts, and approaches," which comprises four chapters. The first chapter examines the history of mental health programs in Chile after 1973, working with former political prisoners, relatives of victims of forced disappearances, relatives of executed persons, and other victims of human rights violations under Dictatorship (1973–1990). The work includes the continuity of several research lines, contributing to memory's field studies after the political transition.

The following chapters refer to clinical, legal, and psychosocial approaches related to forced disappearances in Uruguay and Argentina. The CELS' team chapter reflects the legal and subjective dimensions included, considering forced disappearance as torture in the Argentine case. They contribute to the conceptualization of trauma, the mourning caused by disappearance, and the narration of the trauma in court. The next chapter refers to the appropriation of Uruguayan's children and their conflictive construction of identity. They were located mainly by "Abuelas de Plaza de Mayo" from Argentina. We learn how identity is constructed in these young people through the seven protagonists after discovering them. Some eventually recognize their origin and resume ties with the families from which they were stripped; others reject any possibility of learning about their origins that threaten their constructed "identity" out of loyalty to the adoptive or appropriating family. The circumstances that lead to one or the other decision can only be understood in each story's singularity.

The identity restitution is the matter of the last chapter of this section. The search for people, now adults, who disappeared in their childhood or were born in captivity refers to the story of appropriation and restitution and renews crucial questions about parental functions in extreme situations. This chapter establishes essential perspectives, including the right to identity and the symbolic and subjective value of genetic data; the psychological implications related to the parental function and the role of memory in constructing identity. They also illustrate the psychosocial influence through cinema, literature, and photography, which made this topic a heritage of humanity.

The second section, "Psychosocial assistance and intervention methodologies," comprises two chapters related to different approaches on the psychosocial work with social organizations under sociopolitical violence in Mexico. The first one is the chapter written by professionals of *Aluna Acompañamiento Psicosocial* explaining their method and methodology in contexts of sociopolitical violence. They describe and analyze the case of an organization that defends the territory and has threatened, suffering harassment and other aggressions.

The next chapter describes the construction of a psychosocial care and support model based on the training of peer psychosocial companions. The authors underlined the need to review and reformulate mental health professionals' training. They provide transdisciplinary skills and foster interdisciplinary dialogue, offering a Mexican psychosocial attention and accompaniment model.

The third section, "Psychotherapeutic Interventions," includes three chapters related to therapeutic approaches and practices in Uruguay, Guatemala, and Chile. The Uruguayan experience describes the specific approach carried out by several therapists working from a psychoanalytical perspective with former political prisoners. The research collected the therapist's observations relating to this clinic's particularities, allowing discussions on theoretical and technical aspects of the treatments, including the patient's political experience.

The next chapter illustrates the possibilities of psychosocial reparation for Guatemalan women who have experienced domestic and sexual violence in their lives. A therapeutic workshop based on arpillera patchwork crafts production fosters two parallel paths of psychosocial recovery: one involves re-processing and assimilation of past political conflicts; the other focuses on the capacity to make decisions, transforming the present life situations. Both paths break the cycle of violence. The process allows the experience of recovering control and power over one's own life and strengthen one's identity as a woman.

The last chapter of this section systematizes some of the main therapeutic group strategies developed in Chile by NGOs and social organizations under the civil-military dictatorship and at the beginning of the political transition. The primary theoretical references were group psychotherapy theory, extreme traumatization, and relational psychoanalysis trauma theory. Each therapeutic experience highlighted the space for working through traumatic situations lived at the individual and social levels. The group function as a third party that recognizes and validates, contains, and allows for the restitution of the damaged collective bonds as a specific contribution of the group device.

The fourth section, "Psychological and psychosocial approach and support during forensic examinations and trials," comprises three chapters related to judicial cases. The first one refers to the El Mozote Massacre and the expert research for building psychosocial reparation of victims. The judicial reparations would be based on the psychosocial process carried out with the survivors and their relatives asking for justice for more than 1000 assassinated children, women, and men. The expert psychosocial assessment supports the claim presented by the Association of Victims of El Mozote before the Inter-American Court of Human Rights, rising a methodology constructed to visualize the victims and to listen to their voices.

The second chapter of this section refers to the women of Sepur Zarco. In 2010, 15 indigenous Q'eqchi' women of the Sepur Zarco community in Guatemala filed a legal complaint. They were survivors of violence and sexual and domestic slavery; they suffered in the military post in their community during the Guatemalan armed conflict. As a result of their suit, in 2016, a Guatemalan court convicted an army officer and a former military officer of human rights violations against women. The chapter analyzes the role of these women in the process of seeking truth, justice, and reparations linked to the organizations that accompanied them, making visible their leading role in the search for justice that was part of their recovery and healing. It also describes the psychosocial work carried out with the women in the Sepur Zarco case to address the consequences of human rights violations suffered and empowered them to face the judicial process and claim their rights.

The third chapter refers to the case "*Norin Catriman, Lonkos* and *Mapuche* Indigenous Leaders versus Chile" in the Inter-American System for the Protection of Human Rights. It reviews the contribution of forensic psychology in litigation related to human rights violations concerning indigenous peoples. The Inter-American Court of Human Rights in May 2014 sanctioned the State of Chile for violations of the American Convention and the rights of eight indigenous leaders wrongly convicted under the Antiterrorist Law. In this litigation, the psychological evaluations based on the Istanbul Protocol provided the Inter-American Court with the elements to delineate the effect of the persecutions and convictions under the Antiterrorist Law on a personal, familial, and community level. This case underlines the essential role of psycho-forensic evidence and the role of professional psychologists in accompanying victims in trials in the Inter-American Court. It also outlines the relevance of using culturally appropriate methodologies when documenting the multidimensional effects of human rights abuses that affect indigenous peoples. This case illustrates the importance of using the Istanbul Protocol to document collective and individual abuses that affect indigenous communities on the continent.

The fifth section, "Psychosocial reparations: Challenges of victims recognition," includes two chapters related to Brazilian experiences, and the other one refers to the Colonia Dignidad, a Chilean-German case. The Clinics of Testimony are therapeutic and psychosocial experiences developed in Brazil. Clinical assistance, training of psychologists, and written material regarding its application in the national territory are the main components of this practice. The Rio de Janeiro project addressed persecuted people who had requested their recognition before the governmental reparation body called the Amnesty Commission and their relatives. The testimony contributes to rebuilding social ties, valorizing power to produce personal changes, and constructing individual and collective memory. The other Brazilian chapter narrates a similar experience in Porto Alegre/Rio Grande do Sul. Specifically, it addressed interventions with members of the military who wanted the State to recognize them as victims of political violence when they served in the Armed Forces.

Colonia Dignidad was an enclave of German settlers established in southern Chile in 1961, lasting more than four decades (1961–2005). Germany and Chile linked through this institution on which crimes against humanity and the most various criminal actions were committed and harbored under the umbrella of the Dignity Charitable and Educational Society, a German, Christian, and charitable organization. Different illegal activities were executed, including human rights violations during Chile's civil-military dictatorship (1973–1990). This chapter presents a psychosocial analysis regarding the current situation of the different groups of victims and the complex victim-victimizer configuration in this context.

The sixth section, "Political and psychosocial challenges of transitions," comprises three chapters related to political transition in Colombia, Venezuela, and Peru. The chapter on Venezuela situation describes the impact of a complex humanitarian emergency with international repercussions. During this multidimensional crisis, citizens are fighting for a democratic transition while developing forms of resistance that challenge an authoritarian model that seeks to break the population's will and dignity. The text proposes several ideas for reconstruction of the social fabric fractured by the conflict, the fight against impunity and the search for justice for the victims, as well as the construction of scenarios of a shared common future, which favor peaceful and democratic coexistence in the country.

The chapter related to Colombia describes and reviews contributions that have explored the consequences of the social and armed conflict on victims of human rights violations. This context has been a scenario that has exponentially triggered repeated human rights violations. This chapter proposes a research and intervention model with a multidimensional analysis perspective that demonstrates the role of psychosocial processes such as forgiveness, reconciliation, transitional justice mechanisms in restoring human rights at the individual, community, and social levels. The work of psychology is key to promoting human rights and seeking ways to contribute to sustainable peace.

The last chapter provides a brief review of Peru's process, development, and status of mental health work. It presents the experience of the Mental Health Unit of the Truth and Reconciliation Commission of Peru (CVR) and its contribution to the understanding and management of mental health issues. It proposes a methodology, recognizing how the living conditions associated with submission, abuse, and violence generate emotional suffering in individuals and peoples, giving rise to severe mental health problems that must be addressed comprehensively, prioritizing a community approach.

Conclusions

This book is a retrospective look at professional actions with victims, their families, and communities during and after conflicts. The various chapters illustrate the different approaches and working modalities in processes of reparation and political memory. After the transitions, the experience of victim rehabilitation carried out by non-governmental organizations or private practices during the armed conflict and dictatorships contributed to the formulation of public reparation policies in some countries. Practitioners applied rehabilitation strategies based on different theoretical orientations and models, depending on the political and institutional conditions of the context. They also worked on strengthening organizations and victims to demand their rights.

The collection of texts that make up this book reports on clinical, psychosocial, and community interventions with victims of human rights violations and political violence from Mexico to Chile.

The particularities of the local political and social contexts and their historical moments differentiate the situation of the victims and the work methodologies in each case. At the same time, an approach is outlined from psychology based on ethical and professional options that propose recognition of people's dignity and the rehabilitation and reparation of the victims and their families and communities.

The strategies and comprehensive theoretical models developed in the chapters have in common:

(a) The consideration of the political and social context as an indispensable dimension in psychological work. The sociopolitical, cultural, community, and family contexts are part of the comprehensive analysis and intervention modalities, identifying individual and collective resources, cultural aspects that affect social relations, families, subjects, and situations that affect or frame professional intervention.

(b) The complex needs of the victims generated a theoretical opening beyond the different clinical models commonly used. The search for knowledge that would contribute to understanding the implications and consequences of human rights violations on individuals, families, groups, and work teams broadened visions and practices. The authors describe how they put their work at the service of the needs of the victims.

(c) The professionals have designed interventions suited to the subjects' needs and their contexts. The various methodologies express the creativity of professionals and teams dealing with complex needs in adverse contexts. This book analyzes experiences of workshops, group psychotherapies, community interventions and long-term psychosocial aid experiences, psycho-legal accompaniment in judicial litigation and forensic activities, psychotherapeutic interventions, case analysis and research on psychosocial and political processes.

The chapters offer—in different contexts—a conceptualization of the consequences of political violence on individuals. The diverse experiences recounted are also a way of recording and leaving a mark on the work of psychologists who, in situations of conflict and political violence, use the discipline to contribute to understanding, mitigating, and repairing the human suffering of individuals, groups, families, and communities.

At the beginning of the second decade of the twenty-first century, new social and political movements have emerged in various Latin American countries. They linked to old and recent cross-cutting social demands, incorporating new forms of participation and social organization and new perspectives based on gender, interculturality, and ecology, in globalized contexts. Many authorities of these countries responded to these new demands with repressive strategies that once again implied human rights violations. Once again, violence exercised on bodies, organizations and communities, and against political ideas and practices.

This contingent political and social scenario appeals to psychologists to collaborate with their work and knowledge in different areas. They are documenting, making a memory to learn from the past, and for understanding conflicts' roots. The recognition and reparation of the victims, assuming the irreparable dimensions that violence and state terrorism have caused them, has contributed to the construction of peace and democratic coexistence.

In this new context, this book provides a professional response to the atrocity generated by sustained violence and human rights violations, addressing individual and collective traumatic experiences. The authors' reflections underline the importance of debating these traumatic issues within a human rights framework beyond the clinic and psychosocial approaches.

References

Acuña, C., & Smulovitz, C. (2007). Militares en la transición argentina: del gobierno a la subordinación constitucional. En A. Pérotin-Dumon (Dir.), *Historizar el pasado vivo en América Latina* (pp. 3–94). Universidad Alberto Hurtado. Retrieved from http://ijdh.unla.edu.ar/advf/documentos/2018/03/5aba57caaf2a2.pdf

Centro Nacional de Memoria Histórica. (2013). *¡Basta ya! Colombia: Memorias de guerra y dignidad.* Bogotá, Colombia. Retrieved from http://www.centrodememoriahistorica.gov.co/descargas/informes2013/bastaYa/basta-ya-colombia-memorias-de-guerra-y-dignidad-2016.pdf

Cienfuegos, A. J., & Monelli, C. (1983). The testimony of political repression as a therapeutic instrument. *American Journal of Ortopsychiatry, 53,* 43–51. https://doi.org/10.1111/j.1939-0025.1983.tb03348.x

Comisión de la Verdad para El Salvador. (1993). *De la Locura a la Esperanza. La guerra de 12 años en El Salvador. Informe de la Comisión de la Verdad para El Salvador.* Organización de Naciones Unidas. Retrieved from http://www.derechoshumanos.net/lesahumanidad/informes/elsalvador/informe-de-la-locura-a-la-esperanza.htm

Comisión de la Verdad y Reconciliación. (2004). *Hatun Willakuy: versión abreviada del Informe Final de la Comisión de la Verdad y Reconciliación.* Fondo Editorial PUCP. Retrieved from https://www.verdadyreconciliacionperu.com/admin/files/libros/162_digitalizacion.pdf

Comisión Nacional de Verdad y Reconciliación. (1991). *Informe de la Comisión Nacional de Verdad y Reconciliación.* Santiago. Retrieved from http://pdh.minjusticia.gob.cl/comisiones/

Comisión Nacional por el Derecho a la Identidad (CONADI). (2007). *El trabajo del Estado en la recuperación de la identidad de jóvenes apropiados en la última dictadura militar.* CONADI. Retrieved from http://www.jus.gob.ar/media/1129163/36-conadi_2_el_trabajo_del_estado.pdf

Comisión Nacional sobre la Desaparición de Personas (CONADEP). (1984). *Informe "Nunca más".* Argentina. Retrieved from http://www.derechoshumanos.net/lesahumanidad/informes/argentina/informe-de-la-CONADEP-Nunca-mas.htm

Comisión para el Esclarecimiento Histórico (CEH). (1999). *Informe Guatemala: Memoria del Silencio.* Guatemala. Retrieved from https://www.derechoshumanos.net/lesahumanidad/informes/guatemala/informeCEH.htm

Comisión para la Paz. (2003). *Informe final de la Comisión para la Paz.* Uruguay. Retrieved from https://www.usip.org/sites/default/files/file/resources/collections/commissions/Uruguay-Report_Informal.pdf

Comissão Nacional da Verdade (CNV). (2014). *Relatório Final da Comissão Nacional da Verdade.* Brasil. Retrieved from http://cnv.memoriasreveladas.gov.br/index.php/outros-destaques/576-verdade-e-reconciliacao-dentro-e-fora

Herman, E. (1982). *The real network of terror.* South End.

Joinet, L. (1997). *La administración de la justicia y los derechos humanos de los detenidos. La cuestión de la impunidad de los autores de violaciones de los derechos humanos (civiles y políticos).* Subcomisión de Prevención de Discriminación y Protección de Minorías. Comisión de Derechos Humanos. ONU. Retrieved from http://www.derechos.org/nizkor/doc/joinete.html

Lira, E. (2017). The Chilean human rights archives and moral resistance to dictatorship. *International Journal of Transitional Justice, 11*(2), 1–12. https://doi.org/10.1093/ijtj/ijx015

Martín-Baró, I. (1989). Prólogo. In E. Lira & D. Becker (Eds.), *Derechos Humanos: Todo es según el dolor con que se mira* (pp. 8–10). Ediciones Instituto Latinoamericano de Salud Mental y Derechos Humanos.

Martín-Baró, I. (1990). De la guerra sucia a la guerra psicológica: El caso de El Salvador. *Revista de Psicología de El Salvador, 9*(35), 109–122. Retrieved from http://www.uca.edu.sv/coleccion-digital-IMB/wp-content/uploads/2015/11/1990-de-la-guerra-sucia-a-la-guerra-psicol%C3%B3gica-el-caso-de-El-Salvador.pdf

Proyecto Interdiocesano de Recuperación de la Memoria Histórica (REMHI). (1998). *Guatemala: Nunca Más.* Oficina de Derechos Humanos del Arzobispado de Guatemala. Retrieved from https://www.derechoshumanos.net/lesahumanidad/informes/guatemala/informeREMHI.htm

Ruta Pacífica de las Mujeres. (2013). *La verdad de las mujeres víctimas del conflicto armado en Colombia.* Comisión de Verdad y Memoria de Mujeres. Retrieved from https://rutapacifica.org.co/wp/la-verdad-de-las-mujeres-victimas-del-conflicto-armado-en-colombia-informe-de-comision-de-verdad-y-memoria/

Weinstein, E., Lira, E., & Rojas, M. E. (1987). *Trauma, duelo y reparación.* FASIC/Editorial Interamericana.

Part I
History, Situations, Concepts, and Approaches

Chapter 2
Psychology and Human Rights in Chile: Assistance, Registration, Denunciation, Rehabilitation, and Reparation

Elizabeth Lira and Marcela Cornejo

Introduction

After the coup d'état of September 11, 1973, thousands of people were arrested in Chile. Supporters of the overthrown government were denounced as enemies; courts-martial were set up throughout the country to try them. There was little or no legal for people, yet the press publicized convictions and death sentences (Vicaría de la Solidaridad, 1991). The magnitude of the political repression is reflected in the 18,364 people who reported having been detained during 1973 to the National Commission on Political Prisoners and Torture, a figure equivalent to 64% of the qualified cases (Comisión Nacional sobre Prisión Política y Tortura, 2004, p. 79).

About 12,000 people sought refuge in diplomatic embassies and offices (Del Pozo, 2006; Frenz, 2006; Hiilamo, 2015). It is estimated that between 400,000 and 600,000 Chileans and their families left the country during the dictatorship for political or economic reasons (Cornejo, 2015). Some churches reacted by creating the Committee for Peace in Chile [COPACHI] assisting Chilean people who were persecuted. In 1973, the National Committee for Aid to Refugees [CONAR] helped thousands of refugees, mainly Latin Americans (Harper, 2007). In 1975, the Christian Churches Social Aid Foundation FASIC was created (Orellana & Hutchinson, 1991).

Institutional responses to the emergency involved professional learning in a context of threat and uncertainty. Lawyers, social workers, medical doctors, and psychologists became involved in the defense of people's rights, effectively responding

E. Lira (✉)
Universidad Alberto Hurtado, Santiago, Chile
e-mail: elira@uahurtado.cl

M. Cornejo
Pontificia Universidad Católica de Chile, Santiago, Chile
e-mail: marcela@uc.cl

to victims' needs through the deployment of resources and strategies. This work became a form of moral resistance to the dictatorship (Lira, 2017; Lowden, 1996). This experience and knowledge on psychological care would be the reference for rehabilitation and reparation policies for the victims' health at the end of the dictatorship.

Emergency Psychological Support: 1973–1975

Thousands of people were arrested, and thousands more were dismissed from their jobs for political reasons. They turned to COPACHI for legal and social help. COPACHI initially provided free medical care through a network of volunteers. Mental health care began with volunteer psychologists. The consulting population were relatives of political prisoners, former detainees under a state of siege, relatives of the politically executed, and later relatives of disappeared persons. In 1975, 2166 people in Santiago consulted psychologists, and adult and child psychiatrists. The health program provided a total of 64,986 medical services, including different medical specialist and mental health care (COPACHI, 1975).

In 1975, the Archbishop of Concepción and Arauco, Manuel Sánchez, created the Social Service Department of the Archbishopric of Concepción to provide legal assistance to those affected by the country's emergency laws, to assist their families, and to provide legal assistance regarding labor rights to those who were dismissed from their jobs. This was the origin of the Human Rights Pastoral (Arzobispado de la Santísima Concepción, 1988). After 1982 a health program was created providing medical and psychological services for victims and their families, which closed at the end of the dictatorship.

COPACHI closed due to pressure from the government (Frenz, 2006). In January 1976, the Catholic Church created the Vicariate of Solidarity, incorporating COPACHI's programs and personnel into the new entity. The mental health team expanded, including general medicine and psychiatry. The Vicariate documented the complex life circumstances of the individuals and families who consulted as well as the effects of detention, torture, and persecution, aggravated by impoverishment and unemployment (FUNVISOL—Fundación de Documentación y Archivo de la Vicaria de la Solidaridad, 1978a, b, 1980).

In 1980, the Vicariate health team presented a synthesis of its work at a meeting convened to share human rights organizations' psychological and psychosocial care work. They pointed out that the most frequent reasons for consultation were acute anguish and sleep disturbances. They described the repressive situation as an extraordinary and transitory experience. They prioritized crisis interventions, mobilizing "facilitating" experiences to resume the life project and link it to a social project. They reflected on the therapeutic relationship "(...) not only from the perspective of the therapist's safety, but also in the exercise of the profession itself (...) psychotherapy becomes a dangerous profession. The patients' experiences are of such a quality that the emotional commitment is unavoidable (...). Inevitably the therapist becomes involved far beyond what the previous reality may have demanded of him" (BBJ & SLC, 2017, p. 209).[1]

Massive jobs dismissals for political reasons in the context of hyperinflation and economic crisis in the country, and political repression exacerbated families' conflicts. The Vicariate's health team provided medical, psychiatric, and psychological care and collaborated with the legal defense by providing clinical reports certifying the effects on the physical and mental health of people who had been victims of political repression. They insisted that the political repression and the terror spread by the human rights violations, the uncertainty and insecurity generated, severely affected individuals and their families. Torture, fear, unemployment, and food shortages were all factors that contributed to severe emotional disturbances (FUNVISOL, 1982).

From Emergency to Institutionalization

The Christian Churches Social Aid Foundation [FASIC] began its work in 1975. One of its main programs was facilitating the commutation of prison sentences for thousands of prisoners convicted in courts-martial, supporting applications to foster care programs in more than 70 countries (Garcés & Nicholls, 2005; Reyna, 2005).

The Psychiatric Medical Program [PMS] was created at FASIC in 1977. One year after former prisoners who were leaving the country participated with their families in "exile orientation" groups. Going into exile was contradictory: future conditions were idealized despite not knowing about available opportunities in the destination's country. The potential for later reunion of the family upon leaving the country and the loss of the right to live in their homeland were central points in the psychological work, delving into the implications of this decision, the expectations of the family, and the definitive separation with fellow prisoners (Lira, 1999; Pollarolo & Rojas, 1986).

At the beginning of the PMS-FASIC, the crisis intervention approach prevailed. But demand increased and the complexity of the cases became evident. It was necessary to discuss therapeutic strategies, intervention modalities (individual, group), integration of medical care, social support, and psychotherapy. Documenting and disseminating this work through seminars and publications was also important (Colectivo Chileno de Trabajo Psicosocial, 1982; Lira, 1986).

The Vicariate health team analyzed the effects of forced disappearance on 140 children (FUNVISOL, 1978c). Most of the children were referred to PMS-FASIC. The psychologists who attended them noted that the children suffered destabilizing experiences: "the death or disappearance of their father, hunger and malnutrition, or the imperious need to leave their homeland, friends, grandparents (...) they live immersed in chaos, they are half-informed, not informed, or given very

---

[1] The authors were the psychologists Berta Bravo and Sergio Lucero.

distorted information (...) 'perhaps to protect them from suffering'" (Cerda & Lagos, 2017, p. 180).[2]

The PMS-FASIC psychologists, psychiatrists, and social workers served youth and adults in individual, couple, and family therapy. Psychosocial care was also provided to incarcerated prisoners, entering during visiting hours. They offered therapeutic groups for unemployed former prisoners, some of them also former union leaders who lost their jobs and their organizations (Lira, 1999; Lira & Weinstein, 1982). Therapeutic groups for returnees from exile (Castillo, 1986; Salamovich & Domínguez, 1986; Weinstein, 1986a, b). Groups held with relatives of disappeared and politically executed detainees; with young children of disappeared and politically executed detainees; young tortured marginalized from study or work due to detention. Groups held with children and young people returning to the country (Domínguez & Delpiano, 1986; Kovalskys & Lira, 1983). Beginning in 1978, professionals organized workshops for occupational therapy, working with wood, bone, loom, metal, and leather crafts. The Vicariate teams referred patients who also required psychosocial support to the workshops (Weinstein et al., 1987).

After May 1983, there were periodic massive protests against the dictatorship. The government repressed the protests violently and harshly. The demand for psychological care grew to such an extent that it was necessary to organize workshops in the field, with volunteer professionals' cooperation to deal with the consequences of the violence in the massive raids on poor settlements, followed by the detention of many "pobladores." Teams formed with professionals from the human rights organizations, the Medical Association [Colegio Médico], and Psychological Association [Colegio de Psicólogos] worked together facing the emergency (Lira et al., 1987).

Threats and intimidation against social groups and institutions intensified after 1985. People, including psychologists working with victims of repression and family members, received death threats by telephone or by letter. Some human rights agencies were occupied by state agents for hours, while people on the premises were interrogated, threatened, and mistreated. Psychosocial accompaniment workshops were held for those affected (Castillo & Lira, 1986; Lira et al., 1985). The PMS psychologists of FASIC received the National Award of the Chilean Psychological Association [Colegio de Psicólogos] in 1983 for their professional work (Domínguez et al., 1984).

New Mental Health Programs

Support for victims depended on political and professional conditions in the regions. Through various bishoprics throughout the country, the Catholic Church provided legal and welfare assistance to persecuted persons associated with COPACHI.

---

[2] Rosario Domínguez and Adriana Maggi were the psychologists who carried out this work.

Some professionals sought to expand the capacity for mental health care by creating independent non-governmental organizations. In 1979, the Fundación para la Infancia Dañada por Estados de Emergencia PIDEE was created in Santiago to provide psychological care, psycho-pedagogical support, and recreational workshops to children and young people. The institution created small regional teams that linked up with other human rights organizations in Linares, Talca, Chillán, Temuco, and Valdivia.

Psychologists, medical doctors, social workers, and other professionals documented their work in pamphlets, books, and articles (Álamos, 1986; Álamos et al., 1992; Duarte, 1987; Escorza & Maureira, 1989; PIDEE, 1985). Towards the end of the dictatorship, the institution became part of the Coordinating Committee of Mental Health Teams [CESAM], projecting its experience for the mental health policies concerning victims during the transition from dictatorship to elected civilian government (Espinoza et al., 1989).

PIDEE progressively completed its care work, which reached about 12,000 children and young people. It currently (2021) functions as the PIDEE-CEDIAL Documentation Center. One can find articles, books, and manuscripts on its work during the dictatorship and on the activities carried out up to the present (2020).

In 1980, the Corporation for the Defense of People's Rights CODEPU was created to defend life and denounce nationally and internationally the grave human rights violations committed in the country. A multidisciplinary team structured for the "Denunciation, investigation and treatment of the tortured and their family group" DIT-T. Teams were set up in Valparaíso, Talca, Concepción, and Valdivia. This comprehensive and interdisciplinary approach led to creating a team that included doctors from different specialties, psychologists, social workers, sociologists, and research assistants, who participated directly or indirectly in patients' therapeutic accompaniment. The tortured and political prisoners inside prisons and their families received medical and psychological care. The institution also assisted relatives of the executed, victims of forced disappearance, and returnees from exile.

Paz Rojas, a co-founder of CODEPU, neuropsychiatrist, wrote:

We have placed as one of the central objectives of the activity of the DIT-T team the denunciation of repressive acts (...) because as health and social science professionals we consider it an ethical obligation (...). A totalizing study of the repressed person (in its biographical, social, cultural, political aspects) will allow us to understand the reactions and clinical manifestations better and decide the most appropriate therapeutic interventions (...). Therefore, understanding the damage requires an integrated approach that allows considering it in a framework of values and life choices made by the person who was the victim of political repression (...). As a therapeutic team, we are not neutral towards our patients. We are on the same side. We share the rejection of a totalitarian power system, which systematically violates human rights, making violence, and torture its form of social order. This fact establishes a therapeutic link of a different nature to that found in general medical practice (...). Suppose we would like to identify our work in epidemiological terms. In that case, we could say that the denunciation corresponds to a level of primary prevention insofar as it tries to create awareness and shape opinion to prevent political repression and torture. Our individual and collective therapeutic action is part of secondary prevention. Its attempt to repair the damage and, finally, our intransigent commitment to help build a society in which human rights are truly respected constitutes, in our opinion, the third level of prevention (CODEPU, 1989, p. 1).

CODEPU's treatment and prevention proposal (Raszczynski et al., 1991) was extended in 1987 to the "Truth and Justice" program to identify and reveal the mechanisms of impunity and their consequences on individuals, families, and society (CODEPU DIT-T, 1994, 1996; Rojas, 2017). They created after 1987 a family therapy collective. They registered and documented more than 3000 people assisted until 1991, 600 of them inside prisons (Estrada et al., 1997; Faúndez et al., 1991). CODEPU continues its work in 2021.

In 1984, a mental health program was started at the Methodist Polyclinic in Temuco to assist political prisoners still incarcerated and provide psychosocial services to their families and other victims. This team formed one year after the Regional Mental Health Center CRESAM. They worked with victims' groups, developed human rights education programs, and provided psychotherapeutic care to relatives of disappeared and executed detainees, political prisoners, and returnees from exile. Professionals from FASIC and later ILAS supported the work until CRESAM closure in 1995.[3] The professionals documented their work, focusing mainly on the therapeutic modalities implemented (Aránguiz et al., 1988). More than 500 people received individual psychotherapeutic care, including workers from human rights organizations, during its 10 years of existence. In their writings, CRESAM professionals pointed out that "(...) the harm arises from the direct exercise of violence and the distortion of human relations that it entails" (Aránguiz et al., 1995, p. 35). They concluded that the task of mental health in these conditions consists of "not hiding pain and suffering but unveiling it and participating in the transformation of the conditions that generate it" (Aránguiz et al., 1995, p. 37). In the region of Araucanía, many of the victims of forced disappearance and political execution were of Mapuche origin. The team accompanied the families and the victims' groups in the legal proceedings. CRESAM worked with the community of professionals in the region and with victims groups and held workshops on the consequences of fear, torture, exile and return, and the effects of human rights violations.

In 1985, the Stress Research and Treatment Center CINTRAS was founded in Santiago, with the Rehabilitation Center for Torture Victims in Denmark's [IRCT] support. Its main objective was to provide medical-psychological treatment to victims of serious human rights violations. The team included psychologists, psychiatrists, family therapists, social workers, occupational therapists, physiotherapists, and kinesiologists. They built a psychotherapeutic approach from an integral perspective (Vidal, 1990). Between 1985 and 1991, 1344 people were assisted. The professional teams offered individual, family, and group care (Madariaga & Díaz, 1993). According to their statements, the therapeutic approach implemented theoretical and technical epistemological resources from the different currents of modern psychotherapy (Madariaga, 2002; Vidal, 1993). In addition to kinesitherapy, the

---

[3] ILAS: Instituto Latinoamericano de Salud Mental y Derechos Humanos [Latin American Institute of Mental Health and Human Rights] was created in 1988.

socio-family and work aspects of the persons attended and addressed to occupational therapy workshops implemented as a complement for patients with severe psychic damage.

In 1988, the Latin American Institute of Mental Health and Human Rights [ILAS] was founded, with some professionals coming from FASIC. The team implemented a model of comprehensive psychosocial care, including specialized medical care. Between 1988 and 1992, the ILAS team carried out clinical and psychosocial research. The most important was the study on the prevalence of different illnesses in patients (Vío, 1992) and the effects of fear on political behavior (Lira & Castillo, 1991). The ILAS team participated in seminars with human rights and mental health institutions in Concepción, supported the creation of the mental health program of the Human Rights Pastoral and the training of psychology students from the University of Concepción doing their practical internships in this program, supervising their clinical work and, after 1988, organizing therapeutic groups.

After 1988, therapists of ILAS collaborated with the Psychiatry Service of the Puerto Montt Hospital, supporting therapeutic activities with former political prisoners' organizations. They also collaborated with the Mental Health program of the Methodist Church-PROMESA in Punta Arenas in the care of former prisoners and exile returnees, contributing to a regional census to identify those who required health care. They worked in San Antonio and Valparaíso with groups of former political prisoners in therapeutic workshops. Professionals of ILAS, CRESAM and the Department of Psychology of the Universidad de La Frontera (Temuco) gave a diploma course on "Psychotherapy of extreme traumatization" in 1991.

Main Concepts of the Psychological Approach of Mental Health Teams

Suffering, losses, and traumatic effects of repressive violence motivated people to seek professional help. The gravity of the mental health consequences of political repression observed led professionals to denounce them in articles, public statements, and presentations to various audiences. Their purpose was to unite wills to end human rights violations and to generate responsibility for the victims, emphasizing the non-ethical nature of professional neutrality in the face of human rights violations in a social context of fear, threat, and distrust (Rodríguez, 1978; Rodríguez et al., 1980).

The mental health team of the Vicariate and the PMS-FASIC registered their cases according to the repressive situations admitted by the institutions, documenting in practice a *situational* diagnosis linked to the repressive event. It categorized as "relative of a disappeared detainee," "relative of a politically executed person," or "political prisoner." This situational diagnosis incorporated into the taxonomy applied by the Program for Reparation and Comprehensive Health Care [PRAIS] under the Ministry of Health since 1991.

The PMS-FASIC team described the therapeutic relationship as a "committed bond" with the patient's life and dignity, prevailing over ideological or political considerations. They analyzed the therapist's role in a threatening context and referred to the nature of the bond from an ethical and critical perspective. They reviewed the theoretical visions that framed such work, defining the limits and scope of psychotherapy with political repression victims. The declared purpose was "to repair the repercussions of the traumatic impacts of violence linked to political repression on the damaged subject. The aim is to reestablish the subject's relationship with reality and recover his/her capacity to relate to people and things. Recovering capacities to project his/her work and future, through a better knowledge of him/herself and resources and by broadening his/her awareness of the reality in which he/she has lived" (Lira & Weinstein, 1984, p. 13; Lira, 2016). This vision was shared by the professional mental health teams, as expressed in their research publications. The theoretical approaches of the teams were systemic, psychoanalytic, cognitive-behavioral, phenomenological, and psychiatric. Coincidences in the general conceptualization coexisted with a diversity of therapeutic practices. External researchers highlighted the conceptual and practical similarities observed, identifying a sort of "Chilean model" (Agger & Jensen, 1996).

International and Academic Relations Between Mental Health and Human Rights Teams

Some mental health professionals working in human rights programs in Chile, mainly in FASIC, participated in 1986 in a seminar organized by the Medical Union of Uruguay and the US medical organization Esculapius. This meeting brought together mental health professionals from the Southern Cone (Consecuencias de la represión en el cono sur, 1987). This seminar was the start point for developing collaborative research activities and joint participation in congresses of the Interamerican Psychological Society [IPS], Latin American Studies Association [LASA], American Psychological Association [APA], and in regional congresses in the Southern Cone with North American and Latin American colleagues, giving rise to numerous publications on mental health services and political repression (Aron, 1988; Lira et al., 1990).

At the IPS congress in Buenos Aires in 1989, Ignacio Martín-Baró highlighted the role of a Mental Health and Human Rights Network in Latin America empowering the resources available for the care of thousands of victims, for research and the construction of effective solidarities (Lira et al., 2019). Within the framework of this collaboration, a training program for academics from the School of Psychology of the Universidad Centroamericana José Simeón Cañas [UCA] of El Salvador was carried out in 1988, initiating joint research projects and publications (Becker & Lira, 1989; Becker et al., 1995). Ignacio Martín-Baró, academic vice-rector of the UCA, was assassinated on November 16, 1989.

Recognition and Reparation of Victims

Mental health teams from human rights organizations in Santiago contributed to the human right program for political transition, with proposals on reparations for victims of human rights violations.

Patricio Aylwin headed the first government after the dictatorship in 1990. He promised to identify and repair the victims of human rights violations, clarify the situation of disappeared detainees, facilitate exiles' return, and achieve political reconciliation. Aylwin created the National Truth and Reconciliation Commission in April 1990. The Commission report described the effects of people's disappearance and execution based on the testimonies of their relatives, pointing out the impossibility of mourning associated with the traumatic impact of disappearance and death. It determined that the relatives lived "uncertainty about the fate of their loved ones" (Comisión Nacional de Verdad y Reconciliación, 1991, p. 1141). Under these considerations, the Commission recommended that the Ministry of Health develop a specialized program aimed at the most affected population. The Chilean government, between 1990 and 2010, has recognized 3186 victims of forced disappearance, extrajudicial executions, and political violence until 2021.

In 1991, the Program for Reparation and Comprehensive Health Care for Victims of Human Rights Violations (1973–1990) [PRAIS] was inaugurated as a health reparation policy (Domínguez et al., 1994). In 2004 it was institutionally consolidated with Law 19.980, establishing that the Ministry of Health should ensure the resources for its operation and provide comprehensive care to the children and grandchildren of victims recognized as victims of human rights violations by the Chilean State and those enrolled in PRAIS from its creation in 1991 until 2003. In 2021, the program had more than 750,000 enrolled. The program has operated with 29 teams across the country, consisting mainly of physicians, psychiatrists, psychologists, and social workers, providing comprehensive health care, supporting victims' organizations, accompanying family members in exhumations, and carrying out human rights and memory education activities. From the beginning, PRAIS received support programs in training and supervision established by some mental health teams that worked during the dictatorship, mainly ILAS and CINTRAS.

The Vicaría de la Solidaridad closed in 1992. The archives gathered during its work were made available to the public by creating the Documentation and Archive Foundation of the Vicariate of Solidarity of the Archbishopric of Santiago [FUNVISOL].

From 1990 to 2004, reparation laws were passed that established forms of administrative reparation (pensions, education, and others) and symbolic reparation (monuments, memorials, and others) for victims recognized by the State. In November 2003, the government of President Ricardo Lagos created the National Commission on Political Prisoners and Torture. A total of 28,459 persons were identified as victims of political imprisonment and torture; 1244 were under 18 years of age, and 3621 were women. Ninety-four percent reported having been tortured. The report identified more than 1000 detention centers in the country and established that torture was a systematic practice during the military regime. Law 20.405 created in 2010 the Advisory Commission for the Classification of Disappeared Detainees, Politically Executed and Victims of Political Imprisonment and Torture, which classified 9875 new victims of political imprisonment and torture, and 30 new cases of disappeared detainees. This commission finished its work in August 2011 (Comisión Asesora Presidencial, 2011).

The Past That Still Lives in the Present

The consequences of the dictatorship's policies have been the subject of debate and research to date, seeking to characterize the effects of the past on the present of individuals, families, communities, and national political coexistence. In this text, it is not possible to summarize the countless contributions that have been produced, inside and outside Chile, in books, articles, undergraduate and graduate theses, seminars, and the creation of study centers. Specifically, this part of the text refers to the research in social sciences and psychology initiated during the dictatorship, its follow-ups and the opening of new lines and perspectives have contributed to the broad field of memory's studies. This extremely brief synthesis identifies some key studies on exile, return, forced disappearance, torture, transgenerational transmission of damage, reparation, truth and memory and therapeutic modalities that have become academic research lines.

It is worth mentioning the psychosocial and therapeutic accompaniment to the relatives of disappeared detainees in the unending search for their whereabouts and the destination of their relatives' victims of forced disappearance. These experiences gave rise to studies on impossible mourning (Castillo, 2013), the long-term impact on families (Faúndez et al., 2017), on communities (Durán et al., 1998), and expert opinions for legal claims for reparation (Lira, 2015).

Political memory has become a field of research from different disciplines. People's experiences as political actors and their interpretations of such experiences have been the subject of research (Carvacho et al., 2013; Reyes et al., 2013; Tocornal, 2012). These studies refer to generational differences and delve into the personal or family experience of political repression during the dictatorship as dimensions that mark different ways of remembering, including the protagonism and empowerment of the actors. These studies show the younger generations' demand about their right to remember that past as their sphere, differentiating themselves from their parents. These demands include those who were not born during the dictatorship and are independent of their political position. They claim that what happened [to their parents] marks their present, both in personal and family terms and how the country was organized socially and politically (Badilla, 2020; Cornejo et al., 2020; Frei, 2020; Reyes et al., 2015).

Studies on memories of the coup and the dictatorship include former conscripts who performed compulsory military service in that period (Passmore, 2015); exiles and their children (Cornejo, 2008; Serpente, 2015); women presence in the reports of the truth commissions (Hiner, 2009); tortured Mapuche people not recognized in the reports (Jara et al., 2018). Studies on children's discourses about the past (Castillo-Gallardo et al., 2018; Haye et al., 2013); teaching about the dictatorship in school contexts (Oteíza et al., 2015; Toledo & Magendzo, 2013); and the dynamics of the commemorations of the coup regarding the disputes of memories (Candina, 2002) are part of this matters. Topics that have also been studied are the relationship between memory, space, and materiality, identifying the versions of the past transmitted and constructed in memory sites (Collins & Hite, 2013; Klep, 2012; Piper et al., 2017); the ideological segregation of memorials in the city (Aguilera, 2015); and the emotional experiences of visits to memorials (Hite, 2016). The study of the records of human rights organizations and documentation on state terrorism in the transition account for the continuity of the classifications created during the dictatorship in the care of victims, allowing us to trace their genealogy from the initial archives to the truth commissions and reparation programs (Bernasconi, 2018, 2019).

The effects of torture and repressive violence investigated from clinical and social psychology and reparation policies and the implementation of PRAIS (Lira, 2016). Psychosocial trauma (Martín-Baró, 1988) and extreme traumatization constitute a conceptual map for analyzing the consequences of repressive violence on direct victims, their descendants, and the differentiated impact on various social groups (Lira & Castillo, 1993). Studies have been conducted on the transgenerational transmission of trauma in grandchildren of victims (Faúndez et al., 2014); on the impact of listening to torture on political prison and torture commission professionals (Cornejo et al., 2013) and neighbors of a torture center (Mendoza et al., 2019); the effects of truth commissions on victims and non-victims (Cárdenas et al., 2015); as well as the impact on clinical professionals working with trauma generated by political repression (Morales & Cornejo, 2013).

The previously mentioned research and many others on these topics have taken up many of the last conceptual proposals, reformulating and broadening their scope. The conceptualizations on memory have contributed to a national and international transdisciplinary field.

Social protests since October 2019 in Chile open new questions and revive unresolved demands from the political transition. The main contribution from psychology involves collaborating in recognizing pending conflicts, identifying the scars of the past and its invisible traces in people and society, in the proposals for memory and reparation of victims, in the development of shared reflections and the construction of forms of coexistence in peace.

This chapter summarizes synthetically a complex professional work that sought to respond from psychology to victim's needs. As mentioned earlier, the work's documentation draws a broad map of the consequences of the dictatorship on the victims, their families, their communities, and its relations with political coexistence. Human rights violations and political violence have affected the conditions of democracy in the country from the beginning of the republic to the present. Interdisciplinary research shows the importance of victim's recognition and recovery, and the role of political memory, to reinforce the transformation of social relations and democratic coexistence.

References

Agger, I., & Jensen, S. B. (1996). *Trauma y cura en situaciones de terrorismo de Estado. Derechos humanos y salud mental en Chile bajo la dictadura militar*. Ediciones ChileAmérica-CESOC.

Aguilera, C. (2015). Memories and silences of a segregated city: Monuments and political violence in Santiago, Chile, 1970-1991. *Memory Studies, 8*(1), 102–114. https://doi.org/10.1177/1750698014552413

Álamos, L. (1986). *Repercusiones psicológicas en niños víctimas de la represión política*. Fundación de Protección a la Infancia Dañada por los Estados de Emergencia: PIDEE. Retrieved from https://www.pidee.cl/documentacion/

Álamos, L., Duarte, G., Escorza, E., Espinoza, C., George, M., Maureira, G., Pérez, J. M., & Traverso, A. (1992). *Infancia y represión. Historias para no olvidar. Experiencia clínica de niños y niñas que han vivido la represión política*. PIDEE.

Aránguiz, M. T., Atton, V., Duhalde, L., Eltit, M., Lucero, C., Monteiro, E., Rodríguez, M., Sandoval, I., Sepúlveda, C., & Garcés, M. (1995). *Podrás reconocerte, recordando*. CRESAM.

Aránguiz, M. T., Palavecino, M., & Poffald, L. (1988). *Tratamiento psicoterapéutico en personas afectadas por la represión. Una experiencia en la IX Región*. CRESAM.

Aron, A. (Ed.). (1988). Fuga, exilio y retorno. *La salud mental y el refugiado*. San Francisco Committee for Health Rights in Central America.

Arzobispado de la Santísima Concepción, Departamento Pastoral de Derechos Humanos. (1988). *Por la sagrada dignidad del Hombre. 15 años en la defensa y promoción de los Derechos humanos*. Concepción.

Badilla, M. (2020). The day of the young combatant, generational struggles in the memory field of postdictatorship Chile. *Memory Studies, 13*(2), 191–207. https://doi.org/10.1177/1750698017730871

BBJ & SLC. (2017). Algunas reflexiones en torno a las respuestas de los individuos en una situación de crisis política. Comité de Cooperación para la Paz. Antecedentes del trabajo de los psicólogos. En E. Lira (Ed.), *Lecturas de Psicología y Política. Crisis política y daño psicológico* (pp. 203–209). Ediciones Universidad Alberto Hurtado.

Becker, D., & Lira, E. (Eds.). (1989). *Derechos Humanos: Todo es según el dolor con que se mira*. Ediciones Instituto Latinoamericano de Salud Mental y Derechos Humanos.

Becker, D., Morales, G., & Aguilar, M. I. (Eds.). (1995). *Trauma Psicosocial y adolescentes latinoamericanos. Formas de acción grupal*. Ediciones ChileAmérica-CESOC.

Bernasconi, O. (2018). Del archivo como tecnología de control al acto documental como tecnología de resistencia. *Cuadernos de Teoría Social, 4*(7), 68–87. Retrieved from http://cuadernosdeteoriasocial.udp.cl/index.php/tsocial/article/view/62

Bernasconi, O. (Ed.). (2019). *Resistance to political violence in Latin America documenting atrocity*. Palgrave Macmillan.

Candina, A. (2002). El día interminable. *Memoria e instalación del 11 de septiembre de 1973 en Chile*. Siglo XXI Editores.

Cárdenas, M., Páez, D., Rimé, B., & Arnoso, M. (2015). How transitional justice processes and official apologies influence reconciliation: The case of the Chilean 'Truth and Reconciliation' and 'Political Imprisonment and Torture' Commissions. *Journal of Community & Applied Social Psychology, 25*(6), 515–530. https://doi.org/10.1002/casp.2231

Carvacho, H., Manzi, J., Haye, A., González, R., & Cornejo, M. (2013). Consensos y disensos en la memoria histórica y en las actitudes hacia la reparación en tres generaciones de chilenos. *Psykhe, 22*(2), 33–47. https://doi.org/10.7764/psykhe.22.2.601

Castillo, M. I. (1986). La identidad en adolescentes retornados: una experiencia grupal. En FASIC (Ed.), *EXILIO 1986–1978* (pp. 35–45). Amerinda Ediciones.

Castillo, M. I. (2013). *El (im)posible proceso de duelo. Familiares de detenidos desaparecidos: violencia política, trauma y memoria*. Ediciones Universidad Alberto Hurtado.

Castillo, M. I., & Lira, E. (1986). *Psicología, Justicia y Democracia*. Instituto para el Nuevo Chile.

Castillo-Gallardo, P., Peña, N., Rojas, C., & Briones, G. (2018). El pasado de los niños: recuerdos de infancia y familia en dictadura (Chile, 1973-1989). *Psicoperspectivas, 17*(2), 103–114. https://doi.org/10.5027/psicoperspectivas-vol17-issue2-fulltext-1180

Cerda, M., & Lagos, E. (2017). Los niños y las experiencias de pérdida en el marco de la represión política chilena. En E. Lira (Ed.), *Lecturas de Psicología y Política. Crisis política y daño psicológico* (pp. 179–196). Ediciones Universidad Alberto Hurtado.

Colectivo Chileno de Trabajo Psicosocial. (1982). *Lecturas de Psicología y Política: Crisis Política y Daño Psicológico*. Edición privada.

Collins, C., & Hite, K. (2013). Memorials, silences, and reawakenings. In C. Collins, K. Hite, & A. Joignant (Eds.), *The politics of memory in Chile: From Pinochet to Bachelet* (pp. 133–164). First Forum Press.

Comisión Asesora Presidencial. (2011). *Informe de la Comisión Asesora Presidencial para la Calificación de Detenidos Desaparecidos, Ejecutados Políticos y Víctimas de Prisión Política y Tortura*. Santiago. Retrieved from https://www.indh.cl/bb/wp-content/uploads/2017/01/Informe2011.pdf

Comisión Nacional de Verdad y Reconciliación. (1991). *Informe Comisión Nacional de Verdad y Reconciliación*. Santiago. Retrieved from https://bibliotecadigital.indh.cl/handle/123456789/170

Comisión Nacional sobre Prisión Política y Tortura. (2004). *Informe Comisión Nacional sobre Prisión Política y Tortura*, Santiago. Retrieved from https://bibliotecadigital.indh.cl/handle/123456789/455

Comité de Cooperación para la Paz en Chile (COPACHI). (1975). *Crónica de sus dos años de labor solidaria*. Retrieved from http://www.memoriachilena.gob.cl/602/w3-article-10121.html

Comité de Defensa de los Derechos del Pueblo (CODEPU DIT-T). (1994). *La Gran Mentira. El Caso de las "Listas de los 119". Aproximaciones a la guerra psicológica de la dictadura chilena, 1973–1990*. Santiago. Retrieved from http://www.derechos.org/nizkor/chile/libros/119/

Comité de Defensa de los Derechos del Pueblo (CODEPU DIT-T). (1996). *Crímenes e Impunidad. La Experiencia del Trabajo Médico, Psicológico, Social y Jurídico en la Violación del Derecho a la Vida Chile 1973-1996*. Santiago. Retrieved from http://www.derechos.org/nizkor/chile/libros/med/

Comité de Defensa de los Derechos del Pueblo (CODEPU). (1989). *Persona, Estado, Poder. Estudios sobre Salud Mental. Chile 1973-1989*. Equipo de Denuncia, Investigación y Tratamiento al Torturado y su Núcleo Familiar. Santiago. Retrieved from http://www.derechos.org/nizkor/chile/libros/poder/intro.html

Consecuencias de la represión en el cono sur. (1987). *Conclusiones* (folleto).

Cornejo, M. (2008). Political exile and the construction of identity: A life stories approach. *Journal of Community & Applied Social Psychology, 18*(4), 333–348. https://doi.org/10.1002/casp.929

Cornejo, M. (2015). L'exil après l'exil. Histoires de vie d'exilés chiliens. En J. González-Monteagudo (Ed.), *Les Histoires de vie en Amérique Latine Hispanophone. Entre formation, mémoire historique et témoignage* (pp. 153–183). L'Harmattan.

Cornejo, M., Morales, G., Kovalskys, J., & Sharim, D. (2013). La escucha de la tortura desde el Estado: la experiencia de los profesionales de la Comisión Nacional sobre Prisión Política y Tortura en Chile. *Universitas Psychologica, 12*(1), 271–284. Retrieved from https://www.redalyc.org/articulo.oa?id=64728729024

Cornejo, M., Rocha, C., Villarroel, N., Cáceres, A., & Vivanco, A. (2020). Tell me your story about the Chilean dictatorship: When doing memory is taking position. *Memory Studies, 13*(4), 601–616. https://doi.org/10.1177/1750698018761170

Del Pozo, J. (2006). *Exiliados, emigrados y retornados: chilenos en América y Europa, 1973–2004*. RIL Editores.

Domínguez, R., & Delpiano A. (1986). Volver, un programa de apoyo a los niños del retorno. En FASIC (Ed.), *EXILIO 1986–1978* (pp. 27–31). Amerinda Ediciones.

Domínguez, R., Neumann, E., Weinstein, E., Lira, E., Maggi, A., & Becker, D. (1984). La verdad reparadora. *Mensaje, 326*, 29–31. Retrieved from https://www.mensaje.cl/biblioteca/biblioteca-download.php?file=1984/n326_29.pdf

Domínguez, R., Poffald, L., Valdivia, G., & Gómez, E. (1994). *Salud y Derechos Humanos. Una experiencia desde el sistema público de salud chileno*. Ministerio de Salud.

Duarte, G. (1987). *Tratamiento, reparación, rehabilitación: perspectivas de la reparación del daño causado*. Fundación de Protección a la Infancia Dañada por los Estados de Emergencia: PIDEE. Retrieved from https://www.pidee.cl/documentacion/

Durán, T., Bacic, R., & Perez-Sales, P. (Eds.). (1998). *Muerte y Desaparición Forzada en la Araucanía: Una Aproximación Étnica*. KO-AGA ROÑE'ETA se.x. Retrieved from http://www.pauperez.cat/wp-content/uploads/2017/11/perez-sales-muerte-y-desaparicion-forzada.pdf

Escorza, E., & Maureira, G. (1989). *Talleres experienciales con jóvenes*. Manuscrito.

Espinoza, Ch., Villar, M. I., & López, T. (1989). *Daño-reparación: una aproximación conceptual*. Fundación de Protección a la Infancia Dañada por los Estados de Emergencia: PIDEE. Retrieved from https://www.pidee.cl/documentacion/

Estrada, A., Hering, M., & Donoso, A. (1997). *Familia, Género y Terapia. Una experiencia de terapia familiar sistémica*. CODEPU.

Faúndez, X., Azcárraga, B., Benavente, C., & Cárdenas, M. (2017). La desaparición forzada de personas a cuarenta años del Golpe de Estado en Chile: un acercamiento a la dimensión familiar. *Revista Colombiana de Psicología, 27*, 85–103. https://doi.org/10.15446/rcp.v27n1.63908

Faúndez, X., Cornejo, M., & Brackelaire, J. L. (2014). Narration, silence: Transmission transgénérationnelle du trauma psychosocial chez des petits-enfants de victimes de la dictature militaire chilienne. *Cahiers De Psychologie Clinique, 43*, 173–204.

Faúndez, H., Estrada, A., Balogi, S., & Hering, M. (1991). Cuando el fantasma es un tótem: perturbaciones en las interacciones afectivas de adultos jóvenes, hijos de detenidos desaparecidos. En P. Rojas (Ed.), *Persona, Estado, poder: estudios sobre salud mental. Vol. II: Chile 1990–1995* (pp. 223–241). CODEPU.

Frei, R. (2020). In my home nobody spoke about religion, politics, or football: Communicative silences among generations in Argentina and Chile. *Memory Studies, 13*(4), 570–585. https://doi.org/10.1177/1750698017754249

Frenz, H. (2006). *Mi vida chilena*. LOM Ediciones.

Fundación para la Infancia Dañada por Estados de Emergencia (PIDEE). (1985). *Memoria Anual. Reseña del trabajo efectuado*. Manuscrito.

Garcés, M., & Nicholls, N. (2005). *Para una historia de los DDHH en Chile. Historia Institucional de la Fundación de Ayuda Social de las Iglesias Cristianas. FASIC 1975–1991*. FASIC-LOM Ediciones.

Harper, C. (2007). *El acompañamiento. Acción Ecuménica por los Derechos Humanos en América Latina (1970–1990)*. Ediciones Trilce.

Haye, A., Manzi, J., González, R., & Carvacho, H. (2013). Children's theories of the military coup in Chile 25 years after the events. *Psykhe, 22*(2), 67–81. https://doi.org/10.7764/psykhe.22.2.607

Hiilamo, H. (2015). *La ruta finlandesa. La diplomacia clandestina que salvó a miles de chilenos*. Ceibo Ediciones.

Hiner, H. (2009). Voces soterradas, violencias ignoradas: discurso, violencia política y género en los Informes Rettig y Valech. *Latin American Research Review, 44*(3), 50–74. Retrieved from https://www.jstor.org/stable/40783670

Hite, K. (2016). Teaching the politics of encounter empathic unsettlement and the outsider within spaces of memory in Chile. *Radical History Review, 124*, 217–225. https://doi.org/10.1215/01636545-3160086

Jara, D., Badilla, M., Figueiredo, A., Cornejo, M., & Riveros, V. (2018). Tracing Mapuche exclusion from post-dictatorial truth commissions in Chile: Official and grassroots initiatives. *International Journal of Transitional Justice, 12*(3), 479–498. https://doi.org/10.1093/ijtj/ijy025

Klep, K. (2012). Tracing collective memory: Chilean truth commissions and memorial sites. *Memory Studies, 5*(3), 259–269. https://doi.org/10.1177/1750698012441299

Kovalskys, J., & Lira, E. (1983). Exilio y Retorno: una aproximación psicosocial. *Revista Chilena de Psicología, 1*(4), 27–31.

Lira, E. (1986). Psicología y derechos humanos en una situación represiva: la experiencia de FASIC. En H. Frühling (Ed.), *Represión Política y defensa de los derechos humanos* (pp. 269–291). Academia de Humanismo Cristiano/Ediciones CESOC-ChileAmérica.

Lira, E. (1999). Mirando hacia atrás. Un balance de 20 años de iniciativas en el cono sur. En P. Pérez-Sales (Coord.), *Actuaciones psicosociales en guerra y violencia política* (pp. 139–162). Exilibris Ediciones.

Lira, E. (2015). Chile. Desaparición Forzada 1973-2015. En M. Giusti, G. Gutiérrez & E. Salmón (Eds.), *La verdad nos hace libres. Sobre las relaciones entre Filosofía, Derechos Humanos, Religión y Universidad* (pp. 550–573). Fondo Editorial Pontificia Universidad del Perú.

Lira, E. (2016). Reflections on rehabilitation as a form of reparation in Chile after Pinochet's dictatorship. *International Human Rights Law Review, 5*(2), 1–23. https://doi.org/10.1163/22131035-00502003

Lira, E. (2017). The Chilean human rights archives and moral resistance to dictatorship. *International Journal of Transitional Justice, 11*(2), 1–12. https://doi.org/10.1093/ijtj/ijx015

Lira, E., & Castillo, M. I. (1991). *Psicología de la Amenaza Política y del Miedo.* ChileAmérica-CESOC.

Lira, E., & Castillo, M. I. (1993). Trauma Político y Memoria Social. *Revista de Psicología Política, 6*, 95–116. Retrieved from https://www.uv.es/garzon/psicologia%20politica/N6-5.pdf

Lira, E., Castillo, M.I., & Becker, D. (1990). Psychotherapy with victims of political repression in Chile. En J. Gruschow & K. Hannibal (Eds.), *A therapeutic and political challenge. Health service for the treatment of torture and trauma survivors* (pp. 99–114). American Association for Advancement of Science - Committee on Scientific Freedom and Responsibility.

Lira, E., Michel-Fariña, J. J., & Lykes, B. (2019). La Caricia del tiempo. *Aesthethika, 15*(2), 1–5. Retrieved from https://www.aesthethika.org/La-caricia-del-tiempo

Lira, E., & Weinstein, E. (1982). Desempleo y daño psicológico. *Revista Chilena de Psicología, 4*(2), 69–79.

Lira, E., & Weinstein, E. (Eds.). (1984). *Psicoterapia y represión política.* Siglo XXI Editores.

Lira, E., Weinstein, E., & Kovalskys, J. (1987). Subjetividad y represión política: intervenciones psicoterapéuticas. En M. Montero & I. Martín-Baró (Eds.), *Psicología política latinoamericana* (pp. 317–346). Panapo.

Lira, E., Weinstein, E., & Salamovich, S. (1985). El miedo. Un enfoque psicosocial. *Revista Chilena de Psicología, 8*(1), 51–56.

Lowden, P. (1996). *Moral opposition to authoritarian rule in Chile, 1973–90.* Macmillan Press.

Madariaga, C. (2002). *Trauma psicosocial, trastorno de estrés postraumático y tortura.* CINTRAS, Monografía 11. Retrieved from http://www.cintras.org/textos/monografias/monog_trauma_psicosocial_espanol.pdf

Madariaga, C., & Díaz, D. (1993). *Tercero ausente y familias con detenidos desaparecidos.* CINTRAS, Monografía 10. Retrieved from http://www.cintras.org/textos/monografias/monografia10.pdf

Martín-Baró, I. (1988). La violencia política y la guerra como causa del trauma psicosocial. *Revista de Psicología de El Salvador, 7*(28), 123–141. Retrieved from https://www.uca.edu.sv/coleccion-digital-IMB/wp-content/uploads/2015/11/1988-La-violencia-pol%C3%ADtica-y-la-guerra-como-causas-del-trauma-RP1988-7-28-123_141.pdf

Mendoza, F., Cornejo, M., & Aceituno, R. (2019). Voisins d'un centre clandestin d'emprisonnement politique et de torture durant la dictature civile et militaire chilienne: le savoir de l'horreur. *Cahiers de Psychologie Clinique, 53*(2), 149–182. https://doi.org/10.3917/cpc.053.0147

Morales, G., & Cornejo, M. (2013). Ambivalencias en la escucha de la tortura en Chile: implicancias clínicas y sociales. *Terapia Psicológica, 13*(2), 197–208. https://doi.org/10.4067/S0718-48082013000200006

Orellana, P., & Hutchinson, E. Q. (1991). *El movimiento de Derechos Humanos en Chile, 1973–1990*. Centro de Estudios Políticos Latinoamericanos Simón Bolívar.

Oteíza, T., Henríquez, R., & Pinuer, C. (2015). History classroom interactions and the transmission of the recent memory of memory rights violations in Chile. *Journal of Educational Media, Memory, and Society, 7*(2), 44–67. https://doi.org/10.3167/jemms.2015.070204

Passmore, L. (2015). The apolitics of memory: Remembering military service under Pinochet through and alongside transitional justice, truth, and reconciliation. *Memory Studies, 9*(2), 173–186. https://doi.org/10.1177/1750698015587152

Piper, I., Montenegro, M., Fernández, R., & Sepúlveda, M. (2017). Memory sites: Visiting experiences in Santiago de Chile. *Memory Studies, 11*(4), 455–468. https://doi.org/10.1177/1750698017693667

Pollarolo, F., & Rojas, M. E. (1986). La pérdida del derecho a vivir en su propia patria. En FASIC (Ed.), *EXILIO 1986–1978* (pp. 257–273). Amerinda Ediciones.

Raszczynski, K., Rojas, P., & Barceló, P. (1991). *Tortura y resistencia en Chile. Estudio médico político*. Editorial Emisión.

Reyes, M. J., Cornejo, M., Cruz, M. A., Carrillo, C., & Caviedes, P. (2015). Dialogía intergeneracional en la construcción de memorias de la Dictadura Militar chilena. *Universitas Psychologica, 14*(1), 15–30. Retrieved from http://repositorio.uchile.cl/handle/2250/137010

Reyes, M. J., Muñoz, J., & Vázquez, F. (2013). Políticas de memoria desde discursos cotidianos: la despolitización del pasado reciente en el Chile actual. *Psykhe, 22*(2), 161–173. https://doi.org/10.7764/psykhe.22.2.582

Reyna, V. (2005). La Experiencia de la Fundación de Ayuda Social de las Iglesias Cristianas, FASIC. En E. Lira & G. Morales (Eds.), *Derechos Humanos y reparación: Una discusión pendiente* (pp. 37–44). LOM Ediciones.

Rodríguez, A.C. (1978). Detenidos políticos: sufrimiento y esperanza. *Mensaje, 27*(275), 777–783. Retrieved from http://repositorio.uahurtado.cl/static/pages/docs/1978/n275_777.pdf

Rodríguez, A. C., Fuentes, R., & Arismendi, M. P. (1980). Seis años de situaciones represivas sobre la mujer en Chile. *Revista ChileAmérica, 62–63*, 136–158. Retrieved from http://www.socialismo-chileno.org/PS/ChileAmerica/Chile-America62_63/Chile-America62_63.html

Rojas, P. (2017). Recordar. Violación de Derechos Humanos. *Una mirada médica, psicológica y política*. LOM Ediciones.

Salamovich, S., & Domínguez, R. (1986). Proceso psicológico de desexilio: una respuesta psicoterapéutica. En FASIC (Ed.), *EXILIO 1986–1978* (pp. 47–60). Amerinda Ediciones.

Serpente, A. (2015). Diasporic constellations: The Chilean exile diaspora space as a multidirectional landscape of memory. *Memory Studies, 8*(1), 49–61. https://doi.org/10.1177/1750698014552408

Tocornal, X. (2012). *The Chilean memory debate: Mapping the language of polarisation*. Lambert Academic Publishing.

Toledo, M. I., & Magendzo, A. (2013). Golpe de Estado y dictadura militar: Estudio de un caso único de la enseñanza de un tema controversial en un sexto año básico de un colegio privado de la Región Metropolitana – Santiago, Chile. *Psykhe, 22*(2), 147–160. https://doi.org/10.7764/psykhe.22.2.585

Vicaría de la Solidaridad (FUNVISOL). (1978a). *Algunos problemas de salud mental detectados por el equipo psicológico psiquiátrico*. Santiago.

Vicaría de la Solidaridad (FUNVISOL). (1978b). *Algunos factores de daño a la salud mental. Documento N° 00656-00*. Santiago.

Vicaría de la Solidaridad (FUNVISOL). (1978c). *Informe Trabajo Diagnóstico Niños familiares de detenidos desaparecidos*. Santiago.

Vicaría de la Solidaridad (FUNVISOL). (1980). *Análisis del Programa de Salud. Período 1974–1979*. Santiago.

Vicaría de la Solidaridad (FUNVISOL). (1982). *Séptimo año de Labor, 1982, Memoria*. Santiago.

Vicaría de Solidaridad. (1991). *Jurisprudencia. Delitos contra la Seguridad del Estado. Consejos de Guerra*, 3 vols. Santiago.

Vidal, M. (1990). Daño Psicológico y represión política. Un modelo de atención integral. *Revista Reflexión,   4,   10–14.*   Retrieved   from   http://www.cintras.org/textos/monografias/monografia6.pdf

Vidal, M. (1993). *Lo igual y lo distinto en los problemas psicopatológicos ligados a la represión política.* CINTRAS, Monografía 3. Retrieved from http://www.cintras.org/textos/monografias/monografia3.pdf

Vío, F. (1992). *Atención médica-clínica de pacientes traumatizados extremos atendidos en ILAS.* Working paper.

Weinstein, E. (1986a). Algunas orientaciones acerca de la Psicoterapia con retornados del exilio. En FASIC (Ed.), *EXILIO 1986–1978* (pp. 63–80). Amerinda Ediciones.

Weinstein, E. (1986b). Elementos de la experiencia psicológica del retorno: la instancia grupal una respuesta de salud mental. En FASIC (Ed.), *EXILIO 1986–1978* (pp. 22–135). Amerinda Ediciones.

Weinstein, E., Lira, E., & Rojas, M. E. (1987). *Trauma, duelo y reparación.* FASIC-Editorial Interamericana.

Chapter 3
Method of Forced Disappearance and Trials for Crimes Against Humanity: A Dialogue Between the Legal and Subjective Dimensions—Specifics of the Argentine Case

Mariana Wikinski, Mariana Biaggio, Rosa Matilde Díaz Jiménez, and Marcelo Marmer

Introduction

Two unprecedented events marked and continue to mark the history of Argentina and the collective memories of Argentinians.

From 1976 to 1983, Argentina was governed by successive military juntas that implemented State Terrorism and a systematic method of forced disappearance of people. Confined—in some cases for years—in clandestine detention centers (in Spanish, *centros clandestinos de detención (CCD)*) without any official acknowledgment of their fate, the victims of dehumanization, torture, and extermination were then disappeared again, thrown alive into the river or buried in common graves under no name. The plan to exterminate anyone considered "subversive" was made complete with the stealing, kidnapping, and appropriation of around 500 children and babies, many of them born in captivity.[1]

Implemented since the 1960s, or even earlier, in different Latin American countries, this method of extermination took on unique dimensions in the case of Argentina due to the number of disappearances and the establishment of 350

---

[1]Abuelas de Plaza de Mayo had recovered 130 of the 500 victims of the Systematic Plan to Appropriate Children by June 2019. For more information about the search for grandchildren and the restitution of their identity, see Biaggio (2009).

M. Wikinski (✉) · M. Biaggio · M. Marmer
Members of the Mental Health Team, Centro de Estudios Legales y Sociales (CELS),
Buenos Aires, Argentina
e-mail: mwikinski@gmail.com; mbiaggio@cels.org.ar; marcelomarmer@gmail.com

R. M. Díaz Jiménez
Procuración General de la Nación Argentina, Buenos Aires, Argentina
e-mail: rosmadik@gmail.com

© The Author(s), under exclusive license to Springer Nature Switzerland AG 2022
E. Lira et al. (eds.), *Human Rights Violations in Latin America*, Peace Psychology Book Series, https://doi.org/10.1007/978-3-030-97542-5_3

clandestine detention and torture centers throughout the country.[2] These CCDs—at the same time peripheral (clandestine) to and at the core of the political repression (Calveiro, 2008)—were instituted as lawless spaces (i.e., victims lost their citizenship and the rights therein held) and were essential and complementary to the execution of what Calveiro (2008) termed "disappearance power."

This State Terrorism was carried out on an unprecedented scale aimed at exterminating anyone deemed an "enemy," the results of which were an estimated 30,000 disappeared and 500 children appropriated. Stepan (1988, cited in Schindel, 2003) estimates that for every disappearance or death of a detainee in Brazil, there were 10 in Uruguay and 300 in Argentina.[3] Only in absolutely exceptional cases were some detainees released.

The second unprecedented event was that the trials of those responsible for crimes against humanity in Argentina were arbitrated by the ordinary courts—the only case of this in the world. No democratic government since 1984 has been able to elude taking a position on whether to continue holding these trials or halt them, and this political fact has had a profound impact on Argentine society, the construction of its history, the implementation of policies of memory, and the place of victims.

It is still hard to grasp the dimension of the subjective consequences produced by the confluence of the forced disappearances and the trials, because both have been perpetuated into the present, and because both the number of victims and accused are uncommonly high, while those responsible for the disappearances are uncommonly silent as a whole.

The subjective impact of both events was the defining factor in our clinical approach to victims, but we were also met with the task of bridging the confrontation between what happens in the field of justice and the subjective circumstances that the victims and society go through.

In this chapter, we will first briefly describe the social role played by the trials for crimes against humanity in Argentina and the subjective impact of the disappearances, the framework in which we carry out our clinical work. We will then describe the critical reflections that these circumstances produced in our clinical conceptualization and the complex relationship produced by the interaction between the legal field and the subjective clinical field.

---

[2] The Secretariat of Human Rights (Ministry of Justice and Human Rights) places the number of CCDs during the first year of the dictatorship at around 600. This figure later fell to 350. http://www.jus.gob.ar/derechoshumanos/red-federal-de-sitios-de-la-memoria.aspx

[3] This figure is based on the Nunca Más Report, which only points to some 9000 disappearances. The report was produced in 1984 by the National Commission on the Disappearance of Persons (CONADEP), created by President Raúl Alfonsín.

The Trials and Amnesty Laws

In the first post-dictatorship democratic period, President Raúl Alfonsín (1983–1989) established the Trial of the Juntas (Decree No. 158/83). This trial prosecuted the successive military juntas that governed the country starting with the civil-military coup of March 1976 until 1983. Five of the nine officers tried received sentences ranging from perpetual home-arrest to 5 years in prison; four were acquitted.

Even during the Alfonsín government, there was a major setback in the pursuit of truth and justice when the Full Stop (Law 23492) and Due Obedience (Law 23521) laws were passed in December 1986 and June 1987, respectively. The former put an end to the investigations and possibility of bringing those responsible for the crimes to trial. The latter established that any of the accused under the rank of coronel should not be tried, considering that they had acted following orders from superiors, which they could not disobey. The only exceptions to these laws were trials for the appropriation of children, given that the crimes of kidnapping, appropriation, and falsification of identity in public documents are not subject to statutory limitations in that they are ongoing or permanent crimes that can only cease by restitution of identity. Today both laws are referred to as the "amnesty laws."

In 1989 President Carlos Menem (1989–1999) extended the amnesty by issuing pardons for leaders of the military juntas who had already been tried in the Trial of the Juntas, as well as those found guilty among members of the Army first and second corps, the Minister of Economy, among other officials during the dictatorship, and some civilians.

In response to the impunity, human rights organizations and families of the victims of state terrorism promoted the Truth Trials in cities throughout Argentina in the late 1990s, even though there was no legal possibility of sentencing those found guilty of the crimes. In contrast to the Truth Commissions of South Africa, in Argentina these trials (in which members of the armed forces refused to declare) were not aimed at forgiveness and reconciliation; they were intended to be a link in the process of transitional justice that would ultimately lead to the punishment of the guilty parties (Romanin, 2013).

The road to the investigation and prosecution of those responsible for these crimes was reopened when Judge Gabriel Cavallo declared the amnesty laws null and unconstitutional (case 8686/2000) on March 6, 2000, upheld 5 years later by the Supreme Court. As of that point, the numbers are telling. Between 2003 and 2020, 597 cases have been opened. These cases have tried, are currently trying or will try 3329 accused.[4] Many of the accused have died before their trials began, or during, which has come be termed "biological impunity."

---

[4] Statistical report by the Special Attorney's Office on Crimes Against Humanity. The state of cases on crimes against humanity in Argentina. Data updated on March 6, 2018. https://www.fiscales.gob.ar/lesa-humanidad/?tipo-entrada=estadisticas

The reopening of the trials was not limited to the investigation and prosecution of the security forces but also included previous cases, the prosecution of civilian businessmen involved in crimes during the dictatorship and around 150 members of the judiciary (Filippini & Cavane, 2015).

The government of Mauricio Macri (December 2015–2019) was characterized by a marked setback in the policies of memory, truth, and justice. Human rights organizations noted that the rhetoric of officials under that administration brought back the use of concepts like "dirty war," "complete memory," and "reconciliation." At the judicial level, verdicts for repressors were revoked; the Supreme Court tried to apply the 2x1 law for sentences handed down to repressors[5] (later reversed due to general mobilization against it); legal proceedings slowed down and the number of rulings declined; repressors with life sentences in prison were given access to home-arrest regardless of whether their health posed a factor in their continued incarceration in prison (CELS, 2017).

It is impossible to separate the magnitude of this process from any attempt to comprehend the subjective variables affecting the victims in particular and Argentine society in general.

The Imprint Left by Disappearance on Society: Victims' Efforts in Court

In subjective terms, the imprint is unique when it comes to prosecuting disappearances. Bodies disappeared as well as the documents that could prove these crimes. There are very few survivors. So then how to reconstruct for the courts any sort of truth when there is no data to back it up? The disappearances imbued history with a spectral quality that has left its mark on the way it has been reconstructed both inside and out of the courts.

It wasn't only about the disappearance of bodies. It was also about the systematic and daily effort to make captives unable to trust their own capacities of perception by altering any perceptual parameters that might provide their psyches with any semblance of organization, meaning, anticipation of what would happen or location in time. It was also about the State denying to society what was happening. The precision of the CCDs' effectiveness and their expansive power to produce terror cannot be fully comprehended without considering that it was sustained based on knowledge unrecognized by society. The fact that the State showed it and at the same time denied its existence were the mechanisms that allowed the terrorizing endurance of the power of disappearance.

---

[5] Law 24.390, Article 7 establishes that after two years of pre-trial detention with no trial proceedings commenced, each day of pre-trial detention would be calculated as two in prison or one in confinement. Congress ultimately voted unanimously this article was inapplicable to detainees held for crimes against humanity.

Neither society as a whole nor the families of the disappeared had symbolic tools to allow them to understand what a *disappearance* was. This impossibility to name what was happening posed an insidious obstruction to any efforts to process it.

It was up to the victims to establish legal testimony as proof of the atrocities committed. The victims, in general families of the disappeared, and a few survivors of the CCDs, were ones who gave voice and content to the narration, so history could be reconstructed—and continues to be—in the courts. This effort to put into words what was hidden and denied impacted the witnesses and victims in terms of how they navigated the trauma. It was about revealing what happened and is still happening, where all that's left is emptiness and disappearance. Trusting one's own word and the word of others required psychological work, both individual and collective, to give credibility to the unbelievable.

These political and legal circumstances had an impact on our clinical work with the victims of state terrorism and determined the theoretical work that accompanied it.

Between the Legal and the Clinical

Four key aspects of our clinical work required us to specifically reflect on the circumstances that we just described that bore witness to the complex intersection between the legal dimension and the clinical one: the consideration of the lasting effect disappearance has over time, the trauma around the experiences of captivity in the CCDs, the characteristics of mourning caused by disappearance, and the psychological work involved in the act of narrating and giving testimony of the trauma in court.

Disappearance as Torture: Its Effects on Survivors and the Families of the Disappeared

In 1991, the Mental Health Team at the Center for Legal and Social Studies (CELS) presented to the UN Voluntary Fund for Victims of Torture the reasons why disappearance and its effects on the families should be considered a form of torture without statutory limitations. The enduring suffering brought by an inexplicable absence is, for the families of the disappeared, a form of torture.

Human perception always resorts to a clue, a search for meaning, the evocation of an experience. We usually find a non-contradictory continuum between what we perceive and how we formulate our reading of it. However, in the case of situations where we are the object of an attack on perception, as in the case of people disappeared in the CCDs, this natural process is altered, and we find ourselves faced with a contradiction between the perceived and the interpretation imposed upon us.

Hooding (the placement of hoods or blindfolds to block vision), the loss of spatial and temporal points of reference, posed attacks on people's perception by depriving them of their senses. But the systematic casting of doubt on detainees as to their interpretation of the events they were perceiving was also an attack on their perception.

The surviving detainees tell, almost without exception, of the desperate need to *comprehend* what they experienced during their captivity. The need to construct, in fleeting encounters with other detainees, some interpretation of what was occurring, what their fate might be, where they were, what had happened to a companion, to whom the voices that hooded them belonged, the names corresponding to each nickname. All perceptual resources of the victims were attacked.

Ulloa (1998) suggests that a *tragic trap* is produced when a person subjected to the exercise of cruelty by another also depends on that other, with no third party to appeal to, and describes the act of torture as the paradigm of the tragic trap.

This evident fact that directly affected the disappeared expanded its effects to their families and loved ones. The uncertainty extended over time and placed the family at the crossroads between reporting the disappearance or not, given that the rules preserving the life of their loved one were unknown to them and that spectral space between life and death had a paralyzing effect. The tragic trap was produced in this case because, by refusing to provide information on what had occurred, the apparatus of repression forced—and continues to do so—family and friends to be the ones to decide what to do when someone goes missing, whether to consider their loved one, dead or alive.

Those who have accepted the death of their loved ones as fate, they have done so by internally declaring the end of waiting as the outcome of an intimate effort that bordered on guilt for "sentencing" them to death. The trap is then faced with the disconnect between denying the reality of this infinite absence, or going through the guilt of not waiting anymore for the return of the disappeared or even wishing them dead. Even though this process was first experienced in absolute solitariness, the trials later paved the way for the victims to tell their stories and notably attenuated the moral solitude they had suffered in the construction of their history.

In relation to the therapeutic space and clinical work done over the 18 years in which the amnesty laws were in effect, Wikinski (2016) suggests:

> The absence of justice truly posed ethical challenges to us beyond just listening to the suffering, the risk of victimism, the work of processing the trauma: that slipping into being the only place where victims could finally expect to find one – at least – particular way of doing justice: *"Here I can talk; here I can give testimony of my history; here I am heard, here they believe me"* (pp. 39–41).

To the extent that it was possible to establish justice thanks to the victims' stories, each of them found the way to know their part of a history that would no longer be experienced in solitude, and also the possibility of constructing a principle of reality, contrasting their own story with the telling of others, filling in some part of those gaping spaces of the tortured memory that the methodology of disappearance had condemned them to.

The psychological consequences of disappearance as an unprecedented methodology of extermination led the CELS Mental Health Team to present a detailed description to the UN Voluntary Fund for Victims of Torture on the subjective impact and trauma wrought by this methodology as torture prolonged over time for disappeared persons and for their families. Based on this acknowledgement, and with backing from the Fund to address it clinically, this was established symbolically as the "third party." For the victims assisted by the Mental Health Team, this contribution had the psychological effect of a law of protection.

Trauma in Survivors of Clandestine Detention Centers

The daily experiences victims were subjected to in the CCDs were an attack on their drive levees (Freud, 1905/1974), a cornerstone in the process of establishing the psyche. Disgust, shame (tied to morality), or modesty (what must be kept from the view of others) were threatened in the concentration camp-like experience: defecating in front of others; exposure to the view of others in conditions lacking privacy; experiencing feelings outside their own morality (e.g., wishing for someone's death in order to survive); deprivation of their names; captivity in absolute isolation; daily threats to their lives; no possibility of anticipation or comprehension of the rules governing their lives. All of these experiences exposed prisoners to the extreme trauma of having their basic parameters of existence and belonging to the human race torn down. It is essential to underscore the magnitude of the traumatic impact this attack on the foundational aspects of their psyche had on victims subjected to this experience.

Our clinical experience has shown us that trauma:

(a) Always involves a rupture of the psyche's protective membrane when faced with stimuli that, due to excess, quality or the psyche's lack of preparedness and warning to process them exceeds the person's capacity to metabolize or symbolize them;
(b) Disrupts the balance of the apparatus that controls their functioning;
(c) Renders resources available to victims to find meaning absolutely insufficient;
(d) Must be taken on an individual basis, considering that it may produce different levels of rupture of each subject's psychic membrane, reside in different locations, activate different defense mechanisms, evoke different experiences or reactivate traumas suffered by previous generations;
(e) Is never mute, always produces symptomatic psychic manifestations in the body or language, illustrating the demanding work trauma inflicts on the person's psyche;
(f) There is also an added element to the kind of trauma we are referring to: the fact that it was produced deliberately by someone like them, and even worse, in the name of the State, stripping victims of any possibility of recourse.

The description of the specific trauma of having remained disappeared in a CCD formed part of the plea that CELS, with the specific contributions of its Mental Health Team, submitted in 2016 in the collective lawsuit (Megacausa ESMA III). The plea credibly established to the judges that this type of trauma was not comparable to others. A dialogue was opened in the context of the trial in which the characteristics of this kind of trauma, its existence and magnitude, were submitted for the justice system to consider and prove.

The Mourning of Forced Disappearance: Unregistered Mourning That Never Ends

In psychoanalysis, *mourning* is the work done by the psyche to preserve and reestablish itself in the face of significant loss. The death of a loved one is a potentially traumatic experience because it breaks a link in the network that sustains the individual and causes upheaval of the world scenario in which that person finds self-representation. This upheaval of the individual's representational order triggers the work of mourning.

The mourning process involves attaching and de-attaching libidinal investitures. Attachment is an attempt to hold on to something, an adhesion or fixation of the libido to an object and refusal to let go. In mourning processes that do not follow a pathological course, over time the psychic apparatus begins to let go of some memories and the future expectations associated with someone who is no longer present.

The mourning process requires the exercise of *examining reality* to confirm the absence of the loved one. This work exposes the psyche to the conflict of acknowledging the consequences of this examination and at the same time resisting the withdrawal of the libido from the loss of that person (Freud, 1915/1993).

When that loss is due to death, the possibility of access to the lifeless body of the deceased, funeral rites and burial or similar rituals, contribute to the construction of the proof of reality and offer resistance to its denial, one of the first defense mechanisms of the psychic apparatus in dealing with trauma. Furthermore, insofar as the body of the deceased presents information about their particular mode of death, it provides information that will be integrated into the explicative telling of the event. "Ritual activity usually occurs at transcendental moments of mutation of the individual or collective existence and comes from our own emotions. Ritualization consists of translating those emotions into a story" (Aullé, 1998, p. 69).

The ritual allows the loss to be de-privatized, show signs of pain and navigate—with a collectively constructed story—the vacant place that establishes the absence of the deceased.

The burial ground, in turn, is an installation that occupies a physical space: it is locatable and material. Burying the dead is an act of occupying a physical space with the remains and name of the deceased person, and thus honoring them and paying respect to the human being that lost his or her life, while at the same time providing consolation to the mourners.

The proof of reality configured in this way allows the mourning person to move forward in withdrawing their libidinal investitures from the deceased person and make them available for other vital purposes.

In the case of mourning over forced disappearance, none of the parameters included in the mourning process are met. Such an experience is an attack on the integrity of the psychic apparatus and confronts the individual with the dimension of the unassimilable, which defies symbolization, and as a result produces a truly devastating and irreparable impact on the psyche. The surprise at the person's disappearance (for example, when they don't call) rapidly becomes a search for their whereabouts. The silence, the lack of information, the not knowing, over time are accompanied by the waiting.

The National Commission on the Disappearance of Persons (CONADEP), the Truth Trials, and the criminal trials have provided circulation and coordination of disperse data, but the mourning has not ended, because of the cruel, indolent silence of impunity of the perpetrators.

For some people the search continues. For others, sentences are needed that put the guilty on trial not only for the disappearances, but also for the murders.

The work done by the Argentine Forensic Anthropology Team has allowed some families to recover the remains of their loved ones and go through funeral rites. Estela Carlotto president of the Abuelas de Plaza de Mayo was able to learn that her daughter had given birth, revealed in findings based on the position of her hips.

In addition to the process of dehumanization inflicted on the disappeared during their captivity, they were also deprived of funeral rites, perhaps the most steadfast and transcendent sign of humanization in the history of humanity.

Marmer (2016) refers to a type of mourning that has not been sufficiently accounted for or considered in terms of collective significance: the mourning over disappeared friends. Friends who belonged to the same generation as the disappeared, who likely shared the same political experiences or similar sentimental ones, must process a particularly painful type of mourning in which strong feelings of guilt and uncertainty are also at stake. Marmer (2016) sustains that the disregard for the social impact of losing a friend excludes part of society from the need to process their mourning. It restricts the processing of that loss to the family setting, failing to recognize the expansive power of that pain and thus restricting the quantitative dimension of those considered *affected* by the loss.

After former Marine captain and pilot Adolfo Scilingo publicly confessed in 1995 his role in the death flights in which detainees drugged with pentothal were thrown into the sea, CELS made a number of court filings claiming the *right to the truth* and the *right to mourn* of families of the disappeared. In 1998 different human rights organizations, in view of the Argentine court authorities' rejection of the petition, went before the IACHR to petition the admissibility of the case of Carmen Aguiar de Lapacó, mother of the Plaza de Mayo, and her daughter, Alejandra Lapacó, disappeared in 1977. That action laid the foundation for the later installation of the Truth Trials, paving the way toward the reopening of the trials once the amnesty laws were declared unconstitutional.

The Narration of Trauma in Court

The cases in which trials involved specific testimony from victims required arduous psychological work for them to be able to testify in court. The court setting demands that they give testimony with absolute certainty of what they believe happened, as if their perceptive resources had been available and unaltered during the course of their traumatic experience. This requires the victim to exert unusual effort to transform their experience not only in linguistic terms, but also in legal ones (Wikinski, 2016), a task that must navigate four subjective obstacles: the narration of the trauma, the testimony in court, the shame, and speaking on behalf of others. Part of the Mental Health Team's work involves providing witnesses and victims with clinical and psycho-legal support to help them confront these obstacles in order for them to testify in court.

The work done by victims to process the trauma and build their testimony are concurrent efforts, but some cases require specific support from the therapist at the time of testimony in court. One therapist on our team was providing support for a witness when she was about to begin her statement before the judge. Due to carelessness at the courthouse, the person responsible for her father's disappearance passed by the open door of the room where witnesses were waiting to testify. The defendant looked her right in the eye. The witness became very distressed, putting her ability to testify at risk. The therapist suggested that she include this event in her statement. This allowed her to give her testimony and saved her from having to do so in a state of distress, or from the guilt of not being able to testify.

In Closing: Crimes Against Humanity, Challenges and Support from the Legal and Clinical Dimensions

A clinical practice involving the traumatic effects of crimes against humanity cannot remain removed from the political and legal circumstances in which it is framed.

The fact that the policy of memory has been a policy of state in Argentina has been at the core of the work done by victims to process their mourning. The evolution of the trials, the establishment of the National Genetic Data Bank (a fundamental archive used in the work to identify the remains of victims of forced disappearance, in the identification of appropriated children and in the collection of evidence to determine the commission of crimes against humanity), the establishment of memorial sites, the founding of the Fernando Ulloa Center for Assistance to Victims of

Human Rights Violations, are all examples of the resources available to victims and society to know the truth.

The legal and clinical dimensions of this have mutually transformed each other. The trials, the sanctioning of the perpetrators, the investigation of the events, the opening of the courts to give voice to victims has allowed them to go through their traumatic experience in less solitude. The effect on society is priceless, given that the law has reestablished a societal order that was lost during the dictatorship and prevents the instatement of impunity.

At the same time, the characteristics of traumatic suffering have driven new strategies and legal considerations in the legal context. The consideration of disappearance as torture and the extension of the concept of victim to include the families of the disappeared (even 40 years after their disappearance) has enabled a strategy of specific support in cases where they had to declare in court, and allowed them access to free psychological counseling at the Fernando Ulloa Center for Assistance to Victims of Human Rights Violations.

Our clinical experience confirms that the legal and extra-judicial actions taken to clarify the crimes and punish those responsible for them facilitate the processes of mourning the sequences of violence and cruelty, even when the process of mourning has not been entirely overcome.

Our psycho-legal strategy takes all the clinical concepts analyzed in this article, builds an interpretation of the unique impact of these traumatic experiences on those who have to testify in court. Its chief aim is to contribute not only to a fruitful legal process, but also to protect the psyche of victims and avoid, to the extent possible, having to pay with their own suffering their search for justice (CELS Mental Health Team, 2008; Noailles, 2014a, b).

We have tried to pay heed to the political and legal times and, at the same time, the imperative nature of our ongoing support for the victims' subjective needs and times. There is much left to do, but until now it has been the families, friends, witnesses, and survivors who have charted the ways forward, both to sustain memory as well as in the search for truth and justice.

References

Aullé, M. (1998). La ritualización de la pérdida. *Anuario de Psicologia, 29*(4), 67–82. Retrieved from https://www.raco.cat/index.php/AnuarioPsicologia/article/view/61501

Biaggio, M. (2009). *De las apropiaciones a las restituciones: el reconocimiento de la identidad de los nietos desaparecidos en la última dictadura militar argentina.* (Tesis de Maestría no publicada). Instituto de Altos Estudios Sociales. Universidad de San Martín.

Calveiro, P. (2008). *Poder y desaparición. Los campos de concentración en Argentina.* Colihue.

Centro de Estudios Legales y Sociales (CELS). (2017). *Derechos Humanos en Argentina.* Informe 2017. Siglo XXI Editores.

Equipo de Salud Mental del Centro de Estudios Legales y Sociales (CELS). (2008). *Estrategia psicojurídica en un proceso de litigio por secuestro seguido de torturas y muerte durante la dictadura military* argentina. Argentina. Retrieved from https://biblioteca.iidh-jurisprudencia.ac.cr/index.php/documentos-en-espanol/ prevencion-de-la-tortura/1827-estrategia-psicojuridica-en-un-proceso-de/file

Filippini, L., & Cavane, A. (2015). Procesos contra cómplices judiciales en democracia. En J. Bohoslavsky (Ed.), *¿Usted también, doctor? Complicidad de jueces, fiscales y abogados durante la dictadura* (pp. 381–398). Siglo XXI.

Freud, S. (1974). Tres ensayos de teoría sexual. En *Obras Completas*. Tomo VII. Amorrortu. (Original work published 1905)

Freud, S. (1993). Duelo y Melancolía. En *Obras Completas*. Tomo XIV. Amorrortu. (Original work published 1915)

Marmer, M. (2016, Noviembre). *La singularidad del duelo por un amigo desaparecido. A propósito de la aparición de los restos de Lila Epelbaum*. Trabajo presentado en el IX Seminario Internacional Políticas de la Memoria, Centro Cultural Haroldo Conti, Buenos Aires, Argentina.

Noailles, G. (2014a). La palabra del victimario. Confesar, hablar, declarar, testimoniar. En C. Gutiérrez & G. Noailles (Eds.), *Destinos del testimonio: víctima, autor, silencio* (pp. 161–176). Letra Viva.

Noailles, G. (2014b). El valor del testigo. En C. Gutiérrez y G. Noailles (Eds.), *Destinos del testimonio: víctima, autor, silencio* (pp. 27–46). Letra Viva.

Romanin, E. A. (2013). Decir la verdad, hacer justicia. Los Juicios por la Verdad en Argentina. *ERLACS, 94*, 5–23. https://doi.org/10.18352/erlacs.8389

Schindel, E. (2003). *Desaparición y Sociedad. Una lectura de la prensa gráfica argentina (1975–1978.)*. Disertación inaugural para obtener el Título de Doctor. Departamento de Ciencias políticas y sociales, Universidad Libre de Berlín, Alemania. Retrieved from http://www. rehime.com.ar/escritos/documentos/idexalfa/s/schindel/Schindel%20-%20Desaparicion%20 y%20Sociedad%202003.pdf

Stepan, A. C. (1988). Rethinking Military Politics: Brazil and the Southern Cone. Princeton: Princeton University Press. https://doi.org/10.1515/9780691219639

Ulloa, F. (1998, Diciembre 24). *La encerrona trágica en las situaciones de tortura y exclusión social*. Página 12. Retrieved from http://www.pagina12.com.ar/1998/98-12/98-12-24/ psico01.htm

Wikinski, M. (2016). *El trabajo del testigo. Testimonio y experiencia traumática*. La Cebra.

Chapter 4
Locating Children Appropriated by Dictatorships of the Southern Cone: Questioning Identities

Sonia Mosquera

Traces...

The democratic process has not erased the traces of the dictatorship in Uruguay. The process initiated in 1985 continues to produce an interpretative cliché of that period, in which myths and discourses instituted by the establishment persist and are mechanically repeated.

Argumentative expressions and rhetorical procedures characterized the dominant discourses on political transitions. These created a narrative with a deterministic vision, meant to explain the situation's alleged logical outcome.

Governments instilled the value of "forgetting" as the only way to restore and sustain institutionality (1985–2000). The legitimization of the rule of law established that it was impossible to bring justice to human rights violations.

Impunity prevailed. A hegemonic discourse was installed, legitimized, and recognized as the true story. It was a story anchored upon an objectified past that stands as a reference and confirmation of the present structural arrangements and denies or disqualifies the polyphonic version of memory. It is a homogenizing and reductionist discourse that obscures the field of memory, as well as that of justice.

What kind of logic governs this thinking? Totalitarian logics are binary. They understand the world as two great opposing forces: their own and that of others. Thus, everything that is not identical to itself becomes a threatening other, an imminent or latent danger that must be averted. We refer to a logic that seeks to eliminate diversities and imposes a sole and total reality, circumscribing the world into two camps, in this case, represented by the central nucleus of power: The State (Calveiro, 2005).

S. Mosquera (✉)
Facultad de Psicología, Universidad de la República, Montevideo, Uruguay
e-mail: smosquer@gmail.com

© The Author(s), under exclusive license to Springer Nature Switzerland AG 2022
E. Lira et al. (eds.), *Human Rights Violations in Latin America*, Peace
Psychology Book Series, https://doi.org/10.1007/978-3-030-97542-5_4

43

The Appropriations

Children kidnapped with their parents or born in captivity, constitute one of the most tragic chapters of the recent past. In most cases, the mothers were kept alive until the moment of birth and then murdered and disappeared without a trace. The search to find these children and restore their rightful filiation continues to be a primary objective.

The "appropriation of babies" constituted a systematic plan implemented through multiple illegal procedures. Most of these cases occurred in Argentina, within the framework of the repressive operations coordinated against Uruguayans living in that country, in the so-called Plan Cóndor.[1] At the same time, these repressive operations claimed victims among Argentines residing in Uruguay. Of the 500 children kidnapped and appropriated, 129 have been located over the past 40 years (1978–2020). Many Uruguayans were victims of these crimes, and several children were finally located and regained their original biological belonging.[2]

The appropriators are obliged to omit the birth scene from tragic circumstances. At birth, the child's body implied, in the concentration camp, the death sentence of its mother. She would be kept alive until the delivery; after the birth, she would be disappeared. This fact is essential for the constitution of the subjectivity or identity of these children.

When their parents were kidnapped, some children were left with neighbors who later located relatives to return them; others were handed over to public institutions as NN (no name) and given in adoption to people who acted in good faith. Most of them were appropriated by people linked to the military power, who were convinced of their impunity, according to the psychoanalyst Alicia Lo Giúdice (2005).

The genocidal logic was not satisfied with the physical disappearance of the parents of the abducted children. It went further than that. One of its main objectives was to rupture their filiations, and this led to the disappearance of the child that should have been the denial of the name, of the history, of the great expectations associated with his or her arrival in the world. The consequences of the scheme thus extended to the interruption of the foundational generational fabric of the human order. The rupture it produced is both individual, social, and collective because these children were appropriated and prevented from inhabiting the generational framework that corresponded to them. We refer to the most symbolic facet of expropriation: the possibility of transmission (Kletnicki, 2004).

---

[1] Repressive coordination plan of the Armed Forces during the dictatorships in the Southern Cone: Argentina, Brazil, Chile, Uruguay, Bolivia, and Paraguay.

[2] Since the coup d'état in Uruguay (1973), there was a significant emigration of persecuted Uruguayan citizens to Argentina. In March 1976, the coup d'état took place in Argentina, resulting in the persecution, kidnapping, and disappearance of Uruguayans in that country, including 11 "stolen" children. The seven who participated in the investigation were "stolen" in Argentina; two were born in Clandestine Detention Centers. The remaining five appropriated at the time of their parents' kidnapping. They were also found in that country in five of the cases; two were abandoned in a square in Valparaíso (Chile) by Uruguayan military personnel.

The appropriated children were registered under false names that concealed their real identity, thus endeavoring to obliterate their true history. Nevertheless, there is a "knowledge" that has produced effects in the subjectivity of each one of them.

The presence of the kidnapped child perpetuates and reaffirms the sadistic pleasure and absolute domination of the kidnapper. It is perversion insofar as the abductor knows that he transgresses the law, which is part of his enjoyment. He kills, sure of his impunity, and launches the most audacious challenge of all: to become the father of the one whose father he murdered. Appropriated children function as fetish objects by giving the abductor a sense of completeness.

Fernando Ulloa (1988) considers that the resistance of non-repressive appropriators—refusing to return the child—arises from the need to cover up a cruel and painful reality: sterility, loneliness, complicity. In these cases, the child acts as a stopper in the face of something that is "lacking." Ulloa argues that the bond established by the appropriator is one of addictive power, addictive love. By definition, it is impossible to give up the object of addiction, which explains why they cannot return these children.

Another perverse argument used by the appropriators was that the appropriation was not an abduction because it benefited the child since the mother was doomed to disappear anyway. The child was going to become an orphan. This argument omits the existence of other relatives who have been looking for them since the child's disappearance.

Restitution

The organization "Abuelas de Plaza de Mayo" (Grandmothers of Plaza de Mayo) undertook—and still sustains—the task they define as: "to locate and return to their legitimate families all the children kidnapped and disappeared by the political repression, and to create the conditions so that such a terrible violation of children's rights will never be repeated, demanding punishment to all those responsible" (Abuelas de Plaza de Mayo, 2014).

Their work to date has been very successful, with 129 children identified out of an estimated 500 cases.

A significant achievement of the *Abuelas* has been their sagacious application of universal human rights to the singularity of the historical, social catastrophe of the Southern Cone, mainly Argentina. The right to identity as an ethical principle for the human community was introduced by this organization. Through the establishment of the right to identity they installed their own voices and deconstructed a story established as the sole version intended to be enunciated as the true one (Olivares, 2008; Riquelme, 2004).

They opened paths in the legal sphere, promoting new fictions [narratives] to differentiate between adoption and appropriation, giving rise to new signifiers: the right to identity and restitution.

They succeeded in having the right to identity included in the 1989 United Nations Convention on Rights of the Child. Their search contributed to the emergence of new scientific discoveries: the grandparenthood index is proof of this. Thus, it is now possible to determine kinship through genetic testing, despite the absence of a generation. This kinship is recognized as valid proof by the courts.

They also promoted the creation of the Genetic Data Bank, where the blood samples of the relatives of the cases denounced by the *Abuelas* are kept for genetic tests, and of the National Commission for the Right to Identity (CONADI), under the National Ministry of Justice and Human Rights. The Commission's role is to request documentation in the places that intervened in the registration of the babies and, in the cases that require it, the DNA analysis to the National Bank of Genetic Data.

The Abuelas understood that the appropriation becomes engraved upon the children's subjectivity. However, they also foresaw that their requests for the restitution of identity, would open avenues that enable each grandchild to interrogate the imprints of those engravings, as the beginning of the elaboration and recognition of their "identity."

In a society marked by State terrorism, they contributed to the opening of a space from which to think about the devastating consequences of the bodies. The Abuelas publicly visibilized the criminal act of illegal appropriations, while also succeeding in bringing to trial the perpetrators of the appropriation of their grandchildren, even in times when impunity prevailed.[3]

The Discourse of "Abuelas" Over Time

From 1977 until approximately 1997, the Abuelas searched for their grandchildren in an "almost detective-like" manner (Abuelas de Plaza de Mayo, 2014). They followed clues through small messages communicated at their weekly march in Plaza

---

[3] In 1983, at the end of the Argentine dictatorship, the constitutional government ordered the trial of those most responsible for human rights violations, condemning them for the commission of illegal deprivation of liberty, murder, and torture of hundreds of victims in the Trial of the Juntas. Subsequent amnesty laws prevented the prosecution of the lower commanders, the arms responsible for the torture, disappearances, and murders. The kidnapping of children of the disappeared was excluded from the legislation, which guaranteed impunity for the perpetrators. The judicial processes of child abductions classified them as common crimes, and many of the trials were barred by the statute of limitations without convicting the perpetrators. In 2005, the Supreme Court of Justice of the Nation declared the amnesty laws unconstitutional for violating international human rights principles. The murders, tortures, disappearances, and appropriations of children were classified as crimes against humanity and therefore not subject to any statute of limitations. There are 32 convictions (2012) for the abduction and identity supposition of children of the disappeared, among which are the deliverers of the children, their appropriators, doctors and midwives who falsified the birth certificates.

de Mayo, by telephone, and any clue that might lead to the location of one of the missing children.

Signifiers such as "roots," "ecological niche," "true family," and others can be read in the first newsletters the organization published, when it was only sent outside Argentina. The disappeared children had been uprooted from their natural place, their family was looking for them, and in the meantime, they were prisoners, the *Abuelas* affirmed in each newsletter.

For García Delgado and Palermo, two scholars of the so-called "new social movements," the systematic practice of terror and the suppression of all forms of social and political participation define the "dictatorship situation." In this context of social isolation, the only possible reaction "can only start from the deepest levels: the sphere of basic solidarity: the family" (García Delgado & Palermo, 1989, p. 41, as cited in Vecchioli, 2005, p. 4).

The *Abuelas* insisted from the beginning on the difference between appropriation and theft. By making these distinctions in language, they managed to position illegal appropriation as a crime. Before this, appropriation was seen as something normal in Argentine society, something that happened before the dictatorship and still happens today, without necessarily political motives (Villalta, 2006). What set apart the "children appropriated by the dictatorship" from other appropriations was that the crimes had been committed by State violence.

The analogy between "appropriation" and "adoption" was a construction that Abuelas de Plaza de Mayo sought to dismantle in order to denounce the criminal nature of these practices, leading them to develop meanings of one and the other term.

The "Restitution" Debate

Restitution initially was a point of intense debate fueled by the media that persisted several years. The children themselves, who were quite young, would sometimes plead for their appropriators, and the *Abuelas* were challenged to respond. During the years when the children were still small, the organization debated the limits of the biological family's right to tell the truth to an appropriated child. They were keenly aware of the need to avoid any harm to the child by distancing him or her from the "family" of their appropriators, with whom they had lived, in some cases, until adolescence. In highly publicized restitution cases, the *Abuelas* had to defend the return of the children to their families of origin, fighting against arguments such as the good upbringing, affection, and the best intentions of the appropriators. In this debate, those who advocated keeping silent about the situation characterized the action of restitution as the "second trauma," a position supported by several health professionals, including the prominent French psychoanalyst Françoise Doltó (1986).

At that time (1983–1997), in the social imaginary, grandmothers who are mothers of the disappeared, and therefore victims, were positioned in the media as victimizers, contributing to a mechanism of inversion, capable of producing "evils" and deserving of widespread antipathy. They would play an interchangeable role that is ideologically possible given their condition as a minority group, the relatives of the disappeared.

These two opposing views of "the family" are present in this social imaginary. One, associated with the disappeared, claims the child, while the "other," the adoptive (and or appropriating) family, is the one that aims to represent "order," "good," and "good background." But the latter conceals how they acquired custody of the child, namely, a shady scheme that intended to "whitewash" illegality with "papers." Fueled by the media, the tension between the two seemed to call for the need to bury the memory of the disappeared, expel their personal history from memory. The appropriators also fought to retain their products, their children, but "remake" them, "neutralize" them culturally from their "genetic potential" which they imagined as suspicious. The dictatorship had regarded the detainees as "subversives who could genetically transmit to their children" their ideas and "wanted to destroy the western and Christian civilization." Until the second half of the 1990s, the discourse of dictatorship persisted; the children " may have inherited something from them," which reinforced their self-perception as redeemers of the "children of sin."

After 1996, the *Abuelas'* discourse and strategy changed. Their focus became an appeal to young people of the generation born during 1976–1982, who might have doubts about whether or not they are the children of their parents. During this period of time, the word "identity" became crucial, and was used as a keyword in the media. All activities related to the children illegally appropriated during the dictatorship are convened "For Identity" ("x la Identidad"). Identity is a word associated with doubt, with the search for truth. The question "And you, do you know who you are?" was launched by the Abuelas in 1997, triggered numerous "For Identity" ("x la Identidad") campaigns.

At present, the *Abuelas'* cause has gained visibility, and the restituted children and youngsters increasingly have gained the public space and relevance.

Each recovered child is, above all, a grandchild. And not only grandchildren of their biological grandparents, but for all the grandmothers who comprise the organization. Finding the grandchild of one of them is like finding the grandchild of all of them, the *Abuelas* say.

On the one hand, from the generational perspective, the kinship category of "grandchildren of" defines them as "children of" and, therefore, socially positions them in a generation that shares as origins the act of disappearance, a crime committed by the practices of State terrorism. This perspective refers to the shared commonality or the position that the individuals occupy in a given socio-historical constellation. This subjectivity-shaping setting (Lewkowicz, 2004), fractured between appropriation and restitution, arises from social memory elaboration that unfolds in the autobiographical enunciation of the "grandchildren." Although the transmission of inheritance has dissimilar content, all of them articulate the scenario of State terrorism and the disappearances of at least one parents.

Events That Weave the Story(ies) into Life Narratives: Dis-encounters in the Encounter

In the course of our research, we identified the encounter with the news of the "false identity" as an event that weaves and structures life stories, it is on this basis that these young people speak from the place of dilemma, an inner debate between "the mark of legitimate lineage and the imposture to which the terrible course of history has subjected them" (Arfuch, 2004, p. 69).

In their life journeys, these children traversed different categories of belonging. Before being found, they were the "living disappeared" of which they were unaware. After being located and "their identity restored," they became an "appropriated-recovered children." Their genealogical chain was broken. What makes them unique? The unawareness of their condition until they are looked for and identified. DNA, their genes, and biology confirm filiation. They are children and young people returning from two places where they should never have been: horror and the family of the "others." These places and their differences are constituent elements of their essence.

The dilemma is complex and intense for those who never imagined they might be "disappeared" children, sought by their families of origin. They burst into the public arena, positioned as "victims"—a socially assigned place—without feeling it, without knowing it.

The locating of these people arrives as thunderous news. It produces an "event" plotted in "a before and an after" and the discovery "shakes their previously constructed identity." The "located" are not "called as they have been called." They have another name, another surname. Nor were they born on the date stated in their birth certificate; they must change their birthday as well. In many cases, they are not from the place where they thought they were born. Everything is false, including their birth certificate. Their "parents" are not their parents, and their "siblings" are not either. The whole genealogical chain is broken, with everything submerged in great chaos.

These children not only discover themselves to be "illegitimate children" of those they believed to be their "parents," but "appropriated children" due to the violence of an era that also marked the destiny of their biological parents. Relatives are looking for him/her, and all of them have the right to recompose the family history. As Eva Giberti (1991) says, "completing the absence, the [clearing the] haze from genealogy [...] The children have to know that they were not abandoned but kidnapped and that this kidnapping was the result of the disappearance of their parents" (p. 156).

In the study, a girl located when she was a minor (8 years old), the legal mandate called for an immediate, almost automatic family change. This young girl's account of that episode speaks to us of unprotection and strangeness that we interpret as the goodbyes she had to endure since she had no right to choose. She had no interlocutor for her inner-most doubts: "my 'adoptive parents' love me. My biological grandparents love me. But they don't like each other. Who do I prefer? Who do I have to stay with them? Who do I abandon?" In this contradiction, there is something that does not allow for either rectification or escape, in this case remaining locked inside her. It introduces us into the paradoxical realm where each of the spheres is opposed to the other, with no possibility for synthesis, with its own intrinsic logic.

Knowledge of one's origins, how it was communicated to them, and new information appears in the story of these young people along with their mistrust, disbelief, "bad news." Something is "broken" in them, evident in the entire narration. They are living a paradox of the "mis-encounter in the encounter."

However, these life stories also show us a process of transformation. Through them, we witnessed the universal questions of who am I? where do I come from? why am I here? This event triggers the story that raises—from the new information—questions that have to do with nothing less than their origins. The question "where do I come from?" is always so powerful and mobilizing, that some prefer to defer the search for an answer. They resist having to assume it as "truth," dismissing it with disbelief or postponing their answer, to give themselves time to "confirm" it. At the same time, another question arises, juxtaposed with the previous one: why did they lie to me? Paradoxically, it is indissolubly linked to the previous one and will be the most powerful.

Perhaps the density of this last question marks the moment in which they begin to build an itinerary that embraces "the new" self, although not without another set of dilemmas.

Identity is constituted in this tense duality with other questions that challenge them to choose, accepting or not, that "other history" which is difficult to understand and even more complex to integrate because they did not live it or even have records of its existence.

In this study, perhaps the person who most resisted the discovery of being the "illegitimate daughter" of those who raised her, even in this extreme, poses the dilemma about the foundational lie of appropriation in two sentences: "That is also why my life has shown me that there are no absolute truths, not even what I defended tooth and nail, that it was never going to be so, everything I held as an immovable truth- Life took care of leaving me without truths." She refers to the "truths" about her origins. It is not always possible or even desirable to handle goodbyes. In this case it involved looking at "the others" ("foster parents"), who although they are clearly "appropriators," installed the "horror" as figures who, by giving her love, also falsified her origins, denied the existence of her biological parents and the circumstances of the crimes committed against them.

> The misperceptions about one's origin (in its phantasmatic register) are a hardship and a richness of the human condition. It is a universal and infallible ingredient of an imaginary life and the novels about neurotics. [...] It is what Derrida calls identity uneasiness, the never-ending and human question of who we are, where we come from, and where we are going. It is never-ending because it has no sure or absolute answer but has the function that the Promised Land had for Moses, as a place to which we are always heading but never reach.
>
> In the context of a historical tragedy, such as State terrorism or the Shoah, or other genocides, children have an assigned origin, like the children of kings, although the crown is not one of gold but pain. This assigned place fosters stability and tends to limit movement, wandering in search of identity (Viñar, 2011, p. 4).

Viñar's quote refers to the condition of the "victim" as a socially assigned place. The dictatorships of the 70s and 80s in the Southern Cone caused social catastrophes leaving traces over us. These traces continue to transit on those who lived in those times and our descendants, children, and grandchildren. They comprise the new generations that did not experience the "sinister path." To them we transmit the stories of what happened through "social memory."

From the stories of these localized young people, there emerges the category of people conferred as victims without ever assuming it. In some stories, not only do they feel allocated in the socially assigned place of "victims," but also that they are not allowed to leave it. They feel trapped in the socially constructed category of "appropriate-recovered children" with no option to choose another one.

The memory of the recent past generated by intergenerational dialogue is present in this dimension of those who directly lived through State terrorism (protagonists) and those who know what happened through intermediation (successors). What is the legitimate base of each set of discourses? Their legitimacy arises from the conflict between protagonists and successors (Reyes, 2009). In the case before us that conflict is between protagonists, who are situated in different socio-historical and violent experiences, turning around the issue of filiation. While the Abuelas, the biological family, point to the fracture caused by violence, the appropriated-recovered children place another type of tension at the center. Despite having experienced direct violence, – each person who receives the news of their unsuspected identity lives it differently. A sense of protection and love by the relatives who searched for them (after the necessary time has elapsed) may temper the new knowledge of their origins. Every recovered child can reread it from their own particular subjectivity, but with another perspective.

How the past is interpreted depends on the subject's position in the historical and cultural tradition. There is no true interpretation, but it always is shaped by the socio-historical conditions of production as well as the cultural and linguistic anchors of the system of meanings that articulate it (Gadamer, 1975/1993). The past can be interpreted in multiple ways, but the possibilities and limits set by such conditions are always a historical production (Piper et al., 2013, p. 21).

The reference to the term "victim" obscures different realities and opposing meanings, with substantial implications in fields as diverse as psychosocial, community, legal, and political. The relationship with "the other who suffers" must contribute to developing strengths that protect these individuals from new affronts, with actions that respect social and cultural aspects without augmenting the damage. At this crossroads we encounter the debate on the use of the words "affected," "victimized," "victim," or "survivor" to refer to people who have gone through extreme situations.

Dilemmatic Identities

It seems pertinent, based on what this research revealed to us, to locate the dilemmas in the construction of identity that could be thought of, following Gatti (2008), from the tension between "strong" and "weak" identities.

These young people, after being located, lived a time of choices. Given the magnitude of the chaos and the complex situation of having to choose to change a name, a family, and a date of birth, they move through fictional places, inhabiting a story that is not yet theirs (they were told it is), but they cannot inhabit it because they lived another one. Their language is debated in "twisted words." As victims, they move in a registry in which they lack the words to express an account of their identity constructions... the words stutter. There is a linguistic incongruity. When they speak of "parents," which ones? The biological parents or the foster parents and/or appropriators? In the story there are confusions that forced us to choose signs or different parentheses to differentiate the filiations and affiliations they describe.

This research involved three young people founded when they were adolescents (12 years; 17 years and 16 years), the other three located in childhood (9 years; 4 years and 9 years), and one young person located in adulthood (25 years). The ages and bonds that acted as supports for the episode of "identity restitution" were fundamental. At that moment, the encounters with new information take place, generating the drama of the original question that refers to the continuity-discontinuity "of the legend between generations" (Viñar, 2011). In the case of these children, this universal question has a significant density that confronts them with new actors with expectations of affection and bonds, with a yearning that fosters the passion for the encounter, in a search that had no respite.

Their identity construction oscillates between two places, the one they lived in "before" knowing where they came from and the one, they lived in "after" this episode. There, in some cases, begins the inner struggle between and with a "continuity-discontinuity." The "integration" of both parts is sought in order to transcend this dichotomy, which is a challenging feat. In others, it is a "coming and going" between one place and another with moments of greater intensity that tip the balance towards the blood ties and the permanent questioning about how to live with these two parts.

We also find a case in which the "tragic ambush," described by Fernando Ulloa, has operated through a bond of "possession" (appropriator/appropriated). It does not allow her to accept the truth concerning the "terrible human rights violations" committed by the person who raised her, whom she still calls "Dad." When she learns that her "Dad" is an "appropriator and accomplice of an abominable system," she is "trapped at the crossroads of two incompatible ethics," as Viñar (2011) says. This young woman separates the two, for the time being, when she states: "The person I know as my father has nothing to do with that guy. I am not for one side or the other. I can't integrate the image I have of my dad with that other guy..." (Mosquera, 2014, p. 152).

The cases of "appropriation" (Condor plan) and those of "good faith adoptions" (two appeared in Chile) include the recognition of the love received by their adoptive parents. The encounter and reconnection with the biological family meant new itineraries in their lives and changes in their routines (periodic trips between Chile and Montevideo). The construction of new bonds with their grandmothers/grandfathers who expressed affection for them, which not always reciprocated in the same way, made it necessary, over time, to deploy efforts to inhabit curiosities about the history of their origins.

This event, which we can define as central in the life stories, brought us closer to comprehending the "misunderstandings" that always occur in the first stage. The time and circumstances of life subsequently comprise a spiraling process characterized by movement and varying degrees of intensity. Conditions gradually are generated that enable them to draw closer to the singularity of their origin story, to integrate it and assume it despite their different uneven paths, some encountering more significant obstacles than others.

The Process Within the Socio-Historical Evolution

In the initial years of the search and "recovery" (the last years of the dictatorship and the first years of the constitutional governments, including the 1990s), these children were recognized as victims, specifically in the category of "sacrificial victims," which differentiates them from other victims. It is recognized that they are part of a historical process in which their parents were disqualified from different perspectives and whose disappearance constitutes a compromising illegal act, for those responsible for the action and those who pretend to forget it. They are positioned as bearers of a double deficit: one that could be attributed to their parents (disappeared) and another that corresponds to remembering the dictatorship. From an analysis of the structuring of myths, they become propitiatory victims since "they have something unusual and different," a specific condition for creating that category.

After 2003, we note a change of direction, a new discourse accompanied by governmental actions (in Argentina), taking criticisms and claims from different political and social currents, while a new "memory policy" was made official.

At this stage, measures were taken that allowed the reopening of the trials of those responsible for State terrorism. Notable among such measures were the repeal of Full Stop (Punto Final) and Due Obedience (Argentina) laws and the declaration of unconstitutionality of the pardons (Supreme Court of Justice). All these measures were taken under the protection of international human rights legislation.

The "historical memory" crystallized in museums, monuments and urban nomenclature in a context of debates among human rights organizations about the meaning of this "institutionalized memory" and its function of opening or closing advocacy spaces.

The trials of those responsible for human rights violations during State terrorism in Argentina began in the 2010s. These included the paradigmatic case known as the "Systematic plan for the theft of children and babies," which closed with the court's guilty verdict on July 5, 2012. Several perpetrators were sentenced to life imprisonment, as was the case of Jorge Rafael Videla, former de facto president of the Military Junta in Argentina. Subsequently, the trials have continued up to the present day. Military personnel, doctors, nurses, and "appropriator fathers" have been sentenced to serve time in ordinary prisons.

In this historical process, what is essential are the new conditions propitious for possibilities for entry into the public arena of the issue of human rights violations during the dictatorship. This situation brought an important change in the diversity of expressions that visibilized the magnitude of the social catastrophe and its repercussions, consolidating a framework of action and social reflection. The new generations of children and grandchildren will occupy a place in the "new narratives."

This new scenario has a relevant significance for the seven young people we interviewed. Their life journeys reveal a process of approaching history, which had been relegated to the private sphere space many years. Today they are increasingly curious to know who their biological parents were, what happened to them, why they are missing, despite the diversity of the stories that reveal obstacles and possibilities to achieve this.

We understand that it is necessary to support these young people as they move forward from "that conferred place" to embrace "the human right to close their mourning and live their destiny... making it possible for them to alleviate their burden" (Viñar, 2011, p. 5).

By Way of In-Conclusion

The search for children who "disappeared" because they were appropriated, which is also a search for origin, belonging, and family legacies, has spanned more than 40 years. This scenario's complexity arises from the predominance of psychological issues related to each case and the socio-political context in which the transmission of new identity has been produced. The personal time of each young person interviewed is different in regard to the circumstances of their appropriation and the process of locating them. The processes of recognition, approaching their own story are also different, as well as some cases in which the grown-up children, at least in part, embrace their history and that of their disappeared parents.

The circumstances that lead to recognition of the origin and resumption of relations with the families, or, on the contrary, rejecting them, can only be understood in the singularity of each story. No generalization is possible. At the same time, the life stories of these now young adults avoided us a closer view of the recurrence in their stories of issues shared by most of them that were elements part of their vicissitude and persist in their everyday life.

The child or grandchild located and/or discovered, who placed in the position of having to make a choice, of being able and willing, or, unable and unwilling to assume the history, the life, the culture, the daily life from which they were deprived, faces a dilemma, conflict, confrontation, and inner struggle. These children also face the dilemma of wanting and being able to be the children of whom? Of those who took the place of "parents" without being so? Of their legitimate parents who they never knew and, in most cases, never will, as the majority of these parents are victims of forced disappearance-that means, dead?

These children and youngsters built their family transmission history based on a falsified and violated identity, unaware that they were stolen, and not even suspecting that the appropriators had kidnapped and/or murdered their parents.

These cases raise questions that underscore the complexity of the relationship between the psychological of transmission mechanisms and the socio-political contexts in which they occur. In every single case, the resolution of these questions requires a complex working through process, in which life and family options highlight the conflictive subjectivity with all its density.

It is clear from the seven stories that the family of origin, unknown to them, and therefore alien, does not meet their expectations. In some cases, this is expressed in disbelief, others distrust, while still others have no interest whatsoever in the family. It would be accurate to say that there is a misunderstanding in every case, a paradox associated with the encounter between the family and the child who had been "disappeared" until the moment of his/her location.

In five of the seven stories, the issue of the change of name is a problem, a setback. Not even when located still as a child, did they accept it naturally. When the name had given them public notoriety during the search, the situation was quite tense, especially in Uruguay. Each child receives different answers, but none accepts the change.

Over time, each begins to express themselves and, in some cases, even change their birth date. Despite obstacles they gradually incorporate the process as part of a personal history that links them with their "biological mother," even when she does not occupy an important place in the narration.

The situation's privatization is a recurring theme. This dimension is closely associated with the places for disseminating information. The social imaginaries that are being established regarding these former appropriated children, identify them as innocent "victims" of the social catastrophe. But, placing them at the center of the public scene and giving visibility to their situation—in the periods immediately following their location—also turns them into an object of journalistic curiosity. In one of the stories, the person explained the situation thus: "…for them [journalists] we are news. They do not see us as persons." The prevailing desire is to go unnoticed, to be invisible.

The desire to be invisible also alludes to the difficulty in understanding what was happening to them, especially in the years when there were still no answers to their questions: why did it happen to me? This question inevitably implies an attempt to understand the whys of the appropriations in a time of violence about which they know very little. The knowledge they do have frequently is favorable to the so-called "subversion," from which their biological parents came from. There may also be a sense of shame that gives rise to a need to conceal the history. In some of the stories one notes a refusal to share what is happening to them or only with their closest circle. "With the first [friends he told] I was pretty anguished," one person said, and "they started to cry, they could not believe it," stated another.

Territorial distances (Argentina-Uruguay, Chile-Uruguay) provide an essential element from the point of view of "identity" since they make it possible to experience different subjectivities, which can be connected at times but not always. Discontinuities have produced that question from the point of view that refers to continuity as a distinctive "essential" element of identity.

These stories shed light on the different ways in which these young people feel, think, and act in one country or another. The cultural dimension invites us to delve more deeply into the distinctive features of the three countries: Argentina/Chile/Uruguay. However, we could not overlook the key that this thematic axis brings to the subject problem of this research: the construction of identity/identities.

Now that several are parents, they face the challenge concerning the generational transmission to their children. They feel the need to tell them their story, come to terms with the "truth," and perhaps resignifying that in the past they lived a "lie." In short, they are well aware that only they can tell their children what happened to them.

The question "What happened to my parents?" leads them to ask themselves about their genealogy.

The most personal dimension connects them with the "lie" as the foundation of appropriation, and their filiation falsified by those who "took possession" of them. In the course of this process, new dilemmas emerge.

The process of change put into words in their stories indicates that these young people have incorporated their situation, in some cases their "history," into their lives. Today they inhabit it in different ways, although we hold that the "marks" are still there. Even today, they continue to cope with tensions that cause them, in some cases, to swing between the "previous history" and the "current" identity. Another mechanism for coping is the perpetual avoidance of situations that might place them in more intimate and affective environments with the new figures: their biological family. Indeed, each of these children, over time, will be able to question these "marks" as the beginning of the working through and recognition of their "identity."

References

Abuelas de Plaza de Mayo. (2014). *Centro de Memoria del Conflicto*. Retrieved from http://www.memoriasdelconflicto.com/index.php/memorias-del-cesar/memorias-paralelas/item/56-abuelas-de-plaza-de-mayo

Arfuch, L. (2004, abril 23–24). *Cómo se construye la identidad*. Primer coloquio interdisciplinario de Abuelas de Plaza de Mayo: "Identidad, construcción social y subjetiva". Abuelas de Plaza de Mayo.

Calveiro, P. (2005, abril 8–9). *Ancient and new meanings of politics and violence*. Segundo coloquio interdisciplinario de Abuelas de Plaza de Mayo: "El porvenir de la memoria". Abuelas de Plaza de Mayo.

Doltó, F. (1986). Religión y Psicoanálisis. Entrevista a Francoise Doltó. *Psyche, Periódico de Psicología y Psicoanálisis, 3*, 2–5.

Gadamer, H. G. (1993). *Verdad y método*. Sígueme. (Original work published 1975)

García Delgado, D. & Palermo V. (1989). El movimiento de los Derechos Humanos en la transición a la Democracia en Argentina. En: Daniel Camacho y Rafael Menjívar (coords.), *Los movimientos populares en América Latina*. Siglo XXI.

Gatti, G. (2008). *El detenido-desaparecido. Narrativas posibles para una catástrofe de la identidad*. Trilce.

Giberti, E. (1991). Restitución y adopciones. Una conjunción de sufrimiento e interrogantes. En: *Restitución de niños* (pp. 151–173). Abuelas de Plaza de Mayo. Eudeba.

Kletnicki, A. (2004). Niños desaparecidos: lógica genocida y apropiación ilegal. In D. Feierstein & G. Levy (Comp.), *Hasta que la muerte nos separe. Poder y Prácticas Sociales Genocidas en América Latina* (pp. 163–174). Al Margen.

Lewkowicz, I. (2004). *Pensar sin Estado. La subjetividad en la era de la fluidez*. Buenos Aires, Paidós.

Lo Giúdice, A. (2005). Derecho a la identidad. In A. Lo Giúdice (Comp.), *Psychoanalysis: Restitution, appropriation and filiation* (pp. 29–41). Centro de Atención por el Derecho a la Identidad.

Mosquera, S. (2014). *Huellas de las dictaduras en el Cono Sur: construcción de identidad/es en hijos de uruguayos apropiados y posteriormente localizados* [Tesis de Maestría]. Universidad de la República, Facultad de Psicología, Montevideo. Retrieved from https://hdl.handle.net/20.500.12008/4871

Olivares, M. C. (2008). Del trauma a la ficción. En A. Lo Giudice (Comp.), *Psicoanálisis: identidad y transmisión* (pp. 35–40). Centro de Atención por el Derecho a la Identidad de Abuelas de Plaza de Mayo.

Piper, I., Fernández, R., & Iñiguez, L. (2013). Social psychology of memory: Spaces and politics of remembrance. *Psykhe, 22*(2), 19–31. https://doi.org/10.7764/psykhe.22.2.574

Reyes, M. J. (2009). Generations of memory: A conflicting dialogic. *Revista Praxis, 15*, 77–97.

Riquelme, D. (2004). Saber hacer con la historia. In Abuelas de Plaza de Mayo, *Identidad: construcción social y subjetiva* (pp. 107–113). Primer Coloquio Interdisciplinario de Abuelas de Plaza de Mayo.

Ulloa, F. (1988). La ternura como contraste y denuncia del horror represivo. En Abuelas de Plaza de Mayo, *Restitución de niños* (pp. 1–9). Eudeba. Retrieved from http://conboca.ces.edu.uy/images/recursos/ternura_represion.pdf

Vecchioli, V. (2005). La nación como familia. Metáforas políticas en el movimiento argentino por los derechos humanos. En F. Sabina & G. Soprano (Comp.), *Cultural y Política en Etnografías sobre la Argentina* (pp. 1–22). Ediciones UNQ/Prometeo.

Villalta, C. (2006). Cuando la apropiación fue adopción. Sentidos, prácticas y reclamos en torno al robo de niños. *Cuadernos de Antropología Social, 24*, 147–173. https://doi.org/10.34096/cas.i24.4413

Viñar, M. (2011). Paper at the presentation of the book *Los padres de Mariana. La pasión militante*. Trilce. Retrieved from http://www.trilce.com.uy/libros_online.html

Chapter 5
Photography and Film in the Experience of Identity Restitution: Writing with Light

Juan Jorge Michel Fariña and Florencia González Pla

Introduction: *Mamá Coco* and Her Missing Father

When in 2018, the Abuelas de Plaza de Mayo were nominated for the Nobel Peace Prize, a unique sense of fulfilment flooded our hearts. Their constant and silent battle against oblivion over more than four decades represents a social and historical capital and holds lessons for contemporary thought. This chapter seeks to establish the focal points of that discovery through one of its most sensitive facets: the role of creativity in the search for identity.

When tracing the stories of people whose identity was restored after being appropriated under the military dictatorship, we came to appreciate the importance of photographs during this long and painful process. In this context photography is not merely an instrument of recognition but rather, it pertains to the value of the image to support a symbolic order that arises to heal a wound in real terms.

This work seeks to recover that marvelous detail, endowing it with the value of clinical data by means of different sources. These include press clippings of initiatives carried out by the Abuelas de Plaza de Mayo organization team, testimonies of young people who went through that ordeal and were able to recover the bond with their legitimate families, and film fictions that portray the complex situation of filiation.

We will start with one film, "Coco" (Anderson et al., 2017), which won two Academy Awards, thus evidencing the scope of the topic in contemporary culture. The film is a photographic gem of enormous psychosocial value, with which we will introduce this chapter. But first, let's briefly tell the story: Coco is an older woman on the threshold of death. She has lived a long life and suffers from Alzheimer's disease. She confuses her daughter with her grandchildren and, at times, is unaware of her mother, Imelda, whose memory is lost in a photograph mutilated by the

J. J. Michel Fariña (✉) · F. González Pla
Science and Technique Program, Universidad de Buenos Aires, Buenos Aires, Argentina
e-mail: jjmichelfarina@gmail.coml; florenciagonzalez_07@hotmail.com

neurosis of four generations. But the All Souls' Day is approaching. It is about that wonderful Mexican ancestral ceremony in which, for one night, the ancestors, who are no longer with us, revive—but only if their descendants evoke them with their photograph as on the altar of memories. In this case, however Héctor, the adventurous mariachi, was outcast from the family, and his great-great-grandson, Miguel has never even seen the image of his face. His portrait was discarded, leaving no image to evoke his memory—or his oblivion. Banished from the fantastic beyond of *alebrijes* and skulls, his soul is condemned to wander eternally through the calvary of the living dead, until the enigma that led him, unwillingly, to that purgatory can finally be solved. But this will require not only an effort to survive the second death, but also actions by Coco, the daughter he yearns for, and little Miguel, accompanying her, to perform the miracle that will complete the puzzle of that truncated snapshot. When the words, the names, and the reference points are confused in the fog of Alzheimer's, the body opens way and vibrates in that mysterious cord of sounds and recovered images. The photograph can be completed, and a fourth strand comes to (re)knot what had dissolved in the long span of time.

In the film's imaginary set of circumstances, the ordeal of the living dead is recreated. But what strange territory is this? Once at a press conference, Argentine dictator Jorge Rafael Videla uttered a phrase that became sadly famous: *Neither dead nor alive, but disappeared. It [the situation] is an unknown, and it has no entity.* In the film "Coco," Héctor who occupies this ominous place: both dead and alive, simultaneously. Is such a thing possible? What is the subjective cost for his relatives of this socially unthinkable situation? In the book *El Acta de Nacimiento de los Fantasmas* (2010, The Ghost Birth Certificate), psychoanalysts Françoise Davoine and Jean-Max Gaudillière offer us clues: they coin the term *surviving images* to refer to another type of dead, different and at the same time intimately close to those summoned in the Mexican ceremony. They are ghosts that emerge when anguish is presentified; they are the unburied dead. "The unburied dead live in various social places and live first of all in the pain of their kin, of their parents, of their relatives..." (Davoine & Gaudillière, 2010, p. 59). In Coco's mother, Héctor's ghost dwells in the gaps of memory; in Miguel, on the other hand, he finds, without knowing it, a place in his love for music and in the fragmented identity it offers him. Until, accidentally, a fragment that photograph, hidden during so many years, appears enabling him to recover the figure of his great-great-grandfather. That fragment of image will change the course of the little boy's life and that of the rest of the family, restoring the bonds of kinship.

We will maintain then that photograph can be the imaginary support of an individual's symbolic processes woven around a real-life process. Such images allow the unburied dead to enter into a transmissible history. These photographs enable the transformation of those surviving images into transmissible stories, expressions, and spoken words, so that the reality at stake can be inscribed in the memory of their relatives and society as a whole.

We must recall that the etymology of the word photograph refers to two words, both of Greek origin: "photo" and "graphia," which, respectively, derive from *phos*, which translates as "light," and *graphos*, which translates "to write." In this play of language that comprises experience, photography can be thought of as written light. It captures an event in time that allows the subject to append an unknown point of its history and shed light in a future day.

In "Coco" this ethical dimension is organized in three logical tenses. In the first, we have the image of grandmother Imelda in the picture frame, presiding over the family shrine, revered and unattainable. In the second, Miguelito irreverently and without fully calculating it, enables the unfolding of the photo, revealing its long-suppressed underside. Thus comes the crucial fact of the guitar, but also the mutilated face of the mariachi, which leaves the mystery open. It is a suppressed detail of the story, the missing piece of the structure, its question mark. Miguelito rushes to fill it with meaning, without realizing that this hollowed-out segment is the emptiness of his own existence. The third time will be then and finally that of the subject who comes as such, when he is ready to trace on his body the filigree of a script that has not yet been written.

Appropriation and Restitution of Children: Clinical and Social Consequences

The military dictatorship that ravaged Argentina between 1976 and 1983 systematized a mode of political persecution: the forced disappearance of people and the institutionalization of concentration and extermination camps. A particular repressive modality was thus organized, carried out by specific groups, involving all enclaves of power. The fate of the people affected by state terrorism remains unknown in most cases, giving rise to a new legal concept generated by the military process: the disappeared detainee. Violence was implanted in society as a way of life where terror and paralysis disarmed the social fabric, producing a break in the kinship system, that affected several generations. In this way, the trauma experienced impacted the entire social fabric, becoming a historical trauma (Lo Giúdice, 2005). As we have already formulated synthetically in 1986 in several academic theses on the subject, the issue challenges those affected, the social body, and also analytical listening:

> Thesis VI: Correlatively, the so-called "mourning process" is, in reality, a social unthinkable marked by the absence of any certainty regarding the loss. Far from relieving the relative of his/her responsibility for the 'real' destiny of the missing person, it compromises him/her directly because of the complicity of silence imposed on him. And this repudiation of the reality that is promoted from the seat of Power leads him progressively to a symbolic murder since he is required to consider as dead someone who he is not even sure know is dead, and in this, even the therapist as a witness, is implicated and complicated (Maci & Michel Fariña, 2017, p. 51).

In addition to the sinister practices of kidnapping, torture, and forced disappearance of people, there was another unprecedented fact: the theft of children. The latter became one of the most serious crimes in the history of the continent. It involved the abduction, retention, and concealment of children, of the disappeared detainees, who together with their parents were forcibly disappeared or were born in captivity in clandestine detention centers. The armed forces maintained that the ideology they were trying to suppress could be transmitted through the family bond, and, for this reason, these children and babies were torn from their parents' arms (Lykes & Michel Fariña, 1987).

The violence imposed augmented in the schemes of the appropriators and the State apparatus to erase all links with the child's origins. It was a procedure that manipulated bodies and discourses, as a way of destroying the subjective reality (Lo Giúdice, 2005). It became essential for society as a whole to make an effort to gradually reestablish a juridical, social, generational, and human order.

In order to revert the effects of such devastation, it was necessary to create new legal fictions to accommodate those who had been excluded from the social and generational framework. In the context of a legal vacuum, the struggle for the vindication of rights arose. During the reestablishment of democracy and at the request of the Abuelas de Plaza de Mayo, Law No. 23.511 was passed in 1987 (This law was enacted on May 13, 1987, and promulgated on June 1 of the same year). creating the National Genetic Data Bank. It is located at the Hospital General de Agudos "Carlos G. Durand," in the City of Buenos Aires. The purpose of the Bank is to prepare reports and technical opinions and to carry out genetic tests at the request of a court to determine the identity of a child presumed to be the child of a disappeared person. The creation of the "Abuelismo Index" was a system that made it possible to link grandparents with their grandchildren, inferring the genetic information of the children and determining whether they were their grandchildren.

At the same time, within the framework of the International Convention on the Rights of the Child approved by the General Assembly of the United Nations in 1989, the Abuelas also promoted the incorporation of articles 7 and 8 known as "Argentine" clauses and article 11 on the right to identity. And in 1990 Argentina ratified the Convention with the passage of National Law No. 23.849 (This law was sanctioned on September 27, 1990 and actually enacted on October 16 of the same year). Thus, a paradigm shift took place, a new horizon opened for the protection and defense of children, which is expressed in the recognition of children and adolescents as full subjects of rights. Thus, the State's duty to preserve, care for and protect children and adolescents is established to protect the child's identity in advance, to make reparations, and provide all possible means to restore the child's identity. Finally, in 2005, the Law for the Integral Protection of the Rights of Children and Adolescents was passed, which establishes the right to identity and idiosyncrasy. As mentioned in Article 11: Right to Identity, children and adolescents have the right to a name, to a nationality, to their language of origin, to the knowledge of who their parents are, to the preservation of their family relations in accordance with the law, to the culture of their place of origin and to preserve their identity and idiosyncrasy, except for the exception provided for in Articles 327 and 328 of the Civil Code.

These legal changes have made it possible to gradually hold the trials that ordered the restitution of those children, now adults, who were illegally appropriated. But, does this legal action suffice to relieve the subjective suffering of those who were deprived of the place that awaited them in their family? We understand that this is necessary, but not sufficient.

Let us remember that in the legal discourse the term "restitution" means to return an object to the rightful place from which it has been lost, and repair the damage suffered. Kletnicki (2000) cautions that:

> (...) when the object in question is a subject, the complexity of the situation reveals the limits of the restorative illusion of law. (...) It must be admitted that in the axis of the effects on the subject it is necessary to locate the limit of what can be reestablished, since here we will find the imprint of what is irreparable (pp. 46–47).

In any case, we agree that legal restitution is presented as a sine qua non condition to confront the horror of the sinister lived. *And it stands as a key ethical element to read in intertwined legal and analytical discourses* (Domínguez, 2008, p. 94). A distinction could then be made between legal restitution—sustained by the human rights discourse—and the subjective restitution signaled by psychoanalytic praxis.

Regarding the latter, questions arise as to what it is that can be restituted, its scope, its limits and its conditions of possibility. Since, as the author points out, for the field of subjectivity, it is illusory to sustain a "reconstruction" of subjectivity:

> It is illusory to sustain a "reconstruction" of what has been destroyed, a "repair" of what has been lost, a "reencounter" with what should have been, as could be proposed from other fields of knowledge. (...) The dimension of full coverage of the real dimension by the symbolic that suggests "the reestablishment of previous conditions" is thus dissolved, shipwrecked: if for the legal framework, a law cover what is missing and repairs "what has been broken," psychoanalysis indicates that something of what has been altered does not return to its original place. There is a real dimension there on which it is not possible to go back at all (Kletnicki, 2000, p. 56).

It is to this real dimension and its singular focus, that subjective restitution points. Following this differentiation, we maintain that the truth claimed by law cannot be the same as the truth "claimed" by psychoanalysis. In the emergence of each restitution the subject must decide what to do with the fragments of his history, with the loose pieces of his emergence. In the following episodes we will focus on the subjective aspect of each restitution.

Photography in Clinician Restitution: Imaginary, Symbolic, Real Traces

For psychoanalysis, identity itself is never fully constituted: identity must be distinguished from identification. Identification is the core of identity but it is much more than that (Gómez & Degiorgi, 2010). However, the fact that identity does not attain its absolute determination does not mean that this weakens its consistency. On the contrary, this incompleteness will be essential for the subject. Thus, identity implies a symbolic inscription, and this happens within the kinship system where equality and difference can be recognized, since it is by being different that the subject can be particularized (Lo Giúdice, 2005, p. 37). In each unconscious inscription will be marked the place that the subject occupies in the order of generations, the only one that opens the way to new links in the kinship system.

But if the child was removed from its family nucleus before or immediately after birth, it will grow up and become subjectively constituted in an environment different from the one to which it was destined. The psyche will develop in the midst of an alienated identity and based on the background of a falsified filiation. It does not seem an option to erase these marks, nor to deny that in the link between the appropriators and the children, identification processes were at work (Lo Giúdice, 2005). Then, what about the marks transmitted by the appropriators? And what about those singular marks of the mother tongue that affect the subject even before birth? Will there be something in them that summons a truth for the subject?

In order to situate this question, we propose to look at some stories of children of the disappeared. All of them have a point in common: photographs that become traces of history and leave constituent and indelible traces for the subject.

In general, a photo reminds us of a moment, a place, people. If one finds oneself in it, a memory is triggered, which allows one to recognize oneself as having been there. But what happens in those cases in which the subject has no record of who he was, or who he is? There are a surprising number of people who were appropriated and, during the restitution of their identity, specifically mention encountering images, photographs, graphic documents of themselves and their families of origin. In this regard, in Argentina the National Biographical Archive has carried out an enormous work of compilation, recovery, and reconstruction of each life history, based on oral, written, and photographic material. Given its importance in the reconstruction of identity, this material has even given rise to the publication of memorable books. Abuelas de Plaza de Mayo has published two books whose privileged material is photography: *Fotografías de años en lucha* (2014) and *Historietas por la identidad* (2015).

This leads us to affirm that it is from such circumstances that it is possible to find effects and emotions that have an impact on the subject, introducing some movement with respect to his or her identity.

As we have already mentioned in our introduction, the etymology of the word photograph can be traced to "photo" and "graph," which refer to *phos*, which translates "light," and *graphos*, which translates "to write." Hence, the following definition is usually offered: "… photography is that which graphs light." From the perspective of this work, we will consider photography as a possible imaginary support of a symbolic weft that is woven to circumscribe what is real. There is no experience other than what language builds, always retroactively. And photography can be the fragment of lucidity that makes such writing possible.

We are interested in recovering this aesthetic resource, giving it the value of clinical data through different sources: press clippings of treatments by Abuelas de Plaza de Mayo members, testimonies of young people who went through that ordeal and were able to recover the bond with their legitimate families (Widmer, 2018), and certainly films that of the fiction genre that portray the complex story of filiation.

Consider the following episode about an emblematic restitution case made possible by Abuelas:

P. is the first child restituted. It is a case presented by the team of psychologists of Abuelas de Plaza de Mayo. When she was reunited with her grandmother, "she expressed anger and distrust towards her grandmother's stories, but she agreed to look through photos of when she was a little girl, in her parents' arms. She looked at the photos and cried, but she did recognize herself in one of them" (Lo Giúdice, 2015, p. 1). What led the child to change her attitude? Is her incipient psychic apparatus more permeable to images than to stories? Immediately, her grandmother's initiative brings consequences. The (re)encounter with these images— accompanied by her grandmother's stories, to which P. consents only now, modifies something of her subjective position. Before, she affirmed that the appropriator did not lie to her; now she has doubts, "He didn't lie to me, did he?" she wonders. It is a double denial that produces a first subjective movement in the little girl, who, from the moment she recognizes herself in her parents' arms, permits her to rethink herself as a subject. The instant of her gaze enables a time to understand.

Two other examples: the first from a newspaper article, and the second one from a testimony.

Marcos: *The story of Marcos* (Fainsod, 2001), known as the restituted grandson number 85, is extraordinary. On the day he underwent histocompatibility tests, he saw himself for the first time as a baby... in a photograph. It was in the Argentine soap opera "Montecristo" (Colom, 2006). "There was the actress Viviana Saccone in her role as Victoria, holding in her hands a photo of herself as a baby. That's me," she said, immediately recognizing herself. According to the Abuelas themselves, two photos were shown during that episode of the program, and the choice was absolutely random: "We chose those because they were the clearest."[1] Later that same day, this young man, who had gone to the Durand Hospital Genetic Data Bank due to uncertainty about his identity, found himself in front of the television screen, with an unexpected mirror of his existence. The identification with his silenced history was precipitated, emerging to confirm the genetic data. And the photography and film become intertwined: the expectation of the soap opera becomes the unexpected occasion for a singular situation.

Lucía: This is perhaps one of the most moving cases, because it expresses the emptiness generated by the bitter certainty of not even having a photographic memory, a very frequent situation in cases of appropriation. Lucía is the daughter of the writer and poet Paco Urondo. When in 1976 the police ambushed and killed Urondo, his wife, who was with him in the car, managed to flee badly wounded along with little Lucía, the couple's daughter, who was only 2 years old. Almost four decades later, in 2012 in Guaymallén, Mendoza, a memorial mural was

---

[1] See complete note in: https://luchadores.wordpress.com/2006/09/30/montecristo-ayudo-a-encontrar-un-nieto-desaparecido/

painted at the site of the murder. The faces of Paco Urondo and his wife are depicted there. When Lucía, who was never photographed with her parents, found out about this cultural event, she decided to have a portrait with participants and posed for the camera next to the mural. The scene was portrayed by Gayle Embrey in the film "Beyond the Walls" (Embrey, 2014), further evidence of the value of film, treasuring the snapshot of an experience, in this case, the marvel of Lucía's first photo with her parents.

Film: Filial Photograms

Humans are the only beings that are interested in images of themselves. Animals are interested, but only when images deceived them; when the animal realizes that it is an image, it becomes completely uninterested. In contrast, humans are the only animals that are attracted by images once they know what they are. That is why they are interested in painting and go to the cinema. A definition of humans from our specific point of view could be that humans are the animals that go to the movies. (Agamben, 1998)

"The truth at 24 frames per second" could be an alternative title for this section, which moves from photography to the sequence of frames that organize the experience of film. As a spectacle of the image par excellence, the seventh art has devoted itself to capturing the theme of filiation through a wide gallery of films.[2] In everyone the recognition of an identity restores—announces the image with its trace in the body through a multiplication of marks that is seeks to reclaim. Although this subject is beyond the scope of this chapter, two vignettes will suffice to appreciate the value of cinematographic fictions in the identification process of a subject who, unknowingly, encounters a long-lost filiation.

In *The Mask of Zorro* (Claybourne et al., 1998), little Elena, daughter of Diego de la Vega and Esperanza, is torn from her cradle when the army murders her mother and disappears her father. She has been kidnapped and is taken to Spain by her captor, Captain Montero, who raises her as his own daughter, hiding her origins. At the age of 24, the young girl returns to Mexico, believing that she is stepping foot for the first time on that land when in reality she was born there beautiful and sensitive, she is captivated by the fragrance of a flower that is persistently familiar to her. It is the romalia, native to the Americas that does not grow in Europe. Everything about the young woman's life environment leads her to dismiss the memory, as a confusion.

But the signifier insists on her body and becomes a nagging question, a question without answers. At this point the film takes a crucial turn. For the unsuspecting, it appears to be the film version of the old television series, in which the mark of Zorro only an initial implanted on the prominent belly of Sergeant García. But in the film the mark is transformed into an imprint. An imprint in the memory of a little girl.

---

[2] Other films regarding the Argentine case: *La historia oficial* (Luis Puenzo, 1985), *Vidas privadas* (Fito Páez, 2001), *Los pasos perdidos* (Manane Rodríguez, 2001), *Cautiva* (Gastón Biraben, 2003), *Eva & Lola* (Sabrina Farji, 2010), *El día que no nací / Das Lied in mir* (Florian Cossen, 2010).

The sign becomes significant. To the tangible sign of a social cause—independence from the Spanish crown, the struggle of the oppressed of California—, it now adds another repressed name. But this is not about the morality of good, or the ideal of justice. This sign floats in the air. It is the fragrance of a flower, which, impregnated in the body of a woman, does not forget. Romalia is the name of the rose, to borrow from the beautiful image of Umberto Eco. That is why it defies the passage of time. That is why the seas intensify its fragrance. And that is why, as in all the stories of children whose identity has been stolen, she too lovingly retains the mystery of a filiation.

The second example, *Anastasia* (Bluth & Goldman, 1997) is the animated recreation for children's cinema of the mythical story of the Russian princess lost after the events of 1917. Anastasia, the daughter of czar Nicholas and Alexandria, manages to flee with her grandmother to board the express train that would take them to their exile in Paris. But an accident occurs, and she falls from the train, hits her head and loses her memory. She is rescued and raised by a substitute family, who, like herself, does not know her origins. Twenty years later, a young upstart finds her and given her resemblance to Princess Anastasia, trains her to present her in Paris and obtain the reward offered by her grandmother. Ignoring this circumstance, the young woman lends herself to the game without knowing how close she is to learning the truth. But when the moment of the meeting arrives, the grandmother is already tired of impostors and does not believe the latest candidate. She does not even accept to listen to her studied lesson on the Romanov family trees.

Then something unexpected happens. While the two of them are alone, Anastasia recognizes a fragrance that floods the room: it is a bottle of mint that she spilled on the carpet as a child and hat, persistently still floats in the air. Memories rush in, one after the other, and the grandmother cries because she has found her long-lost granddaughter.

Once again, it is the body that remembers. In tune with this inner quest, the film avoids facile solutions and reserves for the viewer a final and astonishing twist. It is only there that the true core of situational complexity emerges.

We have deliberately taken two films set in historical moments when photographs did not exist or were still rare treasures. The image of the body is organized there from the memory of peppermint, or the fragrance of a flower. These are objects of recognition that the film takes care to capture in sequences of frames that make light a plausible experience for the subject, on both sides of the screen. At the same time, the sequence shows two modes of the restitution of appropriated children: in the first, little Elena is kidnapped as a spoil of war, after the death and disappearance of her parents; in the second, Anastasia is raised by a substitute family that takes her in good faith, unaware of her origins, also marked by historical and political turmoil.

By Way of Synthesis

In the search for those missing children, different scientific disciplines are called upon: genetics, which proves identity even in the absence of the intermediate generation, through that beautiful syntagma called "grandparentality index"; forensic anthropology, which makes it possible to verify pregnancies and births by studying the skeletal remains of the murdered persons; law, which establishes the legal premises for the restitution of identity and the punishment of those responsible for the illegal appropriation; psychology and psychoanalysis, which establish the profound meaning of the knowledge of a person's origins and the mystery of filiation.

But all this knowledge is interwoven with a factor that is not part of science: the political and social activity of the Abuelas. None of the aforementioned disciplines would have dealt with the issue of restitution without the white hand kerchiefed women who circled around the Plaza de Mayo.

Once again, we have proof that great ethical questions arise accompanied by the political turmoil of the history of humanity. The emergence of unprecedented facts subjects the clinician or the researcher to a test of his/her instruments and the social and subjective meaning they entail. But in the case of the Abuelas, this movement exceeds any known framework. It is a genuine invention, an ongoing process that recreates itself with the discovery of each new recovered grandchild. Along with the various scientific disciplines, art has played a crucial role in promoting social awareness of the work of the Abuelas. Music, theater, and especially photography and film have shed new light on the articulation between scientific knowledge and the act of creativity. The artist's aesthetics and style thus represent a powerful conceptual synthesis and, at the same time, an unprecedented contribution to intervention and social change.

This chapter offers a possible route through variants of adulterated filiation, of the many that are present in clinical experience, and whose access is always difficult. The dialectic between identity and identification implies an ethical exercise that is related to the creative activity. These gems through the mediums of photography and film, put us on the track of the theoretical discovery. They thus help us to deploy the conceptual arguments that make these fictions the opportunity for an exercise in thought. Thus, aesthetic creation nurtures the scientific spirit while reminding us that researchers also are creators, with a mind open to the knowledge of reality and a heart willing to transform it.

References

Agamben, G. (1998). Image et Mémoire. *Arts & Esthetique, 14*, 65–76.
Anderson, D. K., Drumm, M. A., Lasseter, J. (Productores), Unkrich, L., & Molina, A. (Directores). (2017). *Coco* (Película animada). Pixar Animation Studios.
Biraben, G. (Director). (2003). *Cautiva* [Film]. Cacerolazo Producciones.

Bluth, D., & Goldman, G. (Productores/Directores). (1997). *Anastasia* (Película animada). 20th Century Fox.

Claybourne, D., Foster, D., Spielberg, S., Parkes, W. F. (Productores), & Campbell, M. (Director). (1998). *La máscara del Zorro* (Película). Sony Pitures.

Colom, M. (Director) (2006). *Montecristo* [TV series]. Telefé Contenidos: Adriana Lorenzón – Marcelo Camaño.

Cossen, F. (Director). (2010). *Das lied in mir* [Film]. Ayerischer Rundfunk (BR), Filmakademie Baden-Württemberg, Mateína Producciones.

Davoine, F., & Gaudillière, J. M. (2010). *El acta de nacimiento de los fantasmas*. Ediciones Fundación Mannoni.

Domínguez, M. E. (2008). Apropiación/restitución: entrecruzamiento discursivo, del caso judicial al caso clínico. En Lo Giúdice, A. (Comp.), *Psicoanálisis: identidad y transmisión* (pp. 93–104). Centro de Atención por el Derecho a la Identidad.

Embrey, G. (Director). (2014). *Beyond the walls* (documental). Power Surge.

Fainsod, J. (2001, May 27). In search of the lost history. *Clarín Magazine*.

Farji, S. (Directora). (2010). *Eva & Lola* [Film]. Cooperativa de Trabajo Felei.

Gociol, J. (2015). *Historietas por la identidad*. Abuelas de Plaza de Mayo.

Gómez, M., & Degiorgi, G. (2010). *Identidad y nombre propio: del estado de excepción al sujeto de la verdad*. Jorge Sarmiento Editor.

Kletnicki, A. (2000). Niños desaparecidos: La construcción de una memoria. En J. J. Michel Fariña & C., Gutiérrez (Comp.), *La encrucijada de la filiación. Tecnologías reproductivas y restitución de niños* (pp. 45–56). Lumen Humanitas.

Lo Giúdice, A. (2005). Derecho a la identidad. En A. Lo Giúdice (Comp.), *Psicoanálisis: restitución, apropiación y filiación* (pp. 29–41). Centro de Atención por el Derecho a la Identidad.

Lo Giúdice, A. (2015). I stuck my tongue out at him.... Case P. Internal material of the seminar interdisciplinary approaches: Incidence of psychoanalysis in public devices. Master in Psychoanalysis, Graduate School of Psychology, UBA.

Lykes, M. B., & Michel Fariña, J. J. (1987). *Can an official story have a happy ending?* Links.

Maci, G., & Michel Fariña, J.J. (2017). Tesis analítica de las desapariciones forzadas de personas tal como se presentan en la experiencia clínica institucional. *Revista Internacional sobre Subjetiividad, Política y Arte, 13*(1), 49–52. Retrieved from https://www.aesthethika.org/IMG/pdf/49-52_maci_michel_farina_tesis_analiticas_sobre_las_desapariciones.pdf

Páez, R. (Director). (2001). *Vidas privadas* [Film]. Circo Beat.

Puenzo, L. (Director). (1985). *La historia oficial* [Film]. Historias Cinematográficas.

Reinoso, A. (2014). *Fotografías de años en lucha*. Abuelas de Plaza de Mayo.

Rodríguez, M. (Director). (2001). *Los pasos perdidos* [película]. Anola Films, Atlanta P.C, Alfa Visión.

Widmer, V. (2018). *Identidad y filiación. Niños desaparecidos durante la dictadura argentina: Una clínica de la singularidad*. Tesis de Doctorado. Universidad de Lausanne, Suiza.

Part II
Psychosocial Assistance and Intervention Methodologies

Chapter 6
The Method and Methodology of Psychosocial Accompaniment Work: A Contribution for At-Risk Defenders in Mexico

Clemencia Correa, Laura Espinosa, and Rodrigo Morales

The Current Sociopolitical Scene in Mexico and the Political Stakes of the Organization "Aluna Acompañamiento Psicosocial" (Aluna Psychosocial Accompaniment)

It is impossible to present a concrete methodology without speaking to the context in which it is implemented, because many theoretical and methodological decisions are closely related to the contextual circumstances that determine how to accompany when faced with specific types of violence. Therefore, we will start by briefly summarizing the general situation that we do our work in.

Beginning in 2006 and continuing on into the present, an authoritarian State has been established in Mexico upheld by a criminal economy that tries to justify its actions with the argument of the fight against drugs, which has unleashed a process of militarizing the country, accompanied by a judicial framework that aims to legitimize and legalize it. Over the last 15 years, a context of cynicism has been experienced in which the Mexican State, for action, omission, or complicity with organized crime and some national and transnational companies, has violated the population's human rights by implementing social control rhetoric and practices whose aim is to subjugate, isolate, and fracture the social fabric in order to guarantee the reproduction of the interests that are underway.

Throughout the country, there has been an exploitation of *sociopolitical violence*, which we understand as the set of acts of power that States—or other actors that pursue specific interests, whether economic, political, ideological, or of another type—exercise over populations with the intention of reproducing the logic and practices of a capitalist system that acts in the benefit of certain privileged sectors

C. Correa · L. Espinosa · R. Morales (✉)
ALUNA Acompañamiento Psicosocial A.C., Ciudad de México, México
e-mail: laura.espinosa@alunapsicosocial.org; psicosocialaluna@gmail.com; rodrigo.morales@alunapsicosocial.org

© The Author(s), under exclusive license to Springer Nature Switzerland AG 2022
E. Lira et al. (eds.), *Human Rights Violations in Latin America*, Peace Psychology Book Series, https://doi.org/10.1007/978-3-030-97542-5_6

and in detriment to the general interests of the population. It is exercised with a clear political intent through practices such as the perpetuation of widespread climates of violence and systematic human rights violations, the exacerbation of acts of repression, the promulgation of government policies to perpetuate acts of dispossession, co-optation, and exploitation of natural resources in territories as well as the militarization of public security developed from a paramilitary logic (Aluna Acompañamiento Psicosocial [AC], 2015).

Paramilitarism has been a significant phenomenon surrounding the entrenching of sociopolitical violence in Mexico, which is related to the proliferation of different groups formed by shock structures—paramilitary groups and, more recently, actors related to drug trafficking such as hitmen and the armed auxiliaries of landowners—that have military training to execute acts of repression. The paramilitary groups are closely linked to the State because, on many occasions, they are the ones who carry out the orders and assignments that the armed forces cannot openly assume, thus recreating violence that attempts to hide their connections and origins (López y Rivas, 2013, 2015).

These are some figures that provide an account of this context: (a) From 2006 to June 2020, a total of 3978 clandestine graves have been found with 6625 bodies (Comisión Nacional de Búsqueda [CNB], 2020). (b) The official figure of the disappearances that took place between 2007 and 2020 is 167,346 (CNB, 2021), although civil society calculates more than 250,000. (c) Rights defenders and journalists face harassment, threats, attacks, and arbitrary detention, among other risks; in addition to this, in 2020 alone, at least six journalists and 24 rights defenders were murdered. (d) Women defenders and journalists also face gender violence; between January and June 2020, 574 attacks against women or women's collectives were registered, of which 47% were against journalists, 42% against women defenders, and 11% against collectives. The attacks were mainly against the right to information and freedom of expression, the right to a life free of violence, and the defense of land and territory (Espacio OSC et al., 2021).

In the severe crisis of violence that the country is facing, those who defend human rights have become one of the main targets of serious human rights violations, given that they are attacked for defending a human right (their own or that of others) and for affecting the political and economic interests that are protected by the actors that have dominion of power. In this text, we understand *human rights defenders* to be women, men, organizations, or groups that take on political projects in defense of human rights and fundamental liberties in order to contribute to social transformation in pursuit of a dignified life as well as social movements and indigenous or rural communities that embark on projects of resistance, although they do not necessarily identify themselves this way.

In these scenarios, fear, horror, and impunity are employed as mechanisms of social control that are operating continuously to perpetuate dynamics that threaten people's lives, integrity, and liberty (Giraldo, 2004; Lira et al., 1991). *Fear*, as a collective emotion, produces confusion when facing a world that has become potentially threatening or dangerous. *Horror* seeks to nullify, objectify, and do away with subjects and social organization through inculcation practices so people accept the living conditions they are immersed in, causing paralysis and inaction when facing other ways of understanding reality. And *impunity* upholds the previous mechanisms by creating vulnerability and instability among the population, provoking feelings of powerlessness, discontent, desperateness, and injustice in a social context in which such events are not investigated or sanctioned.

In view of this context, in 2013, the organization Aluna Acompañamiento Psicosocial AC ("Aluna Psychosocial Accompaniment," hereinafter Aluna) was created in Mexico with the aim of offering tools for mental health and human rights from a psychosocial perspective in order to strengthen political subjects—organizations and collectives, journalists, human rights defenders, indigenous and rural communities—in their human rights defense projects by promoting strategies that would allow them to resist in contexts where they face situations of risk.

The psychosocial perspective makes it possible to expand and complexify the view of the phenomena analysis by recognizing the sociohistorical and cultural conditions that surround those who have suffered borderline experiences and their coping capacity for confronting them. Therefore, by positioning ourselves from this point, we conceive mental health as a sociohistorical process that is under constant construction and is not limited to the individual but is possible to the extent that States provide the political, legal, economic, social, and cultural conditions to guarantee and secure it.

Based on Aluna's experience, we have observed that people who defend human rights are in a constant state of risk due to the context in which they work because they are directly attacked for defending their own rights, for accompanying others in a similar process, and because their work involves constant exposure to the horrors of these events and an inevitable contact with impunity for having to discern the worsening of the contexts that they aim to transform.

On some occasions, these experiences cause *vicarious trauma*, understood as an accumulative impact that is expressed in those who work with people who have lived through traumatic events and that becomes evident when symptoms and effects that are common among victims are experienced (Paniagua, 2015). Nevertheless, although people are exposed to living with this type of effect, their political commitment and empathetic involvement are qualities that allow them gain awareness and identify with the victims by comprehending their feelings and thoughts about the traumatic experiences (Rothschild, 2009, as cited in Paniagua, 2015).

At the same time, in these contexts, human rights defense produces *psychosocial impacts*, which are the sets of personal, family, organizational, and community effects that disrupt individuality and collectiveness; they become evident in different dimensions of people's lives, such as their physical, mental, emotional, and spiritual health in addition to political, social, and economic order. A special characteristic of these impacts is that they are dialectal, cyclical, and multicausal, which is why they are experienced differently depending on gender and other intersectional dimensions (generation, religion, financial condition, ethnic identity, etc.), as well as the particular variables of each situation, such as previous experiences and support networks, to mention a few.

Psychosocial impacts are expressed, among other forms, in different changes and losses, the fragmentation of affective and meaningful bonds, posttraumatic stress, the proliferation of conflicts in families and collectives, the altering of worldviews, and in the presence of feelings of isolation, silencing, powerlessness, frustration, and despair, which affect and disrupt life projects. However, it is also common that, when facing these impacts, *coping mechanisms* are developed in the shape of different actions and strategies that allow for carrying on with work in the pursuit of social transformation.

Moreover, the impacts that human rights defenders experience are cross-cutting in the condition of *being a woman*. Becoming a woman defender means transgressing what has been established in relation to the caregiving role that has traditionally been assigned to the feminine gender. For many of them, this work has meant living with different forms of violence that are embedded in their gender, such as abuses of power, practices of discrimination and contempt, being stripped of their work, reduction of their political or financial support, excessive burdens from the demands of childcare, a lack of access to medical services for sexual and reproductive health, generalized harassment, sexual harassment, rape, and femicide, to mention a few. This is in such a way that the types of violence they experience cover a dimension that ranges from the social to the most private (AC, 2018).

Repression mechanisms seek to subjugate human rights defenders to borderline experiences where their physical and psychological integrity is put at risk in order to bring about deep-seated feelings of pain, despair, fear, powerlessness, and frustration that lead them to question the meaning of their work or to abandon it due to the effects and debilitation it involves. There is reference to intent because human rights violence and violations are systematic, because the sequenced patterns of threats or harassment are not isolated actions, and they are not randomly executed either; rather, they increase in seriousness as time goes by, given that they aim to control, submit, hinder, or dismantle organizational experiences (Correa, 2009).

Human rights defenders must also face an ideological apparatus that State authorities promote through official media channels, which seeks to discredit and criminalize them by constructing social stigmas around their figures in order to make them the target of violent attacks that stem from notions of their work being dangerous and threatening to others. This is a position that isolates them from social and community support by putting their security, liberty, and capacity for protection into question amid the conditions of risk that rise up around them.

Aluna's Psychosocial Accompaniment: Work Method, Model, and Methodology

Facing a context like the one we have described, at Aluna, we have laid our stakes on psychosocial accompaniment as a tool that makes it possible to contribute to strengthening the subjective and collective processes of political subjects. In general terms, the main objective of accompaniment entails lessening impacts and strengthening coping mechanisms based on a multidimensional interpretation of the harm—which links daily experiences with expressions of power developed on different levels—and with the aim of complexifying, understanding, and analyzing the functioning of sociopolitical violence so that human rights defenders in Mexico may continue with their work.

Psychosocial accompaniment is a dialectical and dialogical process through which a variety of scaffolding is constructed when establishing political spaces of trust, reflection, and analysis that allows for strengthening the paths of emancipation and resistance of actors who fight for social transformation. The scaffolding metaphor makes it possible to imagine how the process is promoted by using interconnected scaffolds, one following another, until coping mechanisms are created that develop into strengthening, thus giving priority to the relational approach in which contextual variables (sociopolitical, historical, and cultural conditions) and intersectional variables (gender, generation, ethnicity, etc.) are considered. This construction happens jointly between those who accompany and those who are accompanied, where the former are only facilitators/instigators in these spaces that advance toward the reflection and recovery of the latter's knowledge and resources.

The psychosocial accompaniment practice is based on a series of principles that derive from our experience and denote the ethical-political stance that we adopt: accompaniment *is not considered to be intervention* because those who accompany the process remove themselves from power-knowledge positions in which they are considered to be specialists; *it is not neutral* because it recognizes that subjects are going through a reality of underlying power relations, and, because of this, they are positioned on the side of those who fight to counteract social injustice; *it is not psychotherapy*, although it often contributes to therapeutic processes and because the theoretical-methodological tools are more extensive when political analysis and organizational or collective strategies are integrated in order to understand all the dimensions of violence. And finally, *it advances toward autonomy*, which means acknowledging the political subjects and respecting their processes without trying to influence their decisions, as we recognize that they have resources for facing violence and their own worldview for developing projects for the future.

Based on experiences of psychosocial accompaniment work, we have developed a method that, in short, is characterized by being *deductive*, because it is based on the analysis of the circumstances and experiences of those whom we accompany; *dynamic*, because it changes and adjusts in terms of the different stages of the process; *dialectic*, because it contemplates a constant ebb and flow between theory and practice; and *participative*, because each stage, objective, and action is developed together with the accompanied political subjects.

This method is part of our Psychosocial Accompaniment Model (Aluna Acompañamiento Psicosocial AC, 2017),[1] which is constantly developing and allows us to work from four fields that reflect the dimensions that experiences of

---

[1] Available at: https://www.alunapsicosocial.org

sociopolitical violence disrupt. In the *psycho-emotional* field, emotions, feelings, and meanings surrounding experiences of borderline situations are addressed. In the *security* field, protection strategies are worked on that include reactive and preventive measures for the short, medium, and long term, with consideration for the different levels of risk that are faced. In *internal dynamics*, elements concerning organizational structure (roles, functions, and responsibilities), relationship building, and ways of interacting are addressed, along with communication and coordination processes and practices that contribute to resolving conflicts caused by the generated impacts. Finally, in the *political project*, the ethical-political meaning is reinforced along with the strategic orientations that guide human rights defenders' actions.

The following are the classifications of psychosocial accompaniment that Aluna offers (1) *crisis and emergency assistance,* through specific processes that aim to develop psycho-emotional and security conditions for facing critical situations in which stability is lost, and (2) *organizational strengthening*, which is a long-lasting process in which subjects can recognize the impacts and changes brought about in the different fields in order to develop coping strategies. In both cases, one or more of the fields can be worked on simultaneously—given that they are all interrelated—and group or individual processes can also be addressed according to each case.

Defending Territory Means Fighting for Life…

Aiming to demonstrate the method and methodology that are employed in the accompaniment processes, below, we present an experience carried out with an organization that is devoted to defending land and territory. We will not get into the details of its characteristics or mention the organization's name for reasons of confidentiality and security; however, for a more complete perspective of the context in which they work, we can say they are located in the southeastern region of Mexico, where sociopolitical violence has heightened in recent years due to underlying economic interests in natural resources.[2]

For 20 years, the organization has been doing community work with the aim of improving living conditions for indigenous peoples in the region by promoting and defending collective rights in matters of health, education, and housing; moreover, for 5 years now, they have been involved in legal defense for communities that fight for territory against companies that want to impose hydroelectric and wind-energy megaprojects in the area. Coincidently, organized crime has been positioning itself in the region for 3 years now, and it has attacked the population through dispossession, murders, and abductions in order to gain territorial control. The organization, in particular, has suffered threats, persecution, and harassment. Due to this situation,

---

[2]The presentation of this accompaniment process is done with the informed consent of all the members of the organization.

they requested accompaniment from Aluna in order to strengthen their security strategy.

Like in all the processes we accompany, a participative diagnostic evaluation was done to develop an accompaniment proposal with specific issues, fields, dates, and procedures. The diagnostic phase involves a rigorous and exhaustive evaluation of the situation that the subjects are going through and the needs they express in order to get a full and in-depth view of how their work is being affected; it also contemplates a systematic return of the information that allows for defining a work route. This is essential for the accompaniment process because it makes it possible to provide evidence of the political stakes of those who accompany (the team from Aluna that will carry out the process, which is generally formed in pairs) and those who are accompanied (the political subjects whom Aluna will accompany).

Organizational strengthening accompaniment processes can involve holding three to seven workshops—generally, one workshop takes two workdays and is held once every 2 months—depending on each situation's specifications. To evaluate the development and how the tools are being adopted, periodic evaluations are done—generally once every three workshops—in order to provide feedback on the process and plan for how it could continue. Accordingly, psychosocial accompaniment, as well as the methodological route for carrying it out, becomes flexible by rethinking, making adjustments, and reformulating according to the different moments and needs that arise during the process.

Together with the organization, we determined that the overall objective of the accompaniment process would be to develop a security strategy that could address the risk with consideration for the security incidents—any act or event that can affect personal or organizational security, such as death threats, persecution, or harassment, to mention a few—that they were facing and the collective fear that they were experiencing. It is worth mentioning that this accompaniment process was carried out by three of Aluna's members: a social psychologist and a political scientist with experience in protection strengthened the process together with an educator in order to interweave interdisciplinary efforts.

In the first workshop, elements related to defending territory were made visible in order to comprehend why the risk increased and understand that feeling afraid was normal, considering the seriousness of the events. Therefore, a context analysis was done using the strategic mapping technique in order to visually locate their position according to the companies' interests and the sites where there are intentions to develop the megaproject; it also included an analysis of the actors based on their types of action and repression strategies. The exercise revealed that the megaprojects implemented in the region had a strong correlation to similar practices that had been carried out in neighboring states, which is why the dynamics of dispossession that the residents suffered was part of a broader strategy to exploit resources in this geographic region of the country.

Similarly, an interpretation of the attacks they had suffered was made by using a timeline where they chronologically located the times and types of the different security incidents they were experiencing. The inclusion of the political dimension of the experience allowed them to collectively understand how their territorial defense work was affecting the interests of the aggressors and that the events they had experienced were part of a repressive strategy that was related to their work.

Based on these exercises, two workshops were developed that provided evidence of the impacts that the incidents had caused. After a considerable amount of time, this made it possible to specify how fear was creating processes of silencing and concealing information, as many of the members felt they could not share their emotions because they had assumed that they were individual problems. This situation was affecting bonds between organization members, as they had started experiencing distrust among each other, which can be observed in some of their comments: "We're not like we used to be." "It's hard for me to express myself." "I've isolated myself out of fear because I don't know what to do." Accordingly, with this initial reconciling of the issue of fear, it went from being a private experience to a collective understanding that allowed for visualizing how it was influencing their individual and group dynamics.

While we needed to provide tools for confronting risks, this would not have been possible until we had at least minimally addressed the impact of the effects on bonds, given that one of the core themes of the security strategy necessarily involves developing communication and coordination strategies among those who execute them. Two workshops were devoted to the issue of trust and to providing evidence that another intent of repression is to break apart social fabric. This resulted in a political view of the team's internal dynamics, and communication mechanisms were created for conflict resolution within spaces of dialogue and trust.

After having built a more solid and constructive environment, over the next three workshops, work was done on the issue of fear along with the recognition of their risks. On many occasions, this presents a challenge because it involves interweaving fear between the individual and collective spheres in such a way that, to combine these two dimensions, it has been necessary for organization members to listen to each other with *mirror recognition,* which seeks to reflect the experienced sensation in those of others in order to diminish this sensation. Through these exercises, it became apparent that constructed fantasies regarding the possibility of being the target of attacks or even of being murdered were inflated.

In the accompaniment processes, we have observed that, at times, the risk can be minimized by thinking that everything is fine, even when facing events where one is exposed and harm can be done, but we have also seen that the risk can be maximized by imagining that one could be a murder victim when the probability that it will happen is not high. In view of this, how do we differentiate between the fear that is experienced and the real risk that exists? The concept of risk—the possibility that an incident causing some type of harm will occur—helps us elucidate it, and preventive or reactive security measures can be developed by assessing it.

To work with risk, different dimensions were addressed in one of the workshops: the exercise of analyzing incidents was resumed to demonstrate that, while organization members have risks, they also have different mechanisms to counteract them—such as being figures of reference in the area because of the work they do—and there was collective reflection about the fact that the State would have to assume a very high political cost if it were to murder them. Likewise, a space was opened to exchange experiences about how they were facing risk, where they identified that they had developed different strategies for confronting it; this includes recovering and promoting different strategies to strengthen the meaning of the work based on their validation and sense of belonging, which is why it is important to reinforce activities that range from personal and collective care to spiritual or political beliefs and practices.

Although speaking about fear, socializing it, and learning about how others cope was fundamental for approaching security and risk prevention strategies, it was also important to strengthen individual and team care practices to resignify the sensation of vulnerability with that of protection. In the next three workshops, we developed a variety of mechanisms and protocols—both individual and collective—that have fostered the consolidation of a comprehensive security strategy, which considers measures for digital security and for working and commuting in their territory, spaces for analyzing the context, speaking about fear, and resolving conflicts, as well as the consolidation of networks and alliances at national and international levels.

Through these actions, there has been strategic questioning about how the issue of security is intrinsically related to emotional, communicative, and political mechanisms that can be useful for collectively preventing incidents and harm. It is interesting that the organization has started to work on the issue of protection with the communities it accompanies—that is, from a grassroots level—and they have gradually adapted the strategy based on the multiple forms of violence they face in the territory and from the peoples' idiosyncrasy and autonomy.

The process lasted nearly 3 years, during which time, 14 workshops were developed. Once the organization was strengthened, that process was concluded and, currently, they only have specific assistance sessions in crisis as required. In reflection, we can state that in order to work on security it is necessary to recognize fear, but this does not end when mechanisms and protocols are created, but rather it is resignified in terms of the lessons learned, the tools acquired, and the coping mechanisms that have been developed. In the accompaniment process, we went beyond a viewpoint focused on the security incidents toward the development of a strategic interpretation of the context and the actions that should be taken to strengthen the organization from a collective understanding of security: "I am not alone...I can cope with this better." "Now, I understand why I was so afraid." "Security is everyone's obligation."

Final Reflections

Based on the different accompaniment experiences that we have carried out with political subjects that are in resistance in Mexico, we have faced many challenges and questions about how to continue developing perspectives and tools that transcend the human rights framework and move toward recovering *other* knowledge and worldviews about security, in view of a context where the State is no longer the only actor but rather where it has complexified its political repression strategies hand in hand with actions carried out by organized crime and some companies, whether for action, omission, or complicity.

At Aluna, we have observed the need to formulate an interdisciplinary approach that integrates different knowledge and insight in order to articulate a multidimensional and multifactorial interpretation of the processes of sociopolitical violence. Although we base our work on different theoretical, methodological, and epistemological foundations, we also share common conceptualizations such as the political vision, knowledge of the context, the referential framework of human rights, and ethical-political positionings that allow us to respectfully approach processes of resistance and establish trust-based relationships with those we accompany.

Something else that has deeply enriched our work has been rethinking and reestablishing some notions and tools from the psychological discipline within the framework of the psychosocial perspective. This has made it possible for us to expand our spectrum of work to depathologize mental health and politicize experiences of violence and to also question the normalization of fear, horror, and pain as ways of life that cannot be counteracted with the prospect of generating new paradigms to fight for rights and live with dignity.

Finally, as described throughout this text, the psychosocial accompaniment work that Aluna does is framed within a specific period where we have considered the last 15 years of sociopolitical violence to be a fundamental part of our reference for action and analysis. However, the political change that took place in late 2018 with the inauguration of the new president, Andrés Manuel López Obrador from the party *"Movimento de Regeneración Nacional"* (Morena, "National Regeneration Movement"), has made it necessary for us to adjust our analytical prospects and form different reflections, like the ones we share below.

Although there were many expectations about the possibilities for change with this new administration, they are still unclear. The initial stance demonstrated a different willingness toward the causes that give rise to structural violence in order to have a more comprehensive view when addressing it; however, this has not materialized in actions. While different measures have been adopted from an approach that is more geared toward preventing violence—such as fighting corruption, penalizing impunity, and implementing an austerity policy for public officials—sociopolitical violence has not been reduced; it has even increased in some of its expressions, such as feminicides, gender violence, and murder. Another example of the lack of results is the enforced disappearance of 43 normal school students from Ayotzinapa in 2014, as, while the current president considered the case to be paradigmatic and ordered the creation of an investigative commission, the response continues to be inadequate for finding the students and punishing those responsible.

We should stress that some of the practices of former regimes still persist, and we are deeply concerned about them; they include the continuing focus on militarization for eradicating violence by forming a "National Guard" that authorizes the Armed Forces to carry out security functions and the fact that the strategies implemented on the federal level will not result in changes at the local level, at least not in the same period, especially regarding organized crime's involvement in the municipalities and localities throughout the Mexican territory.

Based on the above, one thing we are certain of is that the effects of repression and fear will not stop nor will they be modified in the short or medium term, and therefore, we will carry forth with the political stakes of psychosocial accompaniment as a tool for producing real paradigm changes from the local level together with political subjects. Consequently, we have more questions to be answered than established certainties: How can tools of resistance that question dominating structures be strengthened to avoid turning into an agency that only responds to situational crises and emergencies? How can we make processes more strategic with organizations that cannot put their work on hold?

This is an invitation for approaches from psychology and the psychosocial approach to continue being woven together with a common principle: the need to carve out paths of hope, dignity, freedom, equity, and justice that are aimed at emancipating those who have been through experiences of repression for taking on projects of political resistance.

References

Aluna Acompañamiento Psicosocial (AC). (2015). *Claves hacia el acompañamiento psicosocial*. Fundación Rosa Luxemburg.

Aluna Acompañamiento Psicosocial (AC). (2017). *Modelo de acompañamiento psicosocial*. Impresiones El Recipiente.

Aluna Acompañamiento Psicosocial (AC). (2018, febrero). *Impactos psicosociales a defensoras en riesgo*. (Documento no publicado). Reporte del Relator Especial de las Naciones Unidas sobre la situación de la defensa de los derechos humanos. México.

Comisión Nacional de Búsqueda (CNB). (2020). *Búsqueda, identificación y registro de personas desaparecidas*. México. Retrieved from https://www.gob.mx/cms/uploads/attachment/file/568163/CNB_13_julio_2020_informe_fosas.pdf

Comisión Nacional de Búsqueda (CNB). (2021). *Registro Nacional de Personas Desaparecidas y No Localizadas*. Retrieved from https://versionpublicarnpdno.segob.gob.mx/Dashboard/Index

Correa, C. (2009). Represión política y miedo como control social: el sexenio del cambio. En *La costumbre de reprimir, el miedo a la verdad y la verdad a medias*. Instituto de Investigaciones Jurídicas de la UNAM. Retrieved from https://archivos.juridicas.unam.mx/www/bjv/libros/7/3461/12.pdf

Espacio OSC, Iniciativa Mesoamericana de Mujeres Defensoras de Derechos Humanos (IM-Defensoras), Red Nacional de Defensoras de Derechos Humanos en México (RNDDHMX), & Centro por la Justicia y el Derecho Internacional (CEJIL). (2021). *Situación de la defensa de derechos humanos y la libre expresión en México a partir de la pandemia por COVID-19*. México. Retrieved from https://articulo19.org/wp-content/uploads/2021/02/Situacion-de-la-defensa-de-DDHH-y-LEX-en-MEX_Digital.pdf

Giraldo, J. (2004, noviembre 24). *El terrorismo de Estado. Desde los márgenes*. Retrieved from http://www.javiergiraldo.org/spip.php?article88

Lira, E., Becker, D., & Castillo, M. (1991). Psicoterapia de víctimas de represión política. En D. Becker & E. Lira (Eds.), *Derechos humanos: todo es según el dolor con que se mira*. ILAS. Retrieved from http://www.psicosocial.net/grupo-accion-

comunitaria/centro-de-documentacion-gac/psiquiatria-psicologia-clinica-y-psicoterapia/
trauma-duelo-y-culpa/109-psicoterapia-de-victimas-de-represion-politica/file
López y Rivas, G. (2013, marzo 29). Paramilitarismo, grupos armados y autodefensas comuni-
tarias *La Jornada*. Retrieved from http://www.jornada.unam.mx/2013/03/29/opinion/015a2pol
López y Rivas, G. (2015, agosto 25). *Paramilitarismo y contrainsurgencia en México, una historia
necesaria*. TeleSURtv. Retrieved from https://www.telesurtv.net/bloggers/Paramilitarismo-y-
contrainsurgencia-en-Mexico-una-historia-necesaria%2D%2D-20150825-0002.html
Paniagua, W. O. (2015). *Afectaciones psicosociales derivadas de la atención a víctimas de violencia armada*. Centro de Investigaciones en Psicología, Universidad de San Carlos de Guatemala,
Nueva Guatemala de la Asunción, Guatemala. Retrieved from http://digi.usac.edu.gt/bvirtual/
informes/puiep/INF-2015-17.pdf

Chapter 7
Construction of a Model of Psychosocial Care and Support: Training of Peer Psychosocial Companions—An Experience from Mexico

José Manuel Bezanilla, María Amparo Miranda, and Juan López

Historical Context

The Cold War was a period of confrontation without direct combat, which marked a change in world geopolitics from multipolarity to bipolarity, with the United States and the then Union of Soviet Socialist Republics (USSR) as focal points. The influence of these superpowers generated polarization within the Latin American continent, forcing nations to take sides, becoming peripheral territories in which ideological confrontations took place (Zurita, 2007).

The Cold War's effects on Latin America were felt in a "second cold war" (Halliday, 2006), formed by polarized national confrontations of national security and economic liberalism against socialism. The Condor Plan produced the coordination of dictatorships in Chile, Argentina, Uruguay, and Brazil, or what in Mexico was known as the Dirty War. This caused strong pressures in the region, and various interventions were unleashed, in the face of national resistance against the hegemonic states (Rodríguez, 1964).

NOTE: This writing is based on author's personal investigation, and in no way represents an institutional position.

J. M. Bezanilla (✉) · M. A. Miranda · J. López
Equipo Mexicano de Atención y Acompañamiento Psicosocial, Naucalpan, México
e-mail: jjmbezanilla@gmail.com; amparo.miranda@gmail.com; lopez.villanueva.xy@gmail.com

© The Author(s), under exclusive license to Springer Nature Switzerland AG 2022   85
E. Lira et al. (eds.), *Human Rights Violations in Latin America*, Peace
Psychology Book Series, https://doi.org/10.1007/978-3-030-97542-5_7

The "Dirty War"

Between the 1950s and 1970s, Mexico underwent a "dirty war," characterized by intense selective repression against the political and social demands of various groups, with the complicit silence of the media. These actions generated serious and systematic human rights violations, such as extrajudicial executions, torture, and forced disappearances, as indicated in the Final Report of the Truth Commission of the State of Guerrero (COMVERDAD, 2014). There are no reliable statistics on the number of people executed and tortured during this period. Estimations of the number of disappearances vary from 500, 532 (Mendoza-García, 2011) and 600, only in the Mexican state of Guerrero (COMVERDAD, 2014).

In this context, the State deployed various actions to suppress the protest mobilizations and control of citizen resistance.

On May 2, 1958, the railroad workers' movement was born that fought for improvements and union democracy. Several demonstrations and protests were repressed by the police and firefighters, and the army occupied the railway workers' union premises. In February 1959, railway workers initiated a general strike, to which the State responded with arrests and massive dismissals and the armed forces again took over union offices and railroad facilities (Guevara-Niebla, 2017).

In 1964, medical interns and residents formed a movement that was repressed, leading to confrontation between the specialists assigned to the November 20 hospital and the nursing staff (Grijalva, 2017).

These episodes were the prelude to the events of the summer of 1968, when protests the Mexico City Olympics held culminated with the armed forced firing upon an estimated 300–400 unarmed students in Tlatelolco on October 2, 1968. The Massacree was characterized as genocide, described as "part of a chain". *Tlaleloco is connected to June 10 and the forced disappearance of the Dirty War in Guerrero. [The facts] are somehow related. There was a systematic and continuous will to end political opposition, armed or not.* (Carrillo-Prieto, 2018).

In 1971, students from the Universidad Autónoma de Nuevo León (UANL) undertook efforts to democratize the university. The movement was met by harsh repression from state forces, resulting in the deaths of a student and a legislator who had supported the movement. In addition, the government discredited the movement in the mass media. and compelled the resignation of Nuevo Leon Governor Elizondo who was replaced by Luis M. Farías, who momentarily calmed the waters (Heredia, 2014).

The Nuevo León student movement had national reverberations, particularly in Mexico City, where support mobilized despite the events of October 2, 1968. On June 10, 1971, a march of students from UNAM and the National Polytechnic Institute was repressed by a paramilitary group known as "Halcones" (Hawks). They first attacked the students with sticks, and when students attempted to defend themselves, they responded with gunfire, finishing off the wounded people in ambulances and torturing the detainees (Castillo-García, 2008; Heredia, 2014; Jiménez-Vázquez, 2016).

This historical period was marked by a state policy that was systematically and widely implemented to "control" the population and exterminate political opponents who were considered dangerous (COMVERDAD, 2014).

> There was brutal repression. Torture was used against the population; the objective was the guerrilla and the people. This fact appears in a document obtained; The Plan Atoyac aims was also to control the people; this confirms the testimonies we received from the people who were prevented from eating and harvesting their crops. It was repression against the population (Noriega & González, 2014).

The "Zapatista Movement," the "Acteal Massacre," and the "Aguas Blancas Massacre"

Despite the apparent end of the "dirty war," the state violence against the dissident or dissident civil population continued. Example is the "Zapatista Movement," the "Acteal Massacre," and the "Aguas Blancas Massacre."

On January 1, 1994, the Zapatista Army of National Liberation (EZLN) arose as an armed movement against what they called the "bad government." The Mexican Government responded by deploying 3000 soldiers, with tanks, helicopters, and airplanes. When the "Zapatistas" retreated to the mountains, they were bombarded by the armed forces. The armed confrontation lasted 12 days. International and national pressure compelled President Carlos Salinas to call for a ceasefire on January 12. In the following years, the government not only sought to discredit the indigenous movement, but also attacked them, and supported armed groups opposed to the "Zapatistas" (Estrada-Saavedra, 2011).

On December 22, 1997, paramilitary groups murdered 45 indigenous Mayans, including women and children from the "Las Abejas" community in Acteal. The attack was meant as a punishment for the struggle undertaken by the inhabitants of San Pedro Chenalhó for self-determination and self-government (Ramírez-Cuevas, 2007).

In the state of Guerrero, on July 17, 1995, 17 people were killed and others seriously injured by police. This massacre occurred in the vicinity of the Aguas Blancas ford when the peasants were on their way to a political meeting in the city of Atoyac de Álvarez. When the attack ended and the survivors were forced to return to their villages of origin, the police officers placed weapons on the deceased, altering the scene to reconfigure events as a justified confrontation (CIDH, 1998).

Femicides in Ciudad Juárez

One of the most egregious manifestations of social violence in Mexico is the systematic murders of women in Ciudad Juárez, Chihuahua. The discovery on January 23, 1993, of the lifeless body of Alma Chavira Farel (A 25 años del primer feminicidio en Juárez, nada ha cambiado en el país, 2018) first brought to light events that had been occurring quite some time. Since then, the murders of women in that border town not only persist but have even increased. Various investigations (Falquet, 2014; Monarrez, 2000) attribute the murders of women to gender violence (femicides). Violence targeting women arises from the politics of difference between the genders that fosters the "brutal" patriarchal order, exacerbated by a perverse "Savage Neoliberalism."

The ONU (2012) indicates that between 1985 and 2010, 36,606 women have been killed, in Mexico and another 7404 between 2012 and 2016 (Denis & Rodríguez, 2017). It also points out that in Mexico, violence against women remains invisible, and has been normalized as part of daily coexistence with persistent judicial impunity in most cases.

The Narco War and the Crisis of Disappearances in Mexico

Parallel to state violence, in Mexico, since the 1990s, there was a breakdown in the security conditions, to such an extent that on November 29, 1997, some 40,000 people marched, demanding government attention to the rising crimes. One of the leaders of this movement was the future President of Mexico, Felipe Calderón (2006–2012) (Las grandes marchas en 17 años, 2014).

On June 28, 2004, community organizations convened the Rescue Mexico nationally to demand greater citizen security amid rampant criminal violence and kidnappings (Illades, 2017).

In December 2006, the new President Felipe Calderón declared the War against "Narcos" (A 10 años de la guerra contra el narco 100 mil Muertos y 30 mil desaparecidos, 2016), aiming to reestablish social security and safety conditions fighting against organized crime. During his 6-year term, violence, insecurity, and systematic violations of human rights intensified a continuation of what had been happening (FIDH, 2017), with significant impacts on the population.

Violence was "privatized" (Pereyra, 2012). The government's incapacity to control criminal groups, led to increased discontent and social resistance. In response, the government implemented what has come to be known as a low-intensity conflict war (LIC) (Finnegan, 2012).

The LIC is viewed as an alternative to conventional warfare, especially when "enemies" cannot be eliminated due to their large number and roots in the territory they are trying to dominate. LIC is characterized by the exercise of targeted physical, judicial, economic, media, symbolic, and psychological violence. It is intended to rupture social cohesion, citizen organization processes by establishing terror as an instrument of control (Von Brostel, 2013).

Low-intensity conflicts are characterized by massive and arbitrary arrests of people (Díaz, 2013), armed attacks against the civilian population (Cervantes et al., 2011), the death of students and citizens in clashes against the security forces

(CNDH, 2012, 2014a, b), torture (ONU, 2014), and other serious human rights violations (CIDH, 2016).

In Mexico, one of the most serious human rights violations is the growing number of disappearances of people (CNDH, 2017a, b; FIDH, 2017), which number more than 77 people (Martínez, 2020). An expression of this repressive mechanism is the disappearance of 43 students from the "Ayotzinapa" Teachers' School (GIEI, 2015, 2016), which gave visibility to this serious structural problem as well as impunity that has prevailed since the Dirty War.

The disappearance of the 43 students from Ayotzinapa is considered "… *extremely serious. The participation of criminals, … in collusion with officials has been exposed; … uncovering the perverse triangle of cover-up, complicity, impunity that has violated a multiplicity of human rights…. The events in Iguala are a clear example of the gradual weakening of the rule of law in the country."* (CNDH, 2018, p. 11).

Assistance Actions and Psychosocial Support

One of the most serious manifestations of violence is the thousands of disappeared people in Mexico, of which 71.3% are men, 45.9% are under 30 years old, and 87.2% are Mexican (Vargas, 2014). A significant fact is the disappearance of women between 15 and 17 years of age and of children, who are generally made invisible (La crisis de desapariciones en México toca ya a niñas y mujeres adolescentes, alerta Redim, 2017).

We approach the phenomenon of disappearance in Mexico with the founding of the movement called United Forces for Our Disappeared in Coahuila (FUUNDEC) in 2009, that became the United Forces for Our Disappeared in Mexico (FUNDEM).

The organization's primary objectives were to promote collective organization processes and develop skills for dialogue with politicians and state actors responsible for conducting the search and investigation of the disappearance.

One of the lessons learned from this experience was that the deep pain and devastation generated by the disappearance of a relative increases the gregarious qualities of human beings, enabling the formation of highly cohesive groups that provide companionship as well as emotional and operational support.

We also were able to actively accompany the search processes of the 43 disappeared students of Ayotzinapa and the members of the *Avispones de Chilpancingo* soccer team who were attacked in the same events. We witnessed the birth of the "Other disappeared" of Iguala, which ruling out that the bodies of the 43 students were buried in 6 clandestine graves discovered on October 4, 2014, in the vicinity of the Guerrero city of Iguala.

Following this organizational effort, in 2015, we assisted in the organization of a national meeting of groups and collectives of relatives of disappeared persons. From this meeting arose the National Links Organization (Organización Enlaces Nacionales), a network that brings together more than 200 organizations from all over Mexico. This organization has enabled relatives to have national visibility, dialogue with highlevel government representatives, and articulate actions like the National Search Brigades, which held five editions.

During this meeting, we became aware of the relevance and ethical implications of the participation of mental health professionals in the search for missing persons. These implications transcend the clinical intervention perspective and require the development of skills to accompany socio-political processes with strong psycho-affective content.

Experience has shown us that the victims we accompany represent a population previously victimized by poverty, marginalization, and exclusion due to an explicit violence (insecurity) and a structural one (La Parra & Tortosa, 2003). The disappearances highlight both types of violence, with an exponential accentuation of the suffering.

> When a disappearance occurs, relatives are taken by surprise and face with an unimaginable situation since most are unaware of the context in which disappearances occur and of the collusion of crime with state agents. At this time, the families initiate desperate and disorganized actions in the hope that the officials will "do their job," wasting valuable time searching for information and tracking down evidence of the act. At this point, officials begin a re-victimization, leading to the families' decision to carry out the search with their own means, despite significant emotional, physical, and economic exhaustion. This stage of the process has been described as follows: '*A path begins, and it is not known when it will end as we are not certain about anything.*' Families become fragmented by the damage caused by the disappearance and the conflicts it unleashes, in addition to significant amount of fear and social resentment (J. Orgen and I. Orgen, personal communication on February 28, 2018, female relatives of disappeared persons and founders of the Uniendo Cristales AC Psychosocial Accompaniment Organization).

From the inception of this phenomenon the groups and collectives of relatives have been accompanied by civil society organizations. However, it is in the context of the organization of the "National Brigades for the Search for Disappeared Persons" that an interdisciplinary team of professionals, teachers, and members of public human rights organizations made up of psychologists, forensic anthropologists, and lawyers, among others, have put their knowledge at the service of people to provide training, care and psychosocial support, expert opinions, and specialized technical advice in various parts of Mexico.

Within this framework, various groups of families of disappeared persons formed "Uniendo Cristales," which is an association that seeks to visibilize and strengthen the psycho-emotional and socio-group processes of the organizations during the searches.

> It is important for the members of the association to identify the abilities and needs of the family members, so that by recognizing them [these skills], they can contribute to the collective processes; that in the process, family life projects can be restructured and, more importantly, to open spaces in which people, through their active contribution to projects, can transform from victims to subjects of social change (J. Orgen and I. Orgen, personal communication on July 23, 2017).

The Mexican Model of Psychosocial Care and Accompaniment (MMAAPSI)

It arises from the reflection and theoretical systematization of the experiences related to the work with victims of serious human rights violations, and disappearance. The model's objective is to strengthen collective, community, family, and personal resources in contexts of social violence and insecurity.

We start from Socionomy (Moreno, 1966), which is the *"science that studies is social laws,"* based on the knowledge of micro-social principles and phenomena, especially of small groups, institutions, and communities (Bezanilla & Miranda, 2012).

It is based on the principle of the *"encounter,"* which is fundamental element to establish healthy relationships, by generating conditions so that those involved in the relationship and interaction have the possibility to acquire a deep and genuine recognition (Moreno, 1972) in the most minimal *"I-you"* existential relationship (Buber, 1984).

To carry out the encounter, the Telé is fundamental. This *"... is constituted as an elemental relationship that can exist between individuals ... and that it develops gradually from birth that gives meaning to interhuman relations. It can be seen as the foundation of all healthy relationships and consists of the feeling and knowledge of the real situation of other people. The Telé usually exists from the first meeting and grows during each subsequent meeting. Occasionally it can be disfigured by the influx of transference fantasies ..."* (Moreno, 1966, p. 49). The Telé is configured as a human capacity for relationship, with which a person is born, and which becomes specialized during the individual's development process.

The concept of *"role"* is defined as the operational form that the individual assumes at the specific moment in which he is in a situation in which she/he enters interaction with other people or objects (Moreno, 1954, as cited in Boria, 2001). The role allows the person in a given *moment/space* to organize all the elements of her personality to respond to the demands of the context.

The socionomic approach that underpins the MMAAPSI allows us to understand that the relatives of disappeared persons play a role in the context of violence in Mexico. That role is fundamental to the implementation of psychosocial assistance and accompaniment strategies, build encounter situations and strengthen the Telé between the members of collectives and family groups.

We understand the *psychosocial perspective "as a multidisciplinary field of articulation that combines knowledge of clinical and social psychology, around the logic of human rights, visualizing the consequences of violence and complex relationships in a social historical context"* (Bezanilla et al., 2019, p. 51).

Santiago-Vera (2007) sustains that the psychosocial view is formed in response to new situations of horror and deterioration of the Latin American reality. The author indicates that this mechanism arises in individuals who face a context of rupture marked structural violence and repeated violations of community integrity, family and individual. Consequently, millions of people find themselves in situations of exclusion and victimizing vulnerability.

For this reason, the approach from the psychosocial perspective constitutes a re-signification of knowledge, actions, and discourses, that reclaim the contributions and identify discipline and professional limitations. We start from a comprehensive dialogical and dialectical opening, where knowledge is at the service of the construction of a society and in which the welfare of minorities is not dependent on the discomfort of the majority. In addition, from this focus, the fulfillment of some does not require the dismissal and denial of others (Iglesia Católica & Francisco, 2015); nor do the interests of a few demands the dehumanization and alienation of the rest (Martín-Baró, 2006).

Thus, the psychosocial perspective is constituted as *"an ethical and existential position-taking, of a commitment to action and an encounter for social transformation, with the victims, families and communities that have faced sociopolitical violence and serious human rights violations."* (Bezanilla & Miranda, 2017, p. 6).

Methodological Approach to the Formation of Peer Psychosocial Companions

The processes of psychosocial assistance and accompaniment that arise from this model take the group as a minimum work unit, which we understand as *"a certain number of people, who 'find themselves' in a given context, who interact with each other, by performing different roles, who are remain united by the Telé and share co-subconscious and psycho-affective contents"* (Bezanilla & Miranda, 2012, p. 160).

The approach to the process with the relatives of disappeared persons employs what Freire (1970) called praxis. This focus fosters the awareness of the context, reflection on the role each person plays in it, and the design of relevant actions to transform it. This implies an ethical commitment (Dussel, 1988).

Methodologically, our approach draws from Participatory Action Research, starting from a critical reading and contextualization of reality, to reveal structural characteristics and, from the collective perspective, to mark the path and meaning for transformation (Melero-Aguilar, 2012).

Based on the above, within the MMAAPSI, psychologists play a fundamental role. By resignifying professional training and meeting with family members (Buber, 1967, 1998), the psychologist establishes the conditions for the accompaniment and the training of peer companions.

The process of training family members as peer psychosocial companions arises as a need to acquire basic skills that enable them to safely manage their affective conditions and enable them to provide others basic support and accompaniment. The process opens with the assumption that the victim's reality is generally not rationalized, neither individually nor in the field of state responsibilities.

Documenting this reality allows participants to define concepts, actors and therefore, priorities, of victims of serious human rights violations.

"Uniendo Cristales" and the EMAAPSI jointly launched this program in various modalities:

- **Face-to-face training**: Workshops for family members to train them to manage and implement Psychological First Aid and develop group processes, paying special attention to risk indicators and the need for channeling for specialized care.
- **Online training**: Developing a virtual course for participants to understand the principles and develop basic skills to provide "First instance psychosocial care and support" to other family members. Topics addressed include human rights; serious human rights violations; consequences of human rights violations; victimization, institutional violence and revictimization; self-care and prevention of "burnout"; psychological first aid; psychosocial accompaniment; principles of group dynamics and conflict resolution, among others. Participants are always counseled virtually and in person by trained psychologists.
- **Technical advice**: Carrying out planning and processing sessions both in the context of preparation for the National Search Brigades, as well as the participation of relatives of disappeared persons in academic forums, holding workshops for other family members and their participation in the media. Such guidance helps open spaces for designing strategies and containment of the emotional states generated by the search tasks and their activism.
- **Double tutoring**: As a result of the training work, the members of "Uniendo Cristales" have begun to train other family members as peer psychosocial companions, both in the collective organization and in the training of groups within the country, always with the accompaniment and advice from specialized EMAAPsi staff.

To date, the work carried out since 2015 with Uniendo Cristales has led to the online training of more than 80 family members who voluntarily provide solidarity as peer companions of other family members. Several are now studying to be psychologists. Furthermore, after much work and discussion, they succeeded in creating the *Psychosocial Commission* within the Movement for Our Disappeared and the National Search Brigades. The work has allowed them to move forward, towards devictimizing processes, despite the omissions and violence of the state institutions.

In parallel, since January 2018, an *"Interinstitutional Seminar for Psychosocial Care and Accompaniment"* has been held at the Faculty of Psychology of the Universidad Nacional Autónoma Mexico (UNAM), with the participation of various UNAM departments, as well as several organizations and institutions such as the National Human Rights Commission (CNDH), the Human Rights Commission of Mexico City (CDHCM), Psychologists Without Borders Mexico (PSFMX), the International Committee of the Red Cross (ICRC), Doctors Sin Fronteras (MSF), the National School of Anthropology and History (ENAH), and the Faculty of Behavioral Sciences (FaCiCo) of the Autonomous University of the State of Mexico (UAEMex). The seminar aims to lay the foundations for the construction of a curriculum for training professionals in the care, and psychosocial support of victims and relatives of violence and human rights violations.

Discussion and Conclusions

In the work of psychosocial care and support for victims of serious human rights violations in the Mexican context, particularly with relatives of disappeared persons, psychologists and companions from other disciplines have been challenged in the deepest foundations of our training. On the theoretical, technical, ethical, and epistemological levels, they carry out profound individual, group, and union reflective processes.

We as clinical psychologists have had to leave our offices, and social psychologists have developed clinical skills to be closer to the people who require our knowledge. This has compelled us to develop transdisciplinary skills and interdisciplinary dialogue, to break down theoretical barriers and build bridges of human and interpersonal encounter to meet the current complex situation.

We have learned that psychology has a transcendent social responsibility with suffering people. This comprises an ethical imperative that forces us to come down from our ivory tower to listen and accompany human pain, strengthening the processes of family and individual healing and collective organization, while establishing channels of interpersonal and institutional dialogue.

Putting the knowledge of the Psi field at the service of family members, relinquishing hegemonic control over them and accompanying the training spaces, has allowed us to witness the strengthening of the processes for the search for truth and justice, and for the restoration of their human and interpersonal attributes. The truth is not limited to the act that created the victim, but to the circumstances prior to it, as part of a broader social construction process that fosters non-repetition measures.

It is necessary to systematically monitor the needs of families and the processes that they are developing in their searches. Arbitrated and flexible instruments are being designed in accordance with their needs and mobility dynamics. It is especially important to detect the foundation and obstacles that groups have for joint and coordinated action with other groups. The current social models of coexistence tend to have serious difficulties for their organizational processes.

The approach with the families must start from encounter and recognition, moving us forward from the place of knowledge to listen to the voices that demand truth and justice, to find those who have disappeared and ensure that no one else disappears. We seek to strengthen group processes, family recomposition, and individual strengthening.

It is essential that, at least in Mexico, psychology training programs are reviewed to transform the profile towards an active and preventive logic, to put an end to passive-welfare vices.

References

A 10 años de la guerra contra el narco: 100 mil muertos y 30 mil desaparecidos. (2016, diciembre 11). *Milenio*. Retrieved from http://www.milenio.com/policia/10_anos_guerra_contra_el_narco-muertos-desaparecidos-homicidios-milenio_0_863913709.html

A 25 años del primer feminicidio en Juárez, nada ha cambiado en el país. (2018, enero 23). *Regeneración*. Retrieved from https://regeneracion.mx/a-25-anos-del-primer-feminicidio-en-juarez-nada-ha-cambiado-en-el-pais/

Bezanilla, J. M., & Miranda, M. A. (2012). La socionomía y el pensamiento de Jacobo Levy Moreno: Una revisión teórica. *Revista de Psicología GEPU, 3*(1), 148–180. Retrieved from https://dialnet.unirioja.es/revista/15248/V/3

Bezanilla, J. M., & Miranda, M. A. (2017). Violaciones Graves de Derechos Humanos: acción inmediata y primer contacto desde una "Mirada Psicosocial". *Cuadernos de Crisis y Emergencia, 1*(16). Retrieved from http://www.cuadernosdecrisis.com/docs/2017/numero16vol1_2017_5_violaciones.pdf

Bezanilla, J. M., Miranda, M. A., & López, J. (2019). Primeras reflexiones sobre la formación de acompañantes psicosociales pares dentro del MMAAPSI. *Alternativas en Psicología, 23*(43), 47–57. Retrieved from http://alternativas.me/attachments/article/214/4%20-%20Primeras%20reflexiones%20sobre%20la%20formaci%C3%B3n%20de%20acompa%C3%B1antes.pdf

Boria, G. (2001). *El psicodrama Clásico: metodología de acción para una existencia creadora*. Ítaca.

Buber, M. (1967). *¿Qué es el hombre?* Fondo de Cultura Económica.

Buber, M. (1984). *Yo y Tú*. Nueva Visión.

Buber, M. (1998). *Yo y Tú*. La Factoría de Ediciones.

Carrillo-Prieto, I. (2018, febrero 25). ¡Hubo confabulación del crimen en 1968! *El Universal*. Retrieved from https://www.eluniversal.com.mx/nacion/sociedad/se-busco-desacreditar-al-ejercito-en-el-68-carrillo-prieto

Castillo-García, G. (2008, junio 9). El halconazo, historia de represión, cinismo y mentiras se mantiene impune. *La Jornada*. Retrieved from http://www.jornada.unam.mx/2008/06/09/index.php?article=018n1pol&section=politica

Cervantes, J., Rodríguez, A., & Campos, L. (2011, septiembre 3). Cuando crimen y política se juntan. *Proceso*. Retrieved from http://www.proceso.com.mx/280396/cuando-crimen-y-politica-se-juntan

Comisión de la Verdad del Estado de Guerrero (COMVERDAD). (2014). *Informe final de actividades*. México. Retrieved from http://congresogro.gob.mx/files/InformeFinalCOMVERDAD.pdf

Comisión Interamericana de Derechos Humanos (CIDH). (1998). *Informe N° 49/97 Caso 11.520 Tomás Porfirio Rondin "Aguas Blancas"*. México. Retrieved from https://www.cidh.oas.org/annualrep/97span/Mexico11.520.htm

Comisión Interamericana de Derechos Humanos (CIDH). (2016). *Situación de los derechos humanos en México*. Washington. Retrieved from http://www.oas.org/es/cidh/informes/pdfs/mexico2016-es.pdf

Comisión Nacional de los Derechos Humanos (CNDH). (2012). *Recomendación N° 1VG/2012: sobre la investigación de violaciones graves a los derechos humanos, relacionada con los hechos ocurridos el 12 de diciembre de 2011, en Chilpancingo, Guerrero*. México. Retrieved from http://www.cndh.org.mx/sites/all/doc/Recomendaciones/ViolacionesGraves/RecVG_001.pdf

Comisión Nacional de los Derechos Humanos (CNDH). (2014a). *Recomendación N° 2VG/2014 sobre la investigación de violaciones graves a los derechos humanos iniciada con motivo de los hechos ocurridos el 9 de julio de 2014, en el Municipio de Ocoyucan, Puebla*. México. Retrieved from http://www.cndh.org.mx/sites/all/doc/Recomendaciones/ViolacionesGraves/RecVG_002.pdf

Comisión Nacional de los Derechos Humanos (CNDH). (2014b). *Recomendación N° 51/2014 sobre los hechos ocurridos el 30 de junio de 2014 en Cuadrilla Nueva, comunidad San Pedro*

Limón, municipio de Tlatlaya. México. Retrieved from http://www.cndh.org.mx/sites/all/doc/Recomendaciones/ViolacionesGraves/RecVG_051.pdf

Comisión Nacional de los Derechos Humanos (CNDH). (2017a). *Informe especial de la Comisión Nacional de los Derechos Humanos sobre desaparición de personas y fosas clandestinas en México*. México. Retrieved from http://www.cndh.org.mx/sites/all/doc/Informes/Especiales/InformeEspecial_20170406.pdf

Comisión Nacional de los Derechos Humanos (CNDH). (2017b). *Recomendación N° 5VG/2017 sobre la investigación de violaciones graves a los derechos humanos, por la detención arbitraria, tortura, desaparición forzada y ejecución arbitraria de V1, V2, V3, V4 y MV, ocurridas el 11 de enero de 2016, en el municipio de Tierra Blanca, Veracruz*. México. Retrieved from http://www.cndh.org.mx/sites/all/doc/Recomendaciones/ViolacionesGraves/RecVG_005.pdf

Comisión Nacional de los Derechos Humanos (CNDH). (2018). *Recomendación N° 15VG/2018 "Caso Iguala"*. México. Retrieved from http://www.cndh.org.mx/sites/all/doc/Recomendaciones/ViolacionesGraves/RecVG_015.pdf

Denis, D., & Rodríguez, A. (2017, marzo 9). Las voces de las silenciadas. Feminicidios en México: una lacra que pervive. *El País*. Retrieved from https://elpais.com/especiales/2017/feminicidios-en-mexico/#

Díaz, G. (2013, enero 18). Denuncian retención ilegal de cuatro hermanos en penal del Hongo. *Proceso*. Retrieved from http://www.proceso.com.mx/331020/denuncian-retencion-ilegal-de-cuatro-hermanos-en-penal-del-hongo

Dussel, E. (1988). *La ética de la liberación: ante el desafío de Apel, Taylot y Vattimo con respuesta crítica inédita de K.O. Apel*. Universidad Autónoma del Estado de México.

Estrada-Saavedra, M. (2011). El levantamiento zapatista de 1994. *Arqueología Mexicana, 111*, 33–60. Retrieved from https://arqueologiamexicana.mx/mexico-antiguo/el-levantamiento-zapatista-de-1994

Falquet, J. (2014, octubre 24). De los asesinados de Ciudad Juárez al fenómeno de los feminicidios: ¿nuevas formas de violencia contra las mujeres? *Viento Sur*. Retrieved from https://www.vientosur.info/IMG/pdf/Art_Feminicidios_Contrettemps-Vientos_Sur_esp.pdf

Federación Internacional por los Derechos Humanos (FIDH). (2017). *México: Asesinatos, desapariciones y torturas en Coahuila de Zaragoza constituyen crímenes de lesa humanidad*. Paris. Retrieved from https://www.fidh.org/spip.php?page=spipdf&spipdf=spipdf_article&id_article=21851&nom_fichier=article_21851

Freire, P. (1970). *Pedagogía del oprimido*. Siglo XXI, Buenos Aires.

Finnegan, W. (2012, julio 2). The Kingpins. The fight for Guadalajara. *The New Yorker*. Retrieved from https://www.newyorker.com/magazine/2012/07/02/the-kingpins

Grijalva, H. (2017, octubre 23). El Día del Médico/Análisis de lo cotidiano. *La Jornada Aguascalientes*. Retrieved from http://www.lja.mx/2017/10/dia-del-medico-analisis-lo-cotidiano/

Grupo Interdisciplinario de Expertos Independientes (GIEI). (2015). *Informe Ayotzinapa: Investigación y primeras conclusiones de las desapariciones y homicidios de los normalistas de Ayotzinapa*. México. Retrieved from https://www.oas.org/es/cidh/actividades/giei/giei-informeayotzinapa1.pdf

Grupo Interdisciplinario de Expertos Independientes (GIEI). (2016). *Informe Ayotzinapa II: Avances y nuevas conclusiones sobre la investigación, búsqueda y atención a las víctimas*. México. Retrieved from https://www.oas.org/es/cidh/actividades/giei/giei-informeayotzinapa2.pdf

Guevara-Niebla, G. (2017, agosto 5). El México anterior a 1968. *Crónica*. Retrieved from http://www.cronica.com.mx/notas/2017/1036954.html

Halliday, F. (2006). *Las Relaciones Internacionales y sus debates*. Centro de Investigación para la Paz. Retrieved from http://www.fuhem.es/media/cdv/file/biblioteca/Informes/Azules/HALLIDAY,%20Fred,%20Las%20relaciones%20internacionales.pdf

Heredia, A. L. (2014, marzo 2). *1971: El año de los jóvenes regios*. El Barrio Antiguo. Retrieved from http://www.elbarrioantiguo.com/1971-el-ano-de-los-jovenes-regios/

Iglesia Católica. Papa (2013-: Francisco)., & Francisco, P. (2015). *Laudato si'. Carta encíclica del Sumo Pontífice Francisco: a los obispos, a los presbíteros y a los diáconos, a las personas* consagradas y a todos los fieles laicos sobre el cuidado de la casa común. Lima: Paulinas. Retrieved from https://w2.vatican.va/content/dam/francesco/pdf/encyclicals/documents/papa-francesco_20150524_enciclica-laudato-si_sp.pdf

Illades, C. (2017, febrero 14). La Marcha Blanca. *MEMORIA*. Revista de Crítica Militante. Retrieved from https://revistamemoria.mx/?p=1339

Jiménez-Vázquez, R. (2016, junio 9). La matanza del 10 de junio no se olvida. *La Jornada*. Retrieved from http://www.jornada.unam.mx/2016/06/09/opinion/016a2pol

La crisis de desapariciones en México toca ya a niñas y mujeres adolescentes, alerta Redim. (2017, marzo 5). *Sin Embargo*. Retrieved from http://www.sinembargo.mx/05-03-2017/3165906

La Parra, D., & Tortosa, J. M. (2003). Violencia social estructural: una ilustración del concepto. *Documentación social, 131*, 57–72. Retrieved from http://www.ugr.es/~fentrena/Violen.pdf

Las grandes marchas en 17 años. (2014, noviembre 20). *Milenio*. Retrieved from http://www.milenio.com/df/Iluminemos_Mexico-_Rescatemos_Mexico-Movimiento_por_la_Paz-Ayotzinapa_0_412759091.html

Martín-Baró, I. (2006). Hacia una psicología de la liberación. *Revista Electrónica de Intervención Psicosocial y Psicología Comunitaria, 1*(2), 7–14. Retrieved from http://www.facso.uchile.cl/psicologia/epe/_documentos/getep/martin_baro_psicologia_liberacion.pdf

Martínez, F. (2020, septiembre 29). Asciende a 77 mil 500 el número de desaparecidos en el país. *La Jornada*. Retrieved from https://www.jornada.com.mx/ultimas/politica/2020/09/29/son-77-mil-150-personas-desaparecidas-en-el-pais-segob-9299.html

Melero-Aguilar, N. (2012). El paradigma crítico y los aportes de la investigación acción participativa en la transformación de la realidad social: un análisis desde las Ciencias Sociales. *Revista Cuestiones Pedagógicas, 21*, 339–355. Retrieved from http://hdl.handle.net/11441/12861

Mendoza-García, J. (2011). La tortura en el marco de la guerra sucia en México: un ejercicio de memoria colectiva. *Polis: Investigación y Análisis Sociopolítico y Psicosocial, 7*(2), 139–179. Retrieved from http://www.redalyc.org/articulo.oa?id=72621412006

Monarrez, J. (2000). La cultura del feminicidio en Ciudad Juárez 1993-1999. *Revista Frontera Norte, 12*(23), 87–117. Retrieved from http://www.scielo.org.mx/scielo.php?script=sci_arttext&pid=S0187-73722000000100004&lng=es&tlng=es

Moreno, J. L. (1954). *Sociometría y psicodrama*. Buenos Aires: Deucalión.

Moreno, J. L. (1966). *Psicoterapia de grupos y psicodram a*. Fondo de Cultura Económica.

Moreno, J. L. (1972). *Fundamentos de sociometría*. Paidós.

Noriega, P., & González, J. E. (2014, octubre 21). Entre el 69 y 79, política de exterminio: represión brutal en Guerrero: Comisión de la verdad. *CNN*. Retrieved from https://aristeguinoticias.com/2110/mexico/entre-el-69-y-79-politica-de-exterminio-represion-brutal-en-guerrero-comision-de-la-verdad-en-cnn/

Organización de Naciones Unidas (ONU). (2012). *Violencia feminicida en México. Características, tendencias y nuevas expresiones en las entidades federativas (1985-2010)*. ONU Mujeres. Retrieved from http://vidasinviolencia.inmujeres.gob.mx/sites/default/files/F05-1feminicidio1985-2010nal.pdf

Organización de Naciones Unidas (ONU). (2014). *Informe del Relator Especial Juan E. Méndez sobre la tortura y otros tratos o penas crueles, inhumanos y degradantes*. Misión a México. Retrieved from http://www.acnur.org/t3/fileadmin/Documentos/BDL/2015/9930.pdf?view=1

Pereyra, G. (2012). México: violencia criminal y "guerra contra el narcotráfico". *Revista Mexicana de Sociología, 74*(3), 429–460. Retrieved from http://revistamexicanadesociologia.unam.mx/index.php/rms/article/viewFile/32219/29638

Ramírez-Cuevas, J. (2007, diciembre 22). La masacre de Acteal, culminación de una política de Estado contra indígenas. *La Jornada*. Retrieved from http://www.jornada.unam.mx/2007/12/22/index.php?article=007n1pol&section=politica

Rodríguez, M. E. (1964). Una interpretación de la guerra fría en Latinoamérica. *Foro Internacional, 4*(4), 517–531. Retrieved from http://codex.colmex.mx:8991/exlibris/aleph/a18_1/apache_media/L5E5T6SGDAVMTAADJ1CCNFXGHQJH9S.pdf

Santiago-Vera, C. (2007). La mirada psicosocial en un contexto de guerra integral de desgaste. *Journal for Social Action in Counseling and Psychology, 1*(1), 14–28. Retrieved from https://scholar.google.com/scholar_url?url=https://openjournals.bsu.edu/jsacp/article/download/17 1/153&hl=es&sa=T&oi=gsb-ggp&ct=res&cd=0&d=4361842050403447656&ei=OY4lYZj zL4WImwHmk7-oCw&scisig=AAGBfm075JuuZ8en4z1v1SxQm_7jaga8IA

Vargas, M. A. (2014, diciembre 10). *¿Cuál es el perfil de las personas que han desaparecido en México?* Expansión. Retrieved from https://expansion.mx/nacional/2014/12/10/cual-es-el-perfil-de-las-personas-que-han-desaparecido-en-mexico

Von Brostel, M. (2013). La guerra de baja intensidad contra las comunidades en resistencia contra la represa el Zapotillo (Primera Parte). *Revista Escaramujo, 40*. Retrieved from http://www.otrosmundoschiapas.org/docs/escaramujo/escaramujo740_gbi_y_presa_zapotillo_i.pdf

Zurita, M. (2007). *La Guerra Fría en el marco de las Relaciones Internacionales.* Ponencia presentada en el II Encuentro de Becarios de la Universidad Nacional de la Plata, Argentina. Retrieved from http://secyt.presi.unlp.edu.ar/cyt_htm/ebec07/pdf/zurita.pdf

Part III
Psychotherapeutic Interventions

Chapter 8
Psychotherapy with Former Political Prisoners in Uruguay: The Vision of the Therapists

María Celia Robaina

Introduction

Between 1968 and 1985, State terrorism curbed social and political mobilizations that were pursuing social justice. The State was responsible for perpetrating torture, illegal, arbitrary imprisonment, homicides, forced disappearance, exile, and banishment from social life. The main methods of repression and disciplining were torture and prolonged imprisonment.

Uruguay has been valued for its democratic tradition. However, before the dictatorship, criminal actions were implemented under the rule of law; it was called the "brutalization of politics" (Rico, 2009). The military dictatorship with civilian support governed from June 27, 1973, to February 28, 1985, and defended society's wealthiest sectors' interests. At first, repression was directed against urban guerrilla groups, then against leftist sectors, until all political opposition to the government was repressed (SERPAJ, 1989, p. 111).

The political transition was negotiated between some political parties and the Armed Forces. Subsequently, amnesty was decreed for political crimes, and political prisoners were released, while tens of thousands of exiles returned. In 1986, impunity was consecrated through Law 15.848 ("Military and police officers. It is recognized that the exercise of the State's punitive pretension has expired concerning the crimes committed up to March 1, 1985"). This law prevented the prosecution of military and police officers for crimes committed for two decades. An attempt was made to annul it in two instances through the vote of the citizens (1989 and 2009), without reaching the required majorities. Between 1985 and 2005 there was a succession of right-wing governments that promoted oblivion and impunity for the crimes of State terrorism.

M. C. Robaina (✉)
Institución Nacional de Derechos Humanos y Defensoría del Pueblo (INDDHH),
Montevideo, Uruguay
e-mail: maricelrobaina@gmail.com

© The Author(s), under exclusive license to Springer Nature Switzerland AG 2022
E. Lira et al. (eds.), *Human Rights Violations in Latin America*, Peace Psychology Book Series, https://doi.org/10.1007/978-3-030-97542-5_8

In 2005 a leftist government, the Frente Amplio, was elected and governed until 2020. Some public policies of recognition and reparation to victims were proposed, and some programs were initiated, although with insufficient resources.

The reparation policies for victims of torture were mainly materialized in Law 18.033 (2006), "Recovery of Pension and Retirement Rights" which grants a "special reparatory pension" (PER) or monthly economic compensation to those who demonstrated labor damages. And Law 18.596 (2009) on Integral Reparation, which among other actions grants:

> Art. 10: "(...) the right to receive, free of charge and for life, if they so request, medical benefits that include psychological, psychiatric, dental and pharmacological assistance to guarantee their comprehensive health coverage within the framework of the Integrated National Health System."

Uruguayan society is unaware of the magnitude of the damage caused by torture to thousands of citizens during the dark period. There is no consensual social narrative repudiating this crime against humanity, although there is awareness of forced disappearance. Victims have filed legal complaints against the repressors, although most enjoy impunity. According to the Luz Ibarburu Observatory (2020), of the approximately 300 judicial cases filed since 1985, only 10% of the accused have been prosecuted.[1] Some of those convicted have died, while others have been given the benefit of home detention.

On Political Prison and Torture

There is no official figure for the total number of political prisoners because some detainees did not register because they did not access justice. The Historical Research team of the University of the Republic, entrusted by President T. Vázquez to reconstruct the events of State terrorism, identified 50 detention centers in the national territory (Rico, 2009) and 5925 prisoners among 1973 and 1984, 739 of them were women.[2] This research sustains:

> The application of torture was a treatment for political detainees went from being an exception denounced and documented in 1970 by a Report of the Chamber of Senators, to becoming a generalized practice, as was verified by the Parliamentary Investigative Commission of the Chamber of Representatives in 1985 (Universidad de la República & Centro de Estudios Interdisciplinarios Uruguayos, 2008, p. 263).

According to the research "Uruguay Nunca Más" [Uruguay Never Again] by the Servicio Paz y Justicia [SERPAJ], the majority of the detainees were young people of medium and medium-high socioeconomic status, political and social activists. This research is based on in-depth interviews and a survey of more than 300 people,

---

[1] Luz Ibarburu Observatory http://www.observatorioluzibarburu.org

[2] Team of historians from the Faculty of Humanities and Educational Sciences of the University of the Republic, hired by the Presidency of the Republic in 2005, to investigate the recent past.

gathering information on human rights violations. According to SERPAJ, the average prison term was 6.6 years for men and 5.7 years for women (SERPAJ, 1989, p. 118). They declared that they had not been tortured: men (1%) and women (2%) (SERPAJ, 1989, p. 144): [...] hood, sit-in, beatings, threats, impeding to going to the bathroom, hunger, thirst, cattle prod, submarine, simulations, hanging, witnessing the torture of other detainees, recordings, trestle, drug-injections, seeing the torture of family members, witnessing rapes, burns, torture with animals, sit-in, dry submarine, dragging, submarine to the heart, witnessing the rape of family members, naked, handcuffs (SERPAJ, 1989, p. 151).

From clandestine detention and torture centers, held incommunicado and temporarily "disappeared," the prisoners were transferred to penitentiary centers (Gil, 1990; Rico, 2009). There were two paradigmatic prisons, one for men, the Libertad Prison or EMR No.1 and the other for women, the Punta de Rieles Prison or EMR No.2.

The military set out to ideologically subdue and defeat the people. According to the bibliography of authorship of victims, this purpose did not obtain significant results. The stories give an account of resistance mechanisms developed individually and in groups. It is pointed out that the jailers, when failing to make the prisoners renounce their ideological convictions, set out to cause them psychic damage to lead them to alienation. They made life in prison unpredictable. Day to day was governed by an omnipresent, capricious, irrational, absurd and arbitrary power (Gil, 1990, p. 126). They applied senseless routines (food, hygiene, sleep); visiting restrictions, censorship of readings, assigned cellmates according to psychopathological criteria; the prisoners were uniformed and identified with numbers (Martín, 2002, pp. 204–205).

Women were savaged by attacking their bodies in their maternal and feminine aspects. During the torture sessions, recordings with children's voices were used to make them believe that they had captured their children. Some women gave birth in captivity, generating early bonds tinged with terror. The children's visits were forbidden to some of them. They were subjected to horrifying acts of sexual and gender-based violence practiced on a widespread basis (nudity, groping, harassment, genital torture, rape).

The social reintegration was prevented by the government when people were released. The release was conditional; they had to sign periodically in military units to guarantee their stay in the city. The families suffered social discrimination and the threat of being arrested again; many families were dismembered having family members in exile or prison.

D. Gil affirms that torture is a scientifically planned practice to dismantle the mechanisms of primary identification, proposing to lead the tortured to the destruction of his self and his symbolic world; in this way, these singular experiences remain in a register before language (Gil, 1990, p. 21). Although torture is applied to the body, it pursues the objective of humiliating, annulling, transforming the person into someone subjected, without ideals or expectations, without will and trust (Gil, 1990, pp. 84–85). Other authors describe torture from the dilemmatic relationship that it installs:

a situation of "double bind" because in a circumstance of maximum in degradation, dispossession, arbitrariness and violence, the victim is required to choose between her physical integrity, on the one hand, and her mental and moral integrity, on the other. Between himself and his companions. Between the integrity of your family and the integrity of your organization. (…) It is a paradoxical situation, in which on the one hand, the human being is despoiled of everything that permits him or her to be identified as such and on the other, one is given the power to make decisions that cannot be made, without destroying essential aspects of oneself (Lira et al., 1989, pp. 24–25).

M. Viñar considers that torture operates in the social space as a symbolic reference to punishment, whose tragic effects point not only to the direct victims the result sought in echo is the intimidation and paralysis of the social group (Viñar, 1993, p. 61).

Psychosocial Care

Torture caused suffering in subjects, families, and society. The demand for psychosocial care in the 1980s led to the formation of non-governmental organizations that offered support programs.[3] The Social Rehabilitation Service [SERSOC 1984–2009] had an interdisciplinary approach to psychology, psychiatry, and social work at numerous consultants' service. In 2009, it closed to lead to the creation of a state-supported repair program. Some SERSOC professionals formed the Cooperativa de Salud Mental y Derechos Humanos [COSAMEDDHH]. As of 2009, the Ministry of Public Health hired COSAMEDDHH to provide free psychological and psychiatric care to reparation beneficiaries (Art. 10, Law 18,596).

From the beginning, SERSOC professionals sought to exchange with colleagues from the region. They identified the particularities of this clinic. Some symptoms could be interpreted in light of the sociopolitical context in which they had occurred and not only concerning the subject's history, which questioned the clinical practice learned.

Therapists understood that the social denial of the trauma experienced affected the therapeutic processes. Some pointed out that social response possibilities affect the personal repair of traumas; the social is the text of subjectivity (Kordon et al., 2002).

The official proposal of oblivion, silence, and impunity, not dealing with the past to look at the future, crossed society. Even in therapeutic spaces, it was cumbersome to talk about torture; there was a particular tacit social agreement not to talk about the dictatorship. However, to elaborate on traumas, it is necessary to speak and contact the emotions associated with them. Thus, the SERSOC members worked for the

---

[3] Between 1981 and 1986, The Peace and Justice Service [SERPAJ-Uruguay], the Commission for the Reunion of Uruguayans, the Orientation and Consultation Center [COYC], Protection of Children Damaged by States of Emergency [PIDEE], the Ecumenical Reintegration Service [SER], the Cardijn Program, and the Social Rehabilitation Service [SERSOC] were created.

"Collective Memory," they disseminated their work in publications or academic events. In 1995 it was published, *Repression and Forgetfulness. Psychological and social effects of political violence two decades later*, edited by Giorgi (1995).

The notion of integral reparation leads therapists to understand that their work represents only one "strand" in the complex web of reparations that the State must provide to victims. During the last decade, the prisoners have filed legal complaints as a group. COSAMEDDHH offers psychosocial accompaniment to a group of 28 former female prisoners who denounced sexual violence during State terrorism, contributing to the elaboration of the lawsuit and their participation in the successive legal proceedings.

Clinic Contributions of SERSOC

SERSOC publications give an account of its work. V. Giorgi warned of the risk of revictimization when assistance institutions consider those who consult as victims, as the only ones affected by State terrorism, as if the institution could assume reparation on behalf of the whole of society (Giorgi, 1995, p. 65). He stated that without social reparation the limits of the therapeutic task should be explicitly defined. He observed some constants in the treatments; he mentioned the silence and isolation of the express on torture both in daily life and in psychotherapy. He described a demanding attitude towards the therapist and the institution. He recommended developing a multidimensional and multifocal approach. He proposed working in different areas: psychic, relational, and corporal, establishing as indicators of the advances of the therapeutic process the expansion and enrichment of the patient's bonding networks. He highlighted the importance of multi-professional teamwork, defining points of urgency in each phase of the process (Giorgi, 1995, pp. 123–129).

On the other hand, A. Martín observed that silences were frequent in the sessions and related them to the loneliness experienced, to defend himself from the other. He highlighted a specific difficulty in freely associating and abstracting therapeutic interpretations. He proposed that the therapist be flexible, that he handles himself with sensitivity and patience. In express withdrawing into themselves, he found a different temporal-spatial relationship, recommending being careful concerning the signs, avoiding referring the patient to bad experiences that he needed to silence (Martín, 2002, p. 210).

In 2002 I described as strategic lines for treatments: Verbalize the affections generated by traumatic episodes processing and circulating the cathexes placed on representations. And, at the same time, dynamize their associative chains; Analyze the meanings given to the traumatic linked to the life story; Put into words the socio-historical-political implications and meanings of trauma; Working through the internalized effects of terror: isolation, authoritarianism, distrust, helplessness (Robaina, 2002, pp. 105–106).

The therapists described as therapeutic goals: (a) to attend the manifest motives for consultation; (b) working through the integration of the experience of the period of State terrorism in their own lives, promoting healthy aspects of the patients.

Clinical strategies included:

- Detecting the internalized effects of State terrorism.
- Preserving some defensive mechanisms.
- Rescuing resilient resources.

Therapists promoted the encounter with those who lived through similar experiences and valued interdisciplinary work. The following were privileged as technical tools: non-neutrality, reliability, analysis of transference and counter-transference aspects, respect for the patient's silences and times. Incorporate the following categories: socio-historical-political; the imaginaries and social discourses; the institutional; the implication and the paradigm of Human Rights (Robaina & Busch, 2007).

Psychotherapy and Late Effects of Torture

I investigated to document the psychic effects that remained in victims of torture and imprisonment and collected the learning achieved in the treatments, to contribute to the public policy of mental health reparation. I interviewed 12 psychotherapists, psychologists, psychiatrists, and psychoanalysts. I selected those who developed clinical work between 2007 and 2013, chosen for their expertise and written production (Robaina, 2014). We inquired about the reasons for consultation of their patients, psychic conflicts, late effects of torture and imprisonment, therapeutic objectives, and theoretical-technical aspects, gathering experiences of three decades of sustained work in this clinic with this population in Uruguay.

Reasons for Consultation and Late Effects[4]

SERSOC and COSAMEDDHH professionals observed that, as of 2005, the need to process torture experiences has emerged as a reason for consultation.

According to those interviewed, public recognition of repressive practices made it possible to express the traumas' silenced aspects. The study revealed that 58.33% consulted for conflicts in significant relationships (more with children born before or during prison); 50% for depression—greater prevalence in women; 33.33% for anxiety disorders; 25% for sleep disorders; 25% for alcoholism—greater prevalence in men; and 25% for ideas of death—greater prevalence in men. A 58.33% linked

---

[4] The interviewees gave informed consent to reproduce excerpts of their words anonymously; the author changed their names, maintaining their gender.

their consultation to some aspect of the traumatic past or social difficulties in processing those traumas.

The psychic conflicts were classified as: (a) family ties; (b) the emergence of the traumatic; (c) psychosocial in sociopolitical situations.

(a) Family ties: ruptures in the family integration and transgenerational transmission of traumatic aspects not elaborated by the first generation. Prolonged imprisonment and persecution led to living underground or exile, imposing a strong uprooting among victims and their family nuclei. Segregations, disputes, and blame were observed. As if those aspects of the violence received had been trapped inside the families. Captivity deprived prisoners of parental roles in the early stages of their children's development. Some parents weighed the distance produced in that bond; some children have accused them of abandoning them. There was no desire for abandonment; the break in the bond was imposed by state terrorism. It is as if there was a "hole" in the bonding web, which continued to cause damage outside the prison. Parents found it difficult to support their children materially and emotionally due to the confinement and social stigma of being a prisoner. By way of hypothesis, it is possible to observe in the closest bonds the raw emergency—in the form of distrust or fear of the other getting so tight that it burns—of those remnants of traumatic experiences that could not be symbolized or metabolized.

(b) The emergence of the traumatic. It refers to the anguish that emerges flashbacks, terrifying memories, acting out, displacement of persecutory aspects to people in the present. This anguish, experienced in traumatic events, not being linked to words, could remain latent and manifest as symptomatology in the body.

(c) Identified psychosocial conflicts that emerge in the face of the sociopolitical processing of historical traumas. Frequently, people manifest intense internal mobilizations and physical symptomatology in the front of political events, due to advance or retreat towards Truth, Justice, and Reparation. Society must recognize the horror and give it a real place of existence for integrating the silenced aspects. However, some people to continue with their life projects, dissociate or deny their emotions and traumas; when horror reappears untimely in the public space, the balances reached shakes, and overflowing feelings resurface. Facing painful situations caused by personal experiences or public events could reactivate the devastating experiences of the past.

The late effects of torture were as follows:

(a) Mistrust, for having known human cruelty in its highest expression; pointed out by 75% of interviewees. If in every psychotherapeutic process paranoid anxiety is visualized, in these patients they are exacerbated.

(b) I called "resistant armor" the psychic envelope, made up of robust defensive mechanisms, built in captivity to control feelings and emotions and not show them to the perpetrators. Armor that later, in different moments of life will be expressed as emotional distance or effective anesthesia, but that in extreme conditions allowed interstices of autonomy not to give in and resist.

(c) The literature on the effects of torture speaks of feelings of guilt that would last. A link established between self-incrimination and what may have happened in the relationship with the torturers, or it is related to having experienced feelings considered miserable. The situation of torture generates confusional states; the mere doubt about what was or was not said can mortify for years. Often a repressor was gentle and deceived the victim about his desire to help him; having believed him can be a motive for self-flagellation. Françoise Sironi (2011) speaks of "the influence of the torturer on the tortured," noting that therapists struck by the importance given to the torturers' words. Those words "remain engraved forever," "literally penetrate their being," "those words gnaw them from the inside." The torturer's influence can be expressed in many other ways, in nightmares, affecting mnemic processes, or self-esteem.

Some late effects of prolonged confinement would manifest themselves as a tendency to passivity and isolation. The authoritarian system in prison did not allow them to make elementary decisions for very long periods: turning on the light, choosing what to eat, and sleeping. Passivity can be expressed in routines of insurance or excessive dependence on loved ones. The tendency to isolation can be observed in the family or the group of inmates, such as the difficulty of integration in social settings, avoiding attending festive events, isolating oneself in alcohol, and even delirium.

Therapeutic Goals

To meet the demand, reduce suffering, alleviate symptoms, resolve intrapsychic conflicts, analyze their causes, make the unconscious conscious, reformulate life projects, and improve life quality were therapeutic objectives as it is in any psychotherapy.

In Uruguay, the professionals used the same approach as in the private clinic, weekly sessions, treatments with an average duration of 2 years, attending to the patient's demands in their entirety. Although the psychotherapies carried out in institutions intended for the care of victims of State terrorism, they worked on the patient's issues, whether or not they were linked to the events of the political past and did not always address the experiences of torture. The professionals worked part-time. The interviewees considered total dedication to be harmful because it is a clinic that comes into contact with the most terrible of the human beings.

Among the therapeutic objectives were identified:

(a) To build a bond of trust.

Torture damages the perception of human being. This population is familiar with barbarity and inhumanity. This experience leads them to demand guarantees to be able to trust the therapist. The interviewees report that there are patients who inquire about the therapist's political ideology before committing to treatment.

They pointed out that they sought to build a relationship between clinician and consultant that reinforces what humanizes. Just as the torturer set out to de-subjectivize, the therapist will have the function of humanizing and sheltering. He/she will have to transmit security, give sustained signs of bearing the listening of stories that display horror; in the face of which it will not be possible to overflow or flee. It is necessary to build a strong bonding network so that the subject can release what he/she is imprisoned in the certainty that he/she will not be abandoned during the process. The therapeutic environment is built as a place of humanization, security, and protection to enable working through helplessness and destruction experiences.

(b) Working through the traumatic.

The aim was to work on the trauma's actual; those remains that reappear in the form of suffering. They point out that what increases the damage is the knotting, the stagnation of vital energy in the traumatic, without finding emancipation ways. Part of the stagnant energy can be recovered if the deadly aspects of the trauma are confronted, and the deployment of new projects directed to the present and the future is enhanced. In the line of "remembering for not to repeat," therapists propose working through the traumatisms, implying taking care of the patient's possible timing, therapist, and treatment process. Professionals have to maintain a favorable atmosphere that makes it possible to "weave" what was damaged, to resignify what happened, to feel again genuine emotions that revolved around the trauma. It is necessary to symbolize, even if only in part, the experiences, linking affections to their respective representations, identifying sensations provoked in the events' heat.

Trauma scholars warn about aspects that will not be able to be symbolized by words; a "hardcore" will remain and could reactivate in the face of certain constellations.

Rafael: "Freud distinguished two things, the living from the experience. A trauma is an experience, but if we put it into words, we transform it into an experience, an experience is what I integrate into my life and it helps me not to stumble over the same stone, as far as possible."

To work on the traumatic with a psychic inscription and also the traumatic with social inscription. The part of the traumatic that is social will depend on political processing in society. The subjective impacts produced by the advances and setbacks of searching for truth, justice, memory, and reparation are analyzed. If society does not recognize political violence and does not take responsibility for it, the victim does not finish processing the traumas. Personal processes are blocked in an environment of impunity, silence, concealment, lies, and oblivion.

(c) De-victimization.

Through psychotherapy, the person is encouraged to find new meanings to what he/she has experienced, learn from it, carry out empowerment processes, develop his/her creativity, and reach gratifying experiences.

The person is accompanied to leave the place of suffering or paralysis, searching for an active and dignifying role. Some interviewees do not use the victim's notion. They consider that this notion refers to the past and point out the psychological connotations associated with the victim's identity as a damaged, demanding paralyzed subject. When therapists speak of de-victimization, they refer to removing the deadly aspects that trap people in a position of suffering and complaint, enabling the development of vital potentialities and resources.

Sebastián: "Whoever has suffered can settle down, lick his wounds and console himself from his melancholy complaint of a victim, or can have a self-repair through work, the creation of a family, all the sublimatory procedures."

Matthew: "What would be an indicator that a person was able to process all those facts? For me, in the possibility of restoring a life project, reformulating his life, from that wound, or taking into account everything that happened, but being able to move forward."

Torture operated like a "machine" that sought to destroy that which sustains the psychism; psychotherapy has to be an environment of ego strengthening, accompanying the patient in self-affirmation processes, allowing the weakening of the reifying experiences produced by the action of the executioner. It will be necessary to dismantle, at an intrapsychic level, the mechanisms of torture, identify the marks of prison and torture, handle them on the plane of consciousness, and seek to overcome the imposed passivity seek empowerment.

(d) Integrating prison time into the history of life.

It is necessary to integrate past, present, and future in the life history of the person. Some ex-prisoners needed to dissociate or minimize what they had experienced during their imprisonment, while others remained fixed to that period.

Florence: "(...) establishing continuity between 'before and after'; not remaining imprisoned on the past. A life that was not the life of ex prisoner."

Working on life history and its continuity from before captivity to the present, and its projection into the future, integrating the split, working on prison experiences, processing mourning, putting words to what silenced.

As they were political militants, some stressed the need to make room for their own and generational meanings of political and social struggles. Militancy occupies a central place in these people's life history and makes it possible to give meaning to prison. The vicissitudes of militancy are as relevant as affective, formative or labor achievements.

One psychoanalyst considered forgetting to be healthy, meaning that the event ceases to occupy "space" in the present consciousness. In COSAMEDDHH, they used verbs such as integrating and working through. They differentiate individual forgetting from social forgetting and value the processes that contribute to the construction of collective memories. Memories are communicable and shareable productions. Other citizens can also take charge of the common tragic past.

The Place of Politics in the Treatments Process

Consultants show a high interest in politics and talk about politics during the sessions. Therapists observe that they comment on the news with a high emotional charge and stress the need to understand this impact on the subject. Some therapists limit themselves to listening; others pointed out that opinions can be exchanged, depending on the bond's strengthening. The political is integrated into the work because this is a "political clinic." They emphasize that this does not happen with other patients. The psychosocial nature of traumatisms could explain this phenomenon; the news could awaken vivid memories. Feelings of relief appeared when the news reports progress in truth, justice, memory or reparation, and setbacks when they obstruct such processes.

The link with politics is typical of a strongly ideologized generation, committed to a political project of building a society with greater social justice. This research was carried out when the left governed Uruguay for a second consecutive period, and many political representatives had been militants or political prisoners.

We observe that improvements in public policies of integral reparation make it possible to release a particular deadly burden that these patients have carried with them. Public discourse orders and legitimizes claims, enabling personal experiences to be transmitted. When an official truth was constructed that recognizes and repudiates the crimes, a performative discourse was enunciated by naming, modifying ways of seeing, thinking, and feeling the shared past. Processes unfold that unearth memories, and new sublimatory modalities emerge that enable the action of reparation.

Analysis of the Experiences of Torture

We inquired if the patient was asked to recount his or her experience of torture. According to the care contexts, differences were found. Private clinic, NGO, and a State reparation program. The therapists' expectations concerning working on experiences of torture were very varied.

> Virginia: "In general, the subject of torture is when something that I can link to it appears. No, I don't ask him how he was tortured."
>
> Mateo: "To ask? not from the beginning, to ask when the subject comes up, that is, not to force."

A professional recommended not to spend too much time talking about torture because he understood that it generates a place where the other becomes an object. All vestige of humanity is lost.

> Josefina: "Now, why this modesty? Because I believe that this is where something that I would call the fundamental prohibition of sociability, of social rules and human rules of considering the Other as a neighbor, is at stake."

When the patient brought up the torture experience, or the therapist approached, looking for links within the discourse, they worked on this experience. But the cruelest moments of torture were executed in the middle of interrogations, making it difficult to ask about it, in the therapists' opinion.

Torture sought the person's destruction, making it extremely difficult to talk about what happened in the relationship with the torturers, which entails unspeakable aspects. Language falls short when describing extreme violence; the impact is so brutal that the psyche will not symbolize events, experiences, emotions, and sensations entirely; there will remain fragments that will not be contained in a coherent account.

Provide More Emotional Support Than Interpretation

The interviewees affirm that they perform fewer interpretations compared to those they serve on other patients. They attach priority importance to the construction of a warm bond before analyzing the deep unconscious aspects. There is a consensus that they work more with the conscious aspects.

> Florencia: "He is a patient who needs not only a cure through words and to make the unconscious conscious. Having lived his vulnerability in isolation and loneliness, he needs support and brings a much deeper affective bond with the therapist."
>
> Mateo: "Perhaps the main instrument is not so much the interpretation as in a more classical treatment; but the restraint that can give, the affective climate."
>
> Mercedes: "Being able to generate warm, trusting bonds, where physical space, body posture, gestures and the handling of silences take on a relevant and diverse meaning, which leads us to be more proactive therapists."

This type of psychotherapy requires offering more affective containment, providing a warm bond and human support. Consultants would reject the in-depth, more classical psychoanalysis interpretations, emphasizing childhood memories and the link with parental figures. The therapeutic environment becomes a space of humanization, offering security and protection, to enable working through extreme violence experiences.

Contributions of Group Psychotherapy

Most of those who consulted SERSOC and COSAMEDDHH requested individual psychotherapy. In both institutions, therapeutic groups formed according to age groups: 18–29 years old, 30–49 years old, and over 50 years old. Participants included prisoners, exiles, relatives of prisoners, relatives of detainees-disappeared, and relatives of the murdered. We worked with operative group techniques, psychodrama, and group dynamics.

> Fernando: "(…) group work enhances much more the possibilities of elaborating what has been lived (…) It also broadens the reading of the social."

> Mercedes: "That heterogeneity, those differences and similarities, are positive, they contribute and help to think about themselves (…) In the groups, links have been generated beyond the clinical, work, friendship and personal space."

Groups help to break isolation, empathize, think with others, and plan joint actions. Solidarity affection unfolds, generate feelings of belonging—deep bonds of fraternity produced by communicating intimate aspects. The group constitute a place for the construction of various types of support.

Those who consult can visualize their dramatic personal or family history interconnected with others, and all of them, within the same national and world-historical context. Life stories with similar traits converge in the group, facilitating the task of finding explanations to unanswered questions and reflecting on what has happened in the country and the region.

Group psychotherapy allows us to think in plurality about the socio-historical-political nature of trauma beyond the individual and family impacts. They were thinking collectively on the treatment given in the public space to the processing of historical trauma and its vicissitudes in the present. One interviewee, a woman, narrates that people who refused to collect the Special Reparatory Pension (PER) or did not dare to testify in a trial, modify their decisions after listening to their peers. They gained momentum or incorporated new arguments, moving from an individual view to a collective and political perspective.

Sharing common affects and experiences allows us to discover other impacts and other ways of elaboration or sublimation. Knowing about different coping ways enriches the range of responses; enable them to move from familiar places, be moved, and offer oneself as a companion.

The group appears as a privileged environment for analyzing bonding conflicts, where diverse bonding modalities expressed with colleagues and therapists are "staged." When acted out, conflicts are visualized and become material for analysis.

Final Thoughts

Identifying particularities in the clinic with former political prisoners contributes to providing knowledge for the public policy of mental health reparation.

The late effects of torture observed in the damage caused to emotional ties and distrust. The psychic envelope built during the torture described as "resistant armor," was built to control feelings and emotions and not to show them to the torturers. But later persistent feelings of self-incrimination appeared, as well as passivity and isolation behaviors.

Some conflictive ties with relatives triggered the consultation, mainly with children born before imprisonment; in other cases, the emergence of aspects of trauma and psychosocial conflicts in the face of political information related to the collective processing of traumas, both by state and social impulse.

Therapists confirmed the dialectic relationship between the processes of social reparation and the processes of personal reparation. It appeared in the manifest reasons for consultation; also, in the patient's need to talk about torture and imprisonment when initiated reparatory public policies in Uruguay (2005). Memories are enabled when society recognizes barbarism and gives it a legitimized place.

The dialectic relationship between the processes of social reparation and the processes of personal reparation was confirmed in the manifest reasons for consultation and in the need to talk about torture and prison when the reparatory public policies began in Uruguay (2005). Memories are enabled when society recognizes barbarism and grants it a legitimate place.

The consultants talked about political news in the sessions, referring to processes of truth, justice, and reparation. The therapists analyzed the personal impact caused by the occurrence of political events in the sessions. It was a sensitive aspect that generated a strong mobilization of feelings and emotions; it was necessary to accommodate it, taking the therapist to a terrain that required experience to attend to his/her reactions, avoid discussing ideas, and recognizing the consultants' needs.

The similarities with technical aspects described in the previous decade, the value assigned to the construction of a strong therapeutic alliance and the priority need to elaborate part of the traumatic, reaffirming the importance of analyzing the continuity of life in one's history. It also confirms that the passage of time does not resolve what could not be integrated by the psyche.

Consultants valued the ideological affinity and commitment of the professionals as human rights activists. SERSOC and COSAMEDDHH assumed this clinic's political character and the need to know the world and regional historical-political events that marked the generation of militants and their ideological and political dilemmas.

It was a finding that the therapists prioritized giving affection to the patient, "containing and supporting," to counteract the machinery of destruction, turning the clinical space into an environment of humanization and shelter, performing fewer interpretations according to the usual technique.

To break the circle of repetition, we sought to set and achieve goals, promote creativity, and conquer gratifying and dignifying experiences. It was necessary to work on the experiences of captivity, feelings, grief, and ruptures to free stagnant psychic energy.

The professionals pointed out that psychotherapy is not enough to repair the damage caused by State terrorism. Parallel processes are required, internally, and collectively, and socially. When a country denies the facts, the damage is more significant. When oblivion and impunity reign, the victims bear the burden of remembering the atrocities. If societies do not assume the lessons learned, the wounds cannot be closed.

Group psychotherapy made it possible to work on psychosocial aspects of traumatisms; people could visualize their personal or family history interconnected with others within the same national and world-historical context. It was possible to "stage" some bonding conflicts through multiple transferential processes, which facilitated their analysis. The groups enable and enhance a working through of the socio-historical-political character of the traumatisms. These therapeutic spaces also provide socialization experiences that combat isolation.

The study deepened the knowledge of a clinic directed to a group of compatriots whose rights were violated fiercely. Beyond theoretical-technical learning, it reaffirms the idea that psychotherapy is a form of reparation, within the measures to be developed by governments and societies. The biggest challenge will be to build subjects aware of these crimes' seriousness and committed to condemn and eradicate torture.

References

Gil, D. (1990). *El terror y la Tortura*. EPPAL.

Giorgi, V. (Comp.). (1995). *Represión y olvido: efectos psicológicos y sociales de la violencia política dos décadas después*. Roca Viva Editorial: SERSOC.

Kordon, D., Edelman, L., Lagos, D., & Kersner, D. (2002). Trauma social y psiquismo. Consecuencias clínicas de la violación de derechos humanos. En D. Kersner, M. A. Jorge, C. Madariaga, & A. Martín (Eds.), *Paisajes del dolor. Senderos de Esperanza. Salud Mental y Derechos Humanos en el Cono Sur* (pp. 283–293). Polemos.

Lira, E., Becker, D., & Castillo, M. I. (1989). Psicoterapia de víctimas de represión política bajo dictadura: Un desafío terapéutico, teórico y político. En D. Becker & E. Lira (Eds.), *Derechos Humanos: Todo es según el dolor con que se mira* (pp. 29–69). Ediciones Instituto Latinoamericano de Salud Mental y Derechos Humanos.

Martín, A. (2002). El fracaso del leteo o la imposibilidad del olvido. En D. Kersner, M. A. Jorge, C. Madariaga, & A. Martín (Eds.), *Paisajes del dolor. Senderos de Esperanza. Salud Mental y Derechos Humanos en el Cono Sur* (pp. 203–213). Polemos.

Rico, A. (2009). *Investigación Histórica sobre la Dictadura y el Terrorismo de Estado en Uruguay (1973–1985)*. CSIC/Ediciones del Sur.

Robaina, M. C. (2002). Tortura e Impunidad. En D. Kersner, M. A. Jorge, C. Madariaga, & A. Martín (Eds.), *Paisajes del dolor. Senderos de Esperanza. Salud Mental y Derechos Humanos en el Cono Sur* (pp. 101–107). Polemos.

Robaina, M. C. (2014). *Psicoterapia y Efectos Tardíos de Tortura y Prisión Política en Uruguay*. Tesis Maestría en Psicología Clínica, Facultad de Psicología, Universidad de la República, Uruguay.

Robaina, M. C., & Busch, S. (2007). Particularidades de la clínica en derechos humanos. Desde la experiencia hacia la construcción de una teoría de la técnica. In *Convocatoria interamericana para sistematizar metodologías de apoyo psicológico a víctimas de violaciones graves a los derechos humanos*. Instituto Interamericano de Derechos Humanos, San José de Costa Rica. Retrieved from https://biblioteca.iidh-jurisprudencia.ac.cr/index.php/documentos en espanol/prevencion-de-la-tortura/1824-particularidades-de-la-clinica-en-derechos/file

Servicio Paz y Justicia (SERPAJ). (1989). *Uruguay. Nunca Más. Informe sobre la violación a los Derechos Humanos (1972–1985)* (3ra ed.). Altamira.

Sironi, F. (2011). *Carrascos e Vítimas. Psicología da tortura*. Terceira Margen.

Universidad de la República & Centro de Estudios Interdisciplinarios Uruguayos. (2008). *Investigación histórica sobre la dictadura y el terrorismo de Estado en el Uruguay (1973–1985)*. Tomo II. Universidad de la República, Comisión Sectorial de Investigación Científica-CSIC; Facultad de Humanidades y Ciencias de la Educación.

Viñar, M. (1993). *Fracturas de memoria: crónicas para una memoria por venir*. Ediciones Trilce.

Chapter 9
Arpilleras of Sexual and Domestic Violence in Post-War Guatemala: Accompaniment in Processes of Psychosocial Reparation

María Luisa Cabrera Pérez-Armiñan

Introduction: Arpilleras, Patches of Repair for Violence Against Women

Women are the social sector that experienced the most significant transformation in Guatemala since the Peace Accords in 1996 (USIP, 1998). Although the political violence related to the armed conflict diminished, ever-rising gender violence appears to have replaced it. Many human rights violations committed against women represent patterns of behavior arising from culturally rooted machismo. These are ingrained values and beliefs that are used to justify situations of oppression and social inferiority, as well as social and domestic mistreatment. The reproduction of these practices reinforces the legitimacy of domestic abuse.

Arpillera patchwork tapestries are a handmade textile craft that have been adapted as a projective and reparation tool in processes of psychosocial intervention and mental health recovery with groups of women survivors of gender, domestic and sexual violence in Guatemala.[1] The process of creating an arpillera may enable addressing the experience of violence and traumatization and its impact on the health, family, and identity of their protagonists (Menjívar, 2014), opening the possibility for transforming their lives. The objective of the handcrafted creations in contexts of reconstruction and social reparation is to communicate painful

---

[1] Arpilleras (burlap, in reference to the fabric on which they are created) are colorful patchwork and embroidered handcrafts that originated in Chile in the 1960s as folk art, resurfacing during the dictatorship of Augusto Pinochet (1973–1990), as visual registries of violence and precarious living conditions. Arpilleras were subsequently adopted by groups of women in other Latin American countries.

M. L. Cabrera Pérez-Armiñan (✉)
Centro de Estudios sobre Conflictividad, Poder y Violencia de Guatemala, CENDES, Antigua, Guatemala
e-mail: mluisacabrera@gmail.com

117

experiences and preventively convey them to the following generations, thus contributing to break the silence and prepare the conditions to seek justice (Lykes & Crosby, 2015).

Suffering from traumatic violence generates high levels of "extreme negative stress, feelings of helplessness, of being at the mercy of others, and of lack of control over one's own life due to uncertainties of the future and feelings of rupture in the continuity of life" (Perren-Klinger, 1996, as cited in Martin, 2010, p. 12). It also causes severe long-term or permanent damage.

We differentiate between structural imbalances in unequal power relations that place women at a social disadvantage and acts of physical, psychological, and sexual violence that constitute "generalized violence" in both public and domestic spaces. For our purposes, we define violence as "intentional physical, sexual or emotional abuse, which generates an environment of fear, lack of communication and silence" (Menjívar, 2014, p. 75).

There is also a form of invisible, symbolic violence that interprets women's behavior and prejudices the meaning of their actions. Consequently, it leaves the victim's reputation badly wounded. The social appearance of what they will say and rumors as a form of social control through "gossip that destroys lives" (Menjívar, 2014, p. 116) fall into this category. "Illnesses, 'nerves', gossip and control over freedom of movement embody the normalization of violence in the female world, a world of fear, suffering, humiliation and lack of attention to the needs of everyday life" (Menjívar, 2014, p. 125).

The structural inequalities that shape their lives are normalized by concealing pain and are justified by certain beliefs and values that legitimize motherhood and child rearing as sacrifice and self-sacrifice, linked to the acceptance of male domination. There is so much violence against Guatemalan women that they are said to live in "a chronic state of emergency" (Menjívar, 2014, p. 79) that may be the precursor to today's intense violence.

Sexual violence and rape are traumatic experiences because these are very invasive and severe attacks on the psychological integrity of the victim, causing persistent memories of the scene and the events and producing emotional numbness that limits and interferes with the expression of tenderness. The stigma of rape, together with the suspicion that the victim provoked it, comprises the taboo of rape as a social shame that must be concealed. The common response is social ostracism and accusations of guilt and mistreatment of the victims, because of the wounded honor of having been with the enemy in wartime contexts or with the aggressor in postwar contexts. This response invisibilizes the causal element of the forced relationship, of slavery, and of the threat to the woman's life.

The Protagonists and the Context of Reconstruction of the Experience

The protagonists of this experience are young and adult women from rural and peri-urban areas of the western highlands of Guatemala, mostly domestic workers or housewives who have scarce economic resources and a low level of schooling. Five adolescent women, who were victims of incest and sexual abuse, two of them adolescent mothers with their respective two- and three-year old daughters, and 21 adult women survivors of sexual and domestic violence were sheltered in a Center for integral Assistance by court order in 2011.

All were victims of sexual and domestic violence and endured physical, sexual, and psychological assault. Domestic violence often combines everything from beatings, threats, and coercion to very debilitating forms of harassment such as insults, humiliation, offenses, and grievances. Many of the protagonists saw their ideals of romantic love transformed into domestic stories of violence, abuse, and contempt.

The protagonists of this project are members of the Asociación Nuevos Horizontes, a Guatemalan women's organization that supports the promotion of human rights with programs of psychological attention, legal and social accompaniment, and labor reinsertion to provide comprehensive care for survivors of violence.[2]

The production of *arpilleras* took place in seven one-day workshops over a period of 6 or 7 months in 2010 and 2011 (Fig. 9.1).

Fig. 9.1 Discrimination against women for domestic violence

[2] The photographs of this chapter were taken by the author during the workshop.

The following chart summarizes the process of the workshops and the construction of the narrative that made it possible for each protagonist to recreate and reinvent her own story (Table 9.1).

Table 9.1 Methodological description of the production process of the *arpilleras*

Differentiated stages	Objectives	Signifiers	Guidelines
Motivational expectation and group disorder	Psychic and corporal immersion in an environment of sensorial stimulation	Warm and welcoming feelings	1st Session Distribution and selection of the material
The group provides containment, social support, and mutual accompaniment	Evocation of the traumatic experience in a personalized space with shared support	Activation of memory of the events (thoughts and recollections)	2nd SessionPre-design. What do you want to represent? Framing the scene and cutting the fabric
Group interaction and communication (observation and mutual learning, sharing)	Representation and staging of episodes of sexual, domestic, and gender violence	When Hands Talk… The strength of pain and hope. Realism and movement of figures	3rd Session Composing the design. Doing, Undoing, Redoing
Fatigue due to the repetitive action of embroidery. Introspective reflection about oneself	Recovery of the sense and re-signification of the lived experience	Emotional expression (guilt and experiences of humiliation, shame). Omnipresence of aggressors vs. insignificance of victims	4th Session Stitching and embroidery of the figures
Begin sharing stories, exchanges, and comparative grievances	Normalization of violent experience: Talking about it without guilt, recognizing social connotations	Decorative appliques reaffirm the intent to transmit "apparent happiness"	5th Session Decorating the scenes and completing the embroidery of the arpillera
Socialization of the stories. Group cohesion and emotional setting of trust and group listening that contains and positivizes the experience	Reintegration of the experience by accepting what happened, without guilt and with preventive lessons	Reassessing the experience of violence and affirming the identity of the protagonists empowers their lives and destigmatizes them	6th Session Finishing the decoration of the arpillera
Social validation of the arpillera as a tool for psychosocial recovery from domestic violence against women	Exhibition of arpilleras, demonstrative effect, and transmission to other groups of survivors	The responsibility of the protagonists does not overcome the feelings of fatalism and resignation	7th Session Group evaluation of workshops and consensus on the final destination of the arpilleras

Dimensions of Psychosocial Analysis of the Arpilleras

In the process of creating the arpillera, certain psychosocial elements emerge that are key to understanding the impact of daily violence, working through the lived experiences, and preventing their consequences.

The psychosocial support is focused not only on the effects of the damage, but also draw from the emotional and social cognitive working through of the lived experience to build new frameworks of meaning and significance while helping to restructure the present and future upon a different foundation.

The embroidered scenes represent a journey into the symbolic sphere that allows the survivors to recognize themselves and gain greater awareness of their own history, to transform it. The setting of creative freedom fosters a reunion with themselves that helps to reintegrate the traumatic experience, regaining control and power over one's life and weaving the social bonds of solidarity, cohesion, and trust in others and in the future.

The evolution observed expresses contained emotions by producing catharsis, talking about the unspoken, recognizing oneself, discovering one's strengths, and transforming the impact of violence into decisions, breaks, and readjustments of life.

The explanations of the Debriefing Model applied to the intervention with victims who have suffered traumatic experiences (Perren-Klinger, 2003) facilitate our understanding that restructuring the traumatic experience requires a preventive reinterpretation of what happened based on new codes. This is possible because the individual now has the capability and resources to face and manage crisis situations.

The processes involved are behavioral, emotional, and cognitive. While **immersion and evocation** help generate the emotional conditions conducive to expressing what happened, **representation and the act of working through** attribute new meaning and significance to the experience by assimilating the fact without feeling guilty about it. However, it does encourage taking responsibility for facing and overcoming its consequences. "Immense cognitive effort is made in trying to understand the experience and produce the necessary changes that require new frameworks of interpretation; the questions of what, what for, how and when contribute to this" (Perren-Klinger, 2003, p. 31). Such questions are generated in an internal dialogue with oneself or in the group sharing with the other protagonists. In addition, emotions and meanings are integrated that foster the appropriation of the experience not only as something alien that hurt me, but as a damage that has remained in me and for that reason, I must transform it and to do so I need to understand who I am and how I can do it with my resources.

Group Process

The objective of the group's formation is to help each other cope with the consequences of daily violence (Martin & Riera, 2003). It comprises recognition that the problem of domestic and sexual violence affects many women, that its disruptive impact can be stopped and reversed, and that the lived experience can be restructured and reintegrated from another vision. The group provides safety and social support, founded on the concept that "my world is contained within the worlds of others."

The group fosters growth and strengthens the individual identity by operating as a transitional space that created the conditions to represent the stories. "The arpilleras are like an open book that tells stories that are being lived," that, when exposed and shared, help to generate changes in life. The group provides strength through mutual support and sets limits of respect for the Other by allowing the development of active listening, emotional empathy, identification with peers, sensitivity, and changes in attitude and behavior.

Drawing from the sense that all are equals, which generates a relationship of trust and security, the group process defines a collective identity that enables each individual to transit from "I" to "we." In so doing, they learn from one another how to cope with violence better by giving each other ideas (Martin & Riera, 2003, p. 210).

During the group process the participants' roles varied in the sessions, alternating between active, unifying leaderships and disruptive attitudes, which had to be redirected.

The collective appropriation of the space and its individual disposition were strategic for the group process. Physical contact between the women evolved from initial inhibition to the formation of bonds and emotional attachment. As the protagonists took control of themselves and recovered control of their own lives, they moved about the place with greater freedom and interacted more with others.

Each protagonist was alone in her personal process but emotionally accompanied by her peers in similar situations. Respect for the rules held the group together, becoming important for its members as a self-referential space for personal growth and social empowerment to deal with violence.

Emotional Setting and Group Cohesion

The emotional setting in a group evolves positively when there are interactions, mutual support, communication, and human warmth. As the protagonists did not know each other, it was necessary to build trust and assure confidentiality of the information shared in the group. The setting evolved from non-communication and withdrawal to warm and welcoming communicative interaction that strengthened the setting of well-being and group cohesion, enabling mutual support to flourish.

Two distinct moments of emotional reaction of the protagonists were observed. An initial moment was when the process of selecting the material provoked a connection of the body with the sensations caused by the fabric texture, creating an initially chaotic and unstructured setting of anxious expectation. The next moment was more paused and focused on personal introspection, evoking memories of the situation and conflicting feelings about the experience. The atmosphere evolved to a quiet joy, arising from the satisfaction of producing something by themselves that they had not thought possible. The best indicator of well-being was the protagonists' reluctance to discontinue the work in the last workshops.

The moods varied as each person evolved. An individual becomes emotionally stable when he or she can turn around the experience and the feelings that overwhelm him or her. This stage usually coincided with the embroidered scene: each participant asked herself why it happened to me and what the perpetrator intended, as can be seen in Fig. 9.2. "I felt satisfied to tell my story. It was a relief to share that burden. It was no longer just me who knew, it was not just me who was hurt. It came out of me, and it no longer hurts as much as it did." This dialogue re-signifies the experience by removing the guilt and reducing the emotional burden.

Group identity, communicative interaction, the emotional setting, and group cohesion are the structural conditions that enable working through conflicts. While the structure becomes the continent where pain and suffering can spill out, silence can be broken under conditions of trust and safety. The content reflects the recurrent themes of domestic violence, allowing emotional wounds and breakdowns to be shared without feeling censured by rumors, stigmas, and prejudice. Marriage condenses everyday forms of abuse whose effects are invisible and normalized. It is a form of violence that internalizes the roles assigned by unequal structures in the division of labor, raising children, respect for equal rights and opportunities, as well as decision-making (Menjívar, 2014).

Fig. 9.2 Attempted Femicide due to jealousy

Symbolic and Projective Representations of Trauma

This captivating technique is a theatrical staging that projects hidden, silenced, or underestimated aspects of our daily life that have hurt us, that have changed our lives and society. Onto an object that lasts materially, it places a story that can be deciphered by others and that does not need to be retold. "The young man tried to throw me off the bridge and told me if you're not going to be mine, you're not going to be anyone's and before that he tried to sexually abuse me, so I said I'd better throw myself off." The strength of the scene is in the emotional expressiveness and corporal plasticity of the human figures, which enhance their movement and giving more realism to the scene, as can be seen in Fig. 9.3.

The human presence was gradually incorporated into the arpilleras. The human absence or its brutal psychological characterization (fierce, invasive, aggressive, imposing) says much about the type of violence suffered and the damage caused, as well as the concealed feelings of guilt, shame, and humiliation. The aggressors are represented as omnipresent and powerful figures, in sharp contrast with the insignificance of the victims who have almost disappeared from the scene, as can be seen in this figure.

The description of the volcano arpillera is a metaphor for the personal growth that takes place when situations of oppression and submission that disrupt romantic imaginaries are transformed into annulled lives. As it can be seen in Fig. 9.4, the eruption of the volcano symbolizes the breakup of a couple and gradually took shape during the time when the protagonist was reaching her decision to face the breakup and reorganize her life.

She was absent from two workshops which she "could not and did not want to be" present. On her return she resumed her production, reinterpreting what had happened. "The eruption and the fire mean pain, frustration. Some bolts of flame came

Fig. 9.3 Sexual violence

Fig. 9.4 Volcano 'arpillera'

out before others; some are more intense. There must be a reason why there are no people in my *arpillera*."

The metaphor "*to grow up there has to be an eruption*" helped the protagonist reinterpret and assimilate the consequences of her family breakdown, the liberation that came from breaking the cycle of violence in her life, and the opportunity to rebuild her beliefs of hope and future in a life without violence.

In Guatemala, the forms of oppression and the manifestations of violence are intimately linked. They are sustained by the same scaffolding of racial, gender, and class structural inferiority that is manifested in the daily violence that subjugates and dominates women. Gender ideologies normalize expressions of violence and provide justification for the punishments inflicted for transgressing designated traditional roles (Menjívar, 2014, p. 77).

The reinterpretation of the facts occurs in a framework of new understanding about the causality of violence. However, this does not imply acceptance of any justification for the act; rather it is placed in context to understand its origin and enable the person to change its effects. The idea is to redirect the responsibilities and ethical duties where they belong, that is, not on the victims, who are subjected to suspicion arising from social presumptions.

Past, present. and future are dimensions that appear in the embroidered scenes, either to denounce situations of oppression and invisibility that were experienced or to highlight the struggle to change such situations. The dimension related to the present is associated more with scenes that portray crises, ruptures, and current changes in life. The dimension of the future is depicted in terms of dreams and aspirations of transformation and reconstruction of a different life without violence. "*I would be a single mother again. I long for the freedom to decide without asking permission.*" Without the dimensions of memory, it would not be possible to strive for change or compare the lived experience.

Psychosocial Impact of Violence

The arpilleras reveal the emotional impact of experiences of grief, depression, sexual abuse, abuse of power, orphanhood, discrimination, authoritarianism, suicide attempts. These and other impacts express the pain of loss, abandonment arising from experiences of contempt, humiliation, and shame caused by gender violence, among which the issues of irresponsible parenting, alcoholism, and incest stand out. They also shared the ways in which they protected themselves from the traumatic experience through silence, concealment, appearance, and projective identification. The fear of not being understood and the isolation of having suffered psychologically very debilitating experiences made some protagonists speak in third person. Another woman denounced discriminatory domestic work by equalizing the attachment between ethnically different people, as shown in Fig. 9.5.

The more resistance or difficulty of representation that emerges during the arpillera production, the greater is the inability to elaborate and overcome the experience. Among the relived memories, blockages emerge, which always indicate a difficulty to be overcome, interrupting the task, or repeating it compulsively in an uninterrupted doing, undoing, and redoing.

Scenes of domestic violence depicted a family context normalized by double standards and subjected to continuous blackmail, pressure, and sexual abuse. Abuse and contempt for women and children is the norm. The influence of the social

Fig. 9.5 'No to discrimination'

imaginaries of romantic love on the aspirations and desires of the protagonists is confronted with life stories marked by contempt and invisibility. The continuous humiliations weaken women's dignity and self-esteem. The attitude of self-sacrifice and sacrifice is expected of obedient and resigned women, both by their own families and social networks that control the moral reputation of women.

The paradox of the beliefs that justify violence is that the women aspire to a different life change yet they themselves reproduce the assigned patterns. This occurs because they do not find a way to break the cycle of violence in which they are trapped. Long-established values provide them security and certainty even in traditional and oppressive contexts, where social control is exercised among the same neighbors through rumors.

"Here are three stages of life change: from suffering to hope for a childhood of domestic violence due to my father's alcoholism, a youth with dating violence, and my adult life and pregnancy with reconciliation and an end to violence." Overcoming violence in this woman's life was an achievement she wanted to socialize.

Today we tend to see the symmetry between the cycle of violence (Walker, 1979) and trans-generational abuse that is the common denominator in many stories of domestic violence that are reproduced from generation to generation (grandparents, parents, daughters). Hence the importance of modifying parenting patterns with children to prevent them from repeating violent behavior patterns. Determinist conceptions of inheritance or early learning can exacerbate feelings of powerlessness as an inevitable fate from which there is no escape. This fight against determinism is a permanent challenge in therapeutic approaches because it confronts the weight of oppression with the options for transformation and change.

The adolescent girls' stories were especially moving because of the scope of the problem posed by incestuous relationships and early motherhood. These relationships are based on the manipulation of abuse or aggression through secrecy and trust, exercised with the violence of force or emotional blackmail, due to the asymmetry of power that exists because of the age difference. The most complex aspect to reintegrate was the guilt for the betrayal of the secret shared with the adult, when the girl understands that her own father took advantage of the vulnerabilities of her age and her emotional and protection needs.

The experience of motherhood as an unexpected and unwanted accident was overwhelming for these girls because of the confusion of roles between a disrupted sexuality and a forced motherhood, resulting in a deep mistrust of the world and others.

> My greatest happiness is my daughter. When I received her at birth, I didn't feel good because I didn't feel like being a mother. At first, I didn't love her, and I rejected her because she was the product of a rape (15 years old, 2011).

The violation of this woman's sexual and reproductive rights deepened her feelings of humiliation, guilt, and shame that weaken her identity while also causing a deep distrust that obstructs the forging of emotional bonds. This explained her refusal to remember the experience. "To be honest I am ashamed of everything that happened and that has to stay in the past. I am sad to remember it again" (17 years old, 2011).

Fig. 9.6 'Acceptance'

Accepting the experience of early motherhood seemed to be an inconsistent challenge in the face of this overlap of needs, roles, and capacities that an incestuous relationship implies, but it was a necessary step in order not to hold these child mothers accountable. Acceptance is a process as shown in Fig. 9.6. It was very important for these young women to normalize their reactions to reduce stigma and rebuild trust. The desire to achieve a life without violence and happiness restored their hope for a different future.

"I am this child, and this is my daughter who is one year and four months old. She is holding my hand and together we are taking our future towards happiness so that violence will never happen again in our lives. I was raped by my father. I felt horrible and wanted to die" (16 years old 2011). Fig. 9.7 reflects this experience.

Reintegration of the Traumatic Experience

The final stage of arpillera production helps to restructure life and personal identity based on experience. This enables the assimilation of what happened, reducing the impact of guilt, shame, humiliation, and social stigma. To encourage this reintegration, it is necessary to evaluate how to project the future and how we can grow personally from the experience (Martin & Riera, 2003, p 138). These questions guided the telling of their stories.

The guidelines for reintegrating the experience were:

DI NO A LA VIOLENCIA
Muchacha adolescente víctima de incesto, 15 años
Asociación Nuevos Horizontes de Quetzaltenango, 2010

"Mi historia empieza así, pues yo fui abusada o prácticamente violada por mi papa. El me tocaba y quede embaraza y tuve una nena de él. Siempre me ha gustado estar con ella y ahora vivo en un albergue de refugio que me ha ayudado a superar todo lo que me paso. Siempre me ha ayudado la psicóloga a superar la tristeza, por todo lo que el pasado me da tristeza. Pero en un futuro pienso sobresalir y darle a mi hija lo mejor de mi, darle lo que sea necesario, siempre con la frente en alto, siempre con la autoestima en alto, siempre hallar la felicidad y siempre con la ayuda de Dios, porque él es el único que nos da el camino y la sabiduría para poder seguir con mi felicidad. Esta es una parte de mi historia".

Luisa Cabrera   10

Fig. 9.7 'Say no to violence'

1. Normalize the experience of violence, find meaning and a reason, by the following.

   (a) Name what happened.
   (b) Realize that your case is not the only one.
   (c) That you are not guilty or responsible for suffering violence.
   (d) At the time, there was nothing I could do to avoid what happened.

2. Work through the experience from a new perspective

   (a) Learn to live with it because it cannot be erased.
   (b) Talk about it without feeling shame or guilt.
   (c) Seek other ways of facing the consequences that are more positive and adapted to their reality.

3. Assimilating the experience builds strength and gives meaning to making decisions for change, such as breaking the cycle of violence and dealing with the consequences.

   (a) Awareness of the difficulties of the process of rupture is gained when the experience of suffering has been recognized and worked through.
   (b) Making breakthrough decisions is nurtured by beliefs in hope and the future that restore the conviction that the world is a benevolent and trustworthy

place. These ideas allow life to be reorganized. *"When I was making my arpillera, I thought of my future that has yet to blossom, but I have hope that it will."*

The process of reintegration is a watershed between the experience of pain or harm and emotional recovery. The memory will represent the before and after events and their meanings, according to the universe of beliefs around violence. The "Soledad" [Loneliness] arpillera (Fig. 9.8) exposes the fantasies of romantic love shattered by the deceitful false promises and the social control exercised through the informal circulation of gossip.

> When I met my husband, I thought that he would not make us suffer, he told me that he would never cheat on me, but from the first day I got married, another girl appeared who was always with him … Five days after the birth of my son, he threw me out of the house.

The protagonist felt psychological relief—"I felt better, as if relieved of a burden"—that comes from recognizing the frustration of her expectations and the loneliness of deception and abandonment.

Comparing their arpilleras or reproducing what other protagonists were doing helped these women compare their experiences. It also increased group awareness ("we") with mutually positive communication conveyed by their respective productions.

Fig. 9.8 'Soledad' [Loneliness]

An unexpected dynamic of understanding and mutual support arose from the spontaneous interaction of the adolescents with other mothers who were adults, reproducing maternal care, advice and interest in their lives, a type of bond they lacked due to their disintegrated family backgrounds. This exchange of tenderness and care had a very effective restorative impact in compensating for their emotional needs. While contextualizing these stories of incest, there emerged experiences of anger, resentment, rage, and pain of growing up with this degree of harassment. The most devastating experience was understanding the meaning of a social taboo that they had ignored and whose social stigma made them ashamed. In these complex situations, shame is intensified by the fact that the victims are burdened with a responsibility that society insinuates, when, in fact, they bear no responsibility in the matter. It was very interesting to observe how the accompaniment of the adult women tolerated and understood this reality without prejudicing it and that was a relief for the adolescents, because they did not feel criminalized or rejected.

The assessment of the reintegration was positive, as participants expressed satisfaction with the perceived changes in their process of re-evaluating the past. In the words of one woman, "it helps to go back to the past and then decide that you don't want that anymore." It was important to incorporate the perspective of not deserving what happened to free themselves of blame. Many women come to question whether there is something wrong with their own nature to deserve so much violence. This sense of deserving what happened resides in feelings of guilt that lead them to question whether their behavior provoked it in any way. Such feelings of guilt are socially legitimized by society's suspicion that the victim provoked the assault against her.

Finally, the experience is reintegrated with a new meaning that allows them to break the situation and the silence. With that step, they are in condition to reconstruct their lives. As a participant expressed it, "There comes a moment when we have to let everything out so that there can be change."

By Way of Conclusions. Creativity and Reparation with Survivors of Violence

The production of an arpillera is a multifaceted technique that facilitates the intersection of various theoretical and methodological perspectives that complement its potential for repairing and transforming lives. The creative and dramatic representation techniques, the dynamics of the group process based on the identification of peers in similar situations, the integration of emotions, the integrated story, and the cognitive-behavioral approach of the experience, as well as the gender and human rights approach contributed to the psychosocial analysis.

The role of the psychologist mediated between the opposing needs and desires of the protagonists, between their fears, mistrust, and expectations, channeling the comparative grievances between them, transforming the blocked situations, and responding to their needs for attention. It also fostered recognition of the potentialities that enable them to progress, safeguarding a respectful and empathetic order and promoting sensitive treatment in the interactions. Discovering that they all had the capacity to do and decide was the key to begin to regain control over their own lives.

The process of producing the arpilleras was more directive in creating the conditions for group framing and application of the technique, but totally free and spontaneous in terms of creative representation of the stories. An initiative that reinforced emotional security and the sense as protagonists in their own lives was to photograph the evolution of the personal process of constructing each arpillera. Observing the changes recorded reaffirmed a better image of themselves and empowered them as women.

The normalization of domestic and sexual violence as a frequent pattern in family systems poses new challenges and dilemmas of intervention on its effects, which confirm the transcendence that violence occupies today in social life. Recovering the importance and meaning of their lives requires that one feel important in a small group, not being indifferent to others with whom we interact, and showing the fear that something will happen to us due to the mistrust and helplessness stemming from the profusion of violence.

The arpilleras are humble in their reparative intent and beautiful in their creative expression of each woman's life reality. The process of creating arpilleras brings out the best in people. It integrates emotions, thoughts, and behaviors that have much personal meaning because of the harm caused and the lessons learned. Becoming aware of this gives hope and confidence in the future, two values that are essential to leave violence behind.

The technique mobilizes emotional processes of memories and feelings that affected our upbringing and developmental maturity, as well as values and beliefs that legitimize it and set-in motion processes of mental representation that build the human experience, without which we could not reinterpret the facts or find a new meaning and sense. The latter is what allows us to generate transformative changes in our reality of life. Only a perspective of change can reverse the resignation of suffering so accepted by women who are used to endure because they are convinced that the sacrifice of their lives and freedoms is their destiny. The real challenge is to change the beliefs that assume a social order of violence and impunity as inevitable because it seems to have always been so.

It is fascinating to observe how the hands of these women can create the living representation of experiences of pain, of loss, of submission, of failure, of hope … without the justifying rationalization of the speeches. Once the production is completed, it is reintegrated into a story with new meanings that explain what happened and frees the victim from responsibility. Dissolving the guilt that paralyzes and immobilizes a woman opens the way for a new understanding of what happened, from which decisions are made and life is transformed.

After suffering an experience of victimization, we all ask ourselves if it is possible to live without violence or if we can learn to confront or avoid it, dispensing with the inevitable determinism of the naturalized order of things. In this sense the arpillera technique constitutes an intervention model that contributes to personal growth and social reparation. This model can be replicable with sexual and domestic violence victims. The model considers the gender perspective and human rights focus evidence the dimensions of affectation in the health and intimacy of women whose lives and the crushing weight of being poor have underestimated potentialities, discriminated and excluded.

References

Lykes, B., & Crosby, A. (2015). Creative methodologies as a resource for mayan women's empowerment. In B. Hamber & E. Gallagher (Eds.), *Psychosocial perspectives on peacebuilding* (pp. 147–186). Springer. https://doi.org/10.1007/978-3-319-09937-85

Martin, C. (2010). *Manual sobre perspectiva psicosocial en la investigación de derechos humanos*. HEGOA-CEJIL-UPV.

Martin, C., & Riera, F. (2003). *Afirmación y resistencia. La comunidad como apoyo*. Editorial Virus.

Menjívar, C. (2014). *Eterna violencia. Vidas de las mujeres ladinas en Guatemala*. Facultad de Ciencias Sociales.

Perren-Klinger, G. (2003). *Debriefing. Modelos y aplicaciones de la historia traumática al relato integrado*. Editorial AKADIA.

USIP (1998) Acuerdo de Paz Firme y Duradera: MINUGUA, United Nations Mission for the Verification of Human Rights in Guatemala. https://www.usip.org/publications/1998/11/peace-agreements-guatemala.

Walker, L. E. (1979). *The battered woman*. Harper and Row.

Chapter 10
Group Therapeutic Strategies and Human Rights. Human Rights Violations in Chile

Germán Morales and María Isabel Castillo

Introduction: Trauma and Groupness

Bruno Bettelheim (1981) coined the term extreme traumatization, alluding to traumatic experiences arising from a deliberate policy of persecution and extermination based on ethnic, religious, cultural, and/or political identity by the group in power. The concept of extreme traumatization was redefined to emphasize that the traumatic situation refers not only to the subjects, but also to society and the harmful effects not only concern the individual, but also the society at large (Becker & Castillo, 1993). The definition emphasizes the destruction and extermination of those who have a different identity and are negatively regarded by the power groups, as Bettelheim pointed out (Lira et al., 1990). Thus, the therapeutic processes of people who have suffered extreme traumatization show that the trauma invades multiple levels of the intrapsychic, relational, and social world (Becker et al., 1990). This definition emphasizes how the State, through its agents, develops actions of repressive violence that qualifies as human rights violations, which produce a specific type of trauma, making it necessary to address relationally the fractured bonds and the socio-group identity of those who were victims.

In contemporary relational psychoanalysis, reclaiming the tradition introduced by Ferenczi regarding the role of personal bonds in the trauma, a metaphor is proposed (Bromberg, 2011) that associates trauma with a "tsunami," to describe the devastating effects of the trauma. Bromberg (2011) proposes that the traumatic effect erupts as an unbearable emotion. Central to its constitution is the absence of an "other" to provide an empathic response and the integrity of the "self" is

G. Morales (✉)
Pontificia Universidad Católica de Chile, Santiago, Chile
e-mail: gpmorale@uc.cl

M. I. Castillo
ILAS Instituto Latinoamericano se Salud Mental y Derechos Humanos, Santiago, Chile
e-mail: micastillovergara@gmail.com

© The Author(s), under exclusive license to Springer Nature Switzerland AG 2022   135
E. Lira et al. (eds.), *Human Rights Violations in Latin America*, Peace
Psychology Book Series, https://doi.org/10.1007/978-3-030-97542-5_10

overwhelmed. The experience is fragmented, dissociated, and depersonalized. Since it stems from a relationship, from that unbearable emotion, but fundamentally from the absent empathic response, dissociation develops as a form of psychic and relational survival in the face of helplessness.

Considering that the traumatic consequence appears linked to helplessness, we must think about how to articulate a group reparative and therapeutic strategy in relation to this lost link, since subjectivity is constituted by the presence of another who recognizes it (Ogden, 1985). Thus, trauma is thought of as a rupture of that recognition, which remains encapsulated in subjectivity, cannot be named, and often appears only through sensations, images, symptoms, which constitute the only traces of emptiness, of the "hole in the mind" (Kingston & Cohen, 1986). These disruptive feelings are chronified due to the isolation and marginalization that characterized the stigmatization of the victims, which implied the loss of social ties, of social and labor insertion, which gave meaning to people's existence. The impossibility of symbolizing these experiences and their containment favored their encapsulation. As Grubrich-Simitis (2007) points out, this encapsulation does not allow memory as such, but prevents the distinction between what is temporal—not even what is real—from the imagination.

One way to break the encapsulation of the traumatic is the process of reconstituting and/or repairing the otherness to recover the link and reestablish the lost continuity of the experience of being, which gave rise to the traumatic (Castillo & Morales, 2011). In the therapeutic group "free association develops a double associative chain, which results from the successive associations of each subject and that is constituted in the succession of associative events of the group members as a whole" (Kaës, 2005, p. 25). We might think that this process of association in group psychotherapy occurs thanks to the development of a group mentality and the emergence of a cooperative inclination among group members (Bion, 1979). As stated by Vinogradov and Yalom (1996), the constitutive basis of the healing factors of group therapy are: cohesion in the sense of feeling a collective belonging and emotional containment that the group provides; the sense of parity in feeling that all group members share a similar experience; and instilling hope from the experience that effective help can arise not only from the therapists but from the group itself.

According to Pichon-Rivière (1964), a group implies the construction of an identity and a task would be it explicit or implicit. The notion of task is related to the function that the group fulfills and the task in turn is constituted as a referent of group identity. The notion of task is related to the function fulfilled by the group and its internal structure is constituted by the task that brings them together. The task, in turn, is constituted as a benchmark of group identity. In the case of therapeutic groups with patients who have undergone extreme traumatization, the purpose of these groups is the working through process of this experience to enable the recovery of the damaged otherness.

Consequences of Political Repression on Groupness

In the repressive strategy of the civil-military dictatorship in Chile (1973–1990) led by General Augusto Pinochet, the loss of collective and group spaces played a central role. Fear and caution were generated among a large part of the population regarding to activities that authorities considered suspicious and perceived as a threat to order. This affected the group identities and belonging of those who had participated in the overthrown Popular Unity government. Thus, the onslaught against organizations and groups that gave meaning to the collective (unions, political parties, cultural, neighborhood, and other associations) affected and fractured a socio-group identity.

The repressive strategies sought to destroy the continuity of links to collective spaces. As a form of resistance to these policies, group strategies were developed, many of which acquired a therapeutic value, although they were not necessarily intended as such.

Shortly after the 1973 coup d'état, thousands of people were detained, executed, and victims of forced disappearance. Early on, various forms of resistance to the dictatorship and its political repression emerged, including organizations formed by victims' relatives, such as the Agrupación de Familiares de Detenidos-Desaparecidos (Association of Relatives of Disappeared Detainees, AFDD), and the Agrupación de Familiares de Ejecutados Políticos (Association of Relatives of Politically Executed, AFEP). To the present day, these organizations have been a source of support in terms of cohesion and group support for thousands of people. They also enabled the continuity of the struggle to know the truth of what happened to their relatives and to demand justice. Moreover, they are spaces of emotional support associated with the traumatic experience.

Furthermore, several non-governmental organizations (NGOs) were founded in the mid-1970s and especially in the 1980s to provide legal support and mental health programs to support victims of human rights violations. Staff professionals of FASIC (Fundación de Ayuda Social de las Iglesias Cristianas), CODEPU (Corporación de Defensa de los Derechos del Pueblo), ILAS (Instituto Latinoamericano de Salud Mental y Derechos Humanos), and other organizations developed therapeutic group activities, systematized their work, and were prolific in the publication of papers in international scientific journals and collective books. Concretely, in victims' organizations, churches, and NGOs, the group was considered a natural space for recovery and/or reconstruction, as a significant space in terms of belonging, cohesion, and identity.

The therapeutic experiences developed in Chile generated group mechanisms that created a space in which people found containment and empathy and shared some notion of the group's healing and reparative capacity. When we speak of group experience and its reparative function, we refer to the practice of listening to similar repressive experiences, and sharing disruptive and ambivalent emotions with others, which generates a possibility of mutual recognition. This empathic recognition allows the deployment of personal and group resources and tools, between those who are listened to, enabling them to show how they have coped with difficulties while providing support that restores the bond and trust with others.

After 1990, many group therapies were organized with people who gave testimony to the National Truth and Reconciliation Commission, while others arose from the exhumations and recognition of skeletal remains of recovered disappeared loved ones or due to the emotional impact of testifying in judicial processes. Professionals associated with these instances referred people; participants came to these groups seeking to cope with the emotional impact of these experiences. Several long-term groups were set up, varying in duration from 6 months to 2 years.

Self-Help Groups, Community Interventions, and Group Interventions

The self-help groups and community interventions functioned in the initial period of group approaches, which were not conceived as therapeutic group interventions but did bring relief to many. These interventions aimed at containing group anxieties, fostering organizational cohesion and identity in terms of mental health support. The group interventions were carried out by pairs of psychotherapeutic facilitators in small groups so as to encourage the expression and verbalization of the experiences endured.

This group containment and listening mechanisms were organized as self-help groups or as group interventions in crisis in community instances, through different institutions. By self-help groups, we mean groups that were not necessarily coordinated by a professional, although they may have been designed by one.

In 1974 the Comité Pro Paz (Pro Peace Committee), and later the Vicariate of Solidarity, received reports from family members, mostly women, who turned to the organizations in anguish after the kidnapping and disappearance of their loved ones and the uncertainty of not knowing their whereabouts. In the context of reaching out to these people, various initiatives were developed to bring them together.

It is important to note the formation of small groups that functioned as workshops in different parts of the country. In these groups women embroidered burlap patchwork, sewing pieces of cloth, wool, and thread, crystallizing their denunciations of the crimes perpetrated by the dictatorship. "The arpilleras are tapestries embroidered and drawn with scraps of fabric and sewn onto a hard cloth. Their origins have been lost over time. They have been found in various Latin American countries with local variations in technique and content. The construction of arpilleras and tapestries employs a great variety of materials and sizes" (Lira, 2014, p. 10). In Chile they comprise a folk tradition, with the patchwork tapestries that portray images of different stories and landscapes. The so-called *Chilean political arpilleras* are recognized as an expression of a form of cultural (and political) resistance during the dictatorship and were produced as solidarity work (Lira, 2014). They are currently disseminated through public exhibitions. After 2008 a traveling collection of arpilleras, organized by Roberta Bacic, a Chilean human rights activist living in Ireland, has been exhibited in different parts of the world. They are also exhibited at the Museum of Memory and Human Rights in Chile, which has recovered part of a dispersed production (Lira, 2014). The various forms of political repression were recorded in the arpilleras that these women replicated with other groups. The production process of these tapestries and the testimonies they depict facilitated therapeutic results; consequently, the groups in which they were produced became instances of group elaboration and symbolization.

From the late 1970s to the mid-1980s, a series of initiatives were developed in working class neighborhoods to solve pressing needs. The "community pots" (soup kitchen) were a collective practice that began with collecting food and taking turns in a community setting to cook food, which was distributed to each family, to take home. Some of these initiatives reached 300 families each day. Another initiative was the organization co-op, "Comprando juntos" [buying together] a strategy by which family purchases were organized and bought collectively to lower costs. Grassroots community health networks also were organized to share health knowledge and support at the primary level. These initiatives also gave rise to local human rights committees in some of the most emblematic neighborhoods that struggled against the dictatorship. With the support of NGOs and some professional associations, the human rights committees provided physical and mental health services to those who were wounded, detained or to the relatives of people killed in the massive repressive actions. Such community interventions included group interventions both with individuals and organizations in neighborhoods that were threatened, apparently by adjacent neighborhoods. Neighbors were called upon to prepare for and resist this aggression (Lira, 1990) when in fact the rumor of such threats originated from the regime as part of its "psychological warfare" operations (Watson, 1982).

In FASIC and the Vicariate of Solidarity, various group activities were carried out with relatives of disappeared detainees, associated both with accompaniment in the search process and in the discovery of corpses, as well as the denunciations of abductions. In this context, "the group instance stands as a privileged place of perception and confrontation of these processes, but also as a feared space, since it caused them to experience the dimension of death and to replace the persistent, years-long denial of this possibility" (Weinstein et al., 1987, p. 187). Experiences of helplessness and ambivalence about death intersected these groups. The potential as well as the limits of these groups were evident. Participants experienced symptomatic relief, especially regarding anguish, encouraging mutual containment of pain, although the full emotional elaboration of the experience was not possible in the groups, probably because it was associated with a threatening and uncertain context. These groups provided accompaniment for the relatives mainly of the Association of Relatives of the Detained Disappeared. In this sense, the groups were conceived more as crisis intervention groups that mitigated some of anguish, improved interpersonal relationships among family members, and fostered a sense of organizational belonging and cohesion.

The interventions were quite diverse, ranging from those centered on the creation of *arpilleras* to neighborhood crisis interventions, or crisis interventions groups. Yet, within this diversity, all these groups shared the objective of emotional containment through verbalization and building group cohesion and identity, either in regular group meetings or as instances for specific intervention needs. Besides these therapeutic objectives, the groups also comprised practices of cultural resistance, organizational support, and reconstruction of the social fabric of those times. And each one of these groups arose as an effort to manage complex moments such as discoveries of the remains of disappeared persons, or disruptive information about the whereabouts of their relatives.

Group Interventions with Returnees from Exile

Group interventions were also a significant contribution to the elaboration of the exile/return experience, seeking to emotionally accompany and support people in their process of reintegration into the country. Thus, in the 1980s several NGO programs were generated to facilitate the reintegration process of those returning from exile. The methodology of choice was the group mechanism, which was used with adults, adolescents, children, and families, with the idea of sharing the experience of reintegration in a country that was generally unknown to them and that evoked fear. The duration of these groups varied greatly. They ranged from welcome days for adults returning from exile, entertaining sessions for children, which lasted a morning, an afternoon, or a couple of days, as well as others with adults, adolescents, and/or children that consisted of a few sessions, while others were therapeutic groups that averaged 12 sessions.

Homogeneous and heterogeneous groups were held with young people. The homogeneous groups were more like welcome and support groups to help ease the process of insertion into Chilean society, while the heterogeneous groups were made up of young people returning from exile and local youth. An example of the heterogeneous groups was those developed by the Casa de la Juventud El Encuentro, towards the end of the 1980s, the objective of which was to welcome and promote the insertion of the sons and daughters of exiles who returned to the country without their parents. In addition to the workshops mentioned above, there were therapeutic groups, in which young people who returned to Chile from various countries of exile participated alongside young people who had never left the country. In these groups, playful and artistic methodologies were used to enable participants to learn cultural codes. However, the most important aspect was that the young people who had lived in exile felt welcomed by peers whose experiences differed from theirs, resulting sometimes in a complex group interaction. Conflicts were expressed related to the notion of the "golden exile" (the regime's propaganda on political exile used this term) by the local youths' attitudes towards the returnees, regarding in terms of the idealization of the living conditions of the exiled families far from the repression on Chilean soil. The young returnees responded with stories about feeling uprooting, as well as being subjected to xenophobic and racist discrimination, in their countries of exile. This enabled the locals to understand the pain of exile and enabled them to open up to share their experience with repression. The interchange favored empathy and mutual recognition between peers.

In a group session held at the Casa de la Juventud el Encuentro, one participant commented on her school experience in a Scandinavian country:

> At school I was called "black head" and sometimes I was beaten when I left school…I never told my parents so they wouldn't worry…and now here it seems that I am not Chilean either (Morales, 1990, p. 15).[1]

After listening to the girl describe her experience, a young man who had always lived in Chile said:

> I'm so sorry. I always thought you guys had a great time… I'm really sorry (Morales, 1990, p. 15).

The experience of emotional containment provided by the groups was key to enable the sharing of notions such as feeling like foreigners in their own country, and in the case of many young people, feeling exiled from the country they grew up in when trying to insert themselves in their parents' country.

Group Processes and Fear

In 1991 the book *Psicología de la Amenaza Política y del Miedo* [Psychology of Political Threat and Fear] (Lira & Castillo, 1991) was published. The book drew from a research project conducted with opponents of Pinochet's military dictatorship (human rights activists, religious leaders, working class families, homemakers, students, and social and political leaders). Conducted in 1988 prior to the landmark plebiscite of October, the study involved 1157 people in small groups in Santiago and in several provinces. The explicit focus of working on "fear" was the common element in every group, all of which had suffered threats, detentions, torture or had relatives who had disappeared. This caused them to feel ambivalent and even afraid of participating in the plebiscite, which asked the electorate to vote either in favor or against Pinochet's continuity as ruler.

These group processes generated conditions that enabled people of working through their own experiences of fear, allowing them to recognize their emotions and understand them in the socio-political context they were living in. The recognition of the political threat, the common and shared nature of the fears experienced by the participants, facilitated the affirmation of these experiences and legitimized anguish and fear as a coherent response to the political threat. Thus, the fear staged in one's imagination could be differentiated in the external reality. This made it

---

[1] The participants gave consent to reproduce excerpts of their words; the author maintained only gender and some general references of the exile's places.

easier for the subjects to work to recover their autonomy to cope with the political threat and the fears generated by it, and, consequently, enable them to manage the political context and recover their role as active citizens (Lira & Castillo, 1991).

Group Psychotherapies with Adolescents and Young People

Group psychotherapies with adolescents and young people are always important spaces. Groups are a natural space for adolescents and the brief format is more conducive for metabolizing the ambivalences of the autonomy/dependence conflict typical of that age. Such was also the case with the adolescent sons and daughters of detainees/disappeared and of the politically executed. Sharing a peer space constituted a place for very powerful, empathetic listening. Various NGOs developed this type of group in the late 1980s and early 1990s.

These groups usually lasted at least 12 sessions, with a maximum of 24 sessions, and were run by pairs of therapists, who used entertaining methodologies and creative techniques. A good example of this kind of group was a project called Four Countries, which included teams from other Latin American countries that worked with groups of children and adolescents from Argentina, El Salvador, Guatemala, and Chile (Becker et al., 1994). The participants had lost their mother and/or father or had been estranged from them for a large part of their lives because of political violence, either in the context of dictatorship or civil war in their respective countries. The participating organizations were the Movimiento de Salud Mental Solidaria in Argentina, associated with Madres de Plaza de Mayo; the Universidad Jesuita José Simeón Cañas in El Salvador; the Asociación de Servicios Comunitarios in Guatemala with the support of academics from the Boston College School of Education; and the ILAS team from Chile. This was a project conceived by Ignacio Martín-Baró, a Salvadoran psychologist and Jesuit priest, who never saw it come to fruition because it was initiated after his assassination as a posthumous tribute to his inspiration to produce collaborative Latin American work in a research/action perspective.

The role of peers can be paradoxical when working with adolescents, given that most of the therapeutic groups of adolescents have been homogeneous groups, according to the type of traumatic experience, such as children of detainees-disappeared and politically executed. The paradox to which we refer is that when a group of sons and daughters of victims is formed, it implies a place of stigmatization and ambivalence, where adolescents are challenged by a dilemma of integration: "If they try to be a typical young person of today, leaving behind the world of the persecuted, marginalized, they lose their family belonging, resulting in an unbearable disloyalty. If, on the other hand, they try to assume the historic legacy, attempting to be loyal to the persecuted parents, then they inevitably enter a marginal and retraumatizing dynamic" (Becker et al., 1994, p. 100). This meant that, despite the need for psychotherapeutic attention requested by mothers, fathers, and organizations, there was a certain resistance on the part of the young people to attend a psychotherapeutic group, which resulted in low attendance. Nonetheless, and even though it is common in therapeutic groups, there was no dropout in the groups conducted. Moreover, many of the young people continued to meet beyond the group therapy setting when it ended.

The techniques used in these groups were psychodrama; thematic illustrations; graphic and artistic resources such as self-portraits, individual and collective collages, masks, murals, and construction of objects with disposable materials; literary resources such as stories, narratives, and poetry; and collective imagery (Morales, 1994). Each session generally used some of these devices, leaving at least one subsequent session for reflection on what had been produced and/or dramatized, to move from the figurative symbolic to verbalization. In all the groups special attention was given to ritualizing the conclusion of the group psychotherapy to encourage the mourning processes, central in the repair of the traumatic, which was a very significant moment.

In one group of adolescents, comprised by daughters and sons of detainees/disappeared persons, an imagery exercise explored a beloved object from childhood. Afterwards each participant commented on the object. The words of a young woman whose mother had been detained and had sent her a doll she had made from imprisonment were quite moving for the group participants. During the following session, each young person constructed objects with different materials, and the girl in question built a very flimsy doll, almost without arms or face (Aguilar & Morales, 1995). In the group, the participants expressed admiration for the affectionate gesture of the girl's mother who had thought of her and had been able to make her a doll from prison. The young woman, moved by her creation and by the group's story, ambivalently noted her need for the group, and that it enabled her to open herself to work through the traumatic experience (Morales, 2000):

> I need to talk to you a lot and I like to listen to what you say, to know what you are like, to know you. It's not that I don't want you to get to know me.
>
> But by letting go or telling you about my life, suddenly I will become so dependent… and if suddenly it changes… I am already afraid of losing you (p. 209).

Faced with this, the therapists observe the open expression of pain and the need for the group. Another participant, a young man, affirms:

> It also pains me to leave, but we are here (Morales & Aguilar, 1994, p. 28).

As we can see, group psychotherapies with adolescents and young people facilitated empathy and emotional containment, fostered symbolization and thus the working through of traumatic experiences in a transitional space where the bond with others is recreated and repaired.

Group Psychotherapy with Adults

In the case of adult victims of torture, relatives of disappeared detainees and politically executed, the group therapeutic space was the mechanism of choice for those who had suffered extreme traumatization during the dictatorship. At the beginning of the transition to democracy this type of group had more prolonged developments in the framework of the recognition by the truth commissions, and especially the National Commission on Political Prisoners and Torture (CNPPT, 2005). The group psychotherapies of those who were victims of torture were differentiated between men and women, as there were experiences of sexual torture that were more difficult to share in mixed groups and these were spaces for working through the direct experience of detention and torture.

The group constitutes a private space of intimacy where the experience of horror and helplessness can be shared. The notion of peers, who have lived through the same traumatic experience, fosters a sense of kinship. Recognition in both public and private spaces allows for the transformation of the socio-political and intersubjective context of these people, constituting a moral third party (Benjamin, 2012). In this way, the fragmented history can be integrated, symbolizing the gaps, reconstructing the damaged subjectivity and otherness (Castillo & Morales, 2011). The group becomes a social space that acknowledges the experience of suffering, which has been denied and questioned in other social spaces (Castillo, 2019).

In group psychotherapy processes, the traumatic stories, impotence, and helplessness give rise to resources that allow participants to "recover." They also allow people to gain the conviction that they can reverse the situation of violence and lack of protection to which they were subjected. It is an attempt to regain control over one's own body, to achieve cohesion and a sense of continuity.

What Benjamin (2006) poses is pertinent. She proposes that we understand the therapeutic process as a process of oscillations between the rupture and the reestablishment of the empathetic connection, a process of destruction and survival, of rupture, and repair of regulation (Beebe & Lachmann, 2002; Castillo et al., 2017). In group psychotherapies these oscillations are experienced in the development of the group process, giving rise to mutual repairs that reconstitute the lost otherness. In the group space, internal tragedies and comedies are staged (McDougall, 1993) as spontaneous dramatizations of conflicts and traumatic situations experienced by each person. This facilitates the creation of new possibilities for psychic change by creating the capacity to address the traumatic experience from a shared experience that is validated by others (Castillo, 2019).

Some women who were participants in a psychotherapy group conducted by ILAS after giving their testimony to the CNPPT (2005) were frightened and even felt guilt at the beginning of these groups. The silence of the detained, tortured, abused, and sexually denigrated women is reinforced by shame and guilt. Often it is the body that speaks, as the physical symptoms are the only place of memory.

The group's initial sessions were very intense. Everyone introduced themselves and although they did not describe details of the torture, they did talk about the experience in detention and the feelings of humiliation, shame, and rage that they still have today. In one group of women survivors of torture, a participant commented (Castillo et al., 2017):

> Why do we have to get together to hear all these painful stories? I have never talked about them, and I don't even know if I will tell them here. I feel like standing up and leaving. I didn't want to come today…. (Castillo et al., 2017, p. 31).

Such complaints from group participants must be understood as a junction in which it is possible for them to shed the sense of submission and subjugation by connecting with the pain as an imposition. It enables them to verbalize the distrust and hopelessness they feel, forming a bond that is generated by mutuality and affective resonance. This makes it possible to express dissociation and to initiate a process that enables the integration of the divided aspects in a group moment, especially when the stories about the torture situations begin to emerge (Castillo, 2019).

> "She would take threads from a blanket that had been given to her to tie each of the buttonholes of her blouse where the buttons had been torn off, so she felt more protected. She also tied a pair of very wide pants that had been given to her after the clothes she had arrived in had been torn off."… After listening to this account, another patient of the group notes in surprise, "I did the same thing. I had forgotten…" (Castillo 2019, p. 16).

Within the group setting, expressions of helplessness and disempowerment give rise to resources that enable participants to feel that they are able to reverse the situation of violence and lack of protection to which they were subjected.

Conclusion

Before the civil-military dictatorship, organizations and collective instances flourished intensely. The group was a daily, natural place of belonging, of change and citizenship. After the coup, the group setting became fragmentary and threatening.

As group devices subsequently began to re-emerge in different settings, they increasingly acquired a psychotherapeutic role with social implications. To the extent that the context validated and recognized the traumatic experience, and the reparation of the damaged otherness permeated Chilean society, group devices also contributed to the political task of reconstructing the social fabric. Thus, it is necessary to state that "while the group recognition of suffering plays a fundamental role in repairing people's interpersonal bonds, it acquires greater strength when such suffering has been recognized by the State…" (Morales & Cornejo, 2013, p. 206). Consequently, we can say that group strategies varied depending on the contexts—although they have always had a reparatory role. By recovering the notion of "us," they foster reparation as a process in society, in groups, and in individuals, even if justice is limited or late.

The trajectory of the self-help groups at the beginning of the dictatorship indicates that the mere fact of giving testimony had the value of endowing it the status of reality. The fact of being heard in the group psychotherapies associated with the recognition by the State confirms the experience suffered, and we observe the emergence of increasingly complex therapeutic devices. However, the group space has value and is effective, not only because it is a space of containment and mutual recognition, but also because psychotherapists play the role of facilitators and activators of resources that are already available in the groups and communities.

References

Aguilar, M. I., & Morales, G. (1995). Children of the persecuted in Chile and their relationship to peers: Adolescence, trauma, and individuation. In H. Adam, P. Riedesser, H. Riquelme, A. Verderber, & J. Walter (Eds.), *Children - war and persecution* (pp. 197–200). Sttiftung für Kinder/UNICEF.

Becker, D., & Castillo, M. I. (1993). El tratamiento Psicoterapéutico de Pacientes Traumatizados Extremos. *Revista Chilena de Psicoanálisis, 10*(1), 50–59.

Becker, D., Castillo, M. I., Gómez, E., Kovalskys, J., & Lira, E. (1990). Subjectivity and politics: The psychotherapy of extreme traumatization in Chile. *International Journal of Mental Health, 18*(2), 80–97. https://doi.org/10.1080/00207411.1989.11449125

Becker, D., Morales, G., & Aguilar, M. I. (Eds.). (1994). *Trauma psicosocial y adolescentes latinoamericanos: Formas de acción grupal*. ILAS/CESOC.

Beebe, B., & Lachmann, F. M. (2002). *Infancy research and adult treatment: Co-constructing interaction*. Analytic Press.

Benjamin, J. (2006). *Sujetos iguales, objetos de amor. Ensayos sobre el reconocimiento y la diferencia sexual*. Paidós.

Benjamin, J. (2012). El Tercero. Reconocimiento. *Clínica e Investigación Relacional, 6*(2), 169–179. www.ceir.org.es

Bettelheim, B. (1981). *Sobrevivir: El Holocausto, una generación después*. Crítica.

Bion, W. R. (1979). *Experiencias en grupos* (5th ed.). Paidós.

Bromberg, P. M. (2011). *The shadow of the tsunami, and the growth of the relational mind*. Routledge.

Castillo, M. I. (2019). Mujeres víctimas de la tortura sexual como consecuencia de la violencia política. *Apertura Psicoanalítica, 61*(2), 1–21. https://aperturas.org/articulo.php?articulo=0001062&pre=1

Castillo, M. I., Díaz, M., & Díaz-Cordal, M. (2017). Reconocimiento social y elaboración del trauma de origen sociopolítico. Una experiencia grupal con mujeres torturadas. *TRAMAS. Subjetividad y Procesos Sociales, 41*, 19–42. https://tramas.xoc.uam.mx/index.php/tramas/article/view/686

Castillo, M. I., & Morales, G. (2011). Psicoterapia grupal y tortura. In G. Morales, B. Ortúzar, & E. Thumala (Eds.), *Psicoterapia psicoanalítica de grupo y vínculos* (pp. 171–190). Orjikh Ediciones.

Comisión Nacional Sobre Prisión Política y Tortura (CNPPT). (2005). *Informe de la Comisión Nacional Sobre Prisión Política y Tortura*. Ministerio del Interior. Gobierno de Chile.

Grubrich-Simitis, I. (2007, julio 25–28). *Realitatsprüfung an Stelle der Deutung: Eine Phase in der psychoanalytischen Arbeit mit Nachkommen von Holocaust Überlebenden*. Congreso Internacional de Psicoanálisis. Berlín, Alemania.

Kaës, R. (2005). *La palabra y el vínculo. Procesos asociativos en los grupos*. Amorrortu Editores.

Kingston, W., & Cohen, J. (1986). Primal repression: Clinical and theorical aspects. *The International Journal of Psychoanalysis, 67*(3), 337–352.

Lira, E. (1990). Guerra psicológica: intervención política de la subjetividad colectiva. In I. Martín-Baró (Ed.), *Psicología social de la guerra. Trauma y terapia* (pp. 138–159).

Lira, E. (2014). Resistencia cultural y memoria política. *Conversaciones del Cono Sur, 1*(2), 8–15. https://conosurconversaciones.wordpress.com/

Lira, E., & Castillo, M. I. (1991). *Psicología de la Amenaza Política y del Miedo*. CESOC.

Lira, E., Castillo, M. I., & Becker, D. (1990). Psychotherapy with victims of political repression in Chile. A therapeutic and political challenge. In J. Gruschow & K. Hannibal (Eds.), *Health service for the treatment of torture and trauma survivors* (pp. 99–114). Committee on Scientific Freedom and Responsibility/American Association for the Advancement of Sciences.

McDougall, J. (1993). *Alegato por una cierta anormalidad*. Paidós.

Morales, G. (1990). *Bitácora sesiones grupales Casa de la Juventud El Encuentro*. Manuscrito no publicado.

Morales, G. (1994). Metodologías de trabajo grupal. En D. Becker, G. Morales & M.I. Aguilar (Eds.), *Trauma psicosocial y adolescentes latinoamericanos: Formas de acción grupal* (pp. 105-158). ILAS/CESOC.

Morales, G. (2000). Adolescencia, trauma y equipo terapéutico. In G. Araujo, O. Desatnik, & L. Fernández (Eds.), *Frente al silencio: testimonios de la violencia* (pp. 209–220). Universidad Autónoma Metropolitana, Unidad Xochimilco (UAM-X) /Instituto Latinoamericano de Estudios de la Familia (ILEF).

Morales, G., & Aguilar, M. I. (1994). *Bitácoras de grupo ILAS*. Manuscrito no publicado.

Morales, G., & Cornejo, M. (2013). Ambivalencias en la escucha de la tortura en Chile: Implicancias clínicas y sociales. *Terapia psicológica, 31*(2), 197–208. https://doi.org/10.4067/S0718-48082013000200006

Ogden, T. H. (1985). On potential space. *The International Journal of Psychoanalysis, 66*(2), 129–141.

Pichon-Rivière, E. (1964). *El proceso grupal. Del psicoanálisis a la psicología social*. Nueva Visión.

Vinogradov, S., & Yalom, I. (1996). *Guía breve de psicoterapia de grupo*. Paidós.

Watson, P. (1982). *Guerra, Persona y Destrucción. Usos militares de la psiquiatría y la psicología*. Nueva Imagen.

Weinstein, E., Maggi, A., & Gómez, E. (1987). El desaparecimiento como forma de represión política. In E. Weinstein, E. Lira, & M. E. Rojas (Eds.), *Trauma, duelo y reparación* (pp. 151–191). FASIC/Editorial Interamericana.

Part IV
Psychological and Psychosocial Approach and Support During Forensic Examinations and Trials

Chapter 11
El Mozote Massacre: Expert Research and Challenges of Psychosocial Reparation

Sol Yáñez

Introduction: "From Madness to Hope": In Context[1]

The twelve years of armed conflict in El Salvador took over the lives and dreams of Salvadoran women and men, populating their existence with fear and mistrust. "It is almost dawn. I haven't slept yet. (…) I was thinking about the future that they are trying to abort here" (Berger, 2009, p. 89). Following John Berger's quote, it could be said that the victims have not yet been able to have a good night's sleep.

The violence, says the Truth Commission, was a merciless firestorm that advanced through the fields of El Salvador, razing villages to the ground, cutting off roads, and destroying means of communication. But its impact was even more devastating when it tore apart families, desecrated sacred sites, burned schools to the ground, and "singled out as enemies anyone not on the list of friends" (United Nations, 1993, p. 3).

Although the true scale of the tragedy represented by this war is still far from being known in its entirety, we do know there were approximately 75,000 fatalities and more than 10,000 missing persons (Cruz, 1997).

The peace negotiations concluded with the Chapultepec Accords in January 1992, one of the fruits of which was the creation of a Truth Commission. The report from that Commission was presented in New York in March 1993. It called for measures that would lead to the restoration of peace, national reconciliation, and the reunification of Salvadoran society. As the text put it, such measures were needed to "move from a universe of confrontation to one of serene assimilation, and to banish it from a future marked by a new and mutually supportive relationship of

---

[1] "From Madness to Hope" is the name of the report of fear and mistrust (UN, 1993).

S. Yáñez (✉)
Universidad Centroamericana "José Simeón Cañas" (UCA), San Salvador, El Salvador
e-mail: syanez@uca.edu.sv

coexistence and tolerance" (United Nations, 1993, p. 255). This transition would only be possible if truth were recovered, with "recognition of what happened," leading to the punishment of the perpetrators, and "the reparation due to the victims and their families" (p. 256). These recommendations were not implemented. An Amnesty Law was decreed in the name of national reconciliation. Although the Commission recommended implementation of a policy of integral reparation for an effective peace and a reconstruction of the Salvadoran social fabric, the majority of the victims have not been recognized or repaired by the State.

The massacre of El Mozote, and in surrounding cantons and villages, is considered the largest in Latin America. The "Operation Scorched Earth," as the Armed Forces called operations carried out by the Atlacatl Battalion, began in Arambala on December 10, 1981. Its devastating path continued through El Mozote, Ranchería, Jocote Amarillo, Los Toriles, La Joya, and Cerro Pando, towns belonging to the Department of Morazán, in northeastern El Salvador, where rural communities cultivated corn, made hammocks and handicrafts with mezcal and metate.[2] For 3 days soldiers burned, murdered, raped, destroyed, and razed the area, turning everything in their path into ashes. Many fled the horror by moving to other places, leaving everything behind to save their lives. The army killed 1044 people[3]; 49% were children under 12 [509]; 6% were adolescents between 13 and 17 [68]; 37% were adults between 18 and 65 [386]: 202 women and 182 men. Only 373 people survived.

The massacre of El Mozote corresponds to the characteristics of what are known as "low intensity conflicts" in which psychological warfare plays a relevant role. The Truth Commission (United Nations, 1993) noted that this massacre exemplified patterns of violence perpetrated by state agents and their collaborators. The objective was to deactivate real or supposed support for the guerrillas or to exterminate their collaborators (p. 59).

Memory and Truth

The recovery of the memory of the victims is a condition for the re-establishment of the truth, as "the first step for working through the damage suffered" (Yáñez, 2013, p. 23). The El Mozote massacre affected a large group of people, and the memory of pain is a shared memory that remains attached to the life of a particular collective for a long period of time.

The massacre constitutes an individual and collective traumatic experience that manifests itself in certain symptoms (persistent re-experiencing the event,

---

[2] Milpa: cornfield; Mezcal: Pita fiber prepared to make ropes; Metate: Grinding stone.

[3] That universe of victims was recorded by the victims' association. The sentence ordered the State of El Salvador to update the casualty's record.

avoidance of stimuli associated with the traumatic event, cognitive and emotional alterations, etc.) Additionally, it has resulted in social damage, comprised by injured interpersonal relationships, the deterioration of primary networks of protection and support (family and community) as well as moral damage.

The diagnosis of post-traumatic stress disorder [PTSD] has noted variations since its first formulations. It indicates that traumatic experiences have as a common frame of reference intentional violence (sexual violence, kidnapping, torture, terrorist attack, fighting on the war front, etc.) (APA, 2013).

Martín-Baró wrote in 1984 that "the most deleterious effect of the war on the mental health of the Salvadoran people must be sought in the undermining of social relations, which is the scaffolding on which we build ourselves as persons and as a human community" (Martín-Baró, 2003, p. 343). The traumatic experience manifests itself in the alteration of interpersonal relationships affected by mistrust, fear, and polarization, interrupting participation in community activities, altering family dynamics due to the loss of some of its members, weakening personal autonomy, and deteriorating relationships within the communities. In contexts of collective violence "a social perception of basic mistrust, helplessness, loss of autonomy, or despair is developed" (Lira & Castillo, 1991, p. 236). These consequences characterize psychosocial trauma and are "the concrete crystallization in individuals of aberrant and dehumanizing social relations such as those that prevail in situations of civil war" (Martín-Baró, 2003, p. 293), the most paradigmatic example of which is the El Mozote massacre. Its impact has been experienced and confronted in a particular way by each person, but at the same time it is a shared experience. The personal impact coexists with the deterioration of social life and moral damage, affecting interpersonal relationships, cultural and community values, community structures and organizations and their corresponding networks of protection and support.

The relevance of collective memory in a process of psychosocial reparation is appreciated in the importance of psychosocial accompaniment as a tool to support victims of human rights violations. It can constitute a space that facilitates the exchange and elaboration of traumatic experiences, the processes of recovery of self-image and self-esteem, and the reconstruction of their need for relationship and emotional ties (Yáñez, 2010, p. 51, 2013). The reconstruction of the social dimension is fundamental in mental health, considered as a "dimension of the relationships between people and groups rather than as an individual state" (Martín-Baró, 2003, p. 336).

The collective memory reconstitutes the truth of the painful reality of which the victims are carriers, to invite us to be honest concerning what is real, to let ourselves be affected by the tragedy and thus open the way to solidarity as a necessary premise of the *"principle of mercy"* (Sobrino, 2008, p. 106, italics in the original).

Methodology, Participants, Objectives, Procedure, and Instruments

Two decades after bringing the lawsuit before the Inter-American Commission on Human Rights and in view of the impossibility of reaching agreements with the government, in 2010, it was transferred to the Inter-American Court, which required a psychosocial expert assessment. The judicial expert investigation was carried out between September 2010 and January 2012, supported by the Association of Victims and community leaders, and a professional team.

Out of a total of 398 recorded victims, 311 participated in the investigation.[4] Persistent fear of reprisals prevented many from daring to testify. After the President of the Republic, in El Mozote square, apologized to the victims during commemorations of the twentieth anniversary of the Peace Accords, the number of respondents increased.

Stages of the Research

1. Construction of a methodology based on reliable data to enable visibility of the faces and voices of the victims in their accounts of the events of the massacre.
2. Learning about the experience's respondents endured, the damage they experienced, and their expectations for reparation.
3. Obtain information on the common impact and identify the possible existence of a pattern of damage caused by the massacre, considering: (a) "before" the events occurred; (b) the impact of the massacre itself; (c) the lack of truth and the effects of impunity; (d) the impact of forced displacement; and (e) expectations for the lawsuit and measures of reparation.

The case was read and studied in light of the complaints, requests, and evidence from legal representatives. Subsequently, the community was informed about the individual interviews and the group work, carrying out 311 personal and family interviews. The interview script was constructed based on several instruments, mainly the "Clinician-Administered PTSD Scale" (Blake et al., 2000) and the IPAT depression scale (Gómez et al., 2000). A pilot test was carried out to validate the methodology. The interviews were recorded and transcribed to accurately reflect the great depth of the expressions and meanings attributed to the experiences, noting the tones of voice and the pauses and silences that accompanied the testimonies. Verbal and non-verbal language was considered an indicator of the emotional state when speaking about the massacre. The transcribed interviews were entered into a

---

[4]The victims and their families voluntarily joined the judicial process before the Inter-American Court. The team requested consent from the participants; most of the victims and family members were interviewed by the author or participated in the groups she led.

database and analyzed by the method of judges, systematizing the data, and establishing the main findings.

Twelve focus groups with 12 people per group were held with victims in El Mozote, Ranchería, Los Toriles, Jocote Amarillo, La Joya, and Cerro Pando, incorporating displaced persons from San Miguel, San Francisco Gotera, Arambala, and Lourdes Colón. Two assemblies were convened in which 300 people participated and nine focus groups were held to explore the demands for collective reparation. A guide instrument was developed for the focus groups to note patterns of damage and expectations for reparation.

Results

Given the broad scope of the results, we present the following summary.

The Horror Map

Surviving a massacre puts people in a situation of extreme vulnerability. One experiences horror, helplessness, and the lack of control over one's own life or the lives of loved ones. It is an extreme situation that breaks one's very existence. In line with the name of the operation (Scorched Earth), people described how their loved ones were annihilated, their possessions, the roof that sheltered them, their cornfields, their animals, their houses, their objects, and memories: in short, everything that constitutes a reference of life and that they had struggled so hard to achieve. All this caused a deep wound that continues to undermine the core of existence itself, stemming from a horror of unimaginable dimensions.

> It was then that the Armed Forces began to stalk us. If we didn't get out, they were going to kill us for no reason. That's how they killed the people who didn't run away to the mountain. She [my mother] couldn't defend herself and they grabbed her in her house and killed her, because that's how my mother was… (*Male survivor*).

The memory of the stench of burnt flesh was similar to the accounts Holocaust survivors tell us about when bodies that had just come out of the gas chambers burned in crematoria. The black smoke enveloped the cantons, and the sound was "like corn exploding when it cooked"—when the bodies burned, are forever etched in their memory. The pile of corpses discarded like animals and the burned bones constitute a map of horror that cannot be processed. To this day it is unfathomable to these respondents that a person could do this, and it is still difficult to talk about. When they told what they saw, what they experienced, they would look off into space, become silent, and their voice would choke: "*I still carry the smell, the noise burning, as if it were yesterday. A human being cannot cope with so much horror. Unspeakable, inexplicable, unbearable,*" says one of the victims.

The unexpected and sudden way in which it happened generated a deep feeling of powerlessness and helplessness because it was impossible to protect one's relatives or even one's own life. Survivors report that the display of extreme cruelty violated the trust they had gained from the soldiers. They were acquaintances; some of them had been living in the community and the women were cooking for them. "*We thought we were safe, but we were tricked.*"

> They said, "if we don't walk around here with knives to kill them, here are ropes to hang them up and we have mescal to set them all on fire". They said, "Just cry and get ready, because you're all going to die b. And I just prayed to God. The lady was hanged … and I have not returned …" (*Woman victim*)

In their own words "*they suffered a deep wound*": their personal, family, and community life were destroyed. The acts of cruelty included extrajudicial killings, rape, use of firearms, use of knives, burning of victims, "as in a holocaust," to leave no trace or track behind. The testimonies are as explicit as they are dreadful:

> And those who were not burned were found dismembered, their limbs cut off or their heads rolled off (*Surviving man*)

They were not allowed to bury their loved ones. Their dignity and emotions were trampled. If someone picked up a body, that person was also subjected to persecution and death. People were forced to "swallow" their pain and not bury their dead. Those who dared, did so at night, with panic at their backs, leaving a sign to recognize the burial site, in the hope of returning at some time in the future to give the victim a dignified burial. There are still places where people do not dare to go because of fear. The intense moral damage is evident in several testimonies:

> A soldier told me that if I didn't have family there, I wouldn't bury them. I told him no. Only these two cipotes [boys] I have here. Look, he told me, "I had a feeling in my soul because they were stretched out face down, and they poured gasoline on them and set them on fire, after they were killed." There were a few children and women left there, and outside there was also a pile of dead men. That's why I don't go to that plain, because when I go, I get sicker than I am (*Woman survivor*)

Women, Girls, and Boys

The soldiers were especially ruthless with the women. They were beaten, tortured, and raped in front of their children or husbands. They were particularly brutal with them. Despite the bond of trust created in the interviews, the stories were especially difficult to tell. They were transmitted in hushed tones.

> Yes, I was raped twice by the military. I was raped by a guard, and I was raped by a soldier. The guard raped me the first few days they started mistreating people. I was pregnant with my oldest daughter and the soldier raped me. He stopped me, took my papers and told me, "Go over there" (*Woman, survivor*)

The attacks on motherhood were manifested in the dismemberments of the belly and breasts. The breasts were cut and severed. They beat women in their abdomen, with sticks and with the tip of a rifle, attacking the vessel of life. Ordered not to leave a seed in place, the soldiers attempted to wipe out the seed of life. The war was extended to women's bodies as a symbol of denying reproduction. It extended as well by humiliating men in their incapacity to protect their women, one of the facets of the indelible pain of the offense and moral harm. The military sought to destroy entire families and truncated numerous life projects. Some surviving women were pregnant or with infant children. They believe that anguish and fear they suffered at the time, along with hunger and thirst, may have caused the learning difficulties or disorders their children had afterwards. The massacre appeared to extend up to the present day in the effects on children.

Victims of the massacre included 509 boys and girls under 12 years of age, barbarism committed "with the idea to prevent them from growing up in a certain ideology." Remove "the water from the fish" was the objective of the operations that murdered children. In one focus group, respondents recalled that after killing children in their home, the soldiers wrote in blood on the wall: "One dead child; one less guerrilla." In this group they pointed out that the boys and girls had been waiting with joy for Christmas, toys, gifts, but instead received bullets and bombs. Ending childhood was another way of ending the community's future.

> The children were playing in the square and waiting for Christmas and toys, and what came to them was death. So many children were massacred (*Woman victim*)

> They killed my children, twenty-four relatives, and on a wall, they wrote blood, "one dead child, one less guerrilla" (*Male victim*)

The Impact on the Community

The community had celebrated its rituals, formed emotional networks, and generated a feeling of belonging by integrating those who were part of it. The massacre dissolved the community and its collective identity, leaving a tremendous social void.

Many testimonies confirm that before the massacre the community lived peacefully, in a climate of support and collaboration, with the normal vicissitudes associated with coexistence. The massacre wiped out everything. The El Mozote Plaza and the squares of the surrounding villages had been places full of life. The convents and churches were places for prayer and reflection and community life. They were turned into spaces of death and horror, cruelty, silence. The judgment of October 25, 2012, of the Inter-American Court of Human Rights, which is binding on the State, refers to the expert opinion, stating: "351. *Now, regarding the psychosocial impact and emotional consequences suffered by the victims, the expert witness Yáñez explained that the massacre dissolved the social networks where the individual and community life project was inserted.*" The judgment states: "352… *it has been verified that the damages suffered by the victims affected not only parts of their individual identity but also to the loss of their roots and community ties.*"

> How did it change? The family disintegrated, and we are no longer the same as before. Some live in Santa Ana, some in the United States, others in Honduras. We no longer know if we have that family or not. The problem is not seeing them again. (*Victim testimony*).

That void has been perceived as "dense and sad." They would like to revive the community and give it a new meaning for the young so that it "comes back to life." The massacre affected the social and symbolic fabric of the community. Houses and significant objects were destroyed, animals were stolen and killed: "they took my cows, chickens," "they took my cows; they killed two bulls." The losses were not only material but also emotional. The forms of organization, leadership, organizational structures, and cooperatives that had united them in their development projects were dismantled. Every form of organization was associated with death. The word "organization" itself was prohibited since for the government and the military it evoked the revolutionary ghost. The rationales were one of total extermination, a complete destruction of social spaces.

> For me the community was definitively broken because some had to flee, and others joined the army that was there. Some went over to one side to take refuge with their children. In other words, the community structure was affected to such an extent that it was destroyed.

Surviving Victims Focus Group Forced Displacement

The survivors had to move to save their lives: "we went left because before, they started killing the dogs and my parents said let's get out of here, it's going to get really ugly, and we've been roaming from one place to another ever since."

Situations of rupture, especially flight and the loss of all personal belongings are described in the narratives. One victim relates that she fled with her two-day-old daughter to San Miguel. To integrate into the town, she did not mention that she came from El Mozote to avoid being identified and stigmatized.

> We had to go out and we had to use garden leaves as our mattresses to sleep on. It hurts me a lot to remember. I have two children with bronchial disease, and I have suffered taking them to the hospital. I feel that it is due to that suffering. We have never returned
> (*Female victim*)

The displacement generated insecurities, fear, a feeling of helplessness and uncertainty about the future. Adaptation to the place of displacement was encumbered by the continuous longing for the place of their origins. Some wanted to return, but only found the ruins of their houses razed and reduced to ashes. An estimated 12% of the survivors moved to Honduras; 86% to San Salvador. An estimated 1% moved to Guatemala and the USA, respectively, and 2% to Nicaragua. Between 1991 and 2009 an estimated 45% returned to El Salvador.

Impunity, Justice, and the Search for the Truth

Impunity was enshrined by the Law of General Amnesty for the Consolidation of Peace (March 1993) and has never been reversed. The Special Law of Transitional Justice, Reparation and National Reconciliation (February 2020) did not change the lack of recognition and reparation of the victims or the impunity of the perpetrators.

The following testimony is clear: *"there has been no ways, no means, because the amnesty practically meant forgetting. No complaint has been filed ed anywhere. And if at some point someone came forward to inquire about a legal claim, the response was silence: it couldn't be done. They did not hear us (…) we have not been listened to by the competent institutions."* Family members have experienced frustration and despair due to the lack of response from the authorities:

> First, after they closed the case and said sorry and let's forget about it, they did not want us to speak hey said this has already been forgotten; we are not going to do anything anymore. Second, to do something like this, one needs support from institutions and someone to give them support (*Male victim*)

The testimonies build a narrative corpus that establishes that impunity has been based on the denial of the facts, on the governmental aggrandizement of the perpetrators, and on the victims' fear, all of which led to a loss of trust in the institutions. The search for and recognition of the truth of the facts is the route needed to demand justice and reparation. It does not suffice to walk this path individually; it requires participation and action and community organization to achieve this objective.

To search for the truth, hundreds of survivors went to dig up the earth to "dig" for the truth. An estimated 66% know where their loved ones were left, whereas the remaining 34% do not know where the remains of their relatives are. Most of those who know the location of their loved one's burial sites could not bury them in a dignified manner.

At the request of survivors, at some point after the massacre, exhumations were made under difficult conditions.

When asked why they sought to exhume their family members' bodies, 22% said that they did it to work through the mourning process. Another 43% stated they did so to have evidence to achieve truth and seek justice, while 33% said that they sought community cohesion, by carrying out collective burials and hoped to achieve a recognition of the facts. Most noted that fear prevented them from grieving.

> Firstly, lack of knowledge for filing a complaint; secondly, the fear that because of a complaint they will kill you and leave the family (*Male victim*)

The loss of trust in institutions affects the hope that the guilty will be tried and convicted. Trust, ultimately, is a fundamental element of the social system of which the judicial system is part.

> There was no trust and there is no guarantee. They have never done anything (*Male victim*)

> There has not been a means of reaching out to one to be able to speak. No one intervened or used any means to reach out to the victims; people are isolated from one another (*Male victim*)

The mourning has been a process on hold for lack of truth and due to the inability to bury their relatives' remains. The never-ending process impedes people from rebuilding their lives or adapting to new conditions after successive traumatization.

Life is tied to the search for the bodies, to their recognition, to the possibility of giving them a dignified burial and, finally, accepting their loss.

> (…) And the truth about us, nobody wants to hear it… our voices were not heard, they weren't heard, this… we couldn't find anyone to turn to; … Nobody, until today (*Male Victim*)

> Not knowing the truth even if it pertains s to your family, your son, gives you a feeling, and it does not let you feel good, or eat well, or sleep well (*Male victim*)

The prevailing official exculpatory story that blames the victims themselves for the massacre, coupled with decades of impunity aggravates the suffering. The distortion of the truth affects the view of reality and engenders mistrust not only of institutions, but also regarding basic beliefs about the world.

> Why go to speak alone, so they'll put you in prison? And the first thing they will tell you is to forget what happened (*Male victim*)

> Money will not bring her back to life. What I ask for is justice (*Woman victim*)

> Clarifying the facts: that would be reparation (*Male victim*)

The newly opened path to justice and reparation has been possible, thanks to the selfless collaboration of people and institutions. It is a route that must be traveled together with the group of victims, including the entire society. The testimonies agree on the need for organization, a term regarded as taboo by public officials who view organized participation as an attack against the established order.

> A single swallow does not make a summer. I go with my mother, and we will face the case, to the extent possible. I do not speak badly about the laws, but sometimes you don't sit well with the judge because he says, this guy wants to reopen something that is over and that is a sensitive matter. Now we have an opportunity to see what can be done (*Male victim*)

The Personal Impact on Health

The ruling of the Inter-American Human Rights Court (Inter American Court, 2012 paragraph 351) states: "The expert witness warned that in general they have not been able to process the pain for lack of space for social validation of their pain, due to the lack of institutional and collective support. It is a pain that is carried deep inside, privately, paralyzing many healthy dimensions, such as the capacity to give or receive affection (…). All this must be repaired at the individual and collective levels."

> Where I lived, they all died. There were eleven people and only I was left. There were seven children. I was in Honduras and when I learn ed about the massacre, something very ugly hit me. I couldn't eat, I couldn't sleep. I couldn't get over it because I didn't have anyone to tell. I heard noises, footsteps, like someone wanted to grab me from behind and that's how I lived for two years, until a man began giving me something (*Male victim*)

My life was peaceful because I had my wife, I had my children, my maguey trees. Afterwards this war broke out. An unparalleled sadness to lose my family. I was orphaned of mom, dad, wife. I am going through three orphanhood and to this day there is an emptiness in my heart that I cannot fill with anything (*Male victim*)

The Memory Narrated as Part of the Psychosocial Repair Process

For three decades the victims were abandoned, and they kept silent about the horror they had endured. The time spent listening to them enabled these people to share their pain. Sensing that their testimony had been heard and respected from solidarity and empathy created a space for psychosocial support. This was not just an individual experience. The work with the focus groups helped to collectively reconstruct the individual stories and to validate their collective experience. When the story was choking them and they could not continue speaking due to the emotion that invaded them, the solidary and support they felt made each respondent feel part of a greater process, generating a sense of belonging.

The investigation reconstructed the events and each person's memories of those events, as well as the suffering and trauma experienced, opening a process that was reparative. The facts reported by the victims allowed us to characterize the political, social, and psychosocial contexts of the massacre. We visited the scenes of the massacre and the places where the victims of forced displacement had lived, confirming the perceptions gathered in the various registries. Traumatic memory had the ability to keep details alive and retain those details in the present in an intrusive and constant way.

The desires and expectations for reparation expressed in the interviews, in the focus groups, and in the psychosocial workshops were collectively agreed upon in an assembly of 300 people.

Rebuild what has been damaged. And it is good that the State repair. Reparations first of all should be a school, a shrine, a soccer field for the children to distract them so they don't get involved in other things that aren't good for them. What I ask for the displaced persons is recognition and recognition for the victims (*Male victim*)

The investigation process contained elements of symbolic reparation. It offered the opportunity to speak to people who had never told their story or had never talked about the nightmares that still torment them. It created a setting of safe relationships, of trust, support, and emotional containment that endowed their experiences with meaning. This validation acquired a significant collective dimension in the groups when each person recognized themselves in the shared memory of the trauma.

The process that had begun as an expert legal investigation validated the possibility of speaking and sharing the experiences lived as part of coping with pain. In the processes of psychosocial care with victims of the war in El Salvador, groups have been observed to instill hope as a space for growing stronger and building trust (Yáñez, 2013, pp. 91–92).

Regarding the impact on women and girls, Leigh Binford confirms the testimonies of the victims who testified for this expert report. One testimony she recorded was the following: "…around noon, the Atlacatl troops arrived at Alfredo Márquez's house. They chose the older girls and the young women and forced them to climb the slopes of the forest hills of La Cruz and El Chingo, where they were repeatedly raped over the next twelve or eighteen hours and then murdered" (Binford, 1997, p. 43). Rufina Amaya recalls how the soldiers murdered "several hundred" children who had taken refuge in a house.

Martín-Baró affirmed that one of the consequences of the war on children was that they learned violence "as the most important response for solving the problems of existence" (Martín-Baró, 2003, p. 301). This lesson children learned, Martín-Baró said, resulted in the deterioration of social life and a callousness to the effects of violence.

Impunity aggravates the psychosocial effects of the traumatic experience: "thus, impunity is not merely a legal-political situation. It has profound psychosocial effects" (Yáñez, 2013, p. 36). In the case of El Mozote, the victims' helplessness and their fight against impunity culminated in the complaint filed before the Inter-American Court of Human Rights as well as the psychosocial expert opinion that gave rise to the investigation presented in this chapter.

Ruling of the Inter-American Human Rights Court

The Inter-American Court ruling orders the Salvadoran State to investigate the facts that generated the human rights violations and to identify, prosecute, and punish the responsible parties; and to locate, identify, and deliver to their next of kin the remains of the victims of the massacres. It also calls for measures such as a development program specifically for El Mozote and nearby places and to provide the conditions to enable displaced victims to return to their places of origin.

Regarding psychological and psychosocial care, it orders:

352. *Having verified the violations and the damages suffered by the victims, the Court considers it necessary to order rehabilitation measures in this case. In this regard, it considers that comprehensive care for the physical, mental, and psychosocial afflictions suffered by the victims in this case is the ideal reparation. In fact, the Court considers that psychosocial assistance is an essential reparative component, since it has been verified that the damages suffered by the victims refer not only to parts of their individual identity but also to the loss of their roots and community ties. Therefore, the Court considers it necessary to establish the obligation of the State to implement, within a period of one year, a program of comprehensive care and treatment of physical, mental, and psychosocial health on a permanent basis.*

The expert investigation process for comprehensive reparation with this sentence achieved its objectives and at the same time comprised a reparative process.

John Berger's words have begun to make sense: we are on the path of replacing darkness with trust, through this process of psychosocial repair. Processes are long, but they make sense when the victims speak from their dignity, spurred by their search for the truth, transforming pain into action and resistance, and keeping the flame of memory alive.

The fear of talking about the past is the fear of narration from the memory of the victims. Their stories uncover the ignominy committed and make the official version that negates it and covers it up to fall apart. This massacre was denied by the authorities for a long time, no matter how much the victims took that truth everywhere, or how much the exhumations uncovered the burned bones, women, and children. The Inter-American Court's sentence validated the victims' pain, right to justice, truth, and memory. It was the recognition of the dignity of the victims and that of their loved ones.

One of the monuments to the victims, built by their families and declared a National Monument after the sentence of the Inter-American Court, has a plaque which reads this embrace: "They have not died, they are with you, with us and with all humanity."

References

American Psychiatric Association (APA). (2013). *Diagnostic and statistical manual of mental disorders* (5th ed.). APA.

Berger, J. (2009). *De A para X. Una historia en cartas*. Alfaguara.

Binford, L. (1997). *El Mozote. Vidas y memorias*. UCA Editores.

Blake, D., Weathers, F., Nagy, L., Kaloupek, D., Klauminzer, G., Charney, D., Keane, T., & Buckley, T. (2000). *Clinician-Administered PTSD Scale (CAPS)*. National Center for PTSD.

Cruz, J. M. (1997). Los factores posibilitadores y las expresiones de la violencia en los noventa. *Estudios Centroamericanos, 588*, 977–992. http://www2.uca.edu.sv/publica/eca/588art4.html

Gómez, D., Saburido, X., Pulido, M., & Couselo, M. (2000). La adaptación española de la escala de depresión IPAT: indices de fiabilidad. *Geriátrika, 16*(8), 299–303. https://pesquisa.bvsalud.org/portal/resource/pt/ibc-9436

Inter American Court of Human Rights (2012). Case of the Massacres of El Mozote and nearby places v. El Salvador Judgement of October 25, 2012 (Merits, reparations and costs). https://www.corteidh.or.cr/docs/casos/articulos/resumen_252_ing.pdf

Lira, E., & Castillo, M.I. (1991). *Psicología de la amenaza política y del miedo*. CESOC.

Martín-Baró, I. (2003). *Poder, ideología y violencia*. Trotta.

Sobrino, J. (2008). *Fuera de los pobres no hay salvación*. UCA Editores.

UN Security Council, Annex (1993). *From Madness to Hope. The 12-year war in El Salvador: Report of the Commission on the Truth for El Salvador*. https://www.usip.org/sites/default/files/file/ElSalvador-Report.pdf

Yáñez, M. S. (2010). *Memoria histórica y Derechos Humanos: un camino de apoyo psicosocial después del conflicto armado en El Salvador.* Tesis doctoral, Universidad del País Vasco.

Yáñez, M. S. (2013). *Heridas abiertas. Atención psicosocial a víctimas de violaciones de Derechos Humanos.* Ministerio de Salud.

Chapter 12
Psychosocial Work in the Transitional Justice Framework: The Women of Sepur Zarco

Susana Navarro García and Paula María Martínez Velázquez

The Armed Conflict in Guatemala

Extreme poverty, concentration of wealth, lack of ideological tolerance, political exclusion, and ethnic discrimination were conditions that led to the Internal Armed Conflict (IAC) in Guatemala (CIIDH, 2013). As Luz Méndez and Amanda Carrera wrote, the IAC was rooted in "acute inequality in the distribution of land, wealth, and income, as well as social and political exclusion. [...] Land tenure had its correlate in the political system, which was monopolized by the landowner oligarchy through dictatorships and military governments" (Méndez & Carrera, 2014, p. 31).

The IAC lasted 36 years (1960–1996). According to the Commission for Historical Clarification (CEH), massive violations of individual and collective human rights were committed.[1] More than 200,000 were killed, and 45,000 human beings disappeared; there were more than one million internally displaced persons (CEH, 1999). The Guatemalan military was responsible for 96% of human rights violations.

Counter-insurgency policies expanded into rural areas; the indigenous population was considered an internal enemy and ally of the guerrillas (Mendía & Guzmán, 2012). 83.33% of the victims were of Mayan origin.

---

[1] The Historical Clarification Commission presented the report *Guatemala, Memory of Silence* on February 25, 1999.

S. Navarro García (✉)
Equipo de Estudios Comunitarios y Acción Psicosocial—ECAP, Ciudad de Guatemala, Guatemala
e-mail: susana.navarro@ecapguatemala.org.gt

P. M. Martínez Velázquez
Equipo Estudios Comunitarios y Acción Psicosocial—ECAP y Protection International, Huehuetenango, Guatemala
e-mail: paulamartvel@gmail.com

Sexual violence was directed against women (99%); 80% were indigenous. Most of the sexual violence took place between 1980 and 1983, coinciding with the scorched earth policy (CEH, 1999). Sexual violence was systematic in massacres and acts of selective, public, and multiple ways of political repression. The CEH established that sexual violence constituted genocide, confirmed in the sentence of the case of Ixil Genocide (Caxaj, 2016):

> The cruel acts committed against women in the armed conflict are explained in relation to the counterinsurgency objectives within a patriarchal system, making it possible that "the multiple oppressive systems, of gender, class and ethnicity, articulated in the context of the armed conflict, were manifested in women's bodies through rape" (Méndez & Carrera, 2014, p. 34).

Women of Sepur Zarco

The Sepur Zarco case includes women who come from the communities of San Marcos, La Esperanza, Poombak, and Sepur Zarco, the geographic center of the area, in the Polochic Valley, which is 460 km from Guatemala City. Its population is 220,000 inhabitants (INE, 2002), 89% of whom are indigenous Quehí and Pocomchí (INE, 2006). These communities are isolated from urban centers and state institutions. Sepur Zarco is an indigenous Q'eqchi' community located between the departments of Alta Verapaz and Izabal.

Social and political conflicts were exacerbated by the community's resistance to the dispossession of their lands by farmers and power groups. Farmers requested military control in the area when they felt threatened (Paredes, 2006). On May 29, 1978, the army committed the first major CAI massacre in Panzós, estimating 53 deaths (Impunity Watch & Alianza Rompiendo el Silencio y la Impunidad, 2017, p. 12).

Eight military posts were installed on private farms in the Polochic Valley. Each detachment had different purposes: extermination, torture, or rest of the troops. The Sepur Zarco detachment, built with local labor at gunpoint, was destined since August 1982 for the "rest of the troop." The army captured men from the community and surrounding communities, processing the legalization of their land's titles; this was enough to consider them insurgents. They were victims of forced disappearance. Their widows were deemed available and subjected to sexual violence and sexual and domestic slavery in the military detachment.

> The women of the community and other neighboring communities were raped in masse in front of their sons and daughters in their homes and even in churches or schools. Other women were raped when they searched for their husbands, others when they were kidnapped and taken to the detachment together with their husbands. Some girls were also raped (Impunity Watch & Alianza Breaking the Silence and Impunity, 2017, p. 13).

Members of the army violated these women's human rights, in some cases for months and in others up to 6 years. The women took turns cooking, cleaning, and washing military uniforms being repeatedly raped, individually and collectively. Some report that they were injected and forced to take medicine to prevent becoming pregnant. Women had to pay for the food they cooked for the soldiers and the soap used to wash their uniforms, for which they had to sell the few remaining material goods, exacerbating their poverty (Impunity Watch & Alianza Rompiendo el Silencio y la Impunidad, 2017).

Sexual violence has been a historical constant, regarded as a natural and inevitable effect of wars. Currently, sexual violence against women in armed conflict is being documented as a violation of women's human rights, and, as such, has been a focus of much of the feminist analysis. The judgments of the ad hoc tribunals of the former Yugoslavia and Rwanda classified sexual violence as a war crime and crime against humanity, linked to other crimes such as torture and genocide.[2] In 1998, the Rome Statute of the International Criminal Court was the first international legal instrument to classify acts of rape, sexual slavery, forced prostitution, forced pregnancy, forced sterilization, and any other form of sexual violence as war crimes.

> In Guatemala, sexual violence has been a crime committed against women long before the internal armed conflict. Still, the IAC exacerbated its use as a weapon of war and a tool of social control over women. Sexual violence differs from other crimes because it occurs in a space that has been considered intimate and as such not related to war crimes or crimes against humanity, which makes it difficult for many to understand that sexual violence is nonetheless used as a weapon of war, and that is, after all, a mechanism with various purposes (Impunity Watch, 2015, pp. 11-13).

The women enslaved in the Sepur Zarco detachment were peasant, illiterate, and indigenous women between 61 and 83 years old (2018), whose Q'eqchi' identity was rooted in the Polochic Valley. They are defined as widows, denoting the meaning that their husbands' disappearances and deaths had for them. As a group of Q'eqchi' women, their cohesion and their way of functioning stand out; each one makes decisions based on those they have made as a group. The search for justice by the women of Sepur Zarco publicly established that sexual violence during the IAC constituted a crime against the obligation of humanity, as stated in the court ruling. The women of Sepur Zarco were victims of human rights violations. The suffering they underwent altered their lives, their sense of themselves, and how their community regarded them.

The Psychosocial Situation of Women at the Beginning of Work

Since they experienced human rights violations in the 1980s, women of Sepur Zarco suffered sadness, fear, silence, and isolation produced by the social stigmatization imposed by the community. The rape exposed them to extreme pain and humiliation; they experienced feelings of frustration, hopelessness, and mistrust toward others. This mistrust caused women to isolate themselves (ECAP, 2009).

---

[2] The International Criminal Tribunals for the former Yugoslavia and Rwanda have as their most direct precedent the International Military Tribunals of Nuremberg and Tokyo, set up by the victorious countries of World War II to try war criminals and criminals against humanity.

Feelings of shame and guilt for the sexual violence to which they had been subjected were aggravated by social norms, beliefs, and customs regarding virginity, honor, and respect. The prevailing sexual morality considered the value of women depends on belonging to a single man. Being considered guilty of not having been faithful to their husband prevented them from playing a significant role in their community (Fulchiron et al., 2009). As a publication issued by the Equipo de Estudios Comunitarios y Acción Psicosocial (ECAP) and the Unión de Mujeres Guatemaltecas explains: "Rape turns women into transgressors of the values assigned to them. (…) Women are held responsible for having broken these sexual norms. That is why they are punished and rejected" (Fulchiron et al., 2009, p. 182).

The disappearance of their husbands broke the meaning of their existence, structured from their role as wives. In the eyes of the community, they were considered guilty of "infidelity." In their own eyes, they felt they had failed. They took refuge in silence, blocking for a long time the mourning for the loss of dead and missing relatives. "Perhaps the most painful consequence of this type of torture was that women came to question their social norms and values, their belonging and cultural identity" (ECAP, 2009, p. 12).

The events suffered left physical consequences; some were consequences of the very poor conditions in which they had lived, and others produced by sexual violence. From 2003 to 2008, ECAP and the National Union of Guatemalan Women-UNAMG, together with feminists at individual level within the framework of the "Actoras de Cambio Consortium: Women in search of justice," they articulate actions and strategies to generate psychosocial work processes of empowerment, historical memory, and access to justice. "This consortium emerged to address the invisibility of women in speeches, writings or actions to recover historical memory" (UNAMG et al., 2012, p. 13). Working together allowed the process to be designed together with women victims and women from other regions.

In March 2010, the Court of Conscience Against Sexual Violence against Women during the Internal Armed Conflict in Guatemala was held, organized by the Alliance Breaking the Silence and Impunity, made up of ECAP, Women Transforming the World—MTM, and the National Union from Guatemala. Women—UNAMG, together with La Cuerda and CONAVIGUA, enabled a symbolic political and social justice space so that women victims can break the silence about the serious violations of their rights and especially sexual violence. The court of conscience was a "symbolic justice action that opened a path, not only to break the silence but to seek effective justice that has taken more than 30 years" (Alianza Breaking the Silence and Impunity, 2013, p. 7). Based on this participation, the women of Sepur Zarco decided to seek justice through the official judicial system.

Psychosocial Work Prior to the Justice Process

ECAP began to work in the Polochic Valley in the accompaniment of families who were looking for their victims of forced disappearance, extrajudicial executions and massacres, and in some exhumations. In 2001, some women searching for their husbands in clandestine cemeteries reported experiencing sexual violence. For the first time, we heard directly from the protagonists of the sexual violence experienced during the IAC. It was the beginning of a work that would articulate a broader group of women victims of sexual violence.

ECAP understands psychosocial work as accompanying individuals, families, and communities to prevent, attend to, and confront the consequences of serious human rights violations. The processes involved promote the victims' psychological understanding of their lived experiences while receiving social and emotional support. They aim to improve the victims' well-being and, ultimately, recover a sense of themselves, strengthen their dignity, and feel energized in acting to seek truth, justice, and integral reparation. ECAP's work also considers the reconstruction and strengthening of social support networks as a central element of the personal and collective process.

ECAP worked with professional teams and mental health promoters, connecting with women of their Mayan languages, which substantially improved the work. The women articulated with other women who had experienced sexual violence. The group's objective was "to promote that woman affected by sexual violence resume their lives and their projects, without forgetting, denying or repressing the past; manage to move from the place of victim to the subject of their own history" (ECAP, 2009, p. 8). An additional benefit of working as a group was strengthening the relationship between women, creating a sorority support network among them, and drawing from each other's social and psychological strengths (Fulchiron et al., 2009).

As a result of the social stigma experienced, the women decided not to explain or share the purpose of the meetings, fearing for the reaction of the family and the community. The decision was upheld until they decided to make the human rights violations that affected them public. In 2004, the group was made up of 20 women from various communities in the Polochic Valley and in 2007 it had 56 women from 11 communities.

The formation and consolidation of the initial group were slow. It required a lot of community articulation with trusted leaders of the women, careful communication, so that they could admit that they had been victims of sexual violence, a secret that was not easy to deprivatize. It was necessary to have a lot of community presence and closeness to women and their families. This long process was the basis for the strengthening of the Sepur Zarco case.

The psychosocial work begun in 2001, the participation of the women of Sepur Zarco in the Actoras de Cambio Consortium: Women in search of justice, as well as in the Court of Conscience, was very significant previous steps in the search for criminal justice.

Initial Elements of Psychosocial Work

Trust construction was a significant factor, establishing the basis to approach each woman. It was carried out through home visits, allowing to know the family dynamics and their living conditions and to have a private and safe space to talk.

ECAP installed an office in the region to maintain the presence and institutional proximity to sustain the work. The team consisted of a psychologist and two community mental health promoters. The latter were local women, recognized leaders in their communities who had been trained by ECAP, and belonged to the ethnolinguistic group of women, which allowed them to communicate in their language, sharing meanings and cultural codes and interpretations of the events they experienced. The cultural elements that affirmed their identity were key to articulating the psychosocial work, seeking the complementarity of knowledge, and establishing a relationship of equals, working as a team.

Women presented genital somatizations and urinary problems that affected sex-genital relations, fertility problems, sexually transmitted diseases, degenerative diseases, high blood pressure, chronic pain, cancer, and diabetes (ECAP, 2009). Specialized medical care and treatment was provided throughout the process.

> "We conceived the support group not only as a therapeutic technique but as a possibility of interaction and collective construction of memory (…) that despite the differences in their histories, they share a common problem, in this case, being a female survivor of sexual violence" (ECAP, 2009, p. 22). We see "group work as a space to 're-socialize' women, value the support they receive from other women, distinguish the personal from the political, gain a sense of self-control, gain power" (Burden, pp. 31, p. 1987 cited in Batres, 1997)

The group facilitated the process of de-privatization of pain, allowing the recognition of each one, the use and value of her words in testimonies, respectful coexistence, and responsible listening, facilitating the collective verbalization of thoughts, feelings, and coping mechanisms, enhancing the solidarity between them. The socio-historical and cultural context where the human rights violations occurred was discussed, making it possible to analyze women's sufferings and experiences as "normal responses to abnormal situations." As ECAP we analyze violence against women as a social problem and not as a personal problem, verifying how the State used sexual violence as a weapon of war.

Approaches used:

1. Cultural approach. The group conformed of Q'eqchi' women required to incorporate the cultural meanings and sense that the surviving women gave to what they lived and their experiences. Experiences such as scare (loss of the soul, for them) worked with tools of culture, as well as communication with the ancestors through dreams, which guided each step of the women on the path of justice.
2. Understand and analyze how the social context and the role that women occupy in society contributed to the origin and perpetuation of problems. Starting from the "(…) evident psychological implications in the life of women, their role in society, the socialization model they face and cultural expectations, in the sense that their personality develops in a framework that defines as a devalued group" (Batres, 2009, pp. 1–2).
3. The human rights approach has been fundamental to empowering women in the knowledge and enforceability of their rights, given the serious violations of which they were victims.

The elements addressed in the group were:

- Elaboration of a psychosocial diagnosis, identifying the physical, psychological, and social consequences.
- They were widows because the army disappeared their husbands and their loss was still very present. In the first sessions, they spoke of the pain experienced by the disappearance and the uncertainty of not knowing where his remains were. They spoke of other family members they had lost and the inhumane way in which they were massacred. Every time she spoke, the group listened to her attentively, accompanied her in pain and then, whatever the wake, they expressed words of strength and support to those who could bravely verbalize their suffering.
- They delved into what they experienced during the CAI and how it has affected them so far by working on their life stories. Activities were generated to address the historical memory and the recovery of the memory of Q'eqchi' women.
- The women felt guilty and ashamed; for years they lived feeling that they had broken the social norms of fidelity to the husband and the proper conduct of a good woman. This was reviewed in group work.
- Talking about their sexuality made it easy to talk about themselves. The orientation they received in their family was investigated. They claimed that it was a topic that was not discussed that it was marked as sin or dirty. The analysis of the social vision of the body of women allowed them to understand how rape was used as a strategy to destroy them.
- Despite the years that had passed, the women feared that the events could repeat themselves. They were afraid of being raped if their story was known. They identified faith as a fundamental element and self-confidence as coping mechanism.
- Justice was a latent aspiration from the beginning of the process. They wanted justice against the men who allowed and exercised sexual violence against them. The need for justice arose to heal their wounds, to get rid of stigma and prejudices, to show society that they did not consent to rape, to shed the shame, to transfer it to the perpetrator.
- Regional meetings were held with women from different regions of Guatemala, who experienced sexual violence during the CAI. These meetings made it possible to raise awareness and dimension the strategy used by the army. The participants developed greater cohesion and strengthening, articulating to share life experiences and various coping mechanisms.
- Through art therapy they expressed and reconstructed their life stories, initiating a work to disseminate historical memory through mobile murals, in strategic places of memory; by means of sculptures, representing his personal history. Visits to educational centers and communities were organized and for 6 months they participated in the exhibition Why are we, how are we? in the Guatemala City.

The Judicial Case of the Women of Sepur Zarco

The case of the Sepur Zarco women's court has been accompanied by the Alliance Breaking the Silence and Impunity since 2010. This alliance emerged as a political initiative within the framework of women's human rights and feminist theory to seek truth, justice, and reparation for women victims of violence sexual during the IAC.

The Sepur Zarco case was developed through strategic litigation, understood as an integral process to access formal justice and involve society as a whole and the instances of the State, to generate "a social impact through the law, strengthen the institutions of the justice system, identify the strengths and weaknesses of the justice institutions, promote public debate and educate society, among others" (Sánchez, 2007, p. 11), guaranteeing justice, non-repetition, and comprehensive reparation to women Survivors of sexual violence from the CAI of Guatemala.

The organizations that have formed the Alliance Breaking the Silence and Impunity have played a fundamental role in the Sepur Zarco case. UNAMG has worked on the empowerment and public positioning of the women who were plaintiffs and worked to establish sexual violence against women by the armed forces as a significant violation of international norms of human rights. MTM is responsible for the judicial strategy and impulse, reaffirming the complaints as subjects of law. ECAP has carried out psychosocial work for the generation of capacities, leadership, and transformation, as well as the psycho-legal strengthening of the witnesses.

In 2011, the 15 Q'eqchi' women from Sepur Zarco filed a complaint about the human rights violations of which they were victims. In 2011 and 2012 exhumations were carried out in Sepur Zarco and in the Tinajas farm by the Forensic Anthropology Foundation of Guatemala, FAFG. The women were looking for their missing husbands. In 2012, the 15 women and four men witnesses presented their statements in a pre-trial testimony[3].

In June 2014, Lieutenant Colonel Esteelmer Francisco Reyes Girón and retired officer former Military Commissioner Heriberto Valdez Asij were arrested. In October 2014, the judge in the case declared the opening of the trial. The court accepted the women's 2012 advance statements, and they did not have to testify again. The oral and public hearing took place between February 1 and 26, 2016, and the two defendants were convicted. The Sepur Zarco case is the first to be presented before the domestic courts of Guatemala for crimes of international significance against women.[4] Days later, the court issued a sentence of dignified reparation with 18 measures (Sentencia Caso Sepur Zarco 2016).

---

[3] The lawsuit in the Sepur Zarco case was filed by 15 women. Doña Magdalena died of cancer shortly after giving her statement. The trial continued with 14 women. In recognition of Doña Magdalena, the 15 women are mentioned.

[4] Crimes against humanity are of universal jurisdiction and characterized by the execution of serious violations that are an attack against humanity as a whole and deeply move humanity's conscience. The Rome Statute of the International Criminal Court states in its preamble that "these grave crimes constitute a threat to the peace, security and well-being of mankind."

Esteelmer Reyes Girón was sentenced to 30 years in incommutable prison for crimes against the duties of humanity, doctrinally conceptualized in its forms of rape, sexual and domestic servitude, and humiliating and degrading treatment. For the murder of Dominga Coc and her daughters. Anita and Hermelinda Seb Coc to a sentence of 90 years of incommutable imprisonment, making a total of 120 years.[5] Heriberto Valdez Asig was sentenced to 30 years in incommutable imprisonment for crimes against [the duties of] humanity, doctrinally conceptualized in their forms of rape and humiliating and degrading treatment, as well as 210 years for the forced disappearance of seven men from the Sepur Zarco community, adding 240 years.

The plaintiffs in the judicial process have been "Women Transforming the World," "National Union of Guatemalan Women," and the "Jalok'U Collective" whose name means "transformation or change" [in Q'eqchi] formed by surviving women who are organized as a Collective in 2014.

The psychosocial strategy developed by ECAP was oriented towards a psycho-legal strategy, conceptualized as the interaction between law and mental health, "in the context of litigation of serious human rights violations (…) fosters an interdisciplinary approach to the case and the reality experienced by the victims" (Pacheco, 2009, p. 64).

> To devise such a [psycho-legal] strategy means employing the appropriate legal and psychosocial techniques to enable the victim to participate in the hearing, to make the courtroom a place for reparation and, for the trial to end with a guilty verdict that makes sense in the victim's culture (Gómez & Loarca, 2007).

Psychosocial work within a psycho-legal strategy implies considering gender justice understood as a process, assuming the meaning indicated by Anne Marie Goetz:

> "It is not just the result, but the process that counts. (…) gender justice as a process allows incorporating the agency of women, their struggles to access justice and, therefore, the struggles for full citizenship. And, on the other hand, it introduces the issue of the responsibility of those institutions created to impart justice" (Goetz cited by Meertens & Gutiérrez, 2015, pp. 21–22).

We understand that justice processes must be restorative for the victims. Reparative actions and relationships should be fostered from the victims' consciousness of being people with the possibility of agency and not dependent on the aid teams, thus enhancing their dignity, autonomy, and freedom. We understand by "agency" the ability "to build their lives and influence social processes in which they participate in interaction with other subjects" (Sautu et al., 2005, p. 44).

The psycho-legal strategy was based on the reality of Q'eqchi' women, taking into account their culture, their coping mechanisms, analyzing "unequal gender relations, the historical exclusion of indigenous women, marked by racism and discrimination, exercised by the State of Guatemala"(Impunity Watch & Alianza Breaking the Silence and Impunity, 2017, p. 28). And the human rights approach.

---

[5] Article 378 of the Guatemalan criminal code defines both war crimes and crimes against humanity as "crimes against the duties of humanity".

We worked with groups formed by:

- Fifteen women who had survived sexual violence and sexual and domestic slavery were the main witnesses in the trial.
- Four male witnesses who had accompanied the main witnesses since the initial complaint and gave pre-trial testimony in 2012.
- Twenty new male witnesses and two new female witnesses who all joined the case because of the legal investigations.
- Twenty-eight community leaders and authorities that formed a local security and support network.
- Twenty-five young people from the women's communities.
- Forty-five other women who had also been victims of sexual violence in the Polochic region, along with other women from different regions of Guatemala who composed networks of solidarity and accompaniment for the main women plaintiffs.
- Forty-one relatives of the women, mostly sons and daughters, made up their main safety and support network in the process.

During the judicial process, the expectations and the sense attributed to justice, the implications of being witnesses, were worked on, seeking to empower women as protagonists of their struggle, strengthening decision-making spaces. The judicial process reactivated in them fears, doubts, and confusion, which were worked on, as well as the cohesion of the group to sustain their search for justice.

Before and after the hearings, we worked with the 15 women and the four witnesses, delving into the meanings attributed to their participation in the process; the witnesses were psychologically prepared for the time of their testimony. Existing fears and fears were addressed, coping mechanisms and individual, family and community strengths were identified, as well as protection tools against their cultural elements. It was important for women to address the feelings that arose during the trial, as it was not easy to sit in front of the accused.

The psychosocial work started a few months before the trial with the witnesses. The spoke for the first time in more than 30 years about the events they had suffered, they spoke about their experiences of the violations of their human rights. It was the beginning of working through process, turning their testimony into a repairing element, searching for justice not only for women but also symbolically for men. They learnt breathing techniques and exercises to manage pain, fear, and distress. The witnesses analyzed the possible scenarios after giving their testimony in court: their statement would be made public; their identity would be known in the media and at the local level. Community authorities carried out strategies to support the safety of female victims, male witnesses, and their families.

Since 2012, the work with community leaders and authorities was intensified, allowing them to learn about the human rights approach, women's rights, and women's history in litigation. These community allies supported them in their quest for justice, countering rumors and attacks against them.

Since 2013, work has been done in educational settings with young women and men from the four communities linked to the women's case on historical memory subjects and identifying sexist practices in their lives Radio campaigns were carried out in the languages of the region on the prevention of violence against women. A network for the prevention of gender violence and training in human rights was created. The *Awineleb* ("Sower") network has been one of the most substantial supports for the women of the Sepur Zarco case in the community.

Before the beginning of the trial, three intergenerational meetings were held between the young men and women of the case, so that the new generations could learn about the historical memory and the women's struggle. The *Awineleb* network attended the court hearings in support of women and currently they disseminate women's stories through theater and troupes, in community spaces, commemorations in the communities, and educational settings.

Women victims of sexual violence from other regions of the country, and other women from the Polochic Valley, formed a network of support and solidarity. Meetings between all these women allowed the women in the case to dimension sexual violence during the CAI in Guatemala and how it affected other women. It was comforting for everyone to feel the solidarity and support among equals.

Since 2015, the women's relatives began to participate, making it possible for the children to know the facts and their search for justice. The identification of the effects of traumatic experiences and their transfer to the following generations has been part of the reflection, containment, and psychosocial work with the groups of sons and daughters.

The groups mentioned above continued to function after the sentence. The sentence could become a tool to prevent violence against women.

Conclusions

The fifteen indigenous women victims of sexual violence, sexual and domestic slavery in the military detachment of the Sepur Zarco community began a long journey, breaking the silence individually and collectively on the traumatic experiences of which they were victims, making visible the collective memory of the indigenous women, until they come to justice.

The violence experienced by women during the CAI, and in particular sexual violence, was not considered by the organizations that accompanied the victims. Sexual violence remained "hidden," prevailing taboo and patriarchy over the Human Rights of women.

Since 2001, the women of Sepur Zarco have been accompanied by ECAP in the working through process of their experiences, making their rights enforceable, seeking justice and de-privatizing the damage, transforming the individual experience into a shared experience. They created social spaces to address many women's traumatic experiences, naming them and breaking the silence. This de-privatization has meant that the community and society recognize that it is not by silencing the facts they ceased to exist, but that they form part of the historical memory from which we must learn so that they are not repeated.

The social support received from "others" has given them back an image of courageous women, with leadership, counteracting the guilt they had for many years.

For these women and other survivors of sexual violence, the road to justice has been a way to heal the wounds. By telling their truth before the State and society, helping to prevent and avoid violations of human rights and violence in general, that is, justice has been a tool to ensure non-repetition.

Women have transformed their pain by empowering themselves and obtaining recognition by the State for the damage done. This recognition has led to a change in the social position and perception of these and other women.

Women have actively participated in the re-signification of their experiences. The Pedagogical actions with the participants in the psycho-legal strategy contributed to this, especially the mental health promoters' work to carry out the translation of emotions from and into their mother tongue.

The families were part of the women's support and emotional security throughout the trial and at present. The articulation of the women to the community's young people of the community strengthened the demand for rights of other women victims of gender violence, allowing them to orient themselves and building routes toward speaking out and greater security.

Exposure to long hours of work listening to and supporting victims and witnesses has psychosocial risks. For that reason, taking care of those doing this is part of the psycho-legal strategy and done in self-care and supervision spaces.

Sepur Zarco's case entailed an advance in gender justice, evidencing what many Guatemalan women experienced during the CAI. The contributions of psychology have been specified in the preparation and psychosocial support, making possible the working through, identifying the repercussions in their lives, in the family, social and community environment. The identification of the resources available to women, the group, the community to face the effects of the violations experienced and to take up or rethink a life project.

References

Alianza Rompiendo el Silencio y la Impunidad. (2013). *Nuestra mirada está en la justicia. Caso Sepur Zarco*. Fondo de Población de las Naciones Unidas-UNFPA.

Batres, G. (1997). *Del ultraje a la esperanza. Tratamiento de las secuelas del incesto*. ILANUD.

Batres, G. (2009). *La Terapia Genero Sensitiva con víctimas y perpetradores de la violencia sexual: Un aporte Latinoamericano*. http://www.giocondabatres.com/modules/news/print.php?storyid=2

Caxaj, B. (2016). *Avances y retos en la respuesta de la justicia transicional para víctimas de violencia sexual durante el conflicto armado en Guatemala, del 2012 al 2016*. Tesis de Licenciatura de Sociologíaa. USAC, Guatemala.

Centro Internacional para Investigaciones de Derechos Humanos (CIIDH). (2013). *Derecho a la Verdad como medida de Justicia Transicional. Negacionismo como expresión de Impunidad. Impactos en el resarcimiento de las víctimas del Conflicto Armado Interno*. Guatemala: CIIDH.

Comisión para el Esclarecimiento Histórico (CEH). (1999). *Informe: Guatemala, Memorias del Silencio*. UNOPS.

Estudios Comunitarios y Acción Psicosocial (ECAP). (2009). *Mujeres rompiendo el silencio. Intervención psicosocial con sobrevivientes de violaciones sexuales durante el conflicto armado interno*. SERVIPRENSA.

Fulchiron, A., Paz, O., & López, A. (2009). *Tejidos que lleva el alma. Memoria de las mujeres mayas sobrevivientes de violación sexual durante el conflicto armado*. Equipo de Estudios Comunitarios y Acción Psicosocial (ECAP)/Unión Nacional de Mujeres Guatemaltecas (UNAMG).

Gómez, N., & Loarca, C. (2007). *Diversidad étnico-cultural y estrategia psicojurídica en casos de violaciones a los derechos humanos*. Instituto Interamericano de Derechos Humanos – IIDH. https://www.iidh.ed.cr/multic/WebServices/Files.ashx?fileID=5965

Impunity Watch. (2015). *¿Dónde está la justicia? El continuum de la violencia contra las mujeres*.

Impunity Watch, & Alianza Rompiendo el Silencio y la Impunidad. (2017). *Cambiando el rostro de la justicia. Las claves del litigio estratégico del caso Sepur Zarco*. Guatemala: Impunity Watch, Alianza Rompiendo el Silencio y la Impunidad.

Instituto Nacional de Estadística (INE). (2006). *Encuesta Nacional de Condiciones de Vida - ENCOVI 2006*. https://www.ine.gob.gt/estadisticasine/index.php/usuario/encovi

Instituto Nacional de Estadística (INE). (2002). XI *Censo Nacional de Población y VI de Habitación 2002*. https://www.ine.gob.gt/ine/censo-2002/

Meertens, D., & Gutiérrez, M.L. (2015). Nociones de justicia. En M.L. Gutiérrez (Ed.), *Mujeres Indígenas y Campesinas. Transicionalidad, justicia y resistencia en Colombia y Guatemala* (pp. 17–22). Editorial Pontificia Universidad Javeriana.

Méndez, L., & Carrera, A. (2014). *Mujeres Indígenas: Clamor por la justicia. Violencia sexual, conflicto armado y despojo violento de tierras*. ECAP/F&G Editores.

Mendía, I., & Guzmán, G. (Eds.). (2012). *Ni olvido, ni silencio. Tribunal de Conciencia contra la Violencia Sexual hacia mujeres indígenas durante el conflicto armado interno en Guatemala*. HEGOA.

Pacheco, G. (2009). *Metodología psicojurídica: un abordaje integral en casos de tortura. En Instituto Interamericano de Derechos Humanos. Atención integral a víctimas de tortura en procesos de litigio. Capacitaciones nacionales y subregionales*. IIDH.

Paredes, C.A. (2006). *Te llevaste mis palabras. Tomo I: Efectos psicosociales de la violencia política en comunidades del pueblo q'eqchi'*. ECAP/F&G Editores.

Sánchez, F. (Coord.). (2007). *El litigio Estratégico en México: La aplicación de los derechos humanos a nivel práctico. Experiencias de la sociedad civil*. CEJA-JSCA.

Sautu, R., Boniolo, P., Dalle, P., & Elbert, R. (2005). *Manual de Metodología*. CLACSO.

Sentencia Caso Sepur Zarco (2016). Sentencia C-01076-2012-00021. Of. 2°. Tribunal Primero de Sentencia Penal, Narcoactividad y Delitos contra el Ambiente Guatemala, 26 de febrero de 2016

Unión Nacional de Mujeres Guatemaltecas (UNAMG), Equipo de Estudios Comunitarios y Acción Psicosocial (ECAP), & Mujeres Transformando el Mundo (MTM). (2012). Rompiendo el silencio sobre la violencia sexual contra mujeres durante el conflicto armado en Guatemala. In I. Mendía, G. Guzmán, & M. Alvarado (Eds.), *Ni olvido, ni silencio. Tribunal de Conciencia contra la Violencia Sexual hacia mujeres indígenas durante el conflicto armado interno en Guatemala*. HEGOA.

Chapter 13
Contribution of the Psycho-forensic Evidence in the Inter-American Court in the Case of *Lonkos* and *Mapuche* Indigenous Leaders Versus Chile

Ruth Vargas-Forman

Introduction

This chapter refers to the case of *Lonkos* and *Mapuche* Leaders versus Chile in the Inter-American System and aims to reflect the role of psychological evidence, as well as the role of the expert psychologist in accompanying victims in litigation in the Inter-American Court in situations of violations against human rights in indigenous communities. In this case, the representatives of the leaders, CEJIL and FIDH, requested an expert opinion on "the psychosocial effects of the prosecutions and convictions for crimes considered terrorist in eight indigenous leaders, their families, as well as the alleged collective effects that the case has represented for the *Mapuche* People" (Vargas, 2017, p. 102).

This experience is framed in the field of clinical psychology and forensic psychology. Clinical-psychological knowledge can contribute to national and international litigation and is especially relevant when seeking recognition, justice, and reparation for violations of individual and collective rights of indigenous peoples. The evaluation of the effects of traumatic experiences and consequences of state violence is ascribed to the field of clinical psychology and extends to the field of forensic psychology when that clinical knowledge is articulated to contribute evidence and thus nurture the determinations that are issued from the justice systems.

For a better understanding of the litigation and the contribution of professional psychologist in the Inter-American System, the role of the Inter-American Court and the Commission of Human Rights is presented. Additionally is presented the development of the international system for the protection of indigenous rights, as well as the relationship of the State with the *Mapuche* People in Chile and the use of the Antiterrorist Law

R. Vargas-Forman (✉)
Center for Legal Defense and Research/CIDSUR, Temuco, Chile/Eugene, OR, USA
e-mail: ruth.vargasforman@options.org

© The Author(s), under exclusive license to Springer Nature Switzerland AG 2022   179
E. Lira et al. (eds.), *Human Rights Violations in Latin America*, Peace
Psychology Book Series, https://doi.org/10.1007/978-3-030-97542-5_13

to sanction indigenous lawsuits. Likewise here is presented the forensic psychosocial research process, its results and its influence on the sentence and the reparation measures in favor of the indigenous leaders as indicated in the verdict.

The Inter-American Human Rights System

The Organization of American States, in 1969, adopted the American Convention on Human Rights which is the basis of a regional system for the promotion and protection of rights and freedoms known as the Inter-American Human Rights System. To ensure observance and compliance with the Convention by the member states, the Inter-American Commission and the Inter-American Court were created. The member states recognize the contentious jurisdiction of the Court, an autonomous judicial institution whose objective is to apply and interpret the Convention, as well as recognize the quasi-judicial functions of the Commission. The Commission receives complaints regarding human rights violations by the States, examines these petitions, and adjudicates their admissibility. The Commission submits cases to the Court when there is a need to develop or clarify the jurisprudence of the Inter-American System for the Protection of Human Rights, as they are transcendent issues in light of the Convention (CIDH, 2013a, b, p. 5–6).

Human Rights and Indigenous Peoples

In the evolutionary development of human rights, the rights of indigenous peoples are among the last and have been obtained by the pressure that indigenous peoples have exercised before states and international organizations. Convention 169 of the International Labor Organization (ILO) is the first international treaty that in 1989 specified the rights of indigenous peoples as subjects of individual and collective rights. In 2007, the United Nations Declaration on the Rights of Indigenous and Tribal Peoples emerged. The Declaration recognizes the right to self-determination, autonomy in internal and local affairs, as well as the free and informed consent of these peoples before making decisions that affect them in legislative, administrative, and projects that affect their lands and territories (Aylwin et al., 2013, p. 31).

At the American level, in recent decades the Inter-American Court has established jurisprudence for the legal protection of indigenous rights in the field of civil and political rights, on the material basis of their ancestrally recognized cultures, land, territories, and natural resources (Aylwin et al., 2013). In 2016, the American Declaration on the Rights of Indigenous Peoples emerged, an instrument of the Organization of American States for the protection of these peoples on the continent.

Convention 169, the UN Declaration on Indigenous Peoples, and the American Declaration on the Rights of Indigenous Peoples are the basis from which States must regulate their relations with indigenous peoples on the continent. Despite the evolution of international and national regulations, indigenous people's rights continue to be strongly violated on the continent and the operationalization of international regulations continues to be a great challenge.

The Mapuche People in Chile

The *Mapuche* People are one of the nine original peoples in Chile and constitute 10% of the country's population, 1,745,147 (Instituto Nacional de Estadistica, 2018). Since the arrival of the Spaniards to *Wallmapu, Mapuche* territory (today Chile and Argentina), millions of hectares have been taken from the original communities. In the *Mapuche* vision, the *che,* person of the land has no meaning without the *Mapu* territory, the *Mapuche* social being is defined in relation to the land and the community (Marimán et al., 2006). According to Mella (2007), although the conflict between the State of Chile and the *Mapuche* people has historical roots, during the military dictatorship between 1973 and 1989, the denial of their rights and the transfer of indigenous lands to private companies and forestry companies intensified. Since 1990, with the return to democracy, the desire for territorial restitution and recognition of violated rights arises in the *Mapuche* People.

Chile in 2007 ratified Convention 169 and endorsed in 2009 the Declaration on the Rights of Indigenous Peoples, although in public policies there is negligence in its implementation and almost total indigenous exclusion in the spaces of political deliberation regarding rights of participation in the State, possible forms of autonomy and self-determination, definition of rights over territories and natural resources, as well as the laws that govern them. The Indigenous World Report indicates that Chile has not recognized indigenous peoples in its constitution (IWGIA, 2020, p. 372).

Antiterrorist Law and Criminalization of Demands for Indigenous Rights in Chile

Indigenous peoples on the continent face a growing criminalization of their claims regarding the search for recognition of their collective rights. Between 2001 and 2019, the State of Chile has invoked the Antiterrorist Law almost exclusively on members of the *Mapuche* People. According to Yáñez and Aylwin (2007), since the return to democracy, *Mapuche* communities have articulated actions in their search for territorial restitution, political and social rights, and not finding an expeditious way to meet their demands they have made use of social protest with occupation of farms and forest estates. Acts of vehicular fires began in 1997 in association with the opposition of hydroelectric, mining and forestry megaprojects imposed in their territories. These actions have been countered by the State of Chile applying the

National Security Law in the 1990s and since 2001 with the application of the Antiterrorist Law.

According to Mella (2014), more than one hundred *Mapuche* have been imprisoned by this law, who have carried out numerous and prolonged hunger strikes in prisons as a last resort to demand their rights before the political and judicial systems. In 2010, due to the pressure exerted by hunger strikes, the law was subjected to modifications, such modifications are not yet in accordance with international human rights standards. The persistent use of the Antiterrorist Law makes it difficult to find political solutions and continues to criminalize indigenous communities.

The abuses associated with the application of the Antiterrorist Law have been denounced by a series of international organizations, commissions, and rapporteurs of the United Nations from which a set of recommendations to the State of Chile has emerged. The United Nations Human Rights Council in its recommendations to Chile in 2014 and 2019 has requested a revision to the Antiterrorist Law because it authorizes prolonged pre-trail imprisment, allows the use of anonymous witnesses, allows convictions based on anonymous testimony, with penalties for prolonged periods in relation to similar crimes that are not treated as terrorism.

Lonkos Case and Mapuche Leaders' vs. Chile in Inter-American Court

Around a hundred *Mapuche* indigenous people have been prosecuted for crimes classified by the Chilean State as terrorism, almost all of them acquitted after long pre-trail imprisonment. The eight leaders who elevated their cases to the Inter-American Court are the first convicted by this law in Chile, all cases associated with the claims for territorial recovery.

Regarding this litigation, the Inter-American Commission between 2006 and 2007 declared admissible the complaints of irregularities in the sentences of traditional authorities of the *Mapuche* indigenous people, who were serving sentences between 5 and 10 years in prison in Chile. In 2010, case 12,576 was submitted by the Commission to the Inter-American Court. In May 2013, the Court met and received the arguments referring to racial discrimination and lack of due process in the application of the Antiterrorist Law to *Mapuche* leaders and authorities in Chile.

The parties before the Inter-American Court were: The State of Chile, accused of violations of the rights enshrined in the American Convention to the detriment of indigenous leaders; the Inter-American Commission in its role as guarantor of compliance with the American Convention on Human Rights; the Center for International Law (CEJIL); and the International Federation for Human Rights (FIDH) as legal representatives of the *Mapuche* leaders.

The crime of terrorism is one of the most ambiguous in international criminal law, and there is currently a tendency to criminalize indigenous claims as a threat to the security of national states. For this reason, the Inter-American Commission, when referring to the importance of this case, stated:

The case presents a current challenge to consider regarding the codification of the crime of terrorism, and the necessary procedures to strictly ensure that the principles of legality and due process must be closely observed by the State. (..)

The Commission has decided to submit the case to the jurisdiction of the Honorable Court, considering the need for justice for the victims and the effect on the members of the *Mapuche* Indigenous People as a group. The Commission has considered that the victims were *Lonkos* and *Werkenes,* the highest authorities of the communities in the *Mapuche* Indigenous People, their convictions under the Antiterrorist Law not only affected their rights individually, but also had a negative impact on the social structure and cultural integrity as a group (Commissioner Rose-Marie Belle Antoine, Inter-American Court Hearing Record. Case 12.576, May, 2013).

Psychosocial Effects of Prosecutions for Crimes Considered Terrorist

In litigation in the Inter-American Court, the parties created a strategy that considers the presentation of expert opinions and testimonies. The representatives of the leaders, CEJIL and FIDH, at the request of the Court, requested an expe`rt opinion on "the psychosocial effects of the prosecutions and convictions for crimes considered terrorist on eight indigenous leaders, their families, as well as the alleged collective effects that the case has represented for the *Mapuche* People" (Vargas, 2017, p. 102).

Documentation Procedure

To respond to the request of the Court and to achieve the trust required for this type of documentation with indigenous victims of human rights violations, a horizontal methodology of constant dialogue was considered that did not reproduce asymmetric relationships organized in the following phases: (a) Information and approval for documentation meetings with *Mapuche* individuals, families, and communities. (b) Individual and family interviews between 2010 and 2012. (c) Communication of the results to individuals and lawyers in October 2012. (d) Issuance of reports by each family and community presented to the Inter-American Court in January (2013). (e) Issuance in May 2013 of "Expert evidence of the psychosocial effects of the Antiterrorist Law on members of the *Mapuche* People" and accompaniment to a court hearing.

Expert Documentation Instruments

The semi-structured clinical interview was used as a tool for collecting information for a better understanding of traumatic experiences following the guidelines of the Istanbul Protocol. The Istanbul Protocol is an international forensic tool that guides the medical, psychological, and legal documentation in victims of torture, cruel, inhuman, and degrading treatment (United Nations, 2004, p. 2).

An in-depth individual clinical interview was conducted with each person in the case, one or more interviews with family members and leaders of the community to which they belong. The interviews were carried out in the communities, in the homes of the families, or in the prisons where they were held. The people and communities evaluated are speakers of *Mapudungun,* the language of the *Mapuche* people, and speak Spanish with variable levels of fluency. In each community the *Machi* and *Lonko* were visited and interviewed. The Machi is the spiritual and health authority and the Lonko is the political-spiritual authority. These visits were made in consideration of their roles as authorities and to inquire about the experiences in their communities.

The psycho-forensic reports were presented in the litigation as evidence of the impact of the circumstances that the eight families experienced. Individual reports were presented for each affected person, which included the consequences experienced by their family, as well as the impact on their community. Furthermore, an expert report was delivered to the Court in which a systematization of the psychosocial effects of the arrests and convictions for the application of the Antiterrorist Law on the eight leaders and the collective implications towards the *Mapuche* people was presented.

Effects of the Prosecutions and Convictions of Mapuche Authorities and Leaders

To facilitate the understanding of the experiences of *Mapuche* individuals and families prosecuted for crimes classified as terrorism, the ecological systemic model and the coexistence model was used (Bronfenbrenner, 2005; Vargas, 2010). Within these models, trauma is understood as a product of interpersonal violence and is considered a socio-political phenomenon and these models are appropriate to approach the psychological impact and moral damage on the petitioners, their families, and their cultural environment.

The World Health Organization has defined violence as the intentional use of physical force or power, threat against oneself or another person, another group or community, which results or may result in injury or death and psychological damage or affect development (WHO, 2002, p. 25). According to Moser and Clark (2001), State violence is understood as the use, tolerance, and threat of force by State agents or their representatives, carried out in an organized manner. Violence is perpetrated by agents such as the police, the armed forces, who have been entrusted with the protection of individuals for the establishment of order and social stability.

The Declaration of Restitution Rights for Victims of Serious Human Rights Violations in 1985 defines victim as:

The person who, individually or collectively, as a result of acts or omissions that violate international human rights norms or international humanitarian law, has suffered damages, including physical or mental injuries, emotional suffering, financial loss or substantial impairment of their fundamental rights. Members of the direct family or dependents of the direct victim may also be considered "victims", as well as persons who, by intervening to assist the victim or prevent other violations from taking place, have suffered physical harm, mental or economic (UN, 1985, p. 2).

Traumatic Events Associated with the Use of the Antiterrorist Law

The systematization of the experiences documented in the psychosocial assessments reveals that the *Mapuche* leaders have faced a series of traumatic events during and after the arrests, pre-trails imprisonment, judicial proceedings, and convictions. All these experiences with consequences on the integrity of each person, family, and with a sense of great threat to the culture to which they belong. In the eight families, the *Mapuche* identity emerges as a central element. They all agree that the impact associated with judicial procedures and the treatment of terrorists from State institutions has profoundly changed them, impacting various dimensions of their lives and of the *Mapuche* People, from the individual to the collective.

> When we started to claim our right to the land, we were considered bad. They sent militarized police as a way to kill us, as a way of making us disappear, making us die. Our fight has been without weapons, it has been one of claims and they give us jail. In prison many times we feel without support and without money to pay lawyers. Over the months they explained to me that I am involved in an illicit terrorist association and in that trial they took us to Temuco city, escorted with helicopters, handcuffed. It was a large caravan of policemen and armored vehicles with sirens. I served a sentence for a terrorist threat, an event never seen in history, we are prosecuted four times for the same cause. It is a shame what they have done and the consequences on my family and children. (*Lonko* P.P., male, 58 years old. Expert opinion. Inter-American Court, 2013).

The experiences lived by the leaders, their families and communities in the judicial system are traumatic experiences. Van der Kolk defines trauma as: "a subjective stressful event that surpasses the existing adaptive mechanisms of people" (Van der Kolk et al., 1996, p. 6) and for Herman, "events are traumatic not because they are rare, but because they exceed the internal resources that generally give us control, connection and meaning" (Herman, 1992, p. 33). Martín-Baró points out that "trauma refers to an experience or experiences that affects the person in such a way that it leaves a permanent residue on them" (Martin-Baró, 1988, p. 135). The Diagnostic Manual of Mental Illnesses defines trauma in its criterion A:

> The person, adult, adolescents, and children (older than 6 years) has been exposed to an actual or threatened death, serious injury, or sexual violence in one or more of the following ways: 1. Directly experiencing the traumatic event(s) 2. Witnessing, in person, the event(s) as it occurred to others. 3. Learning that the traumatic event(s) occurred to a close family member or close friend, the event(s) must have been violent or accidental. 4. Experiencing repeated or extreme exposure to aversive details of the traumatic(s) (e.g., first responders collecting human remains; officers repeatedly expose to details of child abuse) (APA, 2013, p. 271).

The evaluation process encountered a great impact on people and family dynamics, evidencing that, just as individual trauma depletes the resources and coping mechanisms of the person, the same happens with the family and community. When the family and *Mapuche* communities suffer this type of persistent threats over time it generates a severe impact on mental health and damages the traditional *Mapuche* social order.

> I get frustrated constantly. As women we are discriminated against and because we are indigenous, we are discriminated against twice. The *Lonko* was imprisoned for leading the community. The family has been left with a great stigma. People say we are terrorists. All the media should rectify and clarify that they, the *Lonkos* and other *Mapuche,* were imprisoned in processes that were not correct. It gives anger and helplessness because I am *Mapuche*. Carabineros (police) are supposed to guard, but for us the *Mapuche* it is the opposite. They have humiliated us, run over, beaten us. Every time a policeman appears, it scares you, it makes you insecure. In our community there is great pain, in the *Machi*, in the elderly. My mother-in-law, every time the police appear, she shivers, she loses control, sometimes she has fainted. Children sometimes cannot sleep. The Machi in our community is the one who has supported us, she tells us how our spirit is, but for many that is not valid knowledge (E.M. woman, 36 years old. Expert opinion. Inter-American Court, 2013).

The experiences described are not an individualized trauma but part of a process carried out in a historical, social, and political system of discriminatory relationships and of sustained territorial dispossession over time. A cross-cutting element in the interviewed communities refers to the mourning for the loss of territory and the painful impact of voracious exploitation in the territories for which they feel responsibility. These experiences correspond to intergenerational or historical trauma; trauma passed to the following generations that becomes cumulative, if the trauma is not addressed and resolved, it becomes more severe as it passes to the next generation (Duran, 2006, p. 16). Braveheart proposes that historical trauma includes the experiences of cumulative mourning over the massacres to which many indigenous communities have been exposed, spiritual persecution, loss of territory, forced family separations, forced displacement (Braveheart, 1995, p. 6).

The treatment of terrorists that is given by the State institutions exceeds the capacity of the people involved and of the *Mapuche* social structure to handle the circumstances that affect them. *Mapuche* families and communities must rearrange their family relationships and life projects. It is a trauma that affects the leader who has been persecuted and impacts on their role as traditional authorities, *lonko, werken,* or *machi*. It is related to the stigma of terrorist in the person, family, and community. The person suffers a lot of damage due to the violent detentions, pretrail imprisonments due to the series of trials that they must face When this happens the whole family is affected. The couple, the children, the parents all suffer this family tragedy. At the community level there is also social damage due to the militarized violence with which the State enters the communities disrupting all levels of family and community relations. The innumerable house raids, beatings, and injuries suffered by children, adults, the elderly, and even the death of young *Mapuche* people. The home, schools, ceremonial sites have been violated by state officials. In court, families try to understand the charges and the consequences of the judicial processes, as well as the barriers to access to justice, they suffer when they observe their relatives on hunger strikes and even the manipulation of evidence against them (Vargas, 2017).

Cultural Factors and Mapuche Resilience

Parallelly, when recounting the traumatic effects of the experiences, in the family narratives emerges a deep desire to preserve the *filkemongen,* harmonious coexistence, or good living among beings that share a territorial and spiritual space. The people, in their testimonies, express their commitment to modulate their own pain and their desires to preserve the *Mapuche* family, social, cultural, and ecological well-being for which they cultivate traditional cultural activities such as spiritual and health ceremonies, community crops. They go to the judicial hearings of other *Mapuches* affected by the criminalization of their political and territorial claims.

> I am interested in saying that we are not only victims in this process of land recovery and ancestral rights, what moves us is dignity and love for the *Mapuche* way of life, which is why we take responsibility for who we are. We are *Mapuche,* we are responsible for our community, for our environment. We have followed a dignified path. I have had to live in prison, in hiding and in exile. These years have allowed me to mature and appreciate our identity as *Mapuche* people, to mature the love for our family and nature. Prison is not a place for a *Mapuche.* (P.P. man, 28 years old, Expert opinion, Inter-American Court, 2013).

Individual resilience is defined as the adaptive capacity of the person to maintain mental health and to recover from adverse circumstances (Herrman et al., 2011, p. 259). Family resilience is the ability of families to manage and confront disruptive experiences, effectively reorganizing themselves and facilitating the well-being of each of their members (Walsh, 2006, p. 15). In turn, cultural resilience refers to cultural factors that contribute to reorganization in the face of traumatic experiences, distinctive elements of culture that strengthen individuals and the larger group (Denham, 2008, p. 411).

The psychosocial expert report concludes that the application of the Antiterrorist Law has impacted various dimensions of the lives of the leaders and of the *Mapuche* People, from the individual to the collective, with evidence of individual trauma, family trauma, psychosocial trauma, and intergenerational trauma. Experiences that are linked to practices of *Mapuche* cultural resilience, from the individual to the cultural, where leaders and their communities are strengthened to overcome the grievances to which they are subjected during their arrests and sentences with qualifications of terrorism by institutions of the State of Chile (Vargas, 2017, p. 194).

The Condemnation of Chile from the Inter-American Court

The verdict indicates that the State violated a series of rights and guarantees:

> The Court concluded that Chile violated the principle of legality and the right to the presumption of innocence to the detriment of the eight victims in this case for having kept in force and applied Article 1 of Law No. 18,314, which contained a legal presumption of the element subjective of the terrorist type, a fundamental element in Chilean law to distinguish the conduct of a terrorist nature from that which was not. The Court also found that reasoning that denotes stereotypes and prejudices was used in the substantiation of the convictions, which constituted a violation of the principle of equality and non-discrimination and the right to equal protection of the law (Press Release, Inter-American Court, July 29, 2014, Case 12.576, p. 2).

The Inter-American Court, when assessing the psychological evidence and determining the reparation measures, indicates in the judgment:

> This Court has verified through the statements of the victims, their families and the psychological expert opinions prepared by the psychologist Vargas-Forman, the consequences of having been declared responsible as perpetrators of crimes of a terrorist nature in violation of the Convention in different dimensions of their personal, community and family life, the effects of which extend even after they have served - most of them - the custodial sentences (Inter-American Court Judgment, May 29, 2014, Case 12.576, p. 144).

Relevance of the Judgment

The verdict makes jurisprudence by highlighting the responsibility of the States in maintaining democratic practices and respect of human rights in the classification and punishment of terrorism crimes. Likewise, the international court requires the State of Chile to adapt the antiterrorist legislation to the international human rights regulations within a period of 1 year; orders the annulment of the sentences for the improper application of the Antiterrorist law to the eight *Mapuche* leaders; and offers individual reparation measures to those involved in the litigation, their families and their communities. The ruling has provided reparations for individual and collective victims, opening spaces for legislative, political, and institutional changes in circumstances of systematic human rights abuses in the *Mapuche* People in Chile. Despite the ruling, some of the reparation measures are still pending, as well as the modifications that the Court has ordered the State to adapt the Antiterrorist Law. This law continues to be applied, police violence in the communities and the criminalization of indigenous demands persists (Vargas, 2017).

Recently, several cases have been referred to the Inter-American Commission for review. Amnesty International's Unfair Pre-Trials Report (2018) indicates that procedural disadvantages framed in the antiterrorist law and lack of due process persist. The Committee Against Torture in the Periodic Report of Chile (United Nations. Committee against Torture, 2018) expresses concern about the vagueness of the definition of terrorism crimes contained in the current law. In addition, the Committee regrets the decision of the State of Chile to consider as evidence confessions obtained under coercion and torture in trials related to this law and therefore recommends the training of judges and prosecutors so that they are able to effectively investigate complaints of torture in order to dismiss statements obtained under torture (pp. 4–5).

Conclusion

The verdict issued by the Inter-American Court in 2014 favors the victims and accounts for the influence of psychological evidence in determining the sentence, as well as in the reparation measures, as indicated in the sentence. This verdict is the first to condemn the Chilean State for the disproportionate application of the Antiterrorist law against indigenous leaders.

The psychosocial expert report was able to document, articulate, and inform the court of the consequences associated with the persecutions and convictions for crimes with the qualification of terrorism, multidimensional alterations in the dynamics and in the life projects of the person, family, and communities affected by the abuses associated with the application of this law. Individual trauma, family trauma, and psychosocial trauma are linked and deepen the historical trauma to which the members of the *Mapuche* People have been exposed by the colonial violence historically exercised by State organisms. In addition, this experience has made it possible to identify narratives of resilience from the individual to the intergenerational, associated with the use of *Mapuche* cultural continuity and protective practices with which families and communities nurture their political desires, protect the territory to which they belong, and face the multidimensional impact of state violence and barriers to access to justice.

From the perspective of forensic psychology, this experience emphasizes the contribution of psychological evidence in trials by documenting the effects of violations of individual and collective rights in members of indigenous peoples: (a) confirms the severity of said damages, (b) provides evidence to seek justice and reparation for such transgressions, (c) seeks to prevent such grievances by exposing the violations to the communities. It is hoped that such violations will not continue to be perpetrated and will not go unpunished. The documentation has been the product of constant accompaniment and dialogue with those affected, who have expressed the hopeful effect for them and their communities of the condemnation of the State of Chile, as well as disseminating their experiences as protagonists of these events in the form of a book and this chapter.

This experience encourages the use of the Istanbul Protocol and invites professional psychologists to promote sensitive and respectful documentation and accompaniment in alignment to the victims' worldview. It promotes networking between human rights organizations, indigenous authorities, and professionals, as well as with international experts for training in forensic documentation of human rights violations in order to generate specialized skills that facilitate access to justice, reparation, and guarantees of non-repetition. The documentation of the effects of human rights violations in indigenous communities requires forensic psychologists with training in clinical psychology, forensic psychology, human rights, international law of indigenous peoples, understanding of the worldview of indigenous peoples regarding their territories, social order, and culture.

References

American Psychiatric Association. (2013). *Diagnostic and statistical manual of mental disorders* (5th ed.). American Psychiatric Association.

Amnistía Internacional. (2018). *Informe Pre-juicios Injustos: Criminalización del Pueblo Mapuche a través de la Ley Antiterrorista en Chile.* Londres.

Aylwin, J., Meza Lopehandía, M., & Yañez, N. (2013). *Los pueblos indígenas y el derecho.* LOM Ediciones/Observatorio Ciudadano.

Braveheart, M. Y. H. (1995). *The return to the sacred path: Healing from historical trauma and historical unresolved grief among the Lakota.* [Doctoral dissertation]. Smith College School of Social Work.

Bronfenbrenner, U. (2005). *Making human beings human: Bioecological perspective on human development.* Sage.

Corte Interamericana de Derechos Humanos (CIDH). (2013a). *ABC de la Corte Inter-Americana de Derechos Humanos. El cómo, cuándo, dónde y por qué de la Corte Interamericana.* Retrieved from http://www1.umn.edu/humanrts/research/colombia/ABC%20Corte%20IDH.pdf

Corte Interamericana de Derechos Humanos (CIDH). (2013b, May 20 and 29). *Registro audiovisual audiencia Caso Norín Catrimán y otros dirigentes y activistas del Pueblo Indígena Mapuche vs Chile.* Retrieved from http://www.corteidh.or.cr/index.php/al-dia/galeria-multimedia

Corte Interamericana de Derechos Humanos (CIDH). (2014a, July 29). *Comunicado de Prensa. Caso sobre aplicación de Ley Antiterrorista a miembros y activistas del Pueblo Indígena Mapuche.* Retrieved from http://www.corteidh.or.cr/docs/comunicados/CP_10_14.pdf

Corte Interamericana de Derechos Humanos (CIDH). (2014b, July 29). *Sentencia caso Norín Catrimán y otros dirigentes y activistas del Pueblo Indígena Mapuche versus Chile.* Retrieved from http://www.corteidh.or.cr/docs/casos/articulos/seriec_279_esp.pdf

Denham, A. R. (2008). Rethinking historical trauma: Narratives of resilience. *Transcultural Psychiatry, 45*(3), 391–414. https://doi.org/10.1177/13634615080994673

Duran, E. (2006). *Healing the soul wound: Counseling with American Indians and other native peoples.* Teachers College, Columbia University.

Herman, J. (1992). *Trauma & recovery: The aftermath of violence from domestic abuse to political terror.* Basic Books.

Herrman, H., Stewart, D. E., Díaz-Granados, N., Berger, E. L., Jackson, B., & Yuen, T. (2011). What is resilience? *Canadian Journal of Psychiatry, 56*(5), 258–265. https://doi.org/10.1177/070667437110560050.4. PMID:21586191.

Instituto Nacional de Estadistica (2018). *Síntesis resultados Censo 2017.* Santiago de Chile: Instituto Nacional de Estadísticas.

International Work Group of Indigenous Affairs IWGIA (2018) The Indigenous World 2018. Copenhagen. Retrieved from https://www.iwgia.org/images/documents/indigenous-world/indigenous-world-2018.pdf.

Marimán, P., Caniuqueo, S., Millalen, J., & Levil, R. (2006). *Escucha, winka…! Cuatro ensayos de historia Nacional mapuche y un epílogo sobre el futuro.* LOM Ediciones.

Martin-Baró, I. (1988). La violencia política y la guerra como causas en el país del trauma psicosocial en El Salvador. *Revista de Psicología de El Salvador, 28*, 123–141. Retrieved from https://biblat.unam.mx/es/revista/revista-de-psicologia-de-el-salvador/articulo/la-violencia-politica-y-la-guerra-como-causas-del-trauma-psicosocial-en-el-salvador

Mella, E. (2007). *Los mapuche ante la justicia. La criminalización de la protesta indígena en Chile.* LOM Ediciones.

Mella, E. (2014). La aplicación del Derecho Penal Común y Antiterrorista como Respuesta a la Protesta Social de Indígena *mapuche* durante el periodo 2000-2010. *Oñati Socio-Legal Series, 4*(1), 122–138. Retrieved from http://ssrn.com/abstract=2384498

Moser, C., & Clark, F. (2001). *Victims, perpetrators or actors?: Gender, armed conflict and political violence.* Zed Books.

United Nations. Committee against Torture (2018). Concluding observations on the sixth periodic report of Chile. CAT/C/CHL/CO/6 Retrieved from https://atlas-of-torture.org/entity/guvp8l9x hzg?file=1537977316283bpbvqrm3e9o.pdf&page=1

United Nations (1985) Declarations of basic Principles of Justice for Victims of Crime and Abuse of Power. Resolution Adapted by General Assembly A/RES/40/34 Retrieved from https://www.refworld.org/cgi-bin/texis/vtx/rwmain/opendocpdf.pdf?reldoc=y&docid=528df7c24

United Nations. (2004). *Istanbul Protocol: Manual on the effective investigation and documentation of torture and other cruel, inhuman, or degrading treatment or punishment.* New York: United Nations.

Van der Kolk, B. A., Mc Farlene, A. C., & Weisaeth, L. (1996). *Traumatic stress: The effects of overwhelming experience on mind, body, and society.* The Guilford Press.

Vargas, R. (2010) Género y Experiencias Traumáticas en Víctimas de Violencia Política. Tesis Doctoral, Doctorado Psicología Clínica y Salud, Departamento de Personalidad, Diagnóstico y Tratamiento Psicológico, Facultad de Psicología, Universidad de Salamanca, Salamanca, España.

Vargas, R. (2017). *Pewmas / Sueños de Justicia. Lonkos y dirigentes mapuche vs Chile en la Corte Interamericana: Testimonios y evidencia de los efectos psicosociales de la ley Antiterrorista.* LOM Ediciones.

Walsh, F. (2006). *Strengthening family resilience* (2nd ed.). Guilford Press.

World Health Organization (WHO). (2002). *Report on violence and health.* Retrieved from http://whqlibdoc.who.int/publications/2002/9241545615_chap8_eng.pdf

Yáñez, N., & Aylwin, J. (2007). *El gobierno de Lagos, los pueblos indígenas y el nuevo trato. Las paradojas de la democracia chilena.* LOM Ediciones.

Part V
Psychosocial Reparations: Challenges of Victim's Recognition

Chapter 14
Testimony and Symbolic Reparation: *The Clinica do Testemunho* Project in Rio de Janeiro

Vera Vital-Brasil

Background

Latin America's genealogy of violence maintains the most atrocious forms of a model that installed in the fifteenth century by the European colonizers. The brutal violence of that period, which included the elimination of the local populations, pillaging, plundering, and exploitation permeated practices, subjective productions, and profoundly impacted social relations. This violence intensified in specific historical moments and provided the conditions for extremely cruel dictatorial regimes.

Every Latin American country, with variations that reflect the political and historical characteristics, has had to grapple with a violent legacy. In Brazil, there have been brief democratic periods during which social public policies and democratic practices were strengthened. Authoritarian and violent traditions, however, were imposed despite these brief moments of greater tolerance. In periods of political and economic crises, the elites implanted models that served their own interests, intensifying the use of violence against the sectors considered undesirable.

The 1964 Civil-Military Coup and Its Context

In the early 1960s, the struggles to expand citizenship rights were in full force. Nationwide social mobilization revealed a democratic aspiration in all levels of social life. Precarious working conditions were evident. The political reform movements united with the demands for better pay, working conditions, and education. Impoverishment was associated with the dependence on foreign capital that

V. Vital-Brasil (✉)
"Clinical Territories of Memory" (TeCMe), Rio de Janeiro, Brasil
e-mail: veravitalbrasil@gmail.com

extracted Brazilian's natural resources and exported its profits. President João Goulart (1961–1964) proposed foundational reform (Reformas de Base), launching a cycle of social transformation through structural changes that included tax, bank, administrative, and agrarian reform, literacy campaigns, and nationalization of foreign companies (CNV, 2014).

The world was operating within the Cold War bipolarity between the USA and the Soviet Union. The Cuban revolution in 1959 and its relationship with the Soviet government was a decisive factor in guiding US foreign policy. The US State Department started to support military coups that were motivated by anti-Communist ideas with the aim of maintaining control over Latin America. An anti-Communist discourse strongly pervaded Brazil endeavoring to undermine the struggles for better conditions. The USA played an influential role in the political crises of the 1950s and had direct involvement in orchestrating the coup of 1964 [Operation Brother Sam]. Moreover, it stationed its naval squad off the coast of São Paulo, prepared, if necessary, to smother strong opposition to the coup (Napolitano, 2014).

Conservative forces represented by important industrialists, businessmen, bankers, landowners, and other sectors interested in attracting foreign capital associated themselves with the USA and vested the Armed Forces with the mission of "saving the country" on April 1, 1964.

The Brazilian dictatorial model was characterized by its effort to maintain a façade of legality. Direct elections for governors and members of parliament continued, guaranteeing control over government institutions. Many laws and decrees were passed to pave the way for repressive mechanisms, under the guise of the National Security Doctrine. A command formed by the Army, the Navy, and the Air Force formulated and implemented the institutional actions, constitutional norms, and decrees and grant a high level of centralization to administration and politics. Such actions were intended as mechanisms to legitimize and legalize political actions. The National Security Law was passed, associating the idea of security with economic development. This law, which has persistent repercussions to this day, fomented internal struggle, provoked hatred, and enshrined the figure of the "internal enemy" that had to be persecuted and rooted out by the force of arms and torture. The National Information Service (SNI), comprised of civilians and military who reported directly to the President, was created to boost intelligence gathering services for the objective of quashing or eliminating opponents to the dictatorship (Arquidiocese De São Paulo, 1985).

With the consolidation of the state of exception, arbitrariness became the operational norm. Only two political parties, both allied with the dictatorship, were allowed to exist. Sweeping censorship was imposed and university campuses were invaded, while scientists, researchers, and teachers were fired. Police agents were present in classrooms, and wiretapping was prevalent. All such measures aimed to create a social climate of suspicion, mistrust, insecurity, and fear (CNV, 2014). Recreational venues, musical and cultural events, like those of the Black Movement were frequently monitored by the repressive system and their leaders were arrested and tortured. Some indigenous communities were massacred to ensure that the construction of highways across the country would not be obstructed. The ethnical and racial discrimination by the military regime was evident in the cruel treatment of the indigenous communities and the people of African descent (Gómez, 2018).

Repression was maintained through a complex structure of surveillance and sophisticated political propaganda within an apparent institutional normality. With the organization of the repressive apparatus to carry out selective actions aimed at specific targets, the Armed Forces unified with other repressive forces in a single integrated entity, taking on the role of a political police (CNV, 2014).

In 1964, the main targets of repression were the organized sectors, rural and urban trade unions, peasants, professional guilds, student unions, and communities from the periphery. It was estimated in 1968 that there were 50,000 political prisoners. With the passage of the Institutional Act. n.5 (AI-5), repression became harsher, annihilating the strength of the opposition. Layoffs, persecutions, imprisonment, killing and disappearances, exile, and banning sealed the fate of the regime's opponents, including those who had opted for armed struggle in the belief that the institutional avenues had been cut off.

Torture was widely practiced with the intention of breaking the organization of the regime's opponents and to produce evidence for the military justice system (Teles, 2013). Even today, torture is still a common and systematic practice employed by public agents in prisons and in public spaces, targeting the poor sectors of the Brazilian population and demonstrators (CNV, 2014).

The Dictatorship and Its Effect on Subjectivity

The Brazilian military dictatorship, one of the longest in Latin America, lasted 21 years, leaving deep marks on society as a whole—on social relations, on institutions, on subjectivity. Apart from the layoffs, the persecutions, and the violent repression within institutions and in public spaces, the dictatorship employed strategies designed to instill fear and insecurity. The culture of fear, sowed by policies of terror, silenced outcry against political repression. The effects of state violence were felt by the most diverse social sectors and have endured over time. Under the reign of silence that prevailed during dictatorship, and after the recovery of the constitutional period, the groups of relatives of those killed and disappeared and former political prisoners were the only voices of this wounded society that demanded clarification of the circumstances related to the killings and disappearances while also calling for memory, truth, and justice (CEMDP, 2007).

During the initial years of the post-dictatorship constitutional period, the insistence on closing the door on the past—based on the illusion that it would guarantee a promising future—prevailed. It was a strategic message fostered in speeches and cultural expressions, as well as the media, in efforts to maintain the silence and foster "forgetting." The official policy of denial has persisted over many years. The Brazilian Armed Forces have not publicly acknowledged their participation in the barbaric regime or their responsibility in the crimes against humanity. Nor have they neither apologized nor expressed a commitment to the democratic rule of law. Nor did they provide documentation requested by Brazil's National Truth Commission [CNV], that between 2012 and 2014, investigated the crimes of forced disappearances committed by its agents. In other words, the military obstructed the investigations carried out by entities commissioned by the presidential mandate.

The denial and the lack of accountability of perpetrators have sustained impunity and prepared the way for the trivialization of violence and torture. The disappearance of people was the paradigm of this denial of the repressive state's responsibility, as a symbolic registration of this tragic happening.

The damage caused by state terrorism spread over society as a whole and increased in scope over time. The repressive measures caused direct damage to the regime's opponents, their relatives, and their institutional membership groups. Suspicion, mistrust, insecurity, and fear strongly marked the production of subjectivity and developed into transgenerational effects (Cardoso & Mourão, 2015; Kordon & Edelman, 2007; Lira et al., 1989; Scapusio, 2006; Vital-Brasil, 2009).

Reparation

Given the impossibility of bringing back the lives of those who were killed or disappeared, of erasing the experience of torture in the bodies and minds of the prisoners, and of returning to the past to continue these interrupted life projects, symbolic reparation for this type of damage can have many different meanings. Reparation is a process of judicial, political, economic, moral, and psychological dimensions. The symbolic dimension of reparation has a unique value as it permits the construction of new areas of meaning about painful experience. Furthermore, it concerns the entire society that experienced this terror. Transitional Justice (Abrão & Torelly, 2011) to counteract the repercussions of dictatorships and wars points to the importance of reparation of the damages caused by crimes against humanity as a state commitment to society that such an event or regime will not be repeated. Even though the political expressions of the historical events highlight the brutality of war and the violations carried out by police states, this guiding principle is intended to obtain a commitment from the state to respect human rights and to reconstruct the affected social fabric.

Despite living with the persistence of a distinct order that challenges the foundation of the democratic rule of law, some progress has been made since the recovery of the democracy. The Brazilian state, however, has not committed to taking the necessary measures to address the consequences of the violence of the dictatorship on the Brazilian society. Until now those who are responsible have not been taken to court. Measures about how to treat the past have been insufficient—despite the efforts of sectors of civil society and some governmental instances—to contribute to the eradication of impunity and to create citizenship consciousness.

The Struggles for Human Rights and Democracy

The demands for the freeing of "political" prisoners and to investigate the repression used against opponents to the regime, the relatives of those who were killed and disappeared and survivors, opened the way to the reaffirmation of human rights specifically in the field of civil rights in Latin America. They also were influential in the subsequent public recognition of human rights violations and the demands for punishment of those responsible. Joining Latin American similar organizations, these movements, led by the sectors most directly affected by state terrorism, inaugurated the denunciation of grave violations committed by public state agents, the struggle to recognize human rights, and the recovery of democracy. In Brazil, as in other countries, they turned to the Inter-American Human Rights Commission and the Inter-American Human Rights, as well as the United Nations and Human Rights Watch, to report violations and to implement psychological and social support for victims.

In the late 1970s, the struggles for political aperture intensified. This produced mass social mobilization that led to the creation of the Brazilian committees for Amnesty, which rallied behind the slogan of "Broad, general and unlimited amnesty." This social movement reached the national level, with an action program for democratic freedom and massive public mobilization (Arantes, 2013). In August 1979, General Figueiredo signed law no. 6683, a partial and limited Amnesty Law, which permitted the freeing of some prisoners and the return of exiles, estimated at 10,000. Many, however, did not receive amnesty and remained in prison (CEMDP, 2007).

Known as a "self-amnesty," this law permitted the amnesty of torturers, according to an interpretation that persists until now. The sentences issued by the Inter-American Human Rights Court in the Gómez Lund and other cases [known as the Guerrilla de Araguaia, 2010] and the Herzog case [2018] ruled the Amnesty Law incompatible with the American Convention. These rulings demand that the Brazilian state investigate and bring the perpetrators to trial, as well as providing medical, psychological, and psychiatric reparation for relatives, among other provisions. The Brazilian state still has not complied. Currently another two cases—involving Eduardo Collen Leite and Luis José da Cunha—are being studied by the Inter-American Commission on Human Rights.

The first reparational measures, which were implemented quite late, concerned job placement. The Brazilian state, through Law no. 9140 [1995] recognized its responsibility in the killing and forced disappearances of political opponents. The Comissão Especial sobre Mortos e Desaparecidos (Special Commission on Deaths and Disappearances), in charge of investigating the circumstances of these deaths and disappearances, was created. The military archives, however, were off limits and the burden of finding evidence fell on the relatives, causing them further suffering.

Based on an article of the 1988 Federal Constitution, the scope of political reparation was extended through Law no. 10,559 (2002), also called the "Amnesty Law," responsible for the "Amnesty Commission" within the Justice Ministry. Despite the inadequate name, associated with the politics of forgetting, this last law concerns the right to reparation of those affected by "acts of exception" such as torture, imprisonment, exiles, arbitrary layoffs—and consequently suffered material, physical, and psychiatric damage—perpetrated by public agents between 1964 and 1988.

Initially, the Amnesty Commission focused solely on economic reparation but, beginning in 2007, it recognized the repercussions of state violence. Recognizing both the legitimacy of the right of those who opposed the dictatorship to fight against it and that the true criminal was the dictatorial state, the Amnesty Commission introduced various initiatives that brought together the construction of individual and collective memory. One was the project "Marcas da Memória," which created and produced films, exhibitions, publications, and seminars. This project also started the "Caravanas de Anistia" public hearings, which analyzed requests for political amnesty. These events took place all over the country giving voice to the witnesses and providing an opportunity for Brazilian society to find out about what had happened during the dictatorship. The government officials promoted the recognition of the violence that had been perpetrated and the damage caused.

In the hearings the ministry's president formally read out a document of apology to the victims, taking on the state's responsibility and commitment to non-repetition. This event became a ritual representing the state's acknowledgment of the violence perpetrated and the relevance of subjective consequences for the victims. The testimonials, as they were made public, aggregated value to this process of individual and collective reparation (Rousseaux & Vital Brasil, 2016).

In 2012, the Amnesty Commission of the Ministry of Justice expanded reparation measures, including the demands for clinical psychological support for victims of human rights violations. This commitment to psychological reparation can be seen through the pilot project "Clinicas do Testemunho."

From Social Movement to State Commitment: The "Clinica do Testemunho" Project in Rio de Janeiro

During the dictatorships, in the Latin American countries that suffered under state terrorism, there were groups, called upon by human rights organizations, that were concerned with the issue of the mental health of those affected, at risk or in hiding. During this process, mental health professionals recognized that the concepts of psychology, psychiatry, and psychoanalysis were inadequate to address the new clinical problems produced by violations of the dictatorial state (Lira & Aguilera, 2018; Rousseaux & Vital Brasil, 2016).

The Clinical Political Team in Rio de Janeiro presented the *Clinica do Testemunho* project to the Amnesty Commission, through the *Instituto Projetos Terapêuticos RJ*. It arose from an experience—with the Tortura Nunca Mais group in Rio de Janeiro (Grupo Tortura Nunca Mais -GTNM/RJ), founded in 1985 by resistance activists, survivors, relatives, and supporters—that involved clinical support for the political persecuted, torture victims and relatives of those killed and disappeared, and the training of mental health professionals between 1991 and 2010.

This support work opened with financial support from the United Nations Fund for Torture Victims. The GTNM/RJ team was part of the Latin American and Caribbean Network against Torture, Impunity, and other Human Rights violations. This network had been sustained by the International Rehabilitation Council for Torture Victims, [IRCT—Denmark], since its foundation, in 1999, in Montevideo. The European Commission also provided support for a collaborative research project about the Transgenerational effects of Political Repression, with similar organizations in the South Cone—Argentina, Brazil, Chile, and Uruguay—that developed clinical support projects for survivors and relatives. In 2009 a publication about this experience was distributed, explaining the transgenerational repercussions of psychological damage. The systematization of clinical work and training has been published in national and international books and articles.

The inadequacy of the theoretical and technical components in the training of psychology professionals at the national public health service and the lack of awareness about the subjective effects of state violence were evident. This prompted the team to create a training method called clinical political workshops that emerged from an investigation developed jointly with the Psychology Department of the Federal Fluminense University (UFF) (Rauter, 2011). During nearly 20 years the central work of the Group Therapy team of Tortura Nunca Mais (Equipe Clínico-Grupal Tortura Nunca Más/RJ) had been to provide clinical support and professional training. An estimated 600 people received support, and training was carried out in various regions of the country for both public and private health professionals. They also encouraged Regional Psychology Councils to debate the effects of state violence in the past and in the present.

Although the persons benefited from access and care from the civil society professionals, it did not compensate for state reparation that was still missing. When the clinical experience had consolidated and had been systematized of, the Clinical Political team turned their focus to advocacy for memory, truth, justice, and reparation as a state responsibility. In a climate more conducive to political and social demands, the professionals publicly launched the issues of reparation and testimony, until then reserved to a few academic spaces.

The favorable context for expanding the concept of human rights with the participation of state entities and social movements facilitated psychological reparation proposal. The Clinical Political team from Rio de Janeiro played a crucial role, drawing from its clinical experience, enriched by its articulation with other organizations equally interested in making psychological reparation policy visible. Aside from the reparation activities promoted by the Amnesty Commission, the installation of the National Truth Commission (CNV), that arose in response to demands of Brazilian social movements, must be highlighted. Upon creating the Truth Commission in 2012, other local, state, and sectorial commissions were also established.

The political context fostered the disposition to speak. The debate and social organization points to the determination to make headway in relation to the truth about what had happened. Psychologists encouraged by the Federal Psychological Council collected the testimonies of colleagues who had lived through the dictatorship. This led to the publication "Truth is Revolutionary: Testimonies and memories of psychologists on the Brazilian civil-military dictatorship" (*A verdade é revolucionário: testemunhos e memorias de psicologos e psicologas sobre a ditadura civil-militar brasileira*). During this process of mobilization around finding out the truth, social actors organized themselves in collectives and committees for Memory, Truth, and Justice, all over the country. These groups, made up mainly of former political prisoners, relatives, and young activists, presented proposals and accompanied the work being carried out by the commissions.

Since 2010, the Clinical Political Team had participated in international and national seminars about the state's duty to create a Truth Commission and to provide psychological reparation. The team had been involved in debates organized by mental health institutions and universities concerning the value of testimony. It was an experience that strengthened the exchange between clinical teams in Brazil and Argentina while also building the foundation for the Clinicas do Testemunho project.

Upon formally recognizing the effects that state violence has had on subjectivity, in 2012 the Amnesty Commission launched the public convocation for a pilot project, called "Clinicas do Testemunho." It is important to clarify that during its institutional mandate the Amnesty Commission received reparation requests from those who had been persecuted between 1964 and 1988, which were studied to reach a determination concerning whom would be granted political amnesty. The majority of the 77,000 requests were approved, while others are still being assessed. These people awaiting a final decision on their cases were called "amnistiandos" (in process of being granted amnesty). Therefore, those who participated in the project were "amnistiados" (those already granted amnesty), "amnistiandos" (whose cases were pending), and their relatives.

The national convocation proposed the creation of a public policy on psychological reparation. Several teams in different parts of the country took part in the selection process, which comprised three principal points called for in the public convocation: clinical support for the affected and relatives, professional training for psychologists, and the production of methodological and theoretical elements. Four projects were approved- one in Rio de Janeiro, two in São Paulo, and one in Porto Alegre, known as Psychological Support and Attention Centers (Nucleos de Apoio e Atenção Psicologica).

The public debate about these issues fostered the mobilization of the affected persons concerning this project. Survivors and their relatives had not recovered trust in the state, yet now they had the opportunity to break the silence. The Truth Commissions' investigatory work was not limited to the testimonies of public employees or to the documentation that already existed. The Truth Commissions' investigative work was not limited to the testimonies of public officials or existing documentary records; the silenced and denied voices of those who lived through the atrocities of the time collaborated, placing themselves in the spot of the testimony of their time.

Testimonials in the Clinica do Testemunho Project in Rio de Janeiro

Contemporary productions of subjectivity and the most frequently used approaches in psychology contributed to the internalization of the damaging effects because historical and collective dimensions were not considered. The Clinical Political Team, therefore, endeavored to find broader clinical strategies that could contribute to the "de-privatization" of damage and reconstruct the connections destroyed by state violence, as these effects were more evident than the effects of imposed silence and denial.

Given the complexity of the issue of state terror and violence, the Clinical Political Team used a clinical approach which had both a transdisciplinary and ethical-esthetic-political perspective. Political, social, and historical dimensions were also considered, as indispensable factors in the clinical approach. These dimensions comprise the subjectivation that predominates throughout the social territory. We are social beings made up of historical and affective imprints and we can consider memory as a dimension that goes beyond the subconscious, intersecting but not totally but does not encompassing it.

Likewise, extreme experiences are characterized by the impossibility of the psychological integration of the traumatic event, which continues to be working in the psyche of the individual in question. To give testimony about what they experienced in torture can contribute to triggering the process of elaboration, resignifying, and updating of what remained without a space in official history (Kolker, 2015; Szpacenkopf, 2015).

In the face of traumatic experience, to deal with these extreme situations that provoke pain, guilt, and isolation, the main clinical strategy was the use of group mechanisms to unlock these testimonial narratives and promote their collectivization. The recognition of those that give testimony as a valuable agent in this process was a crucial element in the clinical political strategy. The witness is a carrier of potential for constructing narratives and languages in the reconstruction of the event. With the public and collective recognition of their suffering, they can leave the passive position as victim, recover their dignity, and reorder their emotional field, neutralizing the evil that was forced on them. Their testimony, when it is heard and recognized by a state representative, makes other connections possible.

The Implementation of the Project

The group work was a wise strategy. This dynamic permitted facing the perceptions and feelings of people from different generations, as in the case of the survivors with children or grandchildren that had never spoken about this subject with their close relatives. These people lost the fear to speak about this issue supposedly taboo in their families. It permitted the forming of an affective dimension that forged trust.

Among participants of diverse social and political positions, it made the acceptance of difference possible.

To construct a public policy of psychological reparation, we agree with what Fabiana Rousseaux (2015) affirms:

> (…) to go back to opening a possible dialogue with the State within the paradoxical situation of having been the State that embodied these crimes, imparts on us– those who work in this context – a fundamental responsibility to propel and guarantee the necessary conditions to implement reparatory policies, taking special care not to give general, bureaucratic or merely palliative answers that ignore the essential underlying needs of the victims' multiple demands in relation to the State (p. 149).

In this way, the Clinical Political Team in Rio de Janeiro, made up of seven professionals (three psychologists, two psychoanalysts, a psychiatrist, and a body therapist), took on the responsibility of clinical support, training and participated in public hearings, official and civil society activities. The support of the 135 participants, that included survivors, the political persecuted, political exiles, relatives, in their situation of "amnistiados" or "amnistiandos," was carried out through various groups with the following functions: reception, construction of testimonies, therapeutic, specific issues, family therapy, and body therapy, in addition to individual psychological and psychiatric support. Of those who received support, 93 had been directly affected by repression—survivors or those persecuted—and 42 were relatives (children, grandchildren, or siblings) (Instituto Projetos Terapêuticos RJ, 2015).

The reception and welcoming groups provided an introductory moment for the participants. The therapist coordinators explained the different types of available treatment and activities, guiding the choice of the most appropriate treatment for the next stage. They gave to the groups, normally made up of eight people, information about the different approaches to reparation. Many patients only knew about the economic compensation provided by the Commission.

Through the experience of listening to testimonies new specific groups began to take shape by way of the connections and identification and the construction of bonds of trust between the participants. For example, groups were formed by those imprisoned in the Military Hospital of the Army after intense torture sessions (HCE group); others were organized by gender (the Women's group); still others reflected a generational perspective (the children and grandchildren group); and some groups were organized by profession (discharged military, the unemployed).

Participation in the groups of common experiences, through remembering things about the struggles and the suffering of each participant, made the creation of an existential effective level possible. The relations of trust, broken by the traumatic situation could, thanks to the reciprocation of affection, made possible the reordering of their own narratives.

To break the silence surrounding repressed memory, it was necessary to create clinical political strategies. These, in turn, generated innovative approaches to group treatment, making it easier to connect with other groups involved in the promotion of political memory.

The act of accompanying the testimonials in the Truth Commissions created a link with Rio's state Truth Commission (CEV-Rio). The project increased its scope by involving other actors, such as the commission members and their advisors. These people were so stunned by the testimonies that they asked the Clinical Political Team to provide a "qualified hearing" as a better way to approach the survivors who wished to give their testimonials (Losicer, 2014).

Receptivity to new mechanisms turned out to be one of the most adequate investigative strategies for a psychological reparation policy. The aim was to create activities that could contribute to the broadening of the level of transversality, to enable better communication about what had been confined to the private sphere, to foster the production of meaning, to reconstruct social fabric that had been torn by state violence. The "Public Conversations" were one of these mechanisms. Here, diverse social actors participated and contributed with their own experiences during in period: former political prisoners, relatives, human rights activists, political parties, psychologists, among others. Inspired by the name of the project, they launched their public testimonials. Rodrigo Blum (2015) emphasizes that during the experience of the "Public Conversations," "the boundaries between what is public, clinical and debate blurred and created a single territory." Words crossed different universes of experience, constructing a collective memory.

In addition to the "Public Conversations," other mechanisms for collective listening were generated to promote the integration of the different generations that had been affected by repression. People were able to understand the reasons behind their relatives' silence of about what had happened during the period of terror. In meetings to evaluate the project's impact, groups that had never been together—dismissed and persecuted military, former political prisoners, and generations of children and grandchildren—came together for the first time.

The participation of both patients and therapists in public hearings, seminars, plenaries, and heterogeneous collective activities meant that they listened to testimonials together, shifting them into the political and social arena, a common ground of citizenship rights. The creation of networks also made up the main tool of training in the pilot project of the "Clinical Political workshops" that recognized the value of the collective dimension as a strategy for managing violence. Due to its focal aspect—to examine the subjective effects of state violence—and with the "learning by doing" dynamic of the workshops—the training was directed more specifically to mental health professionals. A group methodology was employed with participation of 55 mental health professionals of public services and non-governmental organizations in 3 cities. With a focus on the aspects of clinical work to analyze the impasses and difficulties that arise in the participants' daily routine, tools of awareness, case studies, and theoretical references were used. Through the exchange of experiences, participants enriched their abilities of observation and listening to understand the complexity and singularity of everyone's experience and acknowledge those affected by repression as agents of their own processes. As a result of the extreme characteristics of torture, listening to the testimonials and the accompanying of the patients often have emotional effects on the professionals, for which the continuous exercise of analysis of these effects is recommended, recognizing the importance of self-care.

This methodology cultivated a space for meeting and exchange of knowledge and experiences that enhanced reflection, questioning, the development of critical thinking. The workshops led to the creation of networks that enabled articulation between those involved in providing the clinical support so that this type of exchange to endure.

Conclusions

The perverse impact of totalitarian regimes cannot solely be measured by the amount of blood spilt or by the number of abused and disappeared bodies. How authoritarianism has penetrated social workings, invaded thought, social practices in the society as a whole and persisted over time must also be considered. Thirty years have passed since redemocratization and the Brazilian state has not paid its debts to society, which will pay a price with the result of the last presidential elections.

In comparison with other experiences, whether it be in relation to the entities created to implement the policies, or in relation to their limited social reach, the reparation process in Brazil shows singularities. Two state entities were created to deal specifically with reparation: The Special Commission on Political Deaths and Disappearances, installed within the Secretary of Human Rights, and the Amnesty Commission within the Ministry of Justice.

The Clinicas do Testemunho's experience providing support and training, although incipient, only having a brief period of activity and directed to a specific public, endeavored to process the traumas of a dictatorial context that during decades remained embedded in bodies, due to lack of support and a qualified listening mechanism—a necessary condition for these painful experiences maintained in an individual and private space to reach other destinies. The aim was to improve awareness about and train psychology professionals on the issue of state violence—both in the past and in the present—and the possibilities available to intervene in the silence surrounding these issues.

The testimony was a fundamental agent in this process. In open debates, in public hearings, in workshops, or during clinical support, the testimony was felt through the power of his words.

During the pilot project, through the act of giving testimony, a new communication network was created, and a new social and political protagonism was constructed. The experience of being listened to and to listen mobilized expressive creation in relation to testimony. Poems, drawings, writing, photo exhibitions, theater resulted from this experience. It revealed what the brush stroke or gesture can say beyond that of the written or spoken word; underneath the esthetic force, various expressions were constructed in which the word could not reach. Furthermore, through this experience new groups were born beyond that of the clinical meetings. Acknowledging and recognizing pain through the clinical psychological support of the state mandate crossed over both groups of children and grandchildren.

This experience permitted the shifting of their contributing role as the "true" victims—having held until then an obscure place in the background as family members of those who had been affected. Through the creation of the group Children and Grandchildren for Memory, Truth, and Justice (*Grupo Filhos e Netos pela Memória, Verdade e Justiça*) and by recovering their own story as people also affected by violence, they also became protagonists in the struggle which was no longer exclusive to their parents or grandparents (Cardoso & Mourão, 2015).

The testimonials of truth and the collective construction of memory defeated the mandate of silence, opening the path to other experiences of life and to enable society to access other interpretations of what happened in the past, a priceless legacy for the new generations.

The emphasis on the strategy of constructing networks throughout the team's experience, expressed in the development of this pioneering work, unveiled an open field for innovation within relationships and within methodological constructions. In the professional networks, the exchange of experiences resulted in approaches, strategies, methodologies, the problematization of concepts that, in a horizontal way, sought to break hierarchies and experience more democratic relationships.

In the context of Rio de Janeiro's state Truth Commission, the Clinical Political Team provided support for the commission's advisors and members. In its Final Report, specifically in the chapter on Recommendations, it recognized the partnership with the Clinico Político project in Rio de Janeiro and highlighted the need for a policy on psychological reparation. This was also the case with the National Truth Commission (CEV-Rio, 2014; CNV, 2014).

In relation to the production of methodological and conceptual elements for the implementation of a psycho-social reparation policy, the team contributed by writing a Final Report that described the stages of the development of the project, including testimonials, bibliography, and a publication, "A Clinical Political perspective about symbolic reparation, the experience of the Clinicas do Testemunho in Rio de Janeiro," a compilation of articles, poems, and drawings. More than therapy in the strict sense of the word, the Clinica do Testemunho focused its analysis on what happened and its context, on memory of the past and the repercussions it has on life today.

Although the achievements were stimulating for participants, in their capacity as professionals or as patients, and for those who participated in the public conversations, questions have been raised in relation to the permanence of these positive outcomes in the current context and about the continuity of the project as a psychological reparation policy.

If during the first decade and a half of this century, the scenario in Latin America was of certain political opening and the construction of human rights public policy, the current context forecasts a turnaround, a political closure that has been carried out at an unprecedented speed, and Brazil is no exception. Since 2016 the country has experienced a sequence of abuse, with the government dismantling public policy and passing measures that harm the population and deepen social inequality. New laws dismantled public policy in health and education. Universities and professors have been attacked, censored, accused of administrative misconduct, of corruption, without evidence. Violence has worsened: the killing of rural workers, the indigenous, young black people, revolts, and massacres in prisons—where prisoners are kept in heinous conditions—are part of the daily routine in Brazil.

It is a surprising setback with which the rupture of the democratic process helped the victory of an ultra-right-wing candidate, with a military background, who justifies the dictatorship and torturers, while identifying with the policies of the former US president Trump. The collapse of the rule of law, the dismantling of public policies, the violation of the electoral process—given the volume of "fake news," instrumentalized by companies in favor of the elected candidate, the omission or support of public and repressive instances, demonstrate the attack on the democratic regime.

We cannot ignore that democracy is in crisis throughout the world, but there are singularities for each country. The roots of the current Brazilian crisis are found in the erasing of the crimes of exception and the impunity of the torturers, and the killers paid by the state that were never brought to trial.

The policies on memory, truth, justice, and reparation are privileged targets in this wave of public policy destruction. Moreover, once again the old story of the "Theory of the two devils" has reappeared in the media, to disregard the place of the victims of state violence and their contribution to the narrative about that period.

We can say, however, that these voices that were able to reach the public were responsible for reducing the margin of lies that governed during such a long period in the country, enabling society to question the arbitrariness of the past and its persistence in the present. These voices made possible the expansion of the field of truth and memory. The path to justice and its contributions are priceless in strengthening resistance today when state violence is obscenely directed at the poorest sectors of the country.

For the psychologists that put themselves at risk to design mechanisms for acting before the paradox of a State that took on reparation policies but at the same time became an agent of serious violations, in this moment of the intensification of attacks on human rights, the living experience of this work surfaces as a spark of hope in this new stage of resistance. Although in this time the paths to reparation have been blocked, the cumulative experience that did not disregard the temporal and historical implications indicates to us, in a general way, that the task of constructing an ethic of truth in the way we carry out our lives in society is essential for the strengthening of democracy, because memory sheds light on the past that illuminates the present and constructs the future.

Translated by Amy Jo Westhrop.
Edited by Maxine Lowy.
Written in 2019.

References

Abrão, P., & Torelly, M. (2011). As razões da eficácia da Lei de Anistia no Brasil e as alternativas para a verdade e a justiça em relação às graves violações de direitos humanos ocorridas durante a ditadura militar (1964-1985). In A. M. Prado, C. K. L. Batista, & I. J. Isael (Orgs.), *Direito à memória e à verdade e Justiça de Transição no Brasil: uma história inacabada! Uma República inacabada!* (pp. 189–234). CRV.

Arantes, M. A. (2013). *Tortura: testemunhos de um crime demasiado humano.* Casa do Psicólogo.

Arquidiocese De São Paulo. (1985). *Brasil Nunca Mais: um relato para a história.* Petrópolis Vozes. Retrieved from http://bnmdigital.mpf.mp.br/pt-br/

Blum, R. (2015). Conversa Clínica Pública: o público testemunho. In M. Rodrígues & I. F. Sarraf (Coord.), *Travessia do silencio, testemunho e reparação* (pp. 31–38). Instituto Projetos Terapêuticos. Retrieved from http://www.justica.gov.br/central-de-conteudo/anistia/anexos/travessia_final.pdf

Cardoso, C., & Mourão, J. (2015). Notas sobre o ato de comunicar-se. In C. Cardoso, M. Felipe, & V. Vital-Brasil (Orgs.), *Uma perspectiva clínico-política na reparação simbólica: Clínica do Testemunho do Rio de Janeiro* (pp. 111–120). Projetos Terapêuticos RJ, Comissão da Anistia, Ministério da Justiça. Retrieved from http://www.justica.gov.br/central-de-conteudo/anistia/anexos/livro-on-line-2.pdf

Comissão Especial sobre Mortos e Desaparecidos Políticos (CEMDP). (2007). *Direito à verdade e à memória: Comissão Especial sobre Mortos e Desaparecidos Políticos.* Secretaria Especial dos Direitos Humanos.

Comissão Estadual da Verdade do Rio de Janeiro (CEV-Rio). (2014). *Relatório Final.* Retrieved from http://www.cev-rio.org.br/

Comissão Nacional da Verdade (CNV). (2014). *Relatório Final da Comissão Nacional da Verdade* (Vol. 2). Retrieved from http://cnv.gov.br/index.php/outros-destaques/574-conheca-e-acesse-o-relatorio-final-da-cnv

Gómez, J. M. (2018). *Lugares de Memória: Ditadura Militar e resistências no Estado do Rio de Janeiro.* PUC-Rio.

Instituto Projetos Terapêuticos do Rio de Janeiro. (2015). *Relatório Final. Ministério da Justiça, Comissão de Anistia.* Instituto Projetos Terapêuticos. Retrieved from http://www.justica.gov.br/central-de-conteudo/anistia/anexos/relatorio-final-projetos-terapeuticos-do-rio-de-janeiro-com-anexos.pdf

Kolker, T. (2015). Notas sobre o papel do testemunho e do dispositivo clínico-político no processo de reparação dos afetados pela violência de Estado. In C. Cardoso, M. Felippe, & V. Vital Brasil (Orgs.), *Uma perspectiva clínico-política na reparação simbólica: Clínica do Testemunho do Rio de Janeiro* (pp. 57–74). Ministério da Justiça, Comissão de Anistia, Instituto Projetos Terapêuticos. Retrieved from http://www.justica.gov.br/central-de-conteudo/anistia/anexos/livro-on-line-2.pdf

Kordon, D., & Edelman, L. (2007). *Porvenires de la Memoria. Efectos psicológicos multigeneracionales de la represión de la dictadura: hijos de desaparecidos.* Abuelas de Plaza de Mayo.

Lira, E., & Aguilera. C. (2018). Incluir la Salud Mental en la agenda de los Derechos Humanos. In P. Colombo & C. Salamanca (Coord.), Dossier Regímenes autoritarios, nuevas geografías y espacios de vida en América Latina. *Clepsidra. Revista Interdisciplinaria de Estudios sobre Memoria, 5*(9), 104–121. Retrieved from http://ppct.caicyt.gov.ar/index.php/clepsidra/article/view/LIRA/10968

Lira, E., Becker, D., & Castillo, M. I. (1989). Psicoterapia de víctimas de represión política bajo dictadura: Un desafío terapéutico, teórico y político. In D. Becker & E. Lira (Eds.), *Derechos Humanos: Todo es según el dolor con que se mira* (pp. 29–69). Ediciones Instituto Latinoamericano de Salud Mental y Derechos Humanos.

Losicer, E. (2014). Testemunho e Verdade: Projeto Clínicas do Testemunho do Rio de Janeiro e a interação com a Comissão Estadual da Verdade. In *Clínicas do Testemunho: Reparação Psíquica e construção de Memórias* (pp. 183–188). Sigmund Freud Associação Psicanalítica.

Napolitano, M. (2014). *1964 História do regime militar brasileiro.* Contexto..

Rauter, C. (2011). Percepções da Violência nas Práticas dos Profissionais de Saúde: Famílias Desestruturadas, Tiroteios e Outras Estórias. *Passagens: Revista Internacional de História Política e Cultura Jurídica, 3*(1), 99–116. Retrieved from http://www.historia.uff.br/revista-passagens/artigos/v3n1a52011.pdf

Rousseaux, F. (2015). Vicisitudes de la reconstrucción del lazo entre el Estado y las víctimas del terror de Estado. Gestionar el dolor. In O. Delgado (Comp.), *Consecuencias subjetivas del terrorismo de Estado* (p. 149). Grama Ediciones.

Rousseaux, F., & Vital Brasil, V. (2016). *Reparación simbólica en América Latina como Política de Estado. Simposio Internacional Científico IRCT 10: Cumpliendo la promesa del derecho a la rehabilitación.* México. Retrieved from http://www.microsofttranslator.com/bv.aspx?from=en&to=pt&a=http%3A%2F%2Fwww.events.irct.org%2Farchive%2Fevent%2Fsubtopic%2F193

Scapusio, M. (2006). Transgeneracionalidad del daño y memoria. *Revista Reflexión Derechos Humanos y Salud Mental, 32,* 15–19.

Szpacenkopf, M. I. (2015). Trauma e suas vicissitudes: a reinvenção da sobrevivência. In *Trauma e suas vicissitudes* (pp. 141–162). Cadernos de Psicanálise. Sociedade de Psicanalise da Cidade do Rio de Janeiro.

Teles, J. (2013). Apresentação: Ditadura e repressão no Brasil e na Argentina: paralelos e distinções. In P. Calveiro (Ed.), *Poder e desaparecimento: os campos de concentração na Argentina* (pp. 7–18). Boitempo.

Vital-Brasil, V. (2009). Efectos transgeneracionales del terrorismo de Estado: entre el silencio y la memoria. In B. Brinkman, M. Lagos, V. Vital Brasil, & M. Scapusio Daño (Orgs.), *Transgeneracional: consecuencias de la represión política en el cono sur* (pp. 289–327). Cintras/Eatip/GTNM-RJ/Sersoc. Retrieved from http://www.cintras.org/textos/libros/libro-danotrans.pdf

Chapter 15
The Clinics of Testimony: New Ways of Recognition Through Group Listening to Military Personnel

Alexei Conte Indursky, Ângela Flores Becker, Bárbara de Souza Conte, Carlos Augusto Piccinini, Karine Szuchman, and Lísia da Luz Refosco

Introduction: Description of the Civic-Military Dictatorship and Transitional Justice in Brazil

Although the Brazilian civic-military dictatorship ended in 1985 when the military left the government, it continues to produce psychic, social, and political effects in our society.

Beyond the suffering caused by 21 years of civil-military regime, the more than three decades of struggle for the recognition and legitimization of what was suffered by those affected has marked this process. The State's late recognition of the violence that its agents produced (which only happened in 1995 with the creation of the Special Commission on Political Death and Disappearances), as well as the Armed Forces' perverse denial (denying access to archives, refusal to recognize the violations committed and still honoring State agent perpetrators), makes it difficult for civil society to debate the importance and complexity of this process of elaboration of the democratic transition. The growing expressions calling for the return of the dictatorship are a sign of the dispute over the memory of that period, making this a relevant and current matter. To better explain the policy of psychic reparation that we will discuss here, a brief synopsis of the Transitional Justice agendas in Brazil is essential.

A. Conte Indursky (✉) · C. A. Piccinini
Psychoanalytic Association of Porto Alegre (APPOA), Porto Alegre, Brasil
e-mail: alexei.indursky@gmail.com; piccguto@gmail.com

Â. Flores Becker · B. de Souza Conte · L. da Luz Refosco
Sigmund Freud Psychoanalytic Association - SIG (POA/RS), Porto Alegre, Brasil
e-mail: afbecker5044@gmail.com; bdesouzaconte@gmail.com; lisiarefosco@gmail.com

K. Szuchman
Federal University of Rio Grande do Sul, Porto Alegre, Brasil
e-mail: karineszuchman@gmail.com

Transitional Justice in Brazil can be thought of under two different periods. The first (1969–1995) is characterized by the ideology of the "turned page," meaning the attempt to use forgiving and forgetting as social grammars for reconciling society. The second period (1995–2017) is marked by an emphasis on and reclaiming of memory, truth, and symbolic and psychic reparation. Let us analyze these two periods.

The first period, that of political amnesty in Brazil (law 6.683/79), was characterized by an ambivalent meaning. On the one hand, it arose in response to a movement of vindication of civil society and relatives of prisoners, the dead and the disappeared for truth, memory, and justice, whose mobilization decisively affected the process of democratic transition in the late 1980s.[1]

On the other hand, the appropriation of the proposed agenda (Broad, General and Unrestricted Amnesty, Indursky, 2014) by a "bionic" Senate (composed of senators elected indirectly, who passed law in favor of dictatorial power) produced a semantic effect of forgiving "both sides of the conflict," rationalized as "related crimes" that link the actions carried out by the State agents to political crimes, without even classifying or describing their nature (this logic was also used in Argentina, with the theory of the "two demons," in which dictatorial violence was justified by the allegation of the communist threat). That is, the Brazilian State forgave the crimes against humanity that were committed without identifying their agents and the violations committed. Because the Armed Forces' archives were never opened, a kind of recognition without subject or memory occurred in Brazil. Further, with respect to the amnesty application process, the costs of proving the alleged violence fell to the victims of these crimes.

Drawing from the clinical writings of Sandor Ferenczi (1974), the trauma does not reside exclusively in the act of violence that the subject experiences, but also in the denial inflicted by the adult world and by a social setting that does not recognize the extreme experience as such. The psychic effects of the denial have a direct impact on the level of the subject's Ego, since the episode does not effectively cease to exist; instead, its presence leads to a kind of psychic enclave.

Transferring the Ferenczian hypotheses to our field, we endeavor to read the position of the Brazilian State in this first period from the perspective of the denial. When amnesty is granted without identifying or holding agents and their crimes responsible, the State operates in the social sphere with the same effects of denial revealed in clinical psychoanalytic practice, renewing the suffering experienced through the disavowal of its social recognition.

Borrowing from the famous phrase coined by Octave Mannoni (1979) to describe the operation that structures this perversion (*I know, but still...*), we can read the position of the Brazilian State in 1979 as one in which there was not a real ("hard") dictatorship in Brazil, but rather a *soft* dictatorship (*I know* there was a dictatorship, *but* it was a soft dictatorship).[2]

---

[1] In June 1979, the first body of a politically disappeared person was found: Eurico Lisboa was found by his wife, Suzana Lisboa, in a mass grave in the Perus Cemetery, in the city of São Paulo, among the remains of 1000 homeless people.

[2] Translator's note: The Spanish word "dicta*dura*" ("dictatorship" in English) contains the word "dura" ("hard") in it, which allows for a play between a "soft" and "hard" dictatorship in Spanish

In other words, the recognition of the existence of violations does not result in the accountability of its agents, but rather in a kind of mitigation that justifies and forgives the "excesses," thus denying the violations and their responsibility.

A second period begins to emphasize this semantic outlook, starting with the creation of the Special Commission on Political Deaths and Disappearances (CEMDP) in 1995. It was the first time that the State recognized the existence of citizens who were extrajudicially killed and disappeared for political reasons. The CEMDP coordinates the process of recognition and analysis of requests for financial reparation to family members. In 2007, it published a report that confirmed approximately 400 deaths and disappearances due to the dictatorship (CEMDP, 2007).

In 2002, the Amnesty Commission was created (Law 10.559), which broadened the previous commission's scope of action in terms of the possibilities of financial reparation and analysis of excesses committed by the State. In contrast, the 1979 Amnesty Law did not provide for financial reparation, and the CEMDP was able to develop this possibility throughout its activities with the families of the dead and disappeared. It became the responsibility of the Amnesty Commission to recognize the acts of exception that were carried out between 1946 and 1988, such as torture, imprisonment, exiles, arbitrary job dismissals, appeals, among others, and, in addition, to qualifying the condition of political amnesty for those affected by those acts. It should be noted that the amnesty process is not a legal process, but rather an administrative process of recognition. Nevertheless, in the procedures that this commission stipulates, the burden of proof falls on the amnesty applicant. Thus, the individual who suffered State violence is in the paradoxical position of being judged by the State that violated his/her rights. Moreover, to be recognized, the person must prove their status as a victim. The effects of this form of symptomatic recognition were expressed (1) in the *silencing* of the many affected who refused to request recognition from the State and (2) in the *individualization* of the damage suffered.

In 2007, the Amnesty Caravans and the Marks of Memory project were created.[3] These policies presented new tensions between recognition and redistribution (Abrão & Torelly, 2011, pp. 51–55). Through these projects, the dimensions of memory and the symbolic recognition of those affected are officially carried out by the Brazilian State.

In 2011, the National Truth Commission (CNV, Comissão Nacional da Verdade) and the law on access and transparency to public archives were created, through Law 12.528 and Law 12.527, respectively. The dimension of the right to the truth is thus contemplated through an official report of the Brazilian State on the crimes committed during the Brazilian civic-military dictatorships. The CNV report was published in 2015 and contains 29 recommendations, such as maintaining the policy of psychic reparation for those affected.

Linking it to the trauma resulting from the repressive actions of State terrorism, we observe that the impunity of the regime's agents and the long wait for reparation

---

that is not possible in the English language.

[3] See the documentary "Eu me lembro" (2012), which narrates the work of the Amnesty Caravans.

policies beyond monetary provisions contributed to a second period of trauma. Viewing this in terms of denial, we emphasize the link that articulates the function of testimony with the conditions of society for receiving the testimony, recognizing the suffering of people, and enabling a social elaboration of this recent period of Brazilian history. With this objective, the Clinics of Testimony project, created by the Amnesty Commission, seeks to open spaces for listening that recognize the experiences of suffering that were affected by the dictatorship.

Clinics of Testimony

Testimony as a Clinical-Political Tool

Clinics of Testimony is the first Brazilian project to promote psychic reparation for people directly affected by state violence between 1964 and 1985, in the four states of Rio de Janeiro, São Paulo, Santa Catarina, and Rio Grande do Sul. In this way, when starting the pilot project (2013–2015), we were faced with the question of how this would be received by the affected subjects and their families in the Clinics of Testimony. The State's recognition of the violations committed, whether through amnesty or mechanisms of memory and repair, is a sine qua non condition for the urgent establishment of this clinic (Indursky & Piccinini, 2015). However, in the project's meeting with the people affected by the dictatorship and the democratic transition, the same question was posed insistently: why speak now?

Before answering this question, it is necessary to understand the reasons for the question. As we have previously explained, the subject affected by terror oscillates between the urge to talk about everything and the need to forget about the extraordinary event, as if silence could hold the promise of an appeasement of suffering (Indursky & Piccinini, 2015). The subject inhabits and is inhabited by the unspeakable nature of this experience and by the need to recreate an alternative instance that helps them to leave behind the horror experienced and to open images in search of symbolization (Fedida, 2000). A testimonial process can only begin when the subject, with all the risks that reliving the anguish and sustaining the unspeakable imply, makes the difficult decision to participate in such an intense experience, recognizing that the issue has not dissipated and that it continues to produce effects in the person's life.

Only by working through on a different setting will the person be able to traverse this distance. If traditional psychoanalysis holds that this other setting is utopian, for survivors of extreme violations it is a space that seems entrapped by arbitrary violence. The anguished dreams of many survivors attest to the horror of being captured by totalitarian logic. As such, at all times we face the risks that the power of the word can be captured and lose its symbolic value and its destiny. On this point, we propose to consider the *social conditions for receiving testimony* as a task of rebuilding the victim's willingness to give a testimony.

The Clinics of Testimony's acute sensitivity regarding this issue led it to create "intermediary forms" (Kaës, 1989) between the captured intimacy of the subject and the public spaces of debate, seeking to establish transferential bonds of trust and place. In this way, a type of inflection is made in the relationship between supply and demand: the Clinics of Testimony presume the existence of a demand where there was silence, suspicion, anger, the rejection of subjects that the State had never heard, or the cases of "famous political activists" who never stopped talking. In response to this, we proposed *Public Conversations, Welcoming Groups,* and *Testimony Groups* in which, gradually, the interested subjects began to discuss the proposal and the meaning of the project.

Testimony Group with Military Personnel

One of the demands established for the Clinics of Testimony project in 2015 came in response to a group of military personnel from the three branches of the Armed Forces that, at the time, were giving their testimonies to the National Truth Commission (CNV), seeking approval for their amnesty requests. The Clinics of Testimony, in turn, worked with methodologies and objectives other than those of the CNV, to offer a different listening space, without having to focus on verification of the facts. This opened the possibility for this military public to form a testimony group within the project.

The testimonies of these soldiers in the CNV showed, among other issues, the absence of medical care, the practice of intimidation and silencing of the persecuted soldiers, the impossibility of insertion in the job market, arbitrary prisons, and torture. These soldiers comprise a group, mainly made up of non-commissioned officers, corporals, sergeants, and soldiers, people of low-income backgrounds, who saw in the Armed Forces an opportunity for training and social advancement. These are subjects who had placed the hope of realizing their personal and professional dreams through a military career. (The accounts refer largely to the period of 1974–1978.) The CNV report states, in the chapter entitled Persecuted Military Personnel, that.

> the social group that was fought with the greatest resentment and intolerance by the military elite that seized power in 1964 was the military itself. Approximately 6500 members of the Army, Navy, Air Force and Police Forces were persecuted with extreme violence during the dictatorship. This number includes members of the three branches of the Armed Forces who were targeted for different violations of their human rights for various reasons, as reported throughout this chapter. Military of all ranks were persecuted, but the violence was greater with the lowest military ranks. (CNV, 2014, p. 13).

The group referred to in the CNV report was made up of Air Force corporals. The situation that brought them together was the controversy over Ordinance 1.104, of October 1964, which defined the terms for retaining or discharging of corporals who had not been promoted during the 8-year period. At first, this regulation was viewed as an act of exception, and the corporals that the regulation included would be considered eligible to receive amnesty. In 2014, a series of legal opinions issued by the Ministry of Justice and the Attorney General of the Union (AGU) endorsed the decision to revoke the amnesty granted to 495 former Air Force corporals. Starting in 2011, a new inter-ministerial working group was created to review 2574 of these applications. It is important to highlight that Law 10.559 of 2002 affirms that the Amnesty Commission is the institution of the Brazilian State responsible for analyzing the requests for compensation made by people who were prevented from exercising economic activities for exclusively political reasons from September 18, 1946, to October 5, 1988. Despite creating this Working Group, the issue is in a progressive process of judicialization, making it difficult to consolidate the necessary understanding for removing all legal obstacles that prevent obtaining of rights by former corporals under Ordinance 1.104, 1964. (CNV, 2014, p. 35).

It was mainly those military men (former Air Force corporals) who made up the testimony group within the project. They were not members of the political left. Further, they were mainly nationalistic soldiers, moved by ideals of love of country and, as always, for their respective branch of the Armed Forces. Nevertheless, they suffered intimidation and torture when they refused to do "work" with political prisoners. They were also summarily expelled from their corps, stripped of their rights—many of them had worked for several years in the military regime. They were monitored inside and outside the barracks, before and after they were arrested, suffered various punishments, and were subjected to degrading prison conditions, including torture and humiliation, according to CNV testimonies (CNV, 2014, p. 19).

From the Clinic of Truth to the Clinic of Testimony

Characteristics of the Group

The work that the Clinics of Testimony team began in 2015 was conducted once a month during a period of 4 months in the group's hometown, in a different state from that of the project team members. Each meeting lasted about 6 h, divided into 2 sessions: one in the morning and one in the afternoon. The coordination team consisted of four project psychologists that traveled to the group's hometown specifically for this work. The members of the group came spontaneously after learning of the proposal and remained throughout the four meetings. The group consisted of 15 men and 3 women, representing their husbands (who died during the amnesty application period), who were also beneficiaries.

The methodology used for the testimony group was based on two different theories: the Freudian psychoanalytic method and that of the Pichon-Rivière Operative Group. The first approach arises from our individual psychoanalytic practice and is inscribed in the psychoanalytic method based on the principles of therapeutic frame and the transference and abstinence (Freud, 1990/1912). The Operative Group is organized around a task that the coordinators present in the initial meetings. In this case, the task was that each subject constructs their testimony during the meetings.

As highlighted by Pichon-Rivière (2000), "[the group] focused on the task, which has as its goal to learn to think in terms of solving the difficulties created and manifested by the group [...] that enunciates an occurrence as its own spokesperson and for the group's unconscious fantasies" (Pichon-Rivière, 2000, p. 105). In this sense, we mark our understanding that the symptom occurs in the social bond and that this group experience involves clinical-political intervention.

Clinical Profiles

The arrival of the Clinics of Testimony team in the city where these soldiers lived was awaited with great expectations. The person who met us at the airport told us: "my father has a broken foot, but he wanted to come anyway. It was a struggle to persuade him to stay home. He really wanted to come and pick you up." These words from one leader's son, as well as the eagerness to take photos with the Clinics of Testimony team, the hugs and stories shared on the way to the destination city, spoke to a surprising eagerness. Questions arose. Why did our arrival evoke so much expectation? What were they expecting from our meeting? From the beginning we were struck by their documentary zeal: "we have to record this moment," said another important member when taking the photos in the airport lobby. Were we going to a therapeutic listening encounter or a court hearing? The driver's wrong turn seemed to tell us something: instead of taking the highway towards city's downtown district, he took the route to Brasilia, the Brazil's capital city, where the Amnesty Commission's offices are located.

All the military personnel wanted the Amnesty Commission to recognize that their processes were appropriate and, thus, to grant them amnesty and recognize them as affected by state violence within the very organization which they were part of. Their greatest humiliation and shame had been surrendering their uniforms. "How could they live as civilians if they were useless as military personnel?" This was the complaint that marked their lack of insertion in the position of limbo in which they found themselves: "neither here nor there." In one of our meetings, they recounted an episode that expresses the "non-place" in which they lived: a few years ago, some of them were invited to speak at a city school about their activities in the Armed Forces. Upon completing their narrative, they were booed for stating that they were against certain acts of violence. They could not be categorized as military personnel, but neither were they that of *guerrilleros*. As civilians, they felt powerless. Without their uniforms, they again were relegated to a non-place, from where they tried to express their truth, which could not be recognized as such. The state denial of responsibility also is a factor in creating this place of non-recognition considering that for several years they were trying to "prove" that they had the right to financial and psychological reparation.

The subjects of the group had been meeting monthly for more than a decade and, yet, they did not know their companions' stories, since the meetings had a strictly bureaucratic purpose. The meetings concerned monitoring their processes and actions related to their struggle for amnesty. The meetings were about discussing legal processes, not moments for sharing individual processes. Psychic pain was not recorded in their words but was acutely reflected in the manifestation of physical illnesses. The first group meeting was held in a church where our chairs were placed under the image of Jesus Christ on the cross, a portrait of an oath to tell the truth or the prohibition against lying. This moment between the Clinics of Testimony team and the military personnel seems to clearly show that the initial demand was for the recognition of the veracity of the facts. That is, they hoped that as a "truth clinic"—a failed act that marked the juncture between Testimony of Clinics and the Truth Commission—we would help them obtain financial reparation and amnesty due to the state violence they had suffered.

Invited to speak about their experiences, everyone recalled the expectations of their youth with the military career, the pride of wearing a uniform, the dream that working in the Armed Forces could provide them and their families better financial and living conditions. Many of them had prepared texts for the meeting and, as they spoke, they showed documents and [medical] exams to "prove" the events that they had suffered. Initially, they told stories about having been subjected to persecution, violence, and torture. As the emotions emerged from the papers they read, testimonies of the suffering experienced surfaced, and they expressed the need for containment: "It's better for me not to speak. If I do, I'll cry."

This is how they welcomed us in that first (mis)meeting: they wanted to prove their truths to us through papers and stories that seemed rehearsed, whereas we expected to hear testimonies that would come in a stammering, incomplete, and fictional way (Viñar, 1993). For us, everything that they had experienced inside the barracks had real value, but was not enunciated (sometimes, not even to themselves). For them, we had come from so far to listen and legitimize their truths and thus grant, perhaps, a key to access amnesty. They showed us evidence that until then had been insufficient to receive recognition from the Amnesty Commission. We, then, presented ourselves as there to listen to them not as representatives of that commission, but as facilitators moving in another direction, to enable the initial building of recognition between the peers and the group itself. Our job was to veer the route: to retake the path to their city and not to Brasilia.

Turning statements into testimonies and [personal] devaluation into a demand for recognition was the group's challenge. By testimony we understand, in this context, the accounting of the events, emphasizing their veracity, different from the testimony that puts into words the traumatic experience of what was lived and brings to light the place of that subject in the face of the violence experienced. The first idea we transformed was to put aside the awards, papers, tape recorders, and everything that represented "evidence," so that they could talk about what had happened to them, through their own voices. In this way, we hoped to gradually build a place of authorship for their narratives, that is, to enable them to speak of themselves and for themselves. Our aim was that the work of testing the other would arise as a consequence of a previous task: listening to oneself. According to Dori Laub (1995, p. 70), testimony is "the process in which the narrator (or survivor) vindicates his position as a witness: reconstructs the internal 'you' and, therefore, the possibility of a witness or a listener within himself."[4]

According to Laub (1995), testimony seeks to recapture a truth that was lost, thus connecting with what the group saw as the prime task: proving its truths. However, Laub (1995) points out that the performance of the testimony does not fulfill that promise; rather, it is transformed into a process of confrontation of losses. From this path, we understand that the presence of someone who can listen and recognize those losses is essential for those who experience traumatic situations.

Little by little they brought us back to the silenced time: the torture they had suffered, the humiliation and the shame of handing over the uniform, of being threatened, of having felt marginalized, of being institutionalized in psychiatric wards and subjected to injections that left them unconscious. At this time their diseases began to surface cirrhosis, gallstones, diabetes. In addition, they began to have nightmares, anguish, and panic, an indication of the repetition and internalization of the horror they had experienced. We became witnesses to their testimonies and, thus, we collectively worked on the demand to give voice to the stories that until then were expressed in the body. This enabled them to find words to narrate the experience of torture and suffering.

The initial mistrust marked by the expectation that we would produce a report to support the processes initiated in the Amnesty Commission gave way to the work of transforming the statements into testimonies of their stories and the suffering they had experienced for so many years without having anyone to talk to. As testimonies became increasingly possible, the papers and documents were literally abandoned and within each participant arose the desire to be recognized and valued.

This pattern also occurred in other countries such as Argentina., After "the war ended"—"the war" being a term that included extreme actions such as death flights and the use of torture on military personnel—many of them made public what happened "in times of war." From these stories we removed the phrase "war secrets" from the epigraph that opens this essay. By unveiling these "war secrets," it was possible to make public the extermination policy, which produced forced disappearances and acts of torture, allowing us to know not only the methods used by the State, but who executed them, thus initiating the trials of the Argentine military (Verbitsky, 1995).

---

[4] Translation by the authors.

Final Considerations

Based on the framework of transitional justice, the fight for amnesty, and a psychic reparation policy, which gave rise to the Clinics of Testimony project, it was necessary to build a methodology that could account for the implementation of active listening by professional psychologists and psychoanalysts of what subjects affected by state violence had to say. This space sought to break the silence and to foster the construction of testimonies based on experiences that had never been narrated. This positioned the participants as protagonists of their own stories, which are linked to the collective memory of the period of the dictatorship.

The work's scope was configured by the possibility of shifting the demand for amnesty in another direction, that is, towards the recovery of memory. What other avenues of recognition were there? Following the lines established by transitional justice, reparation does not occur only in the legal sphere. Rather there is also a symbolic/moral sphere as well as the one where we include ourselves, namely that of psychic reparation. Psychic repair, through testimony, is the aperture to new psychic pathways, alternative paths that the word promotes. While the subjects talked about their experiences among themselves, collectively, a new step was being designed between what was initially perceived as the opening of legal proceedings and the diseases in the body, leading towards a symbolic elaboration of psychic processes.

Throughout the group's encounters, the pain that seemed to arise through physical illness became more and more "alive" as deeply held memories were recovered. However, considering the limited time for working with the group, we wondered how to open their black boxes, touch those wounds, and then exit without leaving them open. What approach was possible to build collectively?

On the one hand, the Testimony of Clinics is anchored in State policies, yet, on the other hand, we identify with the current concerns of civil society movements, especially with the demands for "Memory, Truth, and Justice." In the same way that we understand the avenues of repair as indivisible, we visualize the previous demand as a tripod: all sides are equally necessary for a solid construction of what we call a political-clinic foundation.

However, we felt that the group's search for justice seemed to blur memory and even conceal the truth. This was not the truth they asked others to confirm, but the truth that came from the subject. They were revealing things that not even their relatives knew that had happened to them in the years of repression. Had they not been hiding the truths of their experiences from themselves?

We proposed, then, to take a new look at their demands. Taking the tripod of "Memory, Truth, and Justice" as an example, we worked to enable them to write each word—no longer in capital letters and with a single meaning—but rather in the plural, unfolding multiple possibilities. It was then that various memories, truths, and even different justices could emerge. The subjects we listened to occupied an unusual place. They had been affected by violence and their experiences expanded the construction of the memory of the period of the Brazilian civic-military dictatorship that still needed "data accumulation" and a "public record of the effects on victims" (Huggins et al., 2006).

During "stringing together" other ways of recognition through a collective outlet, during the meetings the idea arose that the group writes a book. One participant told us that he had thought of this idea, but that he could not carry it out since what had to be said was already stated in his statement to the Truth Commission. Slowly, the desire arose to pass on their stories, to have them read not only by the commissions of truth and amnesty, but also by their relatives, co-workers, neighbors, young people. A book would allow them to return to the school where they had spoken, but now not only as plaintiffs claiming amnesty, but as authors of their own stories.

When other possibilities for recognition were explored, there emerged a new recipient for this history. Although we have had a short period for this work and, consequently, we have not been able to accompany the construction of the book, the group's changed position was clear. It had shifted from a passive attitude, from "amnesty claimants," from those who claim something external, to active roles in their own stories, and writers of their own narratives. During that period, we witnessed a journey that has not yet come to an end, but which, surely, has already reached a point from which the shape of a new horizon is in sight.

References

Abrão, P., & Torelly, M. (2011). As dimensões da Justiça de Transição no Brasil, a eficácia da Lei de Anistia e as alternativas para a verdade e a justiça. In *Brasil. A Anistia na Era da Responsabilização: O Brasil em Perspectiva Internacional e Comparada. Brasília: Ministério da Justiça* (p. 216). Comissão de Anistia y Oxford University, Latin America Centre.

Comissão Especial sobre Mortos e Desaparecidos Políticos (CEMDP). (2007). *Direito à verdade e à memória: Comissão Especial sobre Mortos e Desaparecidos Políticos*. Secretaria Especial dos Direitos Humanos.

Fedida, P. (2000). Le rêve architecte d'un lieu. *L'inactuel, 3*, 42–49.

Ferenczi, S. (1974). Confusion de langue entre les adultes et l'enfant. In *Œuvres complètes, Psychanalyse IV*. Payot.

Freud, S. (1990). Consejos al médico sobre el tratamiento. In *Obras Completas* (Vol. 12). Amorrortu editores.

Huggins, M., Haritos-Fatouros, M., & Zimbardo, P. (2006). *Operários da Violência*. Editora Universidade de Brasília UNB.

Indursky, A., & Piccinini, C. (2015). Testemunho como ferramenta clínico-política. *Mudanças – Psicologia da Saúde, 23*(1), 1–9. https://doi.org/10.15603/2176-1019/mud.v23n1p1-9

Indursky, F. (2014). Uma análise discursiva da lei de anistia e seus efeitos de sentido. In Sigmund Freud Associação Psicanalítica (Org.), *Clínicas do Testemunho. Reparação Psíquica e Construção de Memórias* (pp. 213–238). Criação Humana.

Kaës, R. (1989). Ruptures catastrophiques et travail de la mémoire. In J. Pujet (Ed.), *Violence d'Etat et psychanalyse* (pp. 169–204). Dunod.

Laub, D. (1995). Truth and testimony: The process and the struggle. In C. Caruth (Ed.), *Trauma: Explorations in memory* (pp. 61–75). John Hopkins University Press.

Mannoni, O. (1979). *Clefs pour l'imaginaire*. Seuil.

Pichon-Rivière, E. (2000). *O processo grupal*. Martins Fontes.

Relatório da Comissão Nacional da Verdade (CNV). (2014). *Brasília* (Vol. 2). Retrieved from http://cnv.memoriasreveladas.gov.br/images/pdf/relatorio/volume_2_digital.pdf
Verbitsky, H. (1995). *El Vuelo*. Grupo Editorial Planeta.
Viñar, M. (1993). *Fracturas de la Memoria – Crónicas para una memoria por venir*. Ediciones Trilce.

Chapter 16
Colonia Dignidad: Lights and Shadows in the Recognition of the Victims

Evelyn Hevia Jordán

General Context

In June 1961, a group of approximately 300 parishioners came to Chile from the Private Soziale Mission (PSM) led by preacher Paul Schäfer. Although there had been allegations in Germany since the mid-1950s against Schäfer for child sexual abuse, he managed to enter the country with recommendations from German and Chilean authorities. Officials were convinced by his stated objective to launch an organization like the German mission to support children and underprivileged youth and to help impoverished communities after the 1960 earthquake that struck southern Chile. Such was the founding of the Dignidad Charitable and Educational Society (SBED).[1]

Schäfer and his trusted men[2] looked for a secluded rural location far from urban centers to install their "promised land." They bought the "El Lavadero" farm located in the Parral foothills in southern Chile. Once installed, they captured support from the public government officials and admiration from their neighbors through the founding of a hospital (Hevia, 2016). Social and geographical isolation allowed them to establish an internal order based on the sexual, physical, and psychic control and subjugation of the inhabitants. These were the main characteristics of this

---

[1] Decree No. 3949 of the Ministry of Justice of Chile (September 1961) granting legal personality to the Charitable and Educational Society Dignity (SBED).

[2] From now on, the expression "hierarch" or "hierarchy" will be used to refer to Paul Schäfer's circle of trust. This is a term used in journalistic, judicial descriptions, and by settlers themselves and former settlers.

E. Helvia Jordán (✉)
Universität Berlin (LAI-FU) Berlin, Deutschland/Universidad Alberto Hurtado (UAH), Santiago, Chile
e-mail: eveheviajordan@gmail.com

colony, which became a "state within a state," whose only laws were those imposed by its leader and the small group that controlled it.

Despite early denunciations and knowledge of the situation to which its inhabitants were subjected, this enclave was able to continue throughout different governments in Chile and Germany (1961–2005), increasing its influence and power during Chile's civil-military dictatorship (1973–1990). Allegations of abuses committed in Colonia Dignidad (CD) led the government of Patricio Aylwin (1990–1994) to take steps to stop new crimes by cancelling the institution's legal incorporated status (1991). However, CD leaders circumvented this legal challenge by creating a new organizational and heritage structure through newly incorporated businesses. Its inhabitants continued to be subject to the control and subjugation of the internal regime. The most serious aspect during this time was CD's deployment of new strategies to confront the government through the creation of patient and the Youth Permanent Vigil committees (Juventud Vigilia Permanente, JVP), comprised of neighbors who protested in various ways the government's decision to close the hospital, allowing new children to attend the activities they offered to attract their neighbors. This consequently led to the sexual abuse of more children. All this happened with complete impunity until 1996, the year in which a Chilean court issued an arrest warrant for Paul Schäfer, who had fled charges of sexual abuse (Hevia, 2016).

In July 1962 the outside world first caught a glimpse of what occurred within this impregnable enclave when Wolfgang Müller (Villarroel, 2020) escaped and made statements to the press about the system of life and the punishments he received inside the Colonia. However, he was recaptured with a court order and returned to CD, where he was harshly punished as an example and warning to other settlers. In 1963 he tried again unsuccessfully to flee the compound. Finally, in 1966, he managed to escape and leave the country. Years later, others managed to flee. The most publicized cases are Hugo Baar (1984), the Packmor couple (1985), and Tobias Muller, who had lived there since he was 10 years old and Salo Luna, a teenager (1997). All of them had testified in different courts both in Chile and abroad; however, their accusations did not suffice to stop the crimes that were being committed (Fernández, 2015).

The first public complaints about the abuses in Colonia Dignidad were recorded by the press in the mid-1960s (Vexler et al., 1966a, b). Subsequently, numerous complaints were presented before international organizations (Amnesty International, 1977; Organización de Naciones Unidas, ONU, 1978); three investigative committees were established in the Chilean Parliament (1968, 1995, 1997), and in the German Bundestag (1998 and 2001) to analyze this case and its complaints. The reports of the National Truth and Reconciliation Commission (Comisión Nacional de Verdad y Reconciliación, CNVR, 1991) and the National Commission on Political Imprisonment and Torture (Comisión Nacional sobre Prisión Política y Tortura, CNPPT, 2004) received testimonies from victims who were tortured at Colonia Dignidad. The relatives of victims of forced disappearance also mentioned that their family members had been taken there. Notwithstanding these complaints filed before the courts and other official bodies both in Chile and Germany, an investigative commission has yet to be established to ascertain the facts, identify and recognize the various victims, and propose reparation measures for the damage caused.

The allegations have brought to light the conditions of abuse to which those who lived within the enclave were subjected and confirm that between 1973 and 1977, it operated as a base and secret detention site of the "Dirección de Inteligencia Nacional" (DINA). Victims of human rights violations have been recognized by the Chilean State in the above-mentioned commissions; however, the identity of all disappeared detainees and persons summarily executed there is unknown. Pressure from victims and activists, coupled with the effect on German foreign policy from the film "Colonia Dignidad. Es gibt kein Zurück" (2015)[3] prompted the German Foreign Affairs Ministry in April 2016 to publicly recognize German diplomats' ineffective actions to assisting the victims. In June 2017 the *Bundestag* unanimously voted on a resolution entitled, "Clarification of crimes and reconstruction of memory in Colonia Dignidad." The resolution was followed by the signing of a memorandum of understanding between the governments of Chile and Germany to create a bilateral Joint Commission to address this case and the situation of the victims.[4]

Description of the Structure and Operation of Colonia Dignidad

To understand the structure and operation of CD it is key to describe and analyze the role played by the victimizer pattern, as a contribution from the field of psychology that enables us to establish a link between the individual consequences and the serious long-term impact on the victims. In regard to the internal system of abuse, control, and punishments, it is also important to note its effects to the present day, which are expressed in the tensions of daily coexistence within one group of victims and mutual recognition (Honneth, 1994/1997) of the experience of victimization lived by other groups, for example, between settlers and victims of the dictatorship.

The notion of a victimizing pattern is useful for this case. It suggests that the practice of violence and abuse was installed and followed a sequence that gave rise to the modeling, strengthening, and reproduction of rules and actions under that scheme. Each member was functional to this pattern, ensuring its continuity and

---

[3] The story of Colonia Dignidad has been brought to the cinema (1985, 2015, 2019, 2021, 2022) and dozens of testimonial books, novels, plays, documentaries have been published, showing interest in documenting this case and reporting the situation of the victims.

[4] This chapter was written in 2017 and revised in 2021, more than 3 years after the Joint Committee there are no public results. However, in May 2019 the German government allocated an aid fund to victims that is being implemented by IOM (International Organization for Migration). Official document available at: https://www.auswaertiges-amt.de/blob/2218760/ea7f764e09c1d8b83db7b2fdefe9c34e/190516-coloniadignidadhilfskonzept-data.pdf, consulted at: October 15, 2020.

effectiveness for decades, generating external articulations, such as serving the purpose of political repression during the dictatorship. Victimizing patterns, which in literature are called patterns of victimization or violence have been useful in explaining ways of criminological victimization beyond lifestyle theories. Paying special attention to the gender dimension and differences with which men and women experience violence in the spheres of work, family life, and public life (Mustaine, 1997). They also are useful for studying these patterns within relationships and their psychological effects (Dutton et al., 2005). Recently, they have been employed by the philosophy of law to reflect on how these patterns shift the ethical borders concerning the legitimacy and assessment of contemporary violence in the USA, as exercised by public institutions, crime, police, gender, and racial violence (Sklansky, 2021). In this way, the notion of a pattern requires differentiations between the different kinds of violence, the arenas in which it is experienced, specific gender difference considerations, and the effect it might have not only on those who receive and exercise it, but also for witnesses and accomplices to violence.

In the case of CD, for example, gender differences were established from the beginning by separating men from women, boys from girls, to facilitate systematic and repeated sexual domination and abuse by Schäfer of the boys.[5] This was reinforced through the configuration of an image of women that is closely associated with sin. Women were often called insulting terms such as *"Schweine"* or pigs, which prevented any kind of relationship based on bonds of intimacy and trust.

Colonia Dignidad was structured as a hierarchical-pyramidal system. At the base of the pyramid, the inhabitants of the enclave were subjected to the internal regime. Above them were members whose loyalty and unconditional obedience earned them the trust of the upper hierarchy who assigned them guarding and security tasks. The next level was comprised of the top-ranking leaders, who were responsible for the economic, productive, intelligence, and external relations support. The highest echelon consisted of Paul Schäfer alone (Gemballa,1990; Heller, 1993; Maier & Stehle, 2015). This organization also had a network of friends, collaborators, and accomplices in different social and political spheres.

Schäfer and his henchmen installed a system of surveillance, a panoptic control, and total domination of residents' bodies and minds (Foucault, 2002), in which the victimizer pattern was sustained by the subjugation of the body through slave labor. "Working is serving God" was the motto that Schäfer imposed on settlers as his own version of the Nazi concentration camp slogan "Arbeit macht frei" (Work makes you Free). Residents were prohibited from engaging in sex life and reproduction, while sexual abuse of children and young men was introduced as a form of generalized subjugation. Those who dared disobey were subjected to violent punishments, enclosed, isolation for extended periods, hospitalizations where they were given psychopharmaceuticals and electroshocks. The subjugation was exercised through the systematic and routine control of the minds, which were dominated mainly by

---

[5] About the experience of women inside the enclave: Rittel and Karwelat (2018). A study is needed that analyzes from a gender perspective the forms of victimization in this case.

confession, a mechanism of psychological and moral control installed by Schäfer, in which he was the sole confessor with the power to humiliate and punish. This implanted the belief that he knew everything that was going on, what the inhabitants of CD thought and even dreamed (Araya & Lecaros, 1999; Biedermann et al., 2006; Gemballa, 1990; Heller, 1993, 2006; Hevia & Stehle, 2015; Rodríguez, 1968, 2009; Schwember, 2006). For many, this belief became a dramatically brutal form of suffering and repression, enforced by a system of denunciation and informants that ensured control through terror and the inability to strengthen any personal relationship based on trust.

The Victimizer Pattern: A Psychosocial Approach

Who are the victims of the former Colonia Dignidad? It is not easy to answer this question due to the complexity and chiaroscuros of the coexistence during more than four decades of a group subjected under a hierarchical structure. This occurred within the confines of a highly sectarian and concentrationary enclave, which during the years of dictatorship was used as a clandestine political prison and torture center by the secret police.

The victimizer structure and the range of violence experienced enables identification of various categories of victims. A first distinction concerns crimes committed inside or outside the enclave as suggested by Maier and Stehle (2015). The victims of the internal regime included those who were deprived of their liberty and subjected to abuses imposed by the slavery and forced labor systems installed since the formation of this colony. At the same time, the external victims were people tortured, killed, and disappeared in dictatorship inside the property. In an "inside/ outside" border area are the cases of children and young people abused during recreational activities on weekends, holidays, or in the boarding school that the colony offered children and youth from the outside neighboring area. This "internal/external victim" distinction is useful; however, it does not reflect the complexity that arises from the confirmed fact that the rights of all these persons were violated and each one was enslaved at various moments. Nor does it reflect that the victimization was perpetrated, in some cases, by individuals such as the leader and the highest echelons, acting on their own, and, in other cases, by agents of the Chilean State, with the collaboration of these top leaders. This confirms a pattern of torture, abuses of various kinds, and forced disappearance[6] of political opponents.

---

[6] "Enforced disappearance is a crime that marks a very special moment in the history of human rights. When, after the 1973 coup in Chile, people were not only killed without any legal procedure but also arbitrarily detained without leaving a trace for the families who searched for them, and when the same practice was even more common after the 1976 coup in Argentina, people began to name that specific crime: detention/disappearance or (en)forced disappearance. Mothers and other relatives started demanding information on the whereabouts of their loved ones, defying the repression of the regimes" (Huhle, 2021, p. 234). Also, Gatti (2018) points out that it is a concept

The description of "internal victims" requires generational distinctions. The victims who were part of the founding group, that arrived in 1961, can be divided among those who were adults, teenagers, or children at the time of their arrival in Chile. There is also a second generation, who were born in the enclave and knew no other form of socialization. Additionally, there are Chileans who were co-opted and/or fraudulently adopted. Today, we might add a third generation of victims, who were born after Schäfer escaped. This third generation has grown up in the context of an identity conflict, having been transmitted the story of trauma, while also a social denial of that past by using tourism to leave behind those experiences and look towards a promised future. The current situation can be described by identifying those who live outside: those who managed to escape the enclave; others, who—after the escape (1997), detention (2005), and death of Schäfer (2010)—left the site and settled down in different regions of Chile, Germany, or other countries. Also, there are those who tried to live outside but returned to live on the property today known as Villa Baviera; and, lastly, there are those who never left.

To understand how most of them could become victims or victims who became victimizers, it is necessary to delve deeper into the victimizer pattern and its consequences at the individual level and in the relationships of intra- and inter-group coexistence of victims. As noted, this enclave was characterized by a pseudo-religious and sectarian dimension. In this regard, Utsch et al. (2012) analyzed trauma from the sectarian-religious dimension, offering a view on the relationship between religiosity and psychopathology. Bauer (2012), following Mussachio de Zan, mentions the four mechanisms of sects that contribute to the depersonalization of its members: "(1) control of information, (2) time control, (3) social control, and (4) psychophysical weakening" (p. 81). This categorization was drawn from direct patient testimonies and literature to explain how each of the mechanisms described applies to the way of life established within this enclave. All these mechanisms contributed to its inhabitants's altered perception of reality, emotional deregulation, and relationships of mistrust and ambivalence (love/hate) related to the figure of the leader. Even years later, without the presence of Schäfer, mistrust, confusion, and ambivalence persist in the relationships between themselves and outwards (Biedermann et al., 2006; Bauer, 2012).

Responsibilities for criminal actions were made possible by the characteristics built into the organization. Each member occupied a place in the structure that made possible its operation, which—in addition to the mechanisms already described—was sustained by obedience and a system of rewards (seduction) and punishments.[7] It is clear that the victimizer pattern has operated on the basis of abusive leadership and the terror those leaders exercised. Yet, the explanation for the absolute obedience can be traced to a historical, political, and legal utilization, the effects of which

---

that has been colonized to refer to other situations of death and disappearance in Mexico or ethnocides in Guatemala. Thus, it would also include that the victim can be a collective or an ethnic group and the victimizer could be not only the State or parastatal violences, but also private violences.

[7] See testimony of Friedhelm Zeitner in Villarrubia (2013).

cannot be ignored if a critical approach is sought to understand the configuration of the victim subject and the complex victim-victimizer relationship. Obedience to authority has been the subject of extensive research in social psychology in the second half of the twentieth century. Several authors have researched the conditions of obedience and exercise of authority (Blanch, 1982; Milgram, 2007; Zimbardo, 2012). It has also been a subject of academic, legal, and political discussion at the international level (Arendt, 2000; Crenzel, 2008). However, following the Nuremberg trials, those claim to simply follow orders when they commit crimes against humanity are not exempted from criminal responsibilities. Still, it is worth noting the interfaced abusive relationship and the internalized submission of individuals, which is reflected in the collective conduct that persists even after the disappearance of the leader.

The story that contends the leader was the only victimizer who held sole legal responsibility has been reinforced after the arrest of Paul Schäfer in 2005. In April 2006, the community of Villa Baviera issued a public statement (Villa Baviera, 2006) in which three objectives are evident: one, to promote a widespread idea that makes no distinction between the victims; two, place ultimate responsibility for criminal actions on their leader; and three, generate an idea of shared unity (community) regarding the past and present. The inhabitants of Villa Bavaria have endeavored for more than a decade to reconstruct a public image of their past, by justifying the responsibilities of some of its members in criminal actions under the concept of "due obedience." Their exculpatory argument for denying responsibility is the condition of having been victims of deception, physical, sexual, and psychological domination by an absolute leader who could not be confronted. These discourses cannot be read in isolation as a "mea culpa" text of a community with a homogeneous voice and an experience of shared victimization (Maier, 2016). It must be read in the context of a heterogeneity and conflict concerning the past and the demands for reparation in the present. Legal proceedings are underway in the courts that seek to identify responsibilities. There are also demands for court sentence compliance and compensation to children who were victims of sexual abuse, that the current administrators of Villa Baviera and its corporate holdings are not willing to pay (Arellano, 2015). This makes coexistence within this group exceedingly difficult and comprises a watershed regarding how to address both the individual responsibilities and those of the organization of which they were part.

The victimizer pattern was built on a structure of relationships between victims and victimizers that is not explained solely from a psychology of the individual (Martín-Baró, 1990; Montero, 1982) nor from a psychopathological taxonomy. To build a critical psychosocial perspective, three approaches that have resonated in social psychology and contemporary social sciences are useful: (1) problematizing lineal explanations (cause-effect) and generalist theories that neglect subjective particularities (Lira, 2017); (2) problematize those explanations of a purely psychological or psychologistic nature (Martín-Baró, 1990), which focus the analysis on intra-psychic factors, such as psychopathology or personality of victims and victimizers, or, conversely, on the sociologistic side, which focuses only on the contextual dimension, neglecting the subjective dimension, and (3) problematizing the idea of neutral knowledge and the expert professional as a non-political actor that involves accepting the political dimension of knowledge and who holds that knowledge (Breuer, 2003).

The psychosocial analysis of the victimizing pattern—the notion of "gray zone" posed by Primo Levi—arises from these foundations to challenge binary victim/victimizer reductionism. In his Auschwitz Trilogy, he describes the complex web relationships that occur within the *lager* (concentration camp), noting: "Offer some individuals in a state of slavery a privileged position, some comfort and a good chance for survival, demanding in return the betrayal of the natural solidarity with their companions, and without a doubt there will be one who accepts" the deal (Levi, 2005, p. 121). This perspective helps explain the behavior of settlers who grew up and survived thanks to the deployment of "better adaptation mechanisms" to the system of domination, proving themselves to be functional individuals for the purposes of the organization and its leader. This produced a relationship interwoven between purely psychological aspects (fear, seduction), and those inherent to the concentration camp—sectarian context (obedience to authority). On the other side, there are others who challenged this principle and put their own existence at risk, suffering exemplary physical punishments with participation of the "assembly" of settlers. These people became symbols of sin, who were subjected to long periods of solitary confinement, forced to carry out denigrating work and/or electroshocks and psychopharmaceuticals, making brainwashing possible (Meerloo, 1956/2009; Taylor, 2004; Zimbardo, 2012). Their "treatment" was a public message about the serious consequences that would face of those who dared to transgress internal control. This makes the distinction between victims and victimizers excessively complex. Some were victims, others were victimizers, still others collaborated with the abuse and subjugation of others, transiting from victim to victimizer.

Victims of political repression during the dictatorship: relatives of the forcibly disappeared detainees and those summarily executed for political motives, as well as survivors of political prison and torture who recognize having been held there were affected by the victimizer pattern that enabled the operation of a torture center that resulted from the alliance with the dictatorship. These victims and their families have demanded that the States of Chile and Germany investigate crimes against humanity and bring to trial the responsible parties. They have also called for the preservation of the place to build a site of memory to remember the victims.

This case has a complex victimizer pattern not only on account of the internal organization and how it functioned. To understand the psychological impact this situation had during decades on the inhabitants (victims, victimizers, witnesses, and accomplices) requires a *hinge* psychosocial analysis, as Martín-Baró (1990) points out. This must encompass a critical perspective that does not overlook the "macro" sphere (the historical, political, sociological, legal, and economic aspects of the enclave), nor ignore the specifics of the psychological and biographical factors, and the damage caused to each and every victim.

Mental Health Interventions

In 2001, *the Bundestag* proposed that the German government cooperates with the capture of Schäfer. It also proposed that the government provides therapeutic support to settlers, the first expression of a mental health concern for those living in the enclave. The first (and, so far, the only) intervention by the Chilean state took place in 2005. That year, President Ricardo Lagos appointed Chilean civil engineer and writer Herman Schwember as a government delegate to develop a diagnosis and a proposal. In a year's time, he drafted a report entitled "Integral Transition Project (Proyecto Integral de Transición, PIT)," released in March 2006, which proposed five-point strategic guidelines to address the situation of present-day Villa Baviera. The Schwember report proposed the following: (1) rebuild a moral and institutional identity as a community; (2) rebuild its economic viability with a system of companies at the service of the community. For these first two points he called for the following: (3) the community reconciliation with the Chilean setting (judicial, political, and ethical); (4) recovery of the emotional health of a significant number of members. Finally, (5) that there be a critical mass of productive members of the community. However, as Schwember himself pointed out, his task came to a premature halt, for lack of sufficient support to implement his proposals and because his task had been politically misunderstood (El Mercurio de Valparaíso, 2006).

Since 2006, the German Embassy has funded a psychosocial support program for residents of the former Colonia Dignidad. The work has been led by psychiatrist Niels Biedermann and despite some lapses in funding, today it has a psychologist and a social worker, who provide individual and group psychosocial and pharmacological support for those still living on the site. For reasons of confidentiality, it has not been possible to know more details about these professionals' diagnosis and work,[8] but there is still a high demand for psychological support for victims living in other locations without access to specialized support.[9] New psychosocial and educational support needs are now emerging among couples and families, as those who were born and raised in the enclave report numerous affective, sexual, and parenting concerns. In addition to the impact on individuals, collective consequences remain that are expressed in the coexistence between Villa Baviera inhabitants and those living off the premises, reflecting different positions regarding the management of the past and the current administration of VB and its heritage.

Victims of human rights violations committed in dictatorship have medical and psychosocial support from the Reparation Program for Integral Care in Health and Human Rights (Programa de Reparación en Atención Integral en Salud y Derechos Humanos, PRAIS), which was created in 1991 as a reparation measure, in

---

[8] Author's interview with Niels Biedermann, 29.03.2017.

[9] Since 2019, many victims have raised this need for medical and psychological support to professionals at the International Office for Migration (IOM) which is the entity that is interviewing victims of the enclave to determine their access to compensation of 7000 euros established by Germany.

compliance with the recommendations of the CNVR (1991). However, the main reparation demand for this group is the clarification of the crimes against humanity committed there, to know the identity of the forcibly disappeared detainees and those executed for political motives, whose bodies were inhumed and exhumed within the framework of the so-called Operación Retiro de televisores [Removal of Television Sets, 1978],[10] bringing those responsible to trial and the construction of a memory site to remember the victims.

In the limited efforts to address the problem of victims, the group that has become more invisibilized is made up of Chilean children who were sexually abused in the 1990s, even though they were the ones who gave the first to wage judicial battle. Their legal actions successfully brought down the system of abuse and slavery that had remained intact for more than four decades. This brought them and their families harassment, threats, and aggression (Fernández, 2015). Despite court recognition of their condition as victims and the psychological care they received from the Sexual Aggression Victim Support Center in the context of judicial processes and police investigations, this support is not ongoing. Today all these men are approaching 40 years of age and most have decided to keep quiet about their experience and try to go unnoticed by public opinion. They are reluctant to talk about what happened to them because they have seen how sexual abuse not only has personal and family consequences, but also gives rise to social stigma and trivialization from the mass media communication.[11]

The Challenges of Historical Memory of Human Rights Violations

What to do with a space where crimes against humanity have been committed? How to address the situation of those who inhabit it? How to address the need for recognition and reparation for such heterogeneous victims? The current situation is expressed publicly in the opposing views accentuated by the recreational and tourist use that is made of the place. This situation poses a tension that is expressed not only in a struggle for memory (Jelin, 2002), but in an unresolved problem between VB's economic and heritage situation and the integration of its inhabitants into Chilean society.

In 2007, the Zippelhaus restaurant was inaugurated, which opened the CD facilities to tourism. Between 2011 and 2012 it received public funding from the Chilean government for the refurbishment and construction of a hotel that opened in 2012.

---

[10] "Removal of Television Sets" was the name given by the dictatorship to the operation by which the bodies of the disappeared detainees were removed. It is estimated that at least 22 of them, who were buried in a clandestine grave located in Colonia Dignidad, were sprayed with chemical accelerants and the ashes thrown into the Perquilauquén River.

[11] Watch an interview with Salo Luna on the TV show "Mentiras Verdaderas" Tv channel La Red, broadcast on March 5, 2013, available on YouTube.

What is now called the *Complejo Turístico Villa Baviera-Parral* (Villa Baviera-Parral Tourist Complex) is a tourist proposal that capitalizes on German folklore traditions (Villa Baviera, 2017). This use is seen as an offense to the memory of the victims. *"Who has seen a marriage held in a place that was used as a concentration camp?!"* is an argument extensively used by relatives of forcibly disappeared detainees, former political prisoners, victims of sexual abuse and some former inhabitants, highlighting the maccabre attraction to this touristic site. The construction of an on-site historical and public memory of the place (Jelin, 2002; Jelin & Langland, 2003; Vinyes, 2009) is one of the main bilateral discussion points between the representatives of the governments of Chile and Germany. Thus far, the Villa Baviera tourism managers have built their own version of their past with a small museum open to the public. However, the museum construction and its narrative have not resulted from a process of dialogue between the different groups of victims.

Since 2014, work has been undertaken with different groups of victims with several[12] educational methodologies. The project addresses the history of Colonia Dignidad and its place in the individual's biography, fostering instances of intra- and inter-group dialogue and visits to memorial sites in Chile and Germany. This has enabled the exchange of different experiences of victimization as well as the gathering of ideas for a future memorial site in a climate of listening and reciprocal recognition. Also, with the inhabitants of Villa Baviera, work has been done to question their prejudices against Chileans and the ideas about "German identity" that still persist.

Memorials and the recovery of former repressive centers in the form of memory sites have been recognized as forms of symbolic reparation to victims (Piper & Hevia, 2012). However, registering the repressive past of this enclave at the scene of the crime will remain a major challenge for all stakeholders, including both states, who must generate the agreements and conditions to resolve the current ownership and resident situation of the site.

Conclusions

The long history of Colonia Dignidad and the diversity of crimes committed there has led the current situation of the victims to a highly complex juncture. The work of recognition and reparation to victims (Lira & Loveman, 2005) from a critical psychosocial perspective must be approached from both the individual and collective dimensions, without neglecting the macro social perspective that frames the past and delimits possibilities of the present for this case.

---

[12] Task that the Ministry of Foreign Affairs German entrusted Dr. Elke Gryglewski and in the context of the Bilateral Commission, since 2019 it has been working together with the experts: Dr. Jens-Christian Wagner, Elizabeth Lira, and Diego Matte in the preparation of a proposal for a memorial site.

The victimizer pattern makes the dividing line between victims and victimizer in categorical and dichotomic terms complex, because precisely what this pattern brings to light is that each member of the enclave was installed in a specific place in the complex web of victimization. In some cases, a single person at different times in their life and under different conditions of subjugation transited from victim to victimizer or vice versa. This approach is not intended to exonerate the high-ranking leaders and perpetrators from responsibility for cooperating in the commission of crimes against humanity, but rather to explain the Colony's structure and operation as well as its individual and collective consequences for the present.

This chapter has sought to show the development of this institution, its internal operation, and its victimizing structure, as well as its cooperation with political repression in dictatorship. The victimizer pattern expressed in the control over individuals, physical, psychological, and sexual subjugation can open a door for us to understand these chiaroscuros in the recognition of victims. It also unveils the importance of a psychological approach that not only addresses the individual consequences for those who were subjected to the internal CD system, but also employs a critical and *hinged* perspective that enables observation of collective and social consequences that are perpetuated in the present day. An example of this is the tensions that occur within and between the different groups of victims regarding the reciprocal recognition of the history of traumatization and the treatment of the past of violence, whose most concrete expression centers on disputes over the construction of a historical memory on the site.

References

Amnesty International. (1977). *Colonia Dignidad. Deutsches Mustergut in Chile-ein Folterlager der DINA*. AI.

Araya, M., & Lecaros, P. (1999). *Se busca: Paul Schäfer ¿Salvador o demonio de Colonia Dignidad?* Cesoc.

Arellano, A. (2015, October 19). Líderes de Villa Baviera niegan validez de acuerdo para indemnizar a víctimas de Schäfer. *Ciper*. Retrieved from https://www.ciperchile.cl/2015/10/19/lideres-de-villa-baviera-niegan-validez-de-acuerdo-para-indemnizar-a-victimas-de-schafer/

Arendt, H. (2000). *Eichmann en Jerusalén, un estudio sobre la banalidad del mal*. Lumen.

Bauer, S. (2012). Psychologische Behandlungsmöglichkeiten für religiös traumatisierte Menschen am Beispiel der Sekte. In M. Utsch, P. Kaiser, S. Bauer, & H. Freund (Eds.), *Pathologische Religiosität. Genese, Beispiele, Behandlungsansätze* (pp. 67–105). Kohlhammer.

Biedermann, N., Strasser, J., & Poluda, J. (2006). Colonia Dignidad' Psychotherapie im ehemaligen Folterlager einer deutschen Sekte. *Zeitschrift für Politische Psychologie, 14*, 111–127. Retrieved from https://www.academia.edu/36442647/_Colonia_Dignidad_Psychotherapie_im_ehemaligen_Folterlager_einer_deutschen_Sekte_Colonia_Dignidad_Psychotherapy_in_the_Former_Torture_Center_of_a_German_Sect_?auto=download

Blanch, J. M. (1982). *Psicologías Sociales. Aproximación histórica*. Hora.

Breuer, F. (2003). Lo subjetivo del conocimiento socio-científico y su reflexión: ventanas epistemológicas y traducciones metodológicas. *Forum: Qualitative. Social Research, 4*(2), 25. Retrieved from https://www.qualitative-research.net/index.php/fqs/article/view/698/1512

Comisión Nacional de Verdad y Reconciliación (CNVR). (1991). *Informe Comisión Nacional de Verdad y Reconciliación*, Band 2 (Vol. 1, pp. 469–470). Santiago.

Comisión Nacional sobre Prisión Política y Tortura (CNPPT). (2004). *Informe Comisión Nacional sobre Prisión Política y Tortura*. Santiago.

Crenzel, E. (2008). *La historia política del Nunca Más. La memoria de las desapariciones en la Argentina*. Siglo XXI.

Dutton, M. A., Kaltman, S., Goodman, L. A., Weinfurt, K., & Vankos, N. (2005). Patterns of intimate partner violence: Correlates and outcomes. *Violence and Victims, 20*(5), 483–497. https://doi.org/10.1891/0886-6708.2005.20.5.483

El Mercurio de Valparaíso (2006, May 7). Los colonos nacieron y vivieron en una prisión

Fernández, H. (2015). Justicia, impunidad y Colonia Dignidad. In E. Hevia & J. Stehle (Eds.), *Colonia Dignidad. Verdad, Justicia y Memoria* (pp. 87–95). El Desconcierto.

Foucault, M. (2002). *Vigilar y castigar: nacimiento de la prisión*. Siglo XXI.

Gatti, E. (2018). Desaparición Forzada. In R. Vinyes (Dir.), *Diccionario de la memoria colectiva* (pp. 137–138). Gedisa.

Gemballa, G. (1990). *Colonia Dignidad*. Cesoc.

Heller, F. P. (1993). *Colonia Dignidad. Von der Psychosekte zum Folterlager*. Schmetterling.

Heller, F. P. (2006). *Pantalones De Cuero, Moños... y Metralletas*. Cesoc.

Hevia, E. (2016). *From hospital "El Lavadero" to hospital "Villa Baviera". Historical reconstruction of the hospital of Colonia Dignidad in Chile. Proposal for consideration in the Doctorate Program at Free University of Berlin*. S/E.

Hevia, E., & Stehle, J. (2015). *Colonia Dignidad. Verdad, Justicia y Memoria*. El Desconcierto.

Honneth, A. (1994/1997). *La lucha por el reconocimiento. Por una gramática moral de los conflictos sociales*. Crítica.

Huhle, R. (2021). 'Urgent actions' for the search for disappeared persons in the specialised bodies of the United Nations. In K. Ansolabehere, B. A. Frey, & L. A. Payne (Eds.), *Disappearances in the post-transition era in Latin America* (pp. 234–241). Oxford University Press.

Jelin, E. (2002). *Los trabajos de la memoria*. Siglo XXI.

Jelin, E., & Langland, V. (2003). *Monumentos, memorias y marcas territoriales*. Siglo XXI.

Levi, P. (2005). *Trilogía de Auschwitz*. El Aleph Editores.

Lira, E. (Ed.). (2017). *Lecturas de psicología y política. Crisis política y daño psicológico*. Universidad Alberto Hurtado.

Lira, E., & Loveman, B. (2005). *Políticas de reparación. Chile 1990-2004*. LOM: Ediciones.

Maier, D. (2016). *Colonia Dignidad. Auf den Spuren eines deutschen Verbrechens in Chile*. Schmetterling Verlag.

Maier, D., & Stehle, J. (2015). Colonia Dignidad: pieza clave en el aparato represor de la dictadura cívico-militar. Orígenes, historia criminal y preguntas abiertas. In E. Hevia & J. Stehle (Eds.), *Colonia Dignidad. Verdad, Justicia y Memoria* (pp. 27–61) El Desconcierto.

Martín-Baró, I. (1990). *Acción e Ideología. Psicología social desde Centroamérica*. UCA.

Meerloo, J. (1956/2009). *The rape of the mind: The psychology of thought control, menticide, and brainwashing*. Progressive Press.

Milgram, S. (2007). *Obediencia a la autoridad: un punto de vista experimental*. Desclée de Brouwer S.A.

Montero, M. (1982). Fundamentos teóricos de la psicología social comunitaria. *Boletín de la AVEPSO, 5*(1), 15–22.

Mustaine, E. E. (1997). The risk of victimization in the workplace for men and women: An analysis using routine activities/lifestyle theory. *Humanity and Society, 21*(1), 17–38. https://doi.org/10.1177/016059769702100103

Organización de Naciones Unidas (ONU). (1978, October 25). *Informe del Consejo Económico y Social. Protección de los Derechos Humanos en Chile*. Santiago. Retrieved from http://www.archivomuseodelamemoria.cl/uploads/5/7/57818/N7826156-1.c.pdf

Piper, I., & Hevia, E. (2012). *Espacio y Recuerdo. Archipiélago de memorias en Santiago de Chile*. Ocho Libros.

Rittel, H., & Karwelat, J. (2018). *Lasst uns reden. Frauenprotokolle aus der Colonia Dignidad.* Smetterling Verlag.

Rodríguez, G. (2009). *Schäfer y Colonia Dignidad. Crónica de una secta hermética.* S/E.

Rodríguez, M. (1968). *Colonia Dignidad ¿enigma o desafío?* S/E.

Schwember, H. (2006). *Informe Proyecto Integral de Transición. Comunidad de Villa Baviera (ex) Colonia Dignidad.* S/Editorial.

Sklansky, D. A. (2021). *A pattern of violence: How the law classifies crimes and what it means for justice.* The Belknap Press of Harvard University Press.

Taylor, K. (2004). *Brainwashing: The science of thought control.* Oxford University Press.

Utsch, M., Kaiser, P., Bauer, S., & Freund, H. (2012). *Pathologische Religiosität. Genese, Beispiele, Behandlungsansätze.* Kohlhammer.

Vexler, E., Ehrmann, J., & Muray, O. (1966a, April 6). *La Colonia del Terror.* Revista Ercilla.

Vexler, E., Muray, O., Ehrmann, J., & Torrente, H. (1966b, March 30). *Tras los Muros de la 'Dignidad'.* Revista Ercilla.

Villa Baviera. (2006, April 24). Carta enviada por la "Comunidad de Villa Baviera" a la opinión pública. *La Opinión.* Retrieved from https://piensachile.com/2006/04/24/carta-enviada-por-la-comunidad-de-villa-baviera-a-la-opinion-publica/

Villa Baviera. (2017, April 20). *Villa Baviera.* Obtenido de Villa Baviera. Retrieved from www.villabaviera.cl

Villarroel, T. (2020). Un enclave de indignidad. La fuga de Wolfgang Müller y los primeros años de Colonia Dignidad en Chile (1961-1966). *Historia, 53*(II), 661–690. https://doi.org/10.4067/S0717-71942020000200661

Villarrubia, G. (2013, September 23). Mi vida bajo el régimen de Paul Schäfer. *Ciper-Chile.* Retrieved from https://www.ciperchile.cl/2013/09/23/%E2%80%9Cmi-vida-bajo-el-regimen-de-paul-schafer%E2%80%9D/

Vinyes, R. (2009). *El Estado y la memoria. Gobiernos y ciudadanos frente a los traumas de la historia.* RBA Libros.

Zimbardo, P. (2012). *El efecto Lucifer. El porqué de la maldad.* Paidós.

Part VI
Political and Psychosocial Challenges of Transitions

Chapter 17
Political Transition and Social Reparation in Venezuela: Challenges of Democratic Reconstruction

Mireya Lozada

From the Illusion of Change to Social Fracture

Different social sectors refer to the end of the social-democratic consensus in Venezuela as "The end of the illusion," "the breaking of the window," "time to draw the curtain" when the Lieutenant Colonel Hugo Chávez arrived at power. He acceded to the Republic's Presidency by way of an election in December 1998 with 56% of the votes, 6 years after staging a coup d'état against President Carlos Andrés Pérez.

One of the Bolivarian project's main promises was to transform the discredited representative democracy into a participative and leading democracy, nevertheless, after more than 20 years of the Bolivarian Revolution; the death of Hugo Chávez (March 5, 2013) and the rise to power of Nicolás Maduro (April 14, 2013), new forms of authoritarianism and militarization of social life have undermined democracy (Lozada, 2020).

The progressive destruction of the institution marked by a corrupted clientelist scheme allowed for the enrichment of a new political-economic elite, in widespread anarchy of irregular and paramilitary groups that fight for territories and resources. Likewise, in this context, extended the rentier model of the providential "Magic State" (Coronil, 2002) in Venezuela to mining rentier behavior [rentierism]. Transnational companies were granted the right to exploit indigenous areas, damaging patrimonial and ecological richness, aligning itself with market control mechanisms, and international domination of natural resources (Terán, 2018).

In the context of multidimensional crises (Legler & Nolte, 2019), and complex humanitarian emergencies—against which multilateral organizations are positioning themselves—the country exhibits the highest hyperinflation rates, violence, and

M. Lozada (✉)
Universidad Central de Venezuela, Caracas, Venezuela
e-mail: mireyaloza@gmail.com

239

impunity in the world. Additionally, a high migratory exodus poses demanding challenges for Latin America.[1]

Facing social anomie, laziness, cynicism, repression, and control by the rulers, citizens have deployed various resistance and protest forms over two decades. Since the struggle between followers and opponents of the government's proposal upon Chávez's arrival to power—which included insurrectionary actions that led to the coup d'état in April 2002—diverse sectors of the Venezuelan opposition have expressed their discontent with the government's policy. They achieved a new correlation of forces that reached a majority in the December 6, 2015, parliamentary elections.

In 2017, there was an escalation of the conflict and widespread social protests throughout the country, as a result of sentences 155 and 156 of the Constitutional Chamber of the Supreme Court of Justice (TSJ) referring to the suppression of parliamentary immunity, the self-assignment of the National Assembly's (NA) parliamentary powers, the extension of constitutional powers and authority to the President of the Republic and the installation of a National Constituent Assembly (ANC), promoted outside the Constitution, by presidential decree.

At the beginning of 2019, the clash of powers in Venezuela entered a new phase. Nicolás Maduro assumed a second presidential term due to an electoral process, considered illegitimate since it did not comply with international standards.[2] Because of the loss of presidential legitimacy, the National Assembly with an opposition majority declares the "usurpation" of the Presidency and the Constitution's defense. Thus, adhering to its Articles No. 233, 333, and 350, on January 23, 2019, Juan Guaidó, the highest authority of said Parliament, is sworn in as President in Charge of the Republic, before an Open Council in Caracas.

The struggle for a change of political regime and the expectations around a problematic and uncertain stage of political transition, after the failure of the dialogue attempts (2016–2019), and of a prolonged confrontation and polarization, continue. The tensions and struggles among national sectors and sanctions and world geopolitical interests appear during the process.[3]

Approaching from a psychosocial perspective the challenges that said transition poses to a country fragmented by successive crises and socio-political violence requires addressing comprehensive reparation processes to search for truth and justice for the victims. Go deepest on the analysis of the Chavismo-anti-Chavez,

---

[1] Complex Humanitarian Emergency refers to "a humanitarian crisis in a country, region or society in which there is a total or considerable breakdown of authority, resulting from internal or external conflict, and which requires an international response that goes beyond the mandate or capacity of any single agency and the ongoing UN country program" (IASC, 1994). https://www.fundacionbengoa.org/noticias/2019/emergencia-humanitaria.asp.

[2] Observatorio electoral venezolano (2013). *Informe final observación elecciones presidenciales 14 de abril de 2013.* https://oevenezolano.org/wp-content/uploads/2020/05/OEV-PRESIDENCIALES-2013-INFORME-FINAL-OEV.pdf.

[3] Shifter M. (2019, Aug. 8). *'It Worked in Panama.' This Is Not True. More sanctions will only hurt the Venezuelan people.* https://www.nytimes.com/2019/08/08/opinion/contributors/venezuela-embargo-trump.html.

government-opposition dilemmas, or the structural factors and conjunctural ups and downs that contributed to exacerbating the conflict exceeds the objectives of this work. It is worth highlighting the challenges posed to the depolarization processes and reparation in a period of democratic transition in the country.

The analysis of information gathered in research and psychosocial support programs during the period 2000-2019, from a qualitative perspective, highlights the studies developed at the Institute of Psychology, Central University of Venezuela, in conjunction with national and international organizations (Lozada, 2007; McCoy & Diez, 2012).

Social Polarization: "Us or Them"?

In the current conflictive Venezuelan context, it is useful to revise the Sumner proposition (1906), related to the fundamental distinction between "us and them" defining whether or not to belong to specific groups. This proposition characterized and resignified the representations of the politically confronted groups—where the adversary is considered an enemy (Sumner, 2010).

The process of polarization (Martín-Baró, 1985; Lozada, 2007) characterized by.

(a) Narrowing the perceptual field and a dichotomous and stereotyped "us-them" scheme occupies the different areas of existence. It is superimposed on any other perceptual structure, conditioning the meaning of all facts, actions, and objects.
(b) Personal involvement and strong emotional charge: any event captured in polarized terms seems to affect the person himself, who rejects without nuances, the individual or group considered contrary.
(c) Exclusion and intolerance: people, families, schools, churches, or other spaces of coexistence position themselves in one of the poles and hold the same attitudes of rigidity, intolerance, and exclusion present in the political confrontation, which deny discussion, dialogue, and debate of diverse positions.

Polarization, an effective and widespread mechanism of socio-political control worldwide, generates serious and varied consequences in Venezuela at the individual and collective level (Lozada, 2016, pp. 10–11):

• Causes a substantial impact on the psyche and social subjectivity, with high personal and collective suffering costs.
• Fractures the social fabric, by causing separations, ruptures, and confrontation in spaces of cohesion and social coexistence: family, school, work, community.
• Produces patrimonial and urban damages.
• Territorialize the conflict. Segment and criminalize states, cities, towns, regions of the country identified as "official" or "opposition" enclaves.
• Reduce activities in public spaces, due to the climate of insecurity and prevailing tension.

- Cracks the foundations of social coexistence and social identity, by socially or institutionally stimulate mistrust and denial of the Other.
- It hinders the democratic and peaceful management of conflicts.
- Increases naturalizes and legitimizes social and political violence.
- Build representations of the conflict and its oversized actors' media.
- It makes the historical and complex structural causality of conflicts invisible socio-political (exclusion, poverty, unemployment, corruption, impunity, exhaustion of the traditional political model, etc.).
- It privileges conflict management and its solution in the political actors' struggle, excluding the rest of the social sectors.
- It impoverishes the public debate, qualifying the issuer and its political position, to the detriment of discussion on content.

It politicizes institutions and values loyalty over the competition, profoundly impacting public action and civil and political rights violations.

It attributes meanings to the Other's discourse and action, from representations stereotyped of class, sex, race, ethnicity, etc.

- Resignification of the politics "heroic" "macho" social imaginaries (based) and reduced to triumphs or defeats against the "Other Enemy."
- It provokes the breaking of social consensus, practices, norms, and symbolic universes shared (cultural, religious, sports, etc.).
- It prolongs and deepens the conflict without offering any prospect of a short or long-term solution or medium term.

In this context, where impunity and social anomy, institutional decomposition and delegitimization also prevail, processes of dehumanization, naturalization, and legitimization of violence occur, which becomes a daily, chronic, permanent experience. This legitimated practice, socially and institutionally, takes the form of contempt for human life, where intolerance, confrontation, or denial of the Other replaces the values of recognition, solidarity, respect, justice, leaving the law in the hands of those who have more power or more weapons.

Antagonistic Social Representations: The Other Enemy

The organization and dichotomous structure of social reality, as well as the assignment of stereotypes that feed polarization, is reflected in social representations (Moscovici, 1988), which emerge in the two politically confronted groups: "chavistas" (government) and "antichavistas" (opposition), and that of a third group called "Ni-Ni" (neither with the government nor with the opposition).

The progressive fracture of the symbolic and affective practices of a supposed collective "we" in Venezuela generated antagonistic representations. The authorities call for adhesion, trust, identification with the group itself, at the same time, they call to despise, distrust, and hate the opposing group considered an enemy, who has to be eliminated in reality or symbolically, in a struggle of exclusive identities (Lozada, 2014).

These delegitimization process and the complex dynamics of denial of the Other expressed in Venezuela have also been reported in conflict and war contexts worldwide (Bar-Tal, 1990; Martín-Baró, 1985). Said processes deny the humanity of said groups and generate fear and contempt in adversaries and the rest of the population. However, as Zavalloni (1990) warns, the emotional and evaluative significance that results from belonging to certain groups and the "natural" in-group favoritism is not enough to explain the "hatred" and "dehumanization" that situates the superiority of the in-group over the inferiority of the exo-group.

The stereotyped representation and denial of the Other expressed in different moments of political conflict in Venezuela reveal the collapse of the "hegemonic representations" (Moscovici, 1988) of democracy in the country and of the imaginary of justice, equality, and equity, as well as the utopia of well-being, development, modernity, and revolution.

Likewise, the social fabric's rupture questions the consensual communicational and dialogical nature of representations of democracy in Venezuela and reinforces the need to analyze the impact of polarization processes in a society fragmented by conflict. Hence, the importance of recognizing the cultural dimension of social thought and the psychosocial mechanisms that in terms of social identity are put into play in the representation of we-them (Moscovici, 1993), along with forms of polarized thought, affective and irrational present in some mass phenomena (Rouquette, 1994).

The Challenges of the Venezuelan Transition

The enormous challenges that Venezuela will face during a process of democratic transition have begun viewed from multiple disciplinary perspectives, international experience, and the ups and downs of the country's economic, political, and social history (Alarcón & Ramírez, 2016; Terán, 2018).

Some of the critical issues to highlight in this process are: the search for necessary mediation and negotiation strategies and mechanisms, considering the failures in previous initiatives; the possibilities of free, competitive, and transparent electoral processes; the role of civilian and military sectors; internal security problems including displaced persons, drug trafficking, and organized crime; economic and social difficulties in a post-regime model; the complexity of a "hybrid" regime change; the tasks of reinstitutionalization and the fight against impunity; the role of the media, political parties, citizen organization, participation and mobilization at the national level, and the role played by multilateral actors.

At the same time, the official denial, distortion, or "forgetting" of the facts and the persecution and criminalization of different organizations and social sectors, when they exercise their right to peaceful protest, the actions of citizens and political organizations advance in the registration, complaint, and request for help for victims.

The Report of the United Nations Independent International Fact-Finding Mission on Venezuela has made complaints of the flagrant violations of human rights in the country. As mentioned earlier, the report deepens and advances the work expressed in the first Report by Michelle Bachelet, United Nations High Commissioner for Human Rights, on human rights in the Bolivarian Republic of Venezuela, highlighting the need for the processes of repair.[4]

Different national and international sectors, facing the systematic violation of human rights, the dissolution of the constitutional order and the disintegration of the rule of law's functioning evaluate these critical factors. They generate proposals for addressing changes in the spaces of power when the political transition occurs, and the process of democratic stabilization is in progress.

However, the urgency of meeting the needs in the economic, political, and institutional spheres should not overlook the importance of the processes of social reparation, the recognition of the victims, and the fight for justice. Likewise, processes must be undertaken to rebuild the social fabric fractured by the conflict and actions aimed at building scenarios of a shared common future, between different confronted sectors that have been considered enemies for decades.

Social Reparation Processes

In situations of polarization and socio-political violence, some primary conditions for reconstructing the social fabric stand out: the fight for truth, justice, social reparation of damage, and the construction of a peace culture, which allows both to face the consequences and fight the causes. The public admission of the facts denied and imposed by the official "truth," the recognition and identification of the victims, the punishment of those responsible, the commemoration and tribute to said victims, the possibility of managing individual and social grief, will contribute to dignification, in the transition towards a critical reconstruction of personal and social memory.

A society fractured by a violent conflict must face the consequences of that violence, support the victims or survivors, and rebuild social relationships, through a process of social reparation.

---

[4] UN Human Rights (2019, July 4) report on Venezuela urges immediate measures to halt and remedy grave rights violations https://www.ohchr.org/EN/NewsEvents/Pages/DisplayNews.aspx?NewsID=24788&LangID=E.

> In the field of human rights, there is talk of 'reparation' to victims as a way to mitigate their suffering and recognize their rights. By reparation, we understand different measures with different orientations: economic and educational compensation, medical or psychological care programs, commemorations and symbolic measures, or guarantees of non-repetition, among others (Martín, 2011, p. 92).

In this regard, the United Nations General Assembly, through resolution A/RES/60/147 of October 24, 2005, approved the "Basic Principles and Guidelines on the Right to a Remedy and Reparation for Victims of Gross Violations of International Human Rights Law and Serious Violations of International Humanitarian Law. Social reparation, a simultaneously socio-political and psychosocial process, seeks to accompany the victims and acknowledge the damage caused.

Lira et al. (1985–1986) describe the psychological characteristics of the processes triggered by fear during the Chilean dictatorship: a feeling of vulnerability, an exacerbated state of alertness, a feeling of powerlessness or loss of control over one's life, and alteration of the meaning of reality, as it becomes impossible to objectively validate one's own experiences and knowledge, among other reasons due to institutionalized lies and mechanisms of coercion and repression exercised by the State apparatuses. From other experiences, Samayoa (1987, pp. 213–225) describes changes caused by dehumanization generated by the collective and prolonged political violence experience. The four cognitive and behavioral changes he identified are impoverishment of the ability to think lucidly; to communicate truthfully; of his sensitivity to the suffering of others, and to hope.

While recognizing the individual suffering of the victims whose rights have been violated by the state, these reparation processes require emphasizing the social character of the injury caused by the prolonged experience of socio-political violence. The "Ethical-political suffering," according to Bader Sawaia (1999), "psychosocial trauma" according to Martín-Baró (1988) due to a socially produced wound, "community coping and Collective post-traumatic growth," according to Páez et al. (2012).

Social reparation also requires trust contexts that favor the construction of symbolic references that can guide the idea of consensus and national unity. This idea implies undertaking social depolarization processes that favor dialogue, debate, and peaceful coexistence among different social and political sectors.

Polarization has played an important role in the maintenance and deepening of the Venezuelan political conflict and its deepening towards extreme and rigid positions that have made its resolution difficult. The political transition and the democratic reconstruction of the country require, among other conditions, social depolarization.

As Martín-Baró (1985, pp. 58–64) points out, polarization is not a consistent and unidirectional process. Its contradictions and exhaustion are expressed through:

- The fatigue of polarized positions produced by a prolonged conflict without "winners."
- The breakdown of polarization due to the collision of rigid schemes with reality.
- The personal and collective suffering that reflects the high cost of the conflict.

In the author's opinion, to contribute to depolarization requires:

(a) Breaking mirror images.
(b) Assess the high personal and collective costs of the conflict.
(c) Advance a process of awareness and de-ideologization that leads to a critical acceptance of one's own mistakes and a more realistic image of the opposite group.

The role of the media is vital in this process. Given the critical role they play in the construction of social conscience and as spaces for political and ideological confrontation, a self-critical vision is required of them that recognizes the role played throughout the conflict, both in increasing the social polarization, such as its media over-representation.

It is urgent to favor and recover the right to citizen information, currently under the control of the public communication hegemony (Bisbal, 2009) consider the impact and the consequences of the propaganda apparatus of the "show business revolution" (Uzcátegui, 2010), and also the mechanisms of disinformation and polarizing cyberactivism (Madriz, 2020).

Similarly, the deepening of the debate on polarization and social reparation requires addressing issues related to:

– Structural causes of political conflicts and social polarization.
– Socio-economic roots of intergroup discrimination and hostility, and its articulation with psychological variables to personal, group, and collective factors.
– Differences in the forms of expression and responsibilities, institutional and social aspects of political polarization, and violence.
– The Political instrumentalization of social fracture and hatred by representatives and public institutions and political organizations.
– Difficulties in advancing mediation processes between different ideological sectors and actors with antagonistic visions of the conflict and its "resolution."
– Management of truth, justice, and memory programs, in a context of institutional fragility and recovery of the rule of law.
– Conduct of amnesty and citizen reconciliation processes, which in the interest of promoting transition and social peace legitimize impunity in the face of human rights violations and crimes against humanity.

The Peace Agenda

The dynamics of polarization impose substantial challenges to peacebuilding. One of the risks of turning conflict resolution into a heritage reserved for political actors has been the political profitability of conflict and dialogue manipulation. No sector is willing to give in, encourage self-criticism, call for citizen participation at the negotiating tables or respect the agreements signed in those spaces.

Several mediation initiatives, dialogue tables, and truth commissions have emerged throughout the conflict in Venezuela. The various commissions for justice and truth, sponsored within the framework of the national government's socio-political conflict have not had continuity. They have lacked a plural and suitable presence of political and social sectors. Likewise, some of these commissions have only emphasized human rights violations against political leaders of the left, committed in Venezuela during the so-called Puntofijismo during the 1960s and 1990s.

Although these initiatives address processes of justice and necessary reparations, they create different memories. These differences originate by denying or covering up the practice of torture, cruel, inhuman and degrading treatment, arbitrary detentions, and serious human rights violations against leaders and different sectors of the opposition that occurred during the Bolivarian Revolution security, military and paramilitary agencies.

Of the mediation initiatives, perhaps the one with the most significant repercussion and impact has been the Table of Negotiation and Agreements installed during November 2002–May 2003, which counted with the government's representation, the opposition, and supportive political and social sectors. Although this effort contributed to stopping the escalation of violence during 2002–2004, most of the agreements of the declaration signed in Caracas on May 29, 2003 were not effectively fulfilled. On the contrary, socio-political violence increased, and disrespect for the Republic's Constitution and laws spread. The failure of three other negotiation attempts (2016–2019), which included international actors, among them the Vatican, and the political cost of their strong criticism in social networks, has made it difficult to advance this alternative, considered the best scenario for a transition between government and opposition.

For Diez (2019), the Venezuelan conflict's central issue has always been the dispute for presidential power. But, currently, such conflict and its resolution transcend the internal confrontation to maintain or achieve it. The parties have multiplied, and tensions, dilemmas, struggles, and international interests are involved.

In the same sense, Legler and Nolte (2019) affirm that the crisis in Venezuela has affected the multilateral structure erected to safeguard continental democracy and multiply the conflict spaces. According to the authors, the Venezuelan crisis has torn the democratic fabric.

In general, multilateral efforts to "defend" or "restore" democracy in Venezuela or those directed at privileging economic, energy, and military interests in Venezuela by other States, for example, The USA, Russia, China, among other global actors, tend to ignore the real demands of the population or structural socio-economic problems.

There are many lessons derived from the solution offered to political conflicts in other countries, which allow us to defend the thesis that it should be the society itself in the conflict that articulates and debates how to confront the problems. All those developed with the population's back turned, sooner or later generate severe social costs. Therefore, it is necessary to support all strategies that assume society as the fundamental subject of change. The political actors should be agents capable of translating into agreements with those initiatives that emerge from the community in conflict.

Only a more equitable and democratic political, economic, and legal order can guarantee lasting peace, heal individual and social wounds, and reduce political violence. Only a democratic regime capable of building citizenship and a culture of peace based on values of dialogue, inclusion, and justice will be ably confronting the current socio-political and economic panorama in Venezuela. Currently, this panorama can be characterized by the discredit of political parties, the fragility of institutions, authoritarianism, society's militarization, social fragmentation, high levels of hyperinflation, unemployment, violence, corruption, and impunity.

Memory-Justice and Truth

There are many challenges to a democratic transition in Venezuela. A society fractured by political violence and social polarization demands reparation processes to search for truth and justice for the victims. From the analysis of the scope and limits of international and Latin American experiences, Martín Beristain (2008) highlights some axes of reflection-action located in the triad: memory-justice and truth:

Human Rights Violations

- Victims and survivors.
- Levels and degrees of the psychological impact.
- Research and psychosocial and psycho-legal support.
- Formation and strengthening of support networks.
- Participation of public and private organizations.
- Expert opinions and case analysis.
- Gathering of testimonies, preparation of hearings, and follow-up.
- Impact on legal representatives and human rights defenders: care and prevention.

Truth Commission

- Selection criteria for committee members. Public consultation.
- Scope and limits of economic, social, psychological reparation programs, spiritual, symbolic.

- Role of human rights organizations, institutions, and external and internal actors.
- Training, support, and technical assistance to Human Rights Organizations, Justice, and commissions established.
- Type of treatment granted to victims.
- Testimonials, preparation of hearings, and follow-up.
- Models of transitional or restorative justice to apply.
- Contribution and limitations of models to the fight against impunity.

Pacification, Reconciliation, Social Peace, and Democratization in Post-conflict Situation and Democratic Transition

- Recommendations for judicial reforms.
- Follow-up of agreements and recommendations.

Training, Research, Social Awareness, Dissemination

- Addressing the problem of impunity, right to truth, justice, and human rights.
- Training in formal and informal educational settings: courses, diplomas, workshops, round tables, seminars.
- Awareness and action in public spaces.
- Research and editorial production.
- Publications in print and digital formats.
- Construction of memory sites and memorials of resistance.

Democratic Reconstruction: The Challenge of Coexistence

As we can see, there is still a long way to go before an effective communication between the confronted sectors is possible. That is to say, where each proposal and each act is not condemning in advance to alter tempers further, deepening quarrels on both sides, denying or postponing the search for a peaceful and democratic transition to the prolonged conflict in Venezuela.

The construction of consensus that allows for the coexistence, participation, and inclusion of the entire Venezuelan population demands the analysis of the formation and maintenance of the oil State; the transits of the political pacts resulting from the "conciliation of the elites" (Rey, 1991); the ruptures that, like the social explosion of the "Caracazo," put an end to the "illusion of harmony" (Naím & Piñango, 1995) and the "model" democracy that Venezuela was experiencing.

In short, the economic model's recurrent crises are addhed to the various demands, struggles, and popular protests and the social-political fragmentation, causing the rupture of the social-democratic imaginary of the so-called Saudi Venezuela. These processes have had a profound social, political, economic, and cultural impact; they have revealed identities that have been denied, marginalized, and made invisible by a large part of the Venezuelan political class at different historical moments. These crises may contribute to alternative searches and horizons to the "national anguish for an identity" (Castro, 1991).

To recognize this process means to assume individually and socially our greatest challenge: to privilege coexistence and deepen democracy, from the critical reconstruction of historical memory, the systematization of social knowledge, and the diversity of experiences lived in this time.

Even though Venezuelan society urgently expects and demands from the political sectors involved in the conflict a way out of the crisis, it will not lead to lasting peace if it does not incorporate into its agenda the plural voice of different national sectors: political, social, cultural, economic, religious, media, etc.

An electoral, peaceful, and democratic solution is required to provide useful answers to the country's serious problems—responses guided by inclusion and justice principles, and for establishing public institutional liability. This democratic solution could allow to ward off the political threats of militarism, authoritarianism, and caudillismo that manipulate emotions and foster blind devotion to a leader, whether military or civilian. This blind devotion encourages the people–anti-people, friends–enemies, patriots–anti-patriots Manichaeism.

The analysis of the objective and subjective obstacles to the deepening of democracy in Venezuela, and in the region, also implies a critique of the reproduction of oppressive models that exclude and deny the Other and reproduce exclusionary, racist, classist, and sexist schemes present in the so called alternative projects. It is necessary to evaluate the consequences of the subordination of the different social sectors to partisan, political, civic-military strategies (armed or not) in power conflicts, in corruption, in the instrumental and populist use, with the consequent decrease in political participation and internal fragmentation.

The promotion and defense of the political, social, economic, and civil rights of the population require resignifying the values of dignity, work, participation, honesty, and solidarity to favor cohesion and reconstruct the social fabric from various fields and disciplines, formal and informal education. It is necessary to deconstruct the values associated with cunning, corruption, and begging present in all kinds of claims and prebends sponsored by the Venezuelan oil state, without mythologizing the popular majorities or disqualifying or excluding other social sectors.

The rescue, the resignification of these values in a post-rentier model, constitutes the ethical condition of change (Esté, 2011) that grants cohesion and collective strength. This process will help overcome the difficulties of dismantling authoritarian practices and following up dialogues, negotiation, and conciliation. In the psychosocial processes of construction of otherness, rather than favoring "exclusionary inclusion" (García-Guadilla, 2003), the emergence of new social subjects can facilitate inclusive and non-antagonistic representations of the Other (Arruda, 1998), recognizing the diversity and plurality of democratic coexistence.

Likewise, the reconstruction processes of a collective memory of the conflict will offer broader and more comprehensive views of different groups and political sectors. Outside the Manichean scheme of polarization, an awareness that what is at stake is not the triumph of one option, but democracy, justice, and peace in Venezuela.

A self-critical look will allow us to recognize our mistakes, excesses or omissions, facts, and individual and collective responsibilities, offering the opportunity to vindicate lessons learned, achievements, sufferings, and joys, giving meaning to the experience of life in its struggle for dignity.

Finally, being all of us one country, guided by a "we" with a common north, we can generate the conditions that allow us to redefine the democratic imaginary as a participatory and inclusive project, felt and shared by different social and political sectors of Venezuela.

References

Alarcón, B., & Ramírez, S. (2016). *El Desafío Venezolano III: La consolidación de una transición democrática*. CEP/UCAB.

Arruda, A. (1998). O ambiente natural e seus habitantes no imaginário brasileiro negociando a diferencia. In A. Arruda (Ed.), *Representando a alteridade* (pp. 17–46). Editora Vozes.

Bar-Tal, D. (1990). Causes and consequences of delegitimization: Models of conflict and ethnocentrism. *Journal of Social Issues, 46*(1), 65–81. https://doi.org/10.1111/j.1540-4560.1990.tb00272.x

Bisbal, M. (2009). *Hegemonía y control comunicacional*. CIC-UCAB.

Castro, L. (1991). *De la patria boba a la teología bolivariana*. Monte Ávila Editores.

Coronil, A. (2002). *El Estado mágico. Naturaleza, dinero y modernidad en Venezuela*. CDCH, Nueva Sociedad.

Diez, F. (2019). El conflicto en Venezuela: La mirada de un mediador. *Foreign Affairs Latinoamérica, 19*(2), 16–23. Retrieved from https://dialnet.unirioja.es/servlet/articulo?codigo=7172820

Esté, A. (2011). *La condición ética del cambio*. Ponencia presentada en VII Jornadas de Investigación Humanística y Educativa, San Cristóbal, Venezuela.

García-Guadilla, M. (2003). *Politization and Polarization of Venezuelan Civil Society: Facing Democracy with two Faces*. Paper for the XXIV International Congress of the Latin American Studies Association, Dallas, UE.

Legler, T., & Nolte, D. (2019). Venezuela: la protección regional multilateral de la democracia. *Foreign Affairs Latinoamérica, 19*(2), 43–51. Retrieved from https://biblat.unam.mx/es/revista/foreign-affairs-latinoamerica/articulo/venezuela-la-proteccion-regional-multilateral-de-la-democracia

Lira, E., Weinstein, E., & Salamovich, S. (1985–1986). El miedo: Un enfoque psicosocial. *Revista Chilena de Psicología, 8*(1), 51–56.

Lozada, M. (2007). El Otro es el enemigo. Representaciones e imaginarios sociales en tiempos de polarización. El caso Venezuela. En A. Arruda & M. de Alba (Coords.), *Espacios imaginarios y representaciones sociales. Aportes desde Latinoamérica* (pp. 381–406). UAM-Iztapalapa.

Lozada, M. (2014). Us or them? Social representations and imaginaries of the other in Venezuela. *Papers of Social Representations, 23*, 178–193. Retrieved from https://repositorioslatinoamericanos.uchile.cl/handle/2250/192979

Lozada, M. (2016). *Despolarización y procesos de reparación social. Los desafíos de la convivencia en Venezuela.* Fundación Friedrich Ebert.

Lozada, M. (2020). Neo-autoritarismos y resistencias sociales en Venezuela: Vida cotidiana de la mitología bolivariana. En D. Uhng Hur & J. M. Sabucedo (Coords.), *Psicologia dos extremismos políticos* (pp. 147–174). Editorial Vozes.

Madriz, M, (2020). *Teoría, procesos y análisis de la desinformación en Venezuela. Parte 1: El contexto de la desinformación.* Observatorio de Desinformación, Rumores y Falsas Noticias ObserVE, Caracas: ININCO, Universidad Central de Venezuela.

Martín Beristain, C. (2008). *Diálogos sobre la reparación. Experiencias en el sistema interamericano de derechos humanos* (Tomo I y II). San José. Instituto Interamericano de Derechos Humanos.

Martín, C. (2011). Violencia, polarización o ¿(re)conciliación?, El caso vasco. En M. Lozada (Coord.), *Polarización social y política en Venezuela y otros países. Experiencias y desafíos* (pp. 79–103). Publicaciones UCAB.

Martín-Baró, I. (1985). *Conflicto y polarización social.* Trabajo presentado en el XX Congreso Interamericano de Psicología, Caracas.

Martín-Baró, I. (1988). La violencia política y la guerra como causas del trauma psicosocial en El Salvador. *Revista de Psicología de El Salvador, 7*(28), 123–141. Retrieved from https://biblat.unam.mx/es/revista/revista-de-psicologia-de-el-salvador/articulo/la-violencia-politica-y-la-guerra-como-causas-del-trauma-psicosocial-en-el-salvador

McCoy, J., & Diez, F. (2012). *Mediación Internacional en Venezuela.* Gedisa editorial.

Moscovici, S. (1988). Notes towards a description of social representations. *European Journal of Social Psychology, 18*(3), 211–250. https://doi.org/10.1002/ejsp.2420180303

Moscovici, S. (1993). *Razón y culturas. Discurso pronunciado con motivo de la investidura como Doctor "Honoris Causa" por la.* Universidad de Sevilla. Universidad de Sevilla. Extensión Universitaria.

Naím, M., & Piñango, R. (1995). *El caso Venezuela: una ilusión de armonía.* Ediciones IESA.

Páez, D., Vázquez, C., & Echeburúa, E. (2012). Trauma Social, Afrontamiento Comunitario y Crecimiento Postraumático colectivo. In M. J. Carrasco & B. Charro (Eds.), *Crisis, vulnerabilidad y superación* (pp. 15–50). Universidad de Comillas.

Rey, J. (1991). La democracia venezolana y la crisis del sistema populista de conciliación. *Revista de Estudios Políticos, 74,* 533–578. Retrieved from https://dialnet.unirioja.es/servlet/articulo?codigo=27121

Rouquette, J. (1994). *Sur la connaissance des masses. Essai de psychologie politique.* PUG.

Samayoa, J. (1987). Guerra y deshumanización: una perspectiva psicosocial. *Estudios Centroamericanos, 461,* 213–225.

Sawaia, B. (1999). O sofrimento ético-político como categoria de análise da dialéctica exclusao/inclusao. En B. Sawaia (Org.), *As artimanhas da exclusao. Analise psicosocial e ética da desigualdade social* (pp. 97–118). Editora Vozes.

Sumner, G. W. (2010). *Folkways: A study of the sociological importance of usages, manners, customs, mores, and morals.* Cornell University Press.

Terán, E. (2018). Une géographie des conflits écologiques au Venezuela. Pétro-État, crise historique et nouvelles frontières des matières premières de haute valeur. Venezuela 1998-2018: Le pays des fractures. *Les Temps Modernes, 697,* 177–196. Retrieved from https://dialnet.unirioja.es/servlet/articulo?codigo=6523443

Uzcátegui, R. (2010). *Venezuela: la revolución como espectáculo. Una crítica anarquista al gobierno bolivariano.* Editorial La Malatesta.

Zavalloni, M. (1990). L'effet de résonance dans la création de l'identité et des représentations sociales. *Revue Internationale de Psychologie Sociale, 3*(3), 407–428.

Chapter 18
Psychology and Human Rights in Colombia: Contributions to Peacebuilding

Wilson López-López (✉), Andrea Correa-Chica, Angélica Caicedo-Moreno, Pablo Castro-Abril, and Carlos Felipe Buitrago-Panader

Introduction

The human rights (HR) proclaimed in the Universal Declaration of the United Nations (1948) are the international instrument that has set the global objective of respecting and guaranteeing human dignity based on the principles of equality and justice (Valdivieso, 2012).

In the Colombian democracy, HR are conceived as guiding and binding principles that shape the government's actions (López, 2012). However, the complex social and state structures have hindered the formulation and implementation of HR policies in Colombia (Herrera & Taylor, 2014). This context is evident in the existing sociopolitical violence, internal armed conflict, and the rationale of state neglect and exclusion (Sikkink, 2009).

W. López-López (✉) · C. F. Buitrago-Panader
Pontificia Universidad Javeriana, Bogotá, Colombia
e-mail: lopezw@javeriana.edu.co; buitrago-c@javeriana.edu.co

A. Correa-Chica
Universidade de Santiago de Compostela, Santiago de Compostela, España
e-mail: jullyandrea.correa@rai.usc.es

A. Caicedo-Moreno · P. Castro-Abril
Universidad del País Vasco, San Sebastián-Donostia, España
e-mail: angelicamoreno8_@hotmail.com; pabloenrique.castro@ehu.eus

Armed Conflict in Colombia

Human rights violations in Colombia's recent history have left cultural, political, economic, social, and psychological scars throughout the country (Centro Nacional de Memoria Histórica [CNMH], 2013). The armed conflict has directly affected more than eight million people (Unidad para la Atención y Reparación Integral a las Víctimas, 2020) through violence against the civilian population such as threats, forced recruitment, disappearances, massacres, killings, and selective executions by multiple actors (e.g., guerrillas, paramilitary groups, state forces, drug trafficking organizations) (CNMH, 2013). Violence has been used systematically to sustain control over the territory in a way that allows land concentration, arms and drug trafficking, and, ultimately, the management of political and economic power both regionally and nationally by a set of elites (Ibáñez & Vélez, 2008).

Since the late twentieth century, peace negotiations were held with some former combatants but with mixed results. Although the demobilization and political participation of some illegal groups were achieved, the lack of institutional and regional support, the resurgence of violent practices, and the political and armed persecution of these new political organizations called into question the State's role as guarantor of human rights of the civilian population and opposing political groups (CNMH, 2018; Comisión Interamericana de Derechos Humanos, 2017).

The many negotiation processes have included multiple transitional justice mechanisms that have had implications for how memory, truth, and reparations for victims have become imperatives. For instance, the Justice and Peace Law 975, that was approved in 2005, established the main formal proceedings of transitional justice (Congreso de la República de Colombia, 2005). Among its goals, this law aimed to disarm the paramilitary groups, reintegrate their members into society, and guarantee the rights of truth, justice, and reparation to the victims. This initiative promoted massive demobilization and created a legal framework to prosecute crimes committed by paramilitary groups. However, this law was decried internationally, warning that it would ensure impunity to those responsible for atrocious crimes while failing to offer guarantees to victims (CNMH, 2013; Villa, 2012).

Subsequently, the Victims Law (Law 1448) was passed in 2011, recognizing the damage caused by armed conflict and seeking mechanisms for attention, assistance, and comprehensive reparation to victims. This scenario fostered the negotiations with the FARC-EP guerrilla in 2016 when a historic peace agreement was reached with this group, achieving demobilization processes and political participation for reintegrating members. The peace accords created one of the boldest transitional justice mechanisms that encompassed a new truth commission, a special justice system for peace, and the missing people's search unit. This mechanism put legal and non-legal reparations measures for the conflict's victims at the forefront of the process. Amid a long and complex armed conflict such as the Colombian one, These measures are a hopeful sign of strengthening the commitment to respect human rights in a context of a long and complex armed conflict such as the Colombian one (United Nations, 2018).

Nonetheless, the agreement was forged in a climate of social polarization, with the government of President Iván Duque (2018–2022) and his party repeatedly speaking out against the peace accord and its implementation. Consequently, the annual reports on the first three years of implementation of the peace agreement documented systematic attacks on HR defenders, social and community leaders. The reports also note difficulty in moving forward with the comprehensive reparation to victims in areas affected in the past by the conflict, due to the lack of coverage, monitoring and guarantees in reintegration and restitution services (United Nations High Commissioner for Human Rights, 2019).

Likewise, as of 2019, combat with other illegal groups (ELN guerrillas, paramilitary, and drug trafficking groups) intensified, reactivating terrorist attacks and forcing new displacements. Paramilitary groups have taken center stage with a subsequent increase in victimization statistics related to the control of illicit economies such as drug trafficking, illegal mining, arms trafficking, and commercial extortion which once again impairs the guarantee of human rights (United Nations High Commissioner for Human Rights, 2019).

It is important to emphasize that the victims continue to be mainly civilians in rural areas (e.g., farmers, indigenous people, Afro-descendants) and community social leaders. During 2020, there were 76 massacres, the highest figure since 2014. There were also 73 homicides of former FARC-EP members and 133 murders of HR defenders (United Nations, 2021).

The prolongation of the armed conflict and the multiplicity of actors involved led to deep societal divisions and have weakened the Colombian state's capacity to respond as a guarantor of HR (Amnistía Internacional, 2018). Promoting the non-repetition of these events and the HR protection, generating policies and measures for the reparation of victims at different levels are indispensable conditions for peace construction.

Psychosocial Consequences of Human Rights Violations During the Armed Conflict

Economic, political, legal, environmental, security, and psychosocial factors must be taken into account when analyzing human rights violations in Colombia (Sikkink, 2009; United Nations High Commissioner for Human Rights, 2019). The context of exclusion, poverty, misery, inequality, the failure to ensure basic security needs, lack of access to health services, and inadequate education resources represent the constant violation of human rights by the Colombian state (Rodríguez, 2004). Moreover, rural inhabitants are the most affected because the war happened in their territory, where there are high levels of poverty and socioeconomic inequality (Naucke, 2017).

Psychology in Colombia has had long participation in community work to mitigate the multiple consequences upon communities and individuals of the armed conflict and the sustained violation of human rights. Psychologists in non-governmental organizations, various initiatives of universities as well as governmental entities have accompanied these challenging processes. The community-based psychology was shaped by the legacy of psychologists such as Maritza Montero, Ignacio Martín-Baró, and by the inspiring work of Elizabeth Lira. Unfortunately, many of these initiatives have not been reported or have been noted only as part of reports that overshadow their actions and impact. However, their contributions are visible in the community practices and the lives of the people who have participated in such programs. In recent years, several new areas of research have emerged regarding the consequences of the conflict and the processes involved in the long and complex peace process.

The field of psychology has sought to understand, specifically, the consequences of the internal armed conflict and the violation of human rights on individual, inter-personal, intra-, and inter-group dynamics (López-López, 2017, 2020). Research has focused on analyzing (a) the consequences on psychological well-being from exposure to traumatic events; (b) the impact on the coexistence of directly and indirectly affected communities; (c) the dynamics of the persistence of violence by analyzing the role of social agents in the legitimization of violent or peaceful practices; (d) the processes of disarmament, demobilization, and reintegration into civilian life of former combatants; (e) the processes of recognition of harm, justice, and comprehensive reparation to victims; and (f) the disposition towards social reconciliation to achieve a shared future of peaceful coexistence.

Some studies on psychological well-being report that people exposed to traumatic events in the context of armed conflict are more likely to suffer mental health disorders as compared to the general population (Cuartas et al., 2019). Post-traumatic stress, depression, and anxiety are frequently encountered (Cudris-Torres & Barrios Núñez, 2018; Gaviria et al., 2016; Hewitt et al., 2016). Research has found that minors directly exposed to a conflict are more likely to have aggressive behaviors, externalizing disorders (e.g., oppositional defiant disorder) (Brook et al., 2007; Cuevas & Castro, 2009), or post-traumatic stress disorder (Pérez-Olmos et al., 2005). Moreover, some studies with children suggest that exposure to violence at an early age or during the gestation period can affect physical and brain development, generating negative consequences in intellectual and interpersonal processes (Cuevas & Castro, 2009; Duque, 2017).

In group and community dynamics, some studies report that the armed conflict generates a decrease in the quality of life and a rupture of the family and social fabric (Castañeda et al., 2019; Hewitt et al., 2016). There is evidence that the relocation and displacement experiences generate new vulnerabilities and ongoing instability in family structures (Mootz et al., 2019).

In territories threatened by different armed conflicts, cohesion, support among community members, and participation in collective decision-making processes make communities less likely to be displaced (Krakowski, 2017). There is even evidence of communities that have mitigated violence against them through peaceful resistance measures such as remaining neutral, avoiding threats, and implementing self-reliance mechanisms to refrain from cooperating with former combatants (Wegner, 2017).

These findings demonstrate that social resources such as trust, cohesion, and solidarity are crucial for the recovery of communities (Krakowski, 2017; Taylor, 2016). There is also evidence of high levels of community resilience, often related to spirituality and religious practices, which have enabled victims to cope and restructure their lives (Hewitt et al., 2016), despite severe conditions of violence.

Regarding the dynamics of persistent violence, broad empirical evidence points to a socio-psychological repertoire shaped by collective beliefs, attitudes, and emotions towards the armed conflict and its actors, which is functional to the members of society to cope with the human and material losses. At the same time, this fosters the continuation of the armed confrontation (López-López et al., 2018).

Likewise, the government discourse concerning the armed conflict has been characterized by a delegitimization of the adversary and legitimization of the use of force (Barreto et al., 2009; Borja-Orozco et al., 2008; López-López et al., 2018). However, some studies also show the transformation of this socio-psychological repertoire in the course of seeking a peaceful resolution to the conflict in recent years. Concretely, impact can be seen in calling for hope for peace, the recognition of victims' rights and the structural causes of the conflict, as well as in the absence or reduction of strategies to delegitimize the adversary (López-López et al., 2018; Rincón-Unigarro et al., 2020).

As for the processes of disarmament, demobilization, and reintegration into civilian life by former combatants, some studies report that the civilian population has little trust or willingness to coexist and work with former combatants of demobilized armed groups (López-López et al., 2016a, b, 2018). In territories where reintegration processes occurred, Kaplan and Nussio (2018) found that former combatants are more likely to participate in community activities when there is high participation of the civilian community members themselves. These are spaces where former combatants also feel useful in the settlement communities. When people are not involved, former organize in isolation, separated from the community, seeking to protect their families and themselves from the effects of the deeply rooted stigmatization of being identified as former combatants (McFee, 2016).

The processes of recognition of harm, justice, and comprehensive reparation for victims present many challenges to overcome. Many initiatives have emerged to repair the damage caused in the conflict by HR groups, state institutions, and the victims themselves to achieve a stable and lasting peace (Arias, 2018). However, the transitional justice mechanisms to achieve comprehensive reparation by providing guarantees to the victims to overcome social helplessness depend on (a) a national budget, which is often insufficient; (b) operational public institutions, often with limited response capacity; and (c) social and political will, sometimes at odds with these objectives (Arias, 2018; Villa & Insuasty, 2016).

Within this context, it is therefore understandable that some studies find that the victim populations do not believe the promised reparations or trials of the perpetrators will ever come about. They simply mistrust state mechanisms (Castrillón-Guerrero et al., 2018).

Lastly (Bloomfield et al., 2003), several studies confirm that structural challenges must be overcome to foster the disposition towards reconciliation and move forward from a divided past to a shared future of peaceful coexistence in Colombia.

In different countries empirical evidence points to the benefits for the psychological well-being of victims derived from reconciliation scenarios such as improved interpersonal relationships, creation of new social networks, strengthening of social capital, overcoming negative emotions, and feelings towards the perpetrator (Cilliers et al., 2016). However, political reconciliation can also increase depression, anxiety, or post-traumatic stress disorder, affecting the psychological well-being of victims (Cilliers et al., 2016). Similarly, although forgiveness is personal and does not condition reconciliation, clearly, it can facilitate participation in the construction of a collective future.

The willingness to forgive and reconcile was studied in Colombia in both the victim and the general population. The research has identified a low disposition to forgive and reconcile—in personal terms—although higher among victims, regardless of the existence of remorse among the perpetrators. Studies also found that during 2016, the year of the peace agreement referendum, the willingness to forgive increased when former combatants participated in peace talks with the state or when there are guarantees of non-repetition (López-López et al., 2013, 2016a, b).

Research on the conceptualizations of forgiveness found that both victims and the general population associated the process with a religious context linked to the idea of *divine justice and forgetting offenses*, partly because there is no credibility in the forms of justice provided by the State (Castrillón-Guerrero et al., 2018; Cortés et al., 2016). Reconciliation, however, is a process usually associated with acceptance and resumption of interactions in which the victim and the victimizer may participate (Castrillón-Guerrero et al., 2018; Cortés et al., 2016; López-López et al., 2016a, b).

In peace processes throughout the world different actors have generated transitional mechanisms associated with justice. This underscores the importance of forgiveness and reconciliation processes in truth commissions and the transitional justice mechanisms. However, it is difficult to achieve effectiveness without conditions of non-repetition and reparation, which is the case in many Colombian local contexts (López-López et al., 2016a, b).

Psychosocial Intervention for the Restoration of Human Rights in the Context of the Colombian Armed Conflict: A Case Study

Thanks to their activism through collective mobilization, the armed conflict victims achieved visibility in the social and political arena, both nationally and internationally. One of the main demands was effective psychosocial care policies from the State (Villa, 2012). Due to this pressure, and with the support of international organizations, the State created a national program focused on psychosocial intervention for armed conflict victims through the Law 1448 of 2011 (Congreso de la República de Colombia, 2011).

Among the different measures contemplated in Law 1448 was the implementation of the Psychosocial Care and Comprehensive Health Program for Victims of the Conflict (PAPSIVI-acronym in Spanish), as part of the health care and physical, mental, and psychosocial rehabilitation measure (Congreso de la República de Colombia, 2011).

The PAPSIVI program has a psychosocial approach, with an ethical commitment, proposing that entities and professionals should recognize the integrality of those who have been victims (Moreno & Díaz, 2016). The aim is to develop comprehensive care services that contribute to the recovery or mitigation of "psychosocial damage, emotional suffering and impacts on the psychological and moral integrity and life project of victims, their families, and communities, as a result of serious human rights violations and breaches of IHL [International Humanitarian Law]" (Ministerio de Salud y Protección Social [MinSalud], 2017a, p. 23, 2017b).

This program intends to address the impacts of violence on the victim population throughout the national territory, at the individual, family, and community levels, taking into account a differential approach, the effective participation of different national institutions, and, above all, highlighting the obligation of the Colombian State to guarantee the victims' human rights (MinSalud, 2017a).

Another psychosocial intervention tool developed as a result of Law 1448 was the Emotional Recovery Strategy at Group Level (ERE-G) promoted by the UARIV (2014), which aims to respond to the psychosocial needs of victims through group work, the construction of meanings, emotional self-regulation, and the representation-symbolization of people's suffering.

According to MinSalud (2019), between 2012 and 2018, the government provided psychosocial care to 692,999 conflict victims. Of this number, 490,708 received care through the psychosocial component of PAPSIVI and 202,291 through the UARIV (within the ERE-G framework). However, the number of psychosocial services provided to date is very low for the proposed target under Law 1448 (24%).

Although the rate of perception of improvement and rehabilitation by the beneficiaries of the PAPSIVI and ERE-G initiatives is suggested to be high (MinSalud, 2019), empirical evidence indicates that not all processes are proving to be restorative for the victims and that these initiatives probably require greater caution and investment.

The criticisms of the psychosocial interventions generated from Law 1448 for conflict victims who have had their HR violated, as shown in Fig. 18.1, are due to structural and professional factors that cause adverse effects in the communities (Aranguren-Romero & Rubio-Castro, 2018; Cuartas et al., 2019; Villa, 2016). For instance, the health system does not prioritize psychosocial care and uses hiring schemes that are often outsourced and precarious. Besides, there is a lack of expertise and training in the multiple interventions in communities and individuals carried out by psychologists and social science and health professionals. Figure 18.1 describes some of the challenges faced at the structural and professional levels.

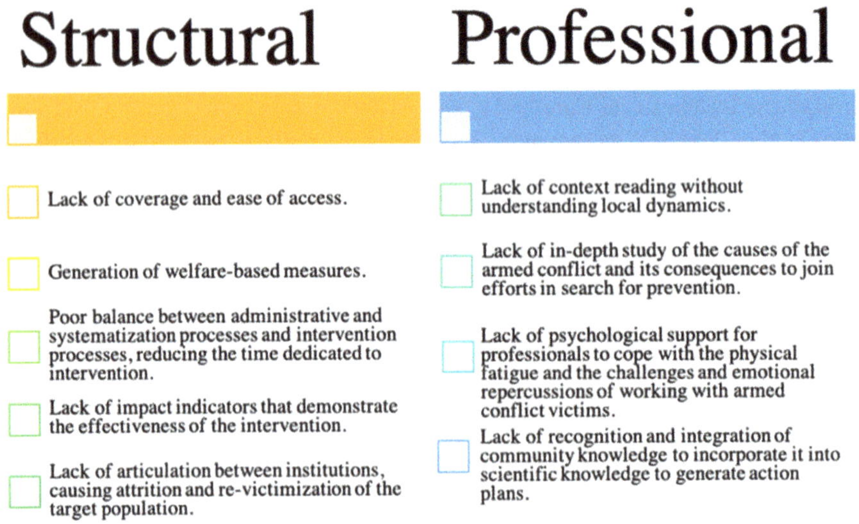

Structural

Lack of coverage and ease of access.

Generation of welfare-based measures.

Poor balance between administrative and systematization processes and intervention processes, reducing the time dedicated to intervention.

Lack of impact indicators that demonstrate the effectiveness of the intervention.

Lack of articulation between institutions, causing attrition and re-victimization of the target population.

Professional

Lack of context reading without understanding local dynamics.

Lack of in-depth study of the causes of the armed conflict and its consequences to join efforts in search for prevention.

Lack of psychological support for professionals to cope with the physical fatigue and the challenges and emotional repercussions of working with armed conflict victims.

Lack of recognition and integration of community knowledge to incorporate it into scientific knowledge to generate action plans.

Fig. 18.1 Structural and professional factors

A Multidimensional Perspective for the Promotion of Human Rights in Colombia

To meet the challenge of building peace in Colombia, as we have previously stated, requires prioritizing the appropriation of human rights in the social and political agenda of the country. In other words, systematic efforts must be focused on prevention, promotion, and protection of human rights, as well as monitoring and denouncing human rights violations. Moreover, we must assume a multidimensional and interdisciplinary perspective of research and intervention to understand the various dimensions of actors, violence, consequences, and processes involved in the pursuit of peace and the defense of human rights. In this sense, López-López (2016, 2017, 2020) proposes in his works to consider a multidimensional research and intervention perspective (see Fig. 18.1).

This perspective contemplates eight dimensions in which agendas should be built, as shown in Fig. 18.2. The transformations proposed for each dimension are:

1. *Socioeconomic:* Reduce inequality in the distribution of wealth.
2. *Sociopolitical:* Promote policies aimed at the inclusion of vulnerable groups and social reconciliation scenarios and implement management mechanisms based on dialogue and consensus.
3. *Socio-legal:* Advance towards the respect for human rights and the reduction of impunity through the application of restorative actions.
4. *Safety:* Establish actions and mechanisms aimed at protecting integrity, privacy, and intimacy.

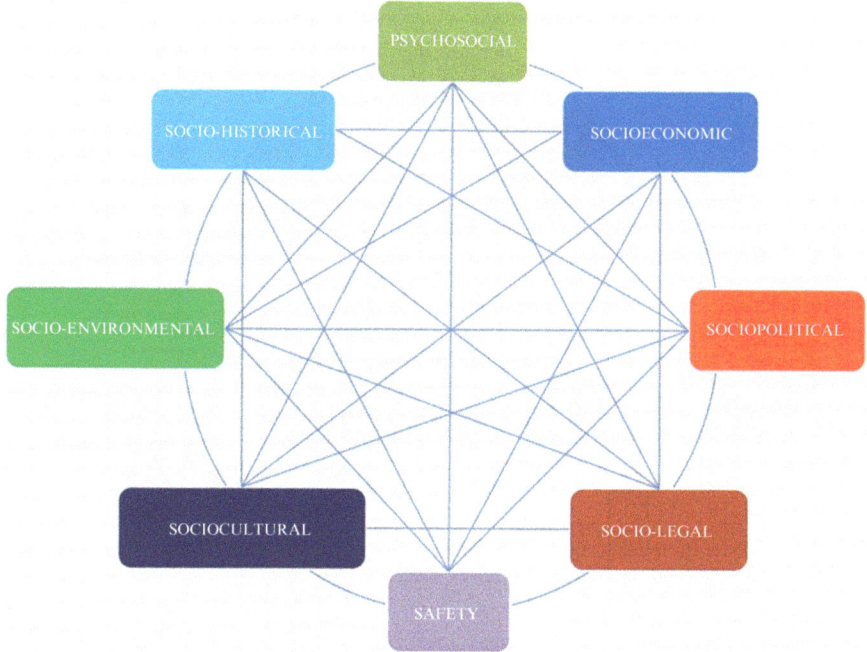

Fig. 18.2 Conflict dimensions. (Adapted from López-López, 2020)

5. *Sociocultural:* Promote practices that encourage tolerance, gender equality, and child-rearing practices and that reject the use of violence and exclusion.
6. *Socio-environmental:* Recognize and transform the environmental crises, the deterioration of natural resources, and violence and move towards economic policies based on sustainable sources and change extractive strategies.
7. *Socio-historical:* Address the communities' experience from a micro- and macro-perspective, taking into account how the socio-historical processes are remembered by the civilian population in the present and the future perspective, thus strengthening collective memory processes.
8. *Psychosocial:* Progress in emotional education processes, reduce asymmetries in interpersonal and inter-group interactions to move towards group cohesion, developing empathy, and giving voice to the communities to advance in the empowerment processes.

Regarding the psychosocial dimension, Fig. 18.3 illustrates an approach based on the identification of a set of actors, violence, consequences, and psychosocial processes. It is an approach that intertwines (a) the ethnic, gender, and developmental differences; (b) experiences of care and community and personal intervention; as well as (c) community and institutional biographies and mediums (López-López, 2020).

This proposed approach understands the psychosocial dimension as a spiral or fabric in which the personal is woven with the relational, the intra- and inter-group,

Fig. 18.3 Model for understanding the conflict with its different actors, forms of violence, processes, and psychosocial consequences (López-López, 2020)

and the societal aspects. Within this fabric, biographies and community and social histories are constructed (López-López, 2020). The evidence of the continuous work of psychologists and other professionals with the communities shows the interaction of the psychosocial dimension with the others (political, economic, environmental, legal) and the importance of transitional justice mechanisms, such as clarifying the truth and achieving social reconciliation. It also suggests that only by articulating this whole set of interactions can sustainable peace processes be built (López-López, 2020).

Proposal for the Future to Advance in the Guarantee of Human Rights from Psychology in Colombia

Peacebuilding in Colombia is a highly complex process that requires, as we have previously stated, a dynamic, multidimensional, interdisciplinary perspective that prioritizes human rights over any other process involved in the reconstruction that seeks to lessen the impact of the social and armed conflict. Thus, protecting the rights and the lives of the most vulnerable communities and those who defend and promote them is an urgent matter. The rise in murders of social leaders and human rights defenders and the lack of government commitment to protect them and clarify, capture, and prosecute those responsible, unfortunately, lead to sustained and escalated conflict.

Furthermore, in a context of permanent transition in which the armed confrontation has not stopped, and the State shows that it cannot respond to the constant violations of human rights, psychology professionals have no alternative but to continue working even in adverse conditions, to contribute to strengthening psychological well-being and the community fabric in the country (Molina, 2017). Therefore, as argued by the multidimensional model of peace proposed by López-López (2016, 2017, 2020), efforts aimed at peacebuilding cannot be limited to a single aspect due to the complexity of the conflict.

The sustained commitment is needed from different social actors, including psychologists, to build, accompany, and install long-term cultural practices of peaceful resistance and care for human rights with communities (López-López et al., 2018). Furthermore, it is necessary to sustain the development of knowledge that allows for understanding and acting in processes associated with the defense of human rights, peacebuilding, and social reconciliation (Velez et al., 2020).

It seems evident that due to the multiple factors that maintain the armed conflict in the Colombian context, there are many challenges that must be addressed to create a setting that guarantees human rights. Therefore, psychology must have a continuous and long-term agenda committed to human rights advocacy that involves psychology as professionals as well as in training and academic research.

References

Amnistía Internacional. (2018). *Informe 2017/2018*. Retrieved from https://www.amnesty.org/es/countries/americas/colombia/report-colombia/

Aranguren-Romero, N., & Rubio-Castro, N. (2018). Formación en herramientas terapéuticas a sobrevivientes del conflicto armado en el Pacífico colombiano. *Revista de estudios sociales, 66*, 18–29. https://doi.org/10.7440/res66.2018.03

Arias, J. D. (2018). Administrative repair to the victims of the armed conflict in Colombia: A fundamental right without warranties. *International Journal of Cultural Heritage, 3*, 91–101. Retrieved from https://www.iaras.org/iaras/filedownloads/ijch/2018/017-0009(2018).pdf

Barreto, I., Borja, H., Serrano, Y., & López-López, W. (2009). La legitimación como proceso en la violencia política, medios de comunicación y construcción de culturas de paz. *Universitas Psychologica, 8*(3), 737–748. Retrieved from http://www.scopus.com/inward/record.url?eid=2-s2.0-77952029175&partnerID=tZOtx3y1

Bloomfield, D., Barnes, T., & Huyse, L. (2003). *Reconciliation after violent conflict a handbook*. IDEA. Retrieved from https://www.idea.int/sites/default/files/publications/reconciliation-after-violent-conflict-handbook.pdf

Borja-Orozco, H., Barreto, I., Sabucedo, J. M., & López López, W. (2008). Construcción del discurso deslegitimador del adversario: Gobierno y paramilitarismo en Colombia. *Universitas Psychologica, 7*(2), 571–583. Retrieved from https://www.redalyc.org/articulo.oa?id=64770220

Brook, J. S., Brook, D. W., & Whiteman, M. (2007). Growing up in a violent society: Longitudinal predictors of violence in Colombian adolescents. *American Journal of Community Psychology, 40*(1–2), 82–95. https://doi.org/10.1007/s10464-007-9126-z

Castañeda, J. G., López-López, W., & Barrero, J. A. (2019). Calidad de Vida en Salud en Población Victima del Conflicto Armado en Colombia. *Psicología Desde El Caribe, 36*(2), 133–148. Retrieved from http://rcientificas.uninorte.edu.co/index.php/psicologia/article/view/10305

Castrillón-Guerrero, L., Riveros, V., Knudsen, M., López-López, W., Correa-Chica, A., & Castañeda Polanco, J. G. (2018). Comprensiones de perdón, reconciliación y justicia en víctimas de desplazamiento forzado en Colombia. *Revista de Estudios Sociales, 63*, 84–98. https://doi.org/10.7440/res63.2018.07

Centro Nacional de Memoria Histórica. (2013). *¡Basta ya! Colombia: Memorias de guerra y dignidad*. Retrieved from http://www.centrodememoriahistorica.gov.co/micrositios/informeGeneral/descargas.html

Centro Nacional de Memoria Histórica. (2018). *Todo pasó frente a nuestros ojos. Genocidio de la Unión Patriótica 1984-2002*. Retrieved from http://centrodememoriahistorica.gov.co/todo-paso-frente-a-nuestros-ojos-genocidio-de-la-union-patriotica-1984-2002/

Cilliers, J., Dube, O., & Siddiqi, B. (2016). Reconciling after civil conflict increases social capital but decreases individual well-being. *Science, 352*(6287), 787–794. Retrieved from http://science.sciencemag.org/content/352/6287/787

Comisión Interamericana de Derechos Humanos (CIDH). (2017). *Informe No 170/17 Caso 11227. Informe de fondo: Integrantes y militantes de la Unión patriótica*. Retrieved from https://www.oas.org/es/cidh/decisiones/corte/2018/11227FondoEs.pdf

Congreso de la República de Colombia. (2005). *Ley de Justicia y Paz 975 de 2005*. Pub. L. No. 975. Retrieved from https://www.fiscalia.gov.co/colombia/wp-content/uploads/2013/04/Ley-975-del-25-de-julio-de-2005-concordada-con-decretos-y-sentencias-de-constitucionalidad.pdf

Congreso de la República de Colombia. (2011). *Ley 1448 de 2011 Por la cual se dictan medidas de atención, asistencia y reparación integral a las víctimas del conflicto armado interno y se dictan otras disposiciones*. Pub. L. No. 1448. Retrieved from https://www.centrodememoriahistorica.gov.co/micrositios/caminosParaLaMemoria/descargables/ley1448.pdf

Cortés, Á., Torres, A., López-López, W., Pérez, C., & Pineda-Marín, C. (2016). Comprensiones sobre el perdón y la reconciliación en el contexto del conflicto armado colombiano. *Psychosocial Intervention, 25*(1), 19–25. https://doi.org/10.1016/j.psi.2015.09.004

Cuartas, J., Karim, L. L., Martínez, M. A., & Hessel, P. (2019). The invisible wounds of five decades of armed conflict: Inequalities in mental health and their determinants in Colombia. *International Journal of Public Health, 64*(5), 703–711. https://doi.org/10.1007/s00038-019-01248-7

Cudris-Torres, L., & Barrios-Núñez, Á. (2018). Malestar psicológico en víctimas del conflicto armado. *Revista CS, 26*, 75–90. https://doi.org/10.18046/recs.i25.2654

Cuevas, M. C., & Castro, L. (2009). Efectos emocionales y conductuales de la exposición a violencia en niños y adolescentes en Colombia. *Revista Internacional de Psicología Clínica y de La Salud, 17*(2), 277–298. Retrieved from https://dialnet.unirioja.es/servlet/articulo?codigo=2998347

Duque, V. (2017). Early-life conditions and child development: Evidence from a violent conflict. *SSM - Population Health, 3*, 121–131. https://doi.org/10.1016/j.ssmph.2016.09.012

Gaviria, S. L., Alarcón, R. D., Espinola, M., Restrepo, D., Lotero, J., Berbesi, D. Y., Sierra, G. M., Chaskel, R., Espinel, Z., & Shultz, J. M. (2016). Socio-demographic patterns of posttraumatic stress disorder in Medellin, Colombia and the context of lifetime trauma exposure. *Disaster Health, 3*(4), 139–150. https://doi.org/10.1080/21665044.2016.1263086

Herrera, P., & Taylor, S. (2014). El Sistema Nacional De Derechos Humanos Y Derecho Internacional Humanitario: ¿Una Nueva Etapa En La Actuación En Materia De Derechos Humanos En Colombia? *Opera, 12*. Retrieved from https://papers.ssrn.com/sol3/papers.cfm?abstract_id=2388181

Hewitt, N., Juárez, F., Parada, A. J., Guerrero, J., Romero, Y. M., Salgado, A. M., & Vargas Amaya, M. V. (2016). Afectaciones Psicológicas, Estrategias de Afrontamiento y Niveles de Resiliencia de Adultos Expuestos al Conflicto Armado en Colombia. *Revista Colombiana de Psicología, 25*(1), 125–140. https://doi.org/10.15446/rcp.v25n1.49966

Ibáñez, A. M., & Vélez, C. E. (2008). Civil conflict and forced migration: The micro determinants and welfare losses of displacement in Colombia. *World Development, 36*(4), 659–676. https://doi.org/10.1016/j.worlddev.2007.04.013

Kaplan, O., & Nussio, E. (2018). Community counts: The social reintegration of ex-combatants in Colombia. *Conflict Management and Peace Science, 35*(2), 132–153. https://doi.org/10.1177/0738894215614506

Krakowski, K. (2017). Resisting displacement amid armed conflict: Community-level conditions that make people more likely to stay. *Journal of Peacebuilding and Development, 12*, 68–84. https://doi.org/10.1080/15423166.2017.1370387

López, J. A. (2012). Las organizaciones no gubernamentales de derechos humanos en la democracia. Aproximaciones para el estudio de la politización de los derechos humanos en Colombia. *Estudios Políticos, 41*, 103–123. Retrieved from http://www.scielo.org.co/scielo.php?script=sci_arttext&pid=S0121-51672012000200006

López-López, W. (2016). La reconstrucción psicológica y social: una prioridad de corto, mediano y largo plazo para el futuro de la paz en Colombia. In G. Niño, J. Escobar, & L. Muñoz (Eds.), *La paz el derecho de la democracia. Elementos de análisis frente a los desafíos del legislador en la implementación del acuerdo final de paz en Colombia* (pp. 149–157). Centro de Investigaciones de Altos Estudios Legislativos – CAEL.

López-López, W. (2017). Contribuciones de Psicología de la Paz: Una Perspectiva Multidimensional. *Innovación y Ciencia, 24*(1), 100–108. Retrieved from https://innovacionyciencia.com/revista/91

López-López, W. (2020). A multidimensional and dynamic perspective of research and intervention in peace psychology. *Peace Psychologist, 29*, 39–41.

López-López, W., Andrade, A. F., & Correa-Chica, A. (2016a). El Proceso de Pedir Perdón como Condición Necesaria para la Construcción de Paz en Medio del Conflicto Armado en Colombia. *Revista Argentina de Clínica Psicológica, 25*(2), 187–194. Retrieved from https://www.redalyc.org/pdf/2819/281946990009.pdf

López-López, W., Pineda, C., Murcia, M. C., Perilla, D. C., & Mullet, E. (2013). Forgiving perpetrators of violence: Colombian people's positions. *Social Indicators Research, 114*, 287–301. https://doi.org/10.2307/24720248

López-López, W., Rincón-Unigarro, C., Correa-Chica, A., & García-Revelo, D. A. (2018). Repertorio socio-psicológico del conflicto colombiano en el discurso presidencial de Juan Manuel Santos. *Interamerican Journal of Psychology, 52*(2), 236–248. Retrieved from https://journal.sipsych.org/index.php/IJP/article/view/491

López-López, W., Silva, L. M., Castro, P., & Caicedo, A. (2016b). Actitudes implícitas de estudiantes universitarios frente al perdón en el marco del conflicto armado colombiano. *Pensamiento Psicológico, 14*(2), 49–62. Retrieved from https://revistas.javerianacali.edu.co/index.php/pensamientopsicologico/article/view/1404

McFee, E. (2016). The double bind of "playing double": Passing and identity among ex-combatants in Colombia. *Peace and Conflict, 22*(1), 52–59. https://doi.org/10.1037/pac0000146

Ministerio de Salud y Protección Social. (2017a). *Programa de atención psicosocial y salud integral a víctimas - PAPSIVI.* Retrieved from https://www.minsalud.gov.co/sites/rid/Lists/BibliotecaDigital/RIDE/DE/PS/Documento-Marco-papsivi-2017.pdf

Ministerio de Salud y Protección Social. (2017b). *Protocolo de atención integral en salud con enfoque psicosocial a víctimas del conflicto armado.* Retrieved from https://www.minsalud.gov.co/sites/rid/Lists/BibliotecaDigital/RIDE/DE/PS/Protocolo-de-atencion-integral-en-salud-papsivi.pdf

Ministerio de Salud y Protección Social, & Social. (2019). *Informe al Congreso de la República 2018-2019.* Retrieved from https://www.minsalud.gov.co/Ministerio/RCuentas/Paginas/informes-gestion.aspx

Molina, N. (2017). Retos de la psicología en la construcción de paz en Colombia: ¿fatalismo o ingenuidad? *Pensamiento Psicológico, 15*(1), 115–126. https://doi.org/10.11144/Javerianacali.PPSI15-1.RPCP

Mootz, J. J., Stark, L., Meyer, E., Asghar, K., Roa, A. H., Potts, A., Poulton, C., Marsh, M., Ritterbusc, A., & Bennouna, C. (2019). Examining intersections between violence against women and violence against children: Perspectives of adolescents and adults in displaced

Colombian communities. *Conflict and Health, 13*, Article 25. https://doi.org/10.1186/s13031-019-0200-6

Moreno, M. A., & Díaz, M. E. (2016). Posturas en la atención psicosocial a víctimas del conflicto armado. *El Ágora USB, 16*(1), 193–213. https://doi.org/10.21500/16578031.2172

Naucke, P. (2017). The memory of resistance: Historicity and remembrance in a Colombian peace community. *The Latin Americanist, 61*(2), 145–168. https://doi.org/10.1111/tla.12127

Pérez-Olmos, I., Fernández-Piñeres, P. E., & Rodado-Fuentes, S. (2005). Prevalencia del trastorno por estrés postraumático por la guerra, en niños de Cundinamarca, Colombia. *Revista de Salud Pública, 7*(3), 268–280. https://doi.org/10.1590/S0124-00642005000300003

Rincón-Unigarro, C., Correa-Chica, A., López-López, W., del Pilar Morales-Sierra, M., & Rivera-Escobar, S. (2020). Media framings of forgiveness and reconciliation in the context of the Colombian armed conflict. *Revista Colombiana de Psicología, 29*(1), 105–123. https://doi.org/10.15446/.v29n1.81505

Rodríguez, F. (2004). La pobreza como un proceso de violencia estructural. *Revista de Ciencias Sociales (RCS), 1*, 42–50. Retrieved from https://www.redalyc.org/pdf/280/28010104.pdf

Sikkink, K. (2009). Comments on the Colombia chapters from the perspective of human rights theories. In E. F. Babbitt & E. L. Lutz (Eds.), *Human rights and conflict resolution in context* (pp. 70–88). S/E. Retrieved from https://books.google.es/books?hl=es&lr=&id=qmTLqCYfoWIC&oi=fnd&pg=PP1&dq=Human+Rights+and+Conflict+Resolution+in+Context&ots=t2PJBRUlH7&sig=LpAo_nqOCdpug7m9jjSy2XS8AmE#v=onepage&q&f=false

Taylor, L. K. (2016). Impact of political violence, social trust, and depression on civic participation in Colombia. *Peace and Conflict, 22*(2), 145–152. https://doi.org/10.1037/pac0000139

Unidad para la Atención y Reparación Integral a las Victimas (UARIV). (2014). *Estrategia de Recuperación Emocional a Nivel Grupal.* Retrieved from https://www.unidadvictimas.gov.co/sites/default/files/documentosbiblioteca/3912-estrategia-de-recuperacion-emocional-nivel-grupal-con-adultos-ereg-v1.pdf

Unidad para la Atención y Reparación Integral a las Victimas (UARIV). (2020). *Registro Único de Víctimas (RUV) RNI - Red Nacional de Información.* Retrieved from https://www.unidadvictimas.gov.co/es/registro-unico-de-victimas-ruv/37394

United Nations. (1948). *Universal declaration of human rights.* Retrieved from http://www.un.org/es/universal-declaration-human-rights/

United Nations. (2018). *National report submitted in accordance with paragraph 5 of the annex to human rights council resolution 16/21 Colombia.* Retrieved from https://www.ohchr.org/EN/HRBodies/UPR/Pages/COIndex.aspx

United Nations. (2021). *Report of the United Nations High Commissioner for Human Rights.* Retrieved from https://www.hchr.org.co/documentoseinformes/informes/altocomisionado/A_HRC_46_76_AdvanceUneditedVersion.pdf

United Nations High Commissioner for Human Rights. (2019). *Annual report of the United Nations High Commissioner for Human Rights and reports of the Office of the High Commissioner and the Secretary-General.* Retrieved from https://reliefweb.int/sites/reliefweb.int/files/resources/G1902543.pdf

Valdivieso, M. A. (2012). La justicia transicional en Colombia. Los estándares internacionales de derechos humanos y derecho internacional humanitario en la política de Santos. *Papel Político, 17*(2), 621–653. Retrieved from https://revistas.javeriana.edu.co/index.php/papelpol/article/view/6545

Velez, G., Twose, G., & López-López, W. (2020). Human rights and reconciliation: Theoretical and empirical connections. In N. S. Rubin & R. L. Flores (Eds.), *The Cambridge handbook of psychology and human rights* (pp. 537–552). Cambridge University Press. https://doi.org/10.1017/9781108348607.037

Villa, J. D. (2012). La acción y el enfoque psicosocial de la intervención en contextos sociales: ¿podemos pasar de la moda a la precisión teórica, epistemológica y metodológica? *El Ágora USB, 12*(2), 349–365. Retrieved from https://dialnet.unirioja.es/servlet/articulo?codigo=4550239

Villa, J. D. (2016). Intervenciones psicosociales en el marco de acciones de reparación a víctimas del conflicto armado colombiano. *ECA: Estudios Centroamericanos, 71*(744), 81–104.
Retrieved from https://dialnet.unirioja.es/servlet/articulo?codigo=5793225

Villa, J. D., & Insuasty, A. (2016). Entre la participación y la resistencia: reconstrucción del tejido
social desde abajo en el municipio de san carlos Más allá de la lógica de reparación estatal.
Agora U.S.B., 16(2), 453. https://doi.org/10.21500/16578031.2442

Wegner, D. (2017). Rethinking civilian protection: How residents of the Colombian peace community in San José de Apartadó resist violence. *Student Journal of Peace and Conflict Studies,
4*(1), 18–29. Retrieved from http://www.paxetbellum.org

Chapter 19
Working Mental Health in Peru

Viviana Valz Gen

Introduction: The Development of Mental Health in Peru
Community Mental Health in the Context of Public Health

The antecedents of community mental health in Peru coincide, from different perspectives, in the political value of contributing to the amelioration of the living conditions of disadvantaged populations, through their transformation. Dr. Hermilio Valdizán (1885–1929) is considered the pioneer, broadening his scope on the population, beyond the disease-focused western medical model, to include cultural expressions of the processes of falling ill and healing. He is recognized as the first representative of cross-cultural psychiatry in Latin America.

Along the same lines, the works of Dr. Humberto Rotondo (1915–1985) and other social psychiatric research identify poverty and slumming as causes of the fragmentation of the social bond, violence within families, and criminal behavior on the streets. However, the model of mental health that was consolidated in psychiatric hospitals and became dominant was the biomedical approach, not interdisciplinary, fragmented, without care continuity, and no consideration for human rights. This dominant approach was severely questioned in the Ombudsman's Office reports: "Mental health and human rights: the situation of the rights of persons interned in mental health facilities," (Defensoría del Pueblo, 2005); and "Mental health and human rights. Supervision of public policies, quality of service and the treatment of vulnerable populations" (Defensoría del Pueblo, 2009). Similar questionings appear in the "Report presented by Mr. Paul Hunt, Special Rapporteur on the right of everyone to the enjoyment of the highest level possible physical and mental health" of the United Nations (2005).

V. Valz Gen (✉)
Wiñastin Salud Mental Comunitaria, La Aurora, Perú
e-mail: vivivalzgen@gmail.com

© The Author(s), under exclusive license to Springer Nature Switzerland AG 2022   269
E. Lira et al. (eds.), *Human Rights Violations in Latin America*, Peace
Psychology Book Series, https://doi.org/10.1007/978-3-030-97542-5_19

A critical moment in the management of mental health public policy was the closure of the Directorate of Mental Health of the Ministry of Health in 1985. It is recognized today as a significant error since it led to a setback by subtracting resources and guidance from recently created community work programs in the field of mental health.

Community Mental Health from the Academia and Civil Society Organizations

Interest in a community approach to mental health grew in university classrooms. The *Universidad Nacional Mayor de San Marcos* (UNMSM) organized a clinical workspace, a psychological clinic (COPSI) aimed at serving the community, thus projecting the university to society. The creation in 1965 by the Catholic Church of the Episcopal Commission for Social Action (CEAS), dedicated to the defense and promotion of human rights nationwide was very important in the process. Years later (1980–2000), it would provide key support to persons, families, and communities affected by the internal armed conflict, including a work line of psychosocial support. Popular Education and the Theology of Liberation (Gutiérrez, 1971) nurtured that process.[1]

The transformation of social conditions through the formation of people, as agents of this transformation, is fundamental (Freire, 1970). This proposal was adopted by many NGOs, strengthening a current committed to social development and collective transformation processes, active participation being key, both in terms of diagnosis (participatory diagnosis) and alternatives to work.

The UNMSM set up the Psychology Service at the Collique Hospital in Comas, closely linked to university teaching (1973). Later (1987) the Community Center for Mental Health (CECOSAM) was established in Villa El Salvador, promoting spaces for dialogue, research, and publication. All those initiatives converged later to shape a certain proposal of community clinical attention, at the time more as shared common sense, product of the experience of daily practice with marginal populations, than an elaborate or consensual proposal.

All these interventions happened almost simultaneously and came together to later shape a kind of community clinical care proposal, at that time more as a shared common sense (product of the experience of daily work with marginalized populations) than as an elaborated and consensual proposal.

In the 1970s, there was a movement among faculty and students of the *Pontificia Universidad Católica del Perú* (PUCP) that developed an orientation to work in mental health outside the scope of private practice. Through the Nuclei of Social Projection of the Departments of Social Science and Psychology, fieldwork was carried out in the outskirts of Lima and some provinces.

---

[1] Paulo Freire was in the country, at the end of the 1960s, advising on education.

The Center for Psychosocial Development and Counseling (CEDAPP) was created in 1976, offering professional internships for students interested in psychosocial issues (Ureta de Caplansky & Soto, 1986).

In 1980, projects for psychological care consolidated in various communities, tending to the needs raised by the communities themselves (Villavicencio, 1986). From a community oriented psychoanalytical perspective, César Rodríguez Rabanal directed two projects that offered services to poor and stressed communities in the outskirts of Lima. The first one lead to the publication of *Cicatrices de la Pobreza: un Estudio Psicoanalítico* (1989), and the second to *La Violencia de las Horas: un Estudio Psicoanalítico de la Violencia en el Perú* (1995), that deals with the work with populations displaced from the emergency zones due to the political violence.

In the early 1990s, an important coordination and articulation effort was made, through the creation of the Mental Health Board (MSM). The aim was to organize the ideas, reflections, and actions of different NGOs regarding the issues of mental health and human rights. It went into a recess in 2002, to re-appear in 2004 as the Mental Health Working Group of the National Human Rights Coordinator (GTSM).[2]

Visions and Interventions

As in other Latin American countries, marginalization, exclusion, and indifference are, unfortunately, some of the features that characterize Peruvian society. Large sectors of the population live in extreme poverty, while small groups enjoy great economic prosperity, and this difference gives rise to others, determining situations of unfair inequality. At the same time, we are a country with a wealth and cultural diversity "broad and alien," paraphrasing Ciro Alegría (1941).

The Internal Armed Conflict

1980–2000 was a period of extreme violence. On May 17, 1980, the Communist Party of Peru-Shining Path (PCP-SL) destroyed and burned amphorae and electoral rolls, in the town of Chuschi (Cangallo-Ayacucho). That event marked the beginning of the "armed fight" led by the PCP-SL, which became clandestine and traveled through many provinces spreading a discourse of social change that soon

---

[2] Personally: Carmen Aldana, Vilma Yarleque, Miryam Rivera y Rosa María Cueto.

Institutions: Asociación Paz y Esperanza, Centro Amazónico de Antropología y Aplicación Práctica (CAAAP), Centro de Atención Psicosocial (CAPS), Comisión Episcopal de Acción Social (CEAS).

Estudio para la Defensa de los Derechos de la Mujer (DEMUS), Red para la Infancia (REDINFA), Unidad de responsabilidad social del Departamento de Psicología de la Pontificia Universidad Católica del Perú (URSpsi-PUCP), Asociación Wiñastin.

became one of terror and submission, unleashing a devastating and cruel war that took the country to unsuspected limits.

The response of the forces of order (the national police, the army, and the navy) was equally violent. A strategy of massive abuse of the rights of Peruvians was adopted (extrajudicial executions, disappearances, torture, massacres, sexual violence, murders). The epicenter of this was the poorest and most abandoned areas of the country, counting on the indifference and passivity, not only of public officials, but of Peruvian society as a whole. Many of the people and communities directly affected felt that what happened to them was as if it happened in "another country," giving account of the feeling of exclusion and indifference that they experienced. In those years, about 69,000 Peruvians died or disappeared, without the country being aware of it. Although it is very clear that the violence in our country did not begin with the internal armed conflict (CAI), it acquired dimensions of tragedy during this period.

> If the proportion of victims estimated for Ayacucho had been the same throughout the country, the internal armed conflict would have caused about 1,200,000 deaths/fatalities throughout Peru, of which approximately 340,000 would have occurred in the city. of Metropolitan Lima, (…) it is clear that rural Peru, Andean and jungle, Quechua and Asháninka, peasant, poor and with little formal education bled for years without the rest of the country feeling and assuming the true dimension of the tragedy of those "alien people within Peru" (CVR, 2003, p. 162).

These figures tell us about the bond between Peruvian men and women and give us a picture of our history that we find difficult to recognize. Additionally, the 1990s were marked by a climate of corruption and a total crisis of the institutions, which ended with the flight of the then president of the country Alberto Fujimori to Japan. The Transitory Government chaired by Dr. Valentín Paniagua created the Truth Commission, responding to the feelings and preoccupation of a sector of our society that was involved in the defense of human rights and has been denouncing the silence and impunity. This notwithstanding, huge sectors of the citizenry continue, even to these days, preferring to deny and ignore what happened. The Truth Commission was ratified and complemented by the elected president Alejandro Toledo (2001–2006), calling itself the Truth and Reconciliation Commission (CVR). It was in charge of clarifying the process, the events that occurred and the corresponding responsibilities, not only of those who executed them but also of those who ordered or tolerated them. Also, the CVR had the task of proposing initiatives that affirm peace and reconciliation among all Peruvians. It started its activities in October 2001 and delivered its Final Report in July 2003.

Mental Health in the CVR Process (2001–2003)

In its Final Report, The CVR included a description of its own working process, including the proposal prepared and developed around mental health.

The task of working on the issue of mental health within the CVR was assumed by psychologists Elsa León and Viviana Valz Gen. The Mental Health Unit was organized with a team made up of psychologists,[3] with the support of local mental health institutions[4] and specialists such as Carlos Martín Beristain, whose contribution was very important.

From a comprehensive, psychosocial approach, the purpose was to contribute to the process, without leaving individual or group care within the limits of the established deadlines. The subjective dimension, the "psi," was considered in a transversal way throughout the process. That is, in the explanation of the historical process of violence, in the collection of testimonies, the public hearings, the exhumation of graves, as well as in the treatment of psychosocial consequences, and the proposal for reparation and recommendations. The transversality of the proposal constituted an important contribution, different from the common notion of many professionals, who consider that mental health must be oriented fundamentally to those who feel bad, break down, overflow, "get sick," a popular notion, associated with mental illness.

An account of the historic process of violence, its genesis and development, was given through a reflection that included the subjective dimension, from the individual to the social. It was proposed that the investigation and clarification of the facts should be in itself a process of recognition and reparation for the persons that had been affected, as for the population in its entirety. Then, strategies were proposed to ameliorate the impact and psychosocial consequences derived from the armed conflict and to diminish unrealistic expectations generated by the work of the CVR itself. Psychosocial sequelae were analyzed, and proposals for reparation and reconciliation were developed.

The methodology used was qualitative: a psychological reflection, from a viewpoint that integrates reality with the subjective processes associated with it. A psychoanalytic framework was put in dialogue with other methodological inputs, which required a quantitative analysis. Thus, for the systematization of psychosocial sequelae, a codebook was prepared which, initially, was worked in coordination with the Information Systems unit, in charge of the process of compiling and quantitative analysis of testimonies. The coding of more specific contents regarding mental health was in charge of the team of the Association for Human Rights Education with Health Application (EdhucaSalud). The results were interpreted from a psychoanalytic point of view, considering the global context of the ongoing

---

[3] Miryam Rivera, Ana Reyes and Claudia Lema (South Central Office), Karina Dianderas (Central Office), Sandy Martel and Luis Cabrera (Nor East Office), Giovana Campos (Andean South Office), Marisol Vega (Lima NOS Office), Fryné Santisteban (Systematization Psychosocial Sequelae) and Elsa León, Francisco Diez Canseco and Viviana Valz Gen (Central Office).

[4] Amazon Center for Anthropology and Practical Application (CAAAP), Social Action Commission (CEAS), Psychosocial Care Center (CAPS), Civil Association for Human Rights Education with Health Application (EDHUCASalud), Mental Health Board (MSM), Paz and Hope and Network for Children and the Family (REDINFA).

process, that is, what had been worked over the last few years and the voice of the people, through their testimonies.

It was very important, although difficult due to the workload and time pressure, to consolidate the accompaniment and support of the team of CVR interviewers who had to move to very remote communities, sometimes under very unfavorable conditions. In the meetings with the affected people, they had to receive and take charge of the complaints and mistrust, as well as the expectations, frustrations, and complaints because they could not receive the testimonies of all who wanted to deliver them. This added to the stress inherent in the process of collecting the testimonies that came with a huge load of suffering and pain that was very difficult to listen to. The interviewers were the essential support of the TRC work in the middle of the pressure inherent to the process. They constituted the face of the TRC in the communities and localities visited.

The Methodology

We proposed a process of psychosocial accompaniment that recognized people as subjects of rights. We intended that every encounter was restorative, based on the recognition of the facts and their impact. We also considered the impact that the silence imposed on individuals, families, communities, and the country. Thus, each testimony should be organized according to the way each person was able to tell their story in their mother tongue, allowing the time necessary according to their individual needs.

We worked with the interviewers to facilitate their understanding of the emotional impact that the years of silence and impunity had had on people. As it happened, together with their painful accounts, they would speak about the suffering from being listened when all those terrible things were happening, from all those years of the State and society covering up and denying what was happening. The CVR, as an instance of the State, had to take charge of that pain and claim.

In each case, this view was included. Emotional support and emotional containment were provided along the different moments and instances of each process: Helping the preparation of the people who came to share their testimonies in the Public Hearings, that is ceremonies in which the affected had to appear in an auditorium in front of the commissioners and with the presence of the public and the press. In coordination with mental health NGOs, some of which had been already accompanying them for a long time, we designed a method for the psychosocial support of the declarants before, during and after their presentations. The fundamental preoccupation in those hearings was the care for the dignity of each person and the community, through a respectful listening to his or her testimony, while allowing them to communicate what had happened during the years of imposed silence.

The same was done during the process of Exhumation of the Graves, a very sensitive and complicated process that confirmed the strategy of forced disappearance, used by the forces of order. Although only three exhumations were made during the CVR process, the need for a National Plan for Forensic Anthropological Investigations was raised, placing the needs of families at the center of attention. The EPAF Forensic Anthropology Team had conducted grave inspections for the CVR, in coordination with the Ombudsman's Office.

One of the most delicate issues in the process was working with the expectations of the population, regarding the demand for truth and the great need to recognize and recover the remains of their relatives. In this process, the relatives spoke of their lives and suffering in the search for their loved ones, with a hope that with the passing of the years remains, since this lawsuit has yet to be resolved. There is a lot of resistance from the institutions involved in these facts to recognize them and offer the necessary information to clarify them.

In 2007, the "Working Group on the Search for Disappeared Persons" was formed, a group of civil society and State organizations that have the common interest of promoting national policies aimed at alleviating the suffering of the families of the disappeared during the CAI, through forensic investigations and psychosocial support.

Its background was the First International Congress of Psychosocial Work in Exhumations, Forced Disappearance, Justice and Truth, held in Antigua, Guatemala (Feb 2007). Its first activity was the promotion and validation of the "World consensus of principles and minimum standards on psychosocial work in search processes and forensic investigations for cases of forced disappearances, arbitrary or extrajudicial executions." After that date, work has continued creating a public policy and disseminating information on the problem of missing persons.

Psychosocial Sequelae

A particularly significant contribution to this process was the preparation of the Psychosocial Sequels Chapter of the CVR Report, systematized and drafted by psychoanalyst Fryné Santisteban Palomino. The organization and content of this chapter collects and at the same time clearly expresses the approach of the Mental Health Unit of the CVR and the previous work of many teams of psychologists and psychoanalysts. What follows is a tight summary of some of the contents of the Psychosocial Sequelae chapter: the effects of CAI on subjectivity are profound, recognizing in them both the impact it left, in terms of sequelae, effects, injury, damage, as well as the resources and potential deployed to deal with this situation (support social networks, for example). The impact and intensity of these events have a destabilizing and de-structuring nature. They challenge and, in many cases, exceed the psychological capacity for defense, leading to serious suffering, both physical and emotional. They provoke intense feelings of insecurity, abandonment, and helplessness and, in some cases, lasting disorders in the psychic organization. We speak of traumatic experiences, lived as a rupture of the vital process, suffered by all those involved in it.

A decisive factor in the traumatic nature of these experiences, as mentioned, was the imposition of silence. Exposure to innumerable acts of violence, for a long time, gave rise to a phenomenon of accumulation with traumatic results. Some effects of the violence appeared at the time of the event, others remained latent to express themselves later. They generally have a lasting impression, they are present, active in the subjective, individual, and collective experience, in the mental representations that each person has today of himself, of society, of democracy, of the possibilities of living with others. Many of these effects go beyond those who suffered it directly, extending to the following generations, we speak then of transgenerational effects.

Although we can describe some common features, trying to be rigorous, it is not possible to generalize about styles and ways of suffering. We recognize the unquestionable uniqueness of each person, each organization, each community. Every human being exposed to dangerous situations resorts to all the psychological defenses available to them, so that psychological reactions to the threatening and destructive impact of violence cannot be considered abnormal or pathological responses, although they may become discomfort, symptoms.

We found, first, fear and mistrust as the strongest effects. Second, that the institution most damaged without a doubt is the family: violence has directly attacked family and community ties, generating irreparable losses and leaving emotional voids expressed mainly in orphanhood and widowhood, from where one experiences what loneliness means in the face of life. There is also the impotence of seeing the family fragment, leaving you without protection or care.

Finally, we observed a set of responses and creative strategies that people generated to confront CAI violence and its effects through forms of solidarity, the support of various organizations and institutions. It became clear that those who had social and emotional support networks were in better conditions to face the violent impact and its consequences throughout these years.

The process of the Mental Health Unit of the CVR has been intense and enriching. Seventeen years later, we continue the tasks proposed in the Final Report.

The Reparation Process

The mental health repair proposal had an approach oriented towards comprehensive recovery, to recognize and promote the capacities of the population.

It was necessary to specify that the reparations proposal should be aimed at addressing and mitigating the impact caused by the CAI violence, being aware that those are facts and processes that leave very large gaps. The accent is on recovering the dignity of individuals and the collective, on compensating them for moral damage, and granting them the recognition of a right to live well.

The CVR proposed a reparations program that should be part of a public health policy for the population, with emphasis on those affected by CAI violence. The transversal incorporation of psychosocial, participatory, intercultural, gender, and symbolic approaches was essential. The development of six programs is recommended: Symbolic Reparations, Health Reparations, Educational Reparations, Reparations in Restitution of Citizen Rights, Economic Reparations, and Collective Reparations (CVR, 2003).

As of 2004, during the government of Alejandro Toledo, public regulations began to be generated aimed at following up on the recommendations of the CVR. The first was the approval of the Programmatic Framework for State Action in matters of peace, reparation, and national reconciliation (2004) and the creation of the High Level Multi-sectorial Commission to follow up on the recommendations of the CVR (CMAN). Finally, a law was given that creates and approves the Comprehensive Repair Plan-PIR (2005) and its Regulations (2006). The health sector is one of the first to commit to the CVR's recommendations on repair issues.

Some instances of the academia and civil society have taken on the reparation proposals and organized activities to enrich and develop them. Notably, the Psychology Department of the Pontificia Universidad Católica del Perú has organized a series of annual meetings (2003 to date) bringing together people who work in different areas of intervention, from individual, family, and group care to community settings, addressing the psychosocial problems of people directly affected by the CAI, and also communities affected by different types of "violence." The idea of these meetings is to summon colleagues who carry out their professional work with populations, from the State, the academy, and civil society organizations.

Considering the shared issues: "it is worth highlighting the consensus regarding ourselves and regarding the populations with which we intervene. About ourselves: strengthen forms of dialogue and exchange that bring us closer, that make the professional support of the mental health of our population a consistent, fluid fabric, nourished by modern conceptions, with a deontology and methods of intervention that are relatively shared and abided by" (Pezo et al., 2008, pp. 23–24). In short, how to achieve a positive impact on people and communities so that they actively seek integral well-being, taking care of their own mental health, consolidating their identities, and being flexible in the face of the rapid changes that life transformations entail modern life.

Ruiz (2016) highlights: "The need to clarify the relationship between the clinical and the community; the importance of the word and dialogue; the idea of 'community listening'; the place of the different 'third', foreigner, alien, in communities marked by poverty and exclusion; the importance of recognition; the power relations and the asymmetry between the community and the 'care agent' or 'mental health agent'; the cultural differences and the different notions of what is healthy and what is ill" (p. 46).

The work carried out by the Wiñastin[5] team (2004–2012) in Ayacucho within the framework of the Mental Health Care and Promotion Project provides a proposal

---

[5] María Ángela Cánepa, Karina Dianderas, Elena Peña Silvia Revilla, Rosa Ruiz, Fryné Santisteban, Viviana Valz Gen and Marisol Vega.

for community mental health, which seeks to put psychoanalytic knowledge and experience at the service of people and populations most in need of care, support, and justice. It is a significant effort that articulates psychological clinical practice, community work, the creation of networks and connections between the various spaces of the community. Also, we consider it is the most interesting and fruitful contribution, the training of agents of mental health, with the conviction that the task of recovery and development of mental health in a community is not exclusive to specialists but to members of the same community.

We believe that one of his most significant and powerful contributions, of psychoanalytic inspiration, is a proposal that seeks to articulate and integrate, in the training processes of local mental health agents, both the reflective dimension through thinking around the discussion and criticism of texts, as well as the practice, organized around the clarification of their concrete experiences of service to their community and the emotional support, essential to elaborate and process their personal difficulties around the work they do in their communities, groups, and/or institutions (Ruiz, 2016).

Towards a Mental Health Law

As part of the follow-up to the recommendations of the CVR, the Institute of Democracy and Human Rights of the Pontificia Universidad Católica del Perú (IDEHPUCP) achieved a Declaration of support for the recommendations of the CVR, signed by 69 congressmen and women on the following topics: (a) educational curriculum, (b) right to identity, and (c) mental health (GTSM, 2006). The Office of Congresswoman Elizabeth León (UPP) invited mental health specialists, mostly members of the mental health workgroup of the National Human Rights Coordinator (GTSM). Thus began a long and inclusive process of dialogue and alliances between different social actors involved in order to arrive at the formulation of a Mental Health Bill that the Congress could approve. The idea was to produce a dialogue between different approaches including psychology, psychiatry, directors of psychiatric hospitals, users, and family members of users, responsible for the departments of Personal Health and Health Promotion of Minsa and with officials of the Department of Mental Health of the same ministry.

A draft Mental Health Law was formulated that comprehensively addresses these issues and integrates, within the framework of national and international human rights instruments, the community mental health approach with the clinical approach with which this problem has traditionally been addressed in the public health of the country.

On June 3, 2008, after 16 months of work, Bill No. 02465—Mental Health Law was presented to Congress, although it was not approved as such, it was a benchmark for some of the modifications that were made. Sadly, however, the Mental Health Law (30947) that was enacted in 2019 has a series of omissions regarding the participation of psychologists. This motivated projects for its modification that to date have been sent to the archive.

Towards a Reform in Mental Health Care (Minsa)

During the years of the CAI (1980–2000), the Minsa made important efforts to serve the affected population with care programs for children and women victims of sexual violence, but as it did not have an adequate approach, this did not work.

Subsequently, it assumed its responsibility in complying with the recommendations of the CVR and intended to implement actions that allow the creation of the best conditions to develop proposals for comprehensive reparation, according to the conceptual and regulatory framework recommended by the CVR.

Efforts were made to strengthen the capacities of personnel working in first and second level establishments, recognizing the need to develop capacities for the care, promotion, and prevention of mental health in areas affected by the internal armed conflict.

The need to care for the affected population mobilized the interest and effort of the different specialized mental health institutions, as pointed out by Dr. Pilar Mazzetti, Minister of the sector (2004–2006), giving an account of the progress made from the National Mental Health Strategy and Culture of Peace, also declaring: "Mental Health: national priority."

In the country, several isolated community experiences have existed that failed to establish themselves as a national public policy. It is about orienting the mental health policies towards a culture of peace, human development, and respect for people's rights, promoting their citizenship. The sanitary strategies of mental health should be those that deepen the analysis of the effects of the violence of the CAI, aimed at the implementation of the Program of Reparations in Health of the Comprehensive Plan of Reparations already approved.

In 2017, the Technical Health Standard that creates community mental health centers was approved. In 2018, the technical document "National Plan for Strengthening Community Mental Health Services 2018-2021" was issued.

The Ministry of Justice and Human Rights incorporates the humanitarian approach, based on the Law for the Search of Disappeared Persons during the period 1980–2000, articulating and providing the measures related to the search, recovery, analysis, identification, and restitution of human remains.

However, there are still several pending challenges, it is necessary to consolidate the community model and place the issue of mental health as a priority on the public agenda. Political proposals cannot remain indifferent to the challenges of public health policies, and especially mental health policies, associated with social unrest and violence. One must think social violence as a mental health problem. Therefore, in the face of a process of consolidation as a democratic society, we hope that it will not go backwards, but rather that the community mental health approach will fully consolidate in our country.

References

Alegría, C. (1941). *El mundo es ancho y ajeno*. Ercilla.
Comisión de la Verdad y Reconciliación (CVR). (2003). *Informe Final*. Perú. Retrieved from https://www.cverdad.org.pe/ifinal/
Defensoría del Pueblo. (2005). *Informe Defensorial N°102: "Salud Mental y derechos humanos: La situación de los derechos de las personas internadas en establecimientos de salud mental"*. Lima. Retrieved from https://www.defensoria.gob.pe/wp-content/uploads/2005/12/informe_102.pdf
Defensoría del Pueblo. (2009). *Informe Defensorial N°140: "Salud Mental y Derechos Humanos. Supervisión de la política pública, la calidad de los servicios y la atención a poblaciones vulnerables"*. Lima. Retrieved from https://cdn.www.gob.pe/uploads/document/file/1189395/informe-defensorial-140-vf20200803-1197146-mde0di.pdf
Freire, P. (1970). *Pedagogía del oprimido*. Tierra Nueva.
Grupo de Trabajo en Salud Mental de la Coordinadora Nacional de Derechos Humanos (GTSM). (2006). *Salud mental comunitaria en el Perú: Aportes temáticos para el trabajo con poblaciones*. Proyecto AMARES.
Gutiérrez, G. (1971). *Teología de la liberación: Perspectivas*. Centro de Estudios y Publicaciones.
Pezo, C., Velázquez, T., Valz-Gen, V., & Pareja, V. (2008). *Encuentros de discusión sobre intervención clínica comunitaria*. Departamento de Psicología, PUCP.
Rodríguez, C. (1989). *Cicatrices de la pobreza: un estudio psicoanalítico*. Nueva Sociedad.
Rodríguez, C. (1995). *La Violencia de las Horas: un estudio psicoanalítico de la violencia en el Perú*. Nueva Sociedad.
Ruiz, R. (2016). *Más allá del consultorio. Aportes del psicoanálisis a la prevención comunitaria*. Tesis para obtener el grado de Magister en Estudios Teóricos en Psicoanálisis, PUCP.
Ureta de Caplansky, M., & Soto, E. (1986). Demanda y asistencia: Dimensiones de una relación humana. Labor psicoterapéutica en sectores populares. *Temas sobre Psiquiatría y Psicología, 2*(2), 14–18.
United Nations (2005) The right of everyone to the enjoyment of the highest attainable standard of physical and mental health. Report of the Special Rapporteur, Paul Hunt: addendum, E_CN.4_2005_51_Add.2-EN.pdf. https://digitallibrary.un.org/record/539922?ln=es#recordfiles-collapse-header.
Villavicencio, R. (1986). Psicoterapia en barrios: Recorriendo un camino. Labor psicoterapéutica en sectores populares. *Temas sobre Psiquiatría y Psicología, 2*(2), 19–26.

Index

Ingram Content Group UK Ltd.
Milton Keynes UK
UKHW020605120523
421636UK00001B/3